Meat Management and Operations

Edward M. Harwell
Herman Friedman
Sam Feig

CHAIN STORE AGE BOOKS
An affiliate of Lebhar-Friedman, Inc.
New York

Prepared for

Cornell University
Home Study Division: Food Industry Management Program
New York State College of Agriculture and Life Sciences
A Statutory College of the State University

The Advisory Board for the Cornell University Home Study Program has reviewed this book and recommends it for use by members of the food industry.

Copyright © 1975, Chain Store Publishing Corporation
2 Park Avenue, New York, N.Y. 10016

All rights reserved. No part of this book is to be reproduced in any form or by any means without permission in writing from the publisher.

Printed in the United States of America
Library of Congress Catalog Card Number: 74-2111S
International Standard Book Number: 0-912016-45-0

To Marilyn G. Harwell

Acknowledgments

This book is the result of the efforts of three authors who took pen to hand and the thousands of others with whom we have brushed shoulders over the past quarter of a century.

Each contact has left its mark, sometimes supporting, other times causing us to re-evaluate opinions that were taken for granted. We have learned as much from our mentors as from our subordinates; our suppliers and customers alike have provided a fertile training ground; and, although exchanges with our peers have probably been the most stimulating part of our learning process, all have helped to shape our thinking, which is reflected in the following pages.

Although those in our past are too numerous to mention, others who were actively involved in the preparation of this text deserve not to remain anonymous.

Particular thanks are due to certain individuals who unselfishly gave of their time to review the original manuscript. Ed Blanton, Publix Super Markets; Ches Wilcox, Dominion Stores; Ken Johnson,

Acknowledgments

National Live Stock and Meat Board; and Gene German, Cornell University, were burdened with the awesome task of reading every typed word and sending back their comments "as soon as possible," which, in the publisher's mind, was always yesterday. It is hoped that by seeing their suggestions in print, these dedicated individuals will know how highly the authors have valued their contribution.

Carol Gulyas, Carl Belanger, Larry Gee, and Dennis Swarbrick, Dominion Stores; Bud Ruth, Publix Super Markets; Reba Staggs, National Live Stock and Meat Board; Tony Khalil, Chuck Pugh, and Roger Frady, Giant Food; and Dr. William Stringer, University of Missouri, each reviewed chapters in their particular areas of expertise, and in many cases provided original source material from which the chapters were developed. Bill Potece, Pic-N-Pay Supermarkets, was a constant source of information and made a very significant contribution to the final text.

The authors are also very much indebted to the National Live Stock and Meat Board for permission to reproduce a considerable amount of the art work that appears in the book, as well as copy for the Glossary and Appendix. The Board's pioneer efforts in bringing the *Uniform Retail Meat Identity Standards* project to fruition, is but one indication of the invaluable service that it provides to all segments of the meat industry.

Recognition is also due to Helene Berlin of the publishing staff for her tireless efforts in bringing this book to print.

A very special word of thanks goes to Arnold D. Friedman, publisher, *Chain Store Age,* who through committing the resources of his publishing company, has played a major role in providing the retail industry with an educational and training library of its own.

There is one individual for whom the authors cannot find words adequate to express their gratitude, and without whom this book could not and would not have been written—Marilyn Greenbaum Harwell —to whom this book is dedicated.

Edward M. Harwell
Herman Friedman
Sam Feig

Contents

Foreword		11
1	The Meat Department—Then and Now	13
2	Meat Department Organizational Structure	29
3	Knowing the Product	43
4	Inspecting and Grading Product	73
5	Recommended Cooking Methods	92
6	Product Procurement	123
7	Central Distributing and Processing	145
8	Store Ordering and Receiving	165
9	Pricing and Merchandising for Maximum Profit	182
10	Sanitation and Safety	216
11	Principles of Retail Operations	246
12	Training Meat Department Employees	281
13	The Role of the Meat Department Manager	315
Appendix		336
Glossary		342

Figures

Chapter 1
Figure 1. Per Capita Consumption of Meat and Poultry 19

Chapter 2
Figure 2. Organization Chart A 33
Figure 3. Organization Chart B 35
Figure 4. Organization Chart C 36
Figure 5. Organization Chart D 37
Figure 6. Organization Chart E 40

Chapter 3
Figure 7. Typical Sales Ranges by Product 45
Figure 8. Primal (Wholesale) Cuts and Bone Structure of Beef 49
Figure 9. Primal (Wholesale) Cuts and Bone Structure of Veal 50

Figures

Figure 10. Primal (Wholesale) Cuts and Bone Structure of Lamb — 51
Figure 11. Primal (Wholesale) Cuts and Bone Structure of Pork — 53
Figure 12. Bones Identifying the Seven Groups of Retail Cuts — 56
Figure 13. The Seven Basic Retail Cuts of Meat — 58
Figure 14. Beef Chart — 60
Figure 15. Veal Chart — 61
Figure 16. Lamb Chart — 62
Figure 17. Pork Chart — 63

Chapter 4

Figure 18. Meat Inspection Stamp — 74
Figure 19. Poultry Inspection Mark — 76
Figure 20. USDA Meat Grades — 80
Figure 21. USDA Meat Grade Stamps — 81
Figure 22. Poultry Inspection Mark, Grade Shield, and Class Name — 85
Figure 23. Yield Grade Stamp — 87
Figure 24. Yield and Value of Cuts from Typical Beef and Lamb Carcasses — 87
Figure 25. Expected Yields of the Four Lean Pork Cuts Based on Chilled Carcass Weight, by Grade — 91

Chapter 5

Figure 26. Suggested Cooking Guide for Beef by Cut and Grade — 93
Figure 27. Timetable for Broiling — 96
Figure 28. Timetable for Roasting — 100
Figure 29. Timetable for Braising — 103
Figure 30. Timetable for Cooking in Liquid — 105
Figure 31. Timetable for Cooking Variety Meats — 109
Figure 32. Roasting Guide for Poultry — 112
Figure 33. Meat Storage Time Chart — 121
Figure 34. Poultry Storage Time Chart — 122

Chapter 8

Figure 35. Order Breakdown Chart — 168

Chapter 9

Figure 36. Contribution to Total Sales and Gross Margin Dollars by Department — 183
Figure 37. Cutting Test on Saw-Ready Round — 187

Chapter 10

Figure 38. Log of Occupational Injuries and Illnesses—OSHA Form No. 100 — 237
Figure 39. Supplementary Record of Occupational Injuries and Illnesses—OSHA Form No. 101 — 238
Figure 40. Summary of Occupational Injuries and Illnesses—OSHA Form No. 102 — 239
Figure 41. Safety and Health Protection on the Job—OSHA Poster — 240

Chapter 11

Figure 42. Man-Hour Requirements for Fixed Functions — 275
Figure 43. Meat Department Tonnage and Man-Hour Forecast — 276
Figure 44. Forecasting and Scheduling System — 279

Chapter 13

Figure 45. Cutting Test on Pork Loin — 331

Appendix

Comparison of Yields of Retail Cuts and Retail Sales Values for Choice Beef Carcasses, by Yield Grade — 340
Comparison of Yields of Retail Cuts and Retail Sales Values for Choice Lamb Carcasses, by Yield Grade — 341

Foreword

When today's meat shopper steps up to the meat counter, she sees a wide variety of products which she generally takes for granted. She does not realize that this tremendous selection of fresh and cured meats before her is the result of a new era in meat operations and merchandising which is just beginning. In fact, more changes in meat operations are expected during the next 15 years than occurred over the last half century.

Today, retailers are serving customers who are entirely different from those they served even a few years ago. The few early "consumerist" voices have called forth an entirely new attitude and awareness on the part of today's shoppers. Progressive retailers are taking notice of the change and are implementing consumer-benefit programs including such innovations as the open-dated freshness code, nutritional labeling, the universal product code, and the uniform retail meat identity standards program.

Despite price controls, feed shortages, consumer boycotts, and inflation, meat retailers must continue to be competitive in efficiency, effectiveness, and economics. These factors are a must for any retailer to sell a product acceptable under today's standards in the market place.

To achieve and maintain contemporary standards, retailers are continually researching new developments such as frozen meats, central cutting operations, boxed meat programs, and the use of textured vegetable protein. The retail meat industry takes advantage of every technological advance in the food industry. New findings in sanitation, temperature control, safety, department layout, inspection, and quality and yield grading are all helping the retailer maintain an effective and economical meat operation.

To improve efficiency, many retailers also conduct training programs for meat personnel. In-store training programs are not only a means of keeping abreast of technical changes in the retail meat industry, but they also aid personnel in understanding the continually growing "consumer awareness."

The man behind the case is the meat industry's principal contact with consumers. Today's meat cutter must know not only "how" to cut, but also "why" to cut a particular way if he is to keep up with the fast changes occurring in the meat industry. I believe this book, *Meat Management and Operations,* will be an invaluable aid in making meat personnel more aware of the demands of today's consumers and will provide store managers and other supervisory personnel with a better understanding of what is required for a successful meat department operation.

> H. Kenneth Johnson
> Executive Director
> Food Science Division
> National Live Stock and Meat Board

1

The Meat Department—Then and Now

Ask the typical food shopper what she is planning for dinner, and chances are the first item she mentions will be meat. Meat is the deciding factor when the consumer plans her shopping list and chooses where to shop. In a national survey of supermarket shoppers, when asked, "which three factors (out of a choice of 11) you consider the most important in selecting a favorite supermarket," consumers mentioned "quality and freshness of meats" more often than any other factor.[1]

The past few generations of consumers have been brought up on the concept of one-stop shopping with almost every convenience built in. Few customers today will regularly shop a store known to have a low-price grocery image if the meat available at that store does not appeal to them. The customer plans her shopping list around her meat menu; and the store that cannot fill that need loses the competitive edge, for no other item stocked by the store will attract or

---
[1] *1971 Study of Supermarket Shoppers* (Cincinnati: Burgoyne, Inc.).

repel her more quickly. The unique capacity of this item to draw traffic to and through the entire store makes the meat department the most important unit in any supermarket.

CONTRIBUTION TO SALES AND GROSS PROFITS

In addition to its magical qualities in merchandising the entire store, meat generates a considerable dollar volume and makes a very substantial contribution to total store performance in terms of gross profit dollars. In 1973, supermarket meat sales (excluding poultry and fish) totaled $14.5 billion, or almost two-thirds of the total meat industry volume. In striking contrast, all canned goods sold through supermarkets during the same period totaled $6.64 billion.[2] Moreover, although accounting for only 25 percent of store sales, the meat department typically contributes 34 percent of a store's gross profit dollars while dry groceries and non-foods contribute an average 55 percent of the gross profit dollars on 67 percent of sales, and produce generates 11 percent of the gross profit dollars on 8 percent of sales.

Meat department sales typically range from a low of 20 percent of store volume to a high of 30 percent with the average at 25 percent. This figure can vary considerably from one company to another depending on which items are rung on the meat key at the cash register. For example, luncheon meats, fish, or cheese may be rung on the meat key in one company and on the delicatessen or dairy key in another, thus affecting the distribution (the percentage of sales to total store volume) of these departments. However, in either case, meat typically contributes more gross profit dollars than is represented in its percentage of total store sales.

HISTORY OF THE DEPARTMENT

Before 1930, small butcher shops were the major outlet for meat sales, and the successful ones were often located adjacent to a food store and a fruit and vegetable market. The synergistic effect of each store's drawing power quickly became apparent; and in the early 1930's, general stores were opened which sold meat, produce, dry groceries, and some houseware items under one roof. This marked

---

[2] *Chain Store Age Sales Manual* (July 1974), p. 65.

the beginning of merchandising meat through food store outlets and the decline in importance of the local butcher shop.

In the early days the meat department basically consisted of a service display case and a cooler, and offered a limited variety of fresh meat, poultry, and some canned items. Service was the byword, unions were few, labor was inexpensive and plentiful, and there was little mechanization. Chicken feathers, for example, were plucked out by hand by employees who earned 50 cents to 70 cents an hour and who were responsible for cleaning the department, disposing of garbage, and performing other menial chores.

In those days the word sanitation had little scientific meaning; the effect of bacteria on product was unknown to the merchant. As one old-timer reminisced, "We had a lot of shrinkage without even knowing anything was shrinking. We would leave the product in the backroom which was not properly refrigerated—we'd take hamburger meat and grind it into a lug, press it down, and just let it sit in the backroom. We would double-handle product, which is unthinkable at today's labor rates. We would stock product in the counter as high as it could go and then put canned hams or salamis on top of the counter so high that we couldn't see the customer."

From that background of experience, it was quite a venture to go into self-service operations. But it didn't take the supermarket operator (the successor to the general store) too long to sharpen his skills and knowledge. The year 1946 marked the advent of his entry into self-service meat operations.

Fairly rapidly after World War II, a number of progressive supermarket companies started converting their display equipment to self-service cases. However, fearing that the consumer was not psychologically ready for such an abrupt change, many companies maintained service and self-service counters side by side. The conversion to self-service, to the extent that it exists today, was still a number of years away.

The major objective of the switch to self-service was, of course, to decrease labor costs while increasing volume, even though labor rates at that time were still comparatively low. Butchers earned $1.80 an hour and part-time meat cutters were paid $1.20.

While the self-service store of 1946 required fewer employees than the service store, the number of people on the payroll was still far greater than would be found in a meat department today. The same store that would require three meat wrappers today would have had 10 to 12 people in 1946, wrapping product by hand, using sealing irons or plates and cellophane. However, because of the tremendous increase in labor rates since 1946 (in many parts of the country meat cutters currently earn over $5 an hour, plus fringe benefits), payroll costs as a percentage of sales are 50 percent higher today.

CURRENT PRACTICES

What most distinguishes the supermarket of today from its predecessor are the improvements that have been developed in methods, equipment, packaging materials, processing, and product flow, all of which have led to marked increases in productivity. Also, more items are being stocked today and more processing is being done by the packer, so that more items are coming into the store prepackaged or processed to a greater degree than ever before. Beef liver, for example, is often sold sliced, with seams removed, and usually frozen (as it is highly perishable), ready to be placed in trays, and wrapped at the store. The appeal to the retailer is not only that slicing liver is a "messy" job, but also that it can be done more economically at the packer level than at store level.

Similarly, luncheon meat traditionally was sliced and wrapped two or three times a week at the store because of its limited shelf life. Today, partly due to preserving additives, but more so because of the development of vacuum packaging, practically all supermarkets buy prepackaged luncheon meats with a shelf life of 15 to 30 days, or longer, depending on the item. Moreover, as packaging continues to improve, shelf life will be further extended.

Twenty years ago, turkey was sold through supermarkets perhaps two or three times a year, and always as a fresh bird. Today, most supermarkets carry turkeys 52 weeks a year, and primarily as frozen product. It is interesting to note that the cost and retail price of today's frozen bird is almost the same as 20 years ago, but today's product represents a much better value to the consumer. The so-called "New York dressed" fresh turkeys, from which only the feathers had been removed, typically cost the store from 39 cents to 49 cents a pound 20 years ago. Today's fully-dressed frozen turkey, which costs and sells at comparable prices, is not only far less expensive in terms of the purchasing power of today's dollar, but it is also cleaner (about 95 percent of the bacteria has been eliminated), and more of the non-edible parts (heads, guts, feet) have been removed. With bigger farms and increased automation, turkey producers have been able to effect considerable savings, much of which has been passed on to the retailer and the consumer.

With regard to fresh meat, practically all cattle was broken down at store level 20 years ago, although, on occasion, some primal cuts (sections cut from the whole carcass) were available for purchase. Today, any retailer who cannot move whole carcasses can readily buy the more expensive primals from a number of sources. Moreover, many stores are served by their own distribution centers which buy whole carcasses, perform the breaking operation, and ship primals or subprimals (sections of primals) to the stores. For whatever processing is done at store level, there is more automated equipment and more sophisticated tools with which to work. Although there have been few changes in the basic breaking and cutting operations, there has been a significant increase in productivity due to better saws, rails, scales, wrapping machines, film, and so on. Additionally, better refrigeration and a greater awareness of the need for cleanliness and sanitation have given longer shelf life to product.

The improvements made at the retail level in terms of productivity, refrigeration, and sanitation have had tremendous effects on the product that is offered to the consumer today; but the producers who raise the animals and the slaughterers who process them also have made significant advances.

Most producers and slaughterers operate far more economically today than in years past. A primary reason is that competition has forced the smaller growers and producers out of business. Those that have survived can function as large-scale operations, reaping all the benefits that traditionally accrue to high-volume enterprises.

Through selective breeding and improved feeding practices, producers have greatly improved the efficiency of their operations so that animals with a higher ratio of lean to fat and bone are fed for shorter lengths of time and are brought to market much sooner.

The slaughtering/processing/packing operation has benefited from improved techniques and equipment for aging, cutting, packaging, and shipping product. In addition to the efficiency that has resulted from more automation, the slaughterer is also able to utilize many products that were formerly discarded, and now somewhat offsets his increased labor rates by selling by-products such as fertilizer from waste products.

Through the efforts of these three groups—the retailer, the producer, and the slaughterer—the American consumer has available today higher quality meat in more variety and quantity.

Despite all her complaints about higher food prices, the average consumer in 1973 spent 2.62 percent of her disposable income for beef; in 1960 she spent 2.61 percent for beef—surely one of the lowest true food price increases she has faced during an era of rapidly rising prices.[3]

Viewed from a slightly different vantage point, in 1973, it cost the average person 17 cents more a day for food over the previous year, but wages increased $1 a day per person during the same period. While it takes the average American wage earner 27 minutes of work to buy a steak, it takes 75 minutes for the average Londoner to earn enough for the same steak and 5½ hours for the average Tokyo worker to buy his steak. Food is taking a smaller share of income than it did 20 years ago, in spite of recent price jumps. In 1953, food accounted for 22 percent of the per capita disposable personal income, but in 1973, food costs were only 15.7 percent of the $4,295 per capita disposable income.[4]

PER CAPITA CONSUMPTION

There is little question that Americans are the best fed people in the world, both in terms of quality and quantity; and that their number one choice of meat is beef. (See Figure 1.) Per capita consumption for beef and poultry reached all-time highs in 1972. The slight drops in 1973 were due partly to the general reduction in consumption in 1973, when the consumer price index rose for almost all consumable goods and produced a resultant drop in purchasing power.

Beef

Per capita consumption of beef reached an all-time record high of 116 pounds in 1972, compared to 85 pounds in 1960. Although consumption decreased to 109.5 pounds in 1973, due to economic factors which affected the supply and therefore the price, it is safe to forecast that the high demand will continue.

Keeping pace with the demands of the American consumer over

---

[3] United States Department of Agriculture (USDA).
[4] *Chain Store Age* (September, 1974), p. 29.

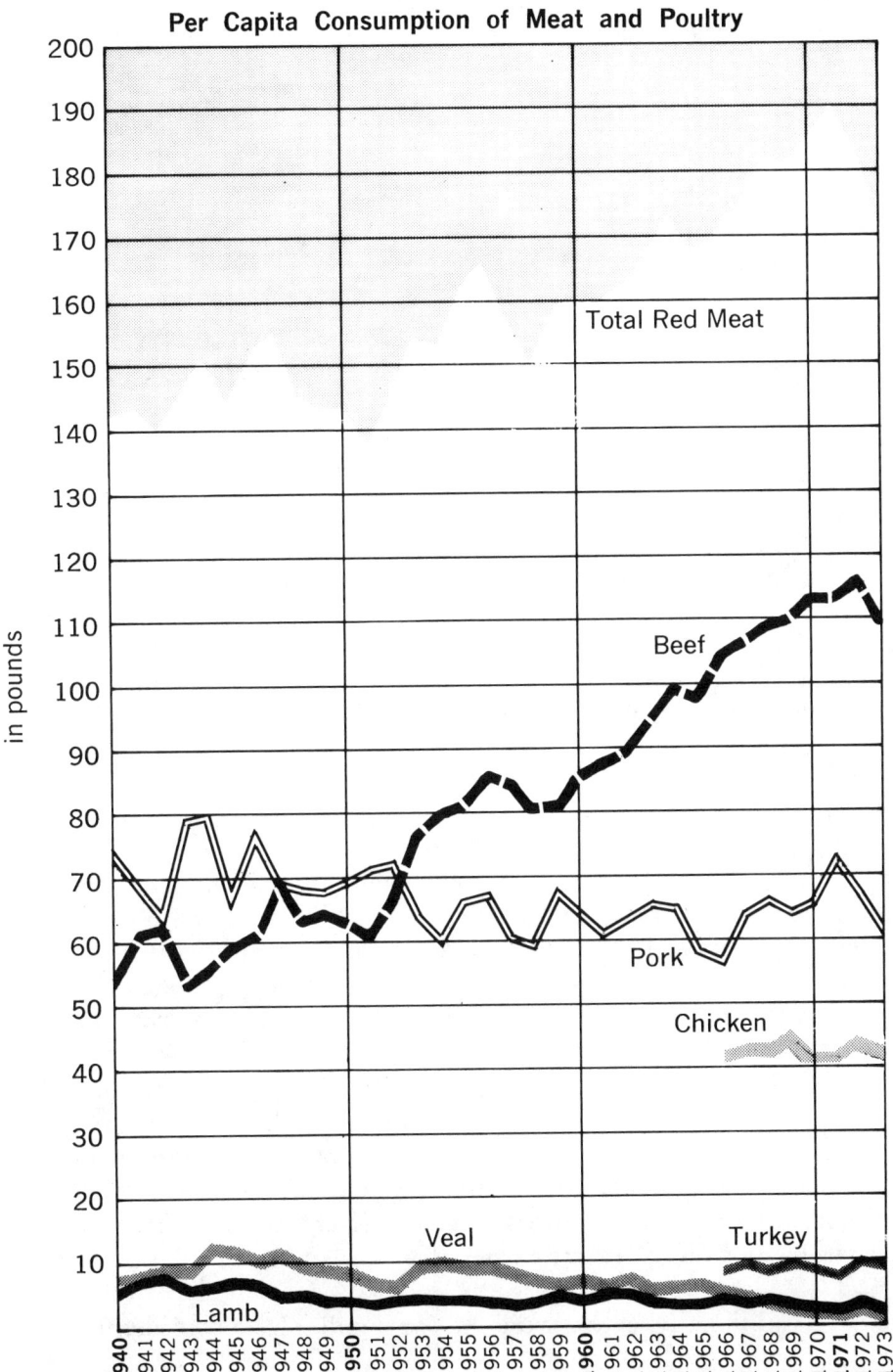

the past 20 years, beef production has risen sharply, due primarily to four major factors:

 1. The proportion of beef cows to dairy cows increased from a one-to-one ratio in the mid-1950's to a ratio of nearly four beef cows to one dairy cow at present.

 2. Since the 1950's, the calf crop per 100 cows increased from 86 to 90, resulting in 2 million more calves annually for the present cow herd.

 3. Calves slaughtered for veal decreased from 12.9 million in 1955 to 3.2 million in 1972. Thus, some 9 million calves were grown out to be beef carcasses at approximately 600 pounds each, instead of veal carcasses at roughly 120 pounds each.

 4. Cattle and calves on farms and ranches in the U.S. on January 1, 1974, numbered 127.5 million head, a record high.[5]

While the first three factors led to an enormous increase in beef output, they have more or less run their course and will have only a modest effect on future supplies. Therefore, the increased production that will be needed to satisfy the needs of the consumer in 1980 will most likely have to come from an expanded cow herd. Whether or not the cattle grower will be encouraged to continue to increase the size of his herd will undoubtedly depend on whether the economics are attractive to him.

Veal

Contrary to the increase in beef consumption, per capita consumption of veal decreased from 6 pounds in 1960 to 1.8 pounds in 1973, due primarily to the decrease in the number of calves slaughtered. With the tremendous increase in demand for beef, farmers found it far more profitable to hold back calves from market, making feeders out of them for cattle.

 Feeders are grass-fed until about 12 months of age and then grain-fed in a feed lot for three to six months, where they gain weight more rapidly—about 2¾ pounds a day. They are generally sold to a slaughterer as yearlings when their weight reaches 1,000 to 1,100 pounds. Most cattle growers have found it far more profitable to make feeders out of calves rather than to have them slaughtered for veal.

 Traditionally, calves were fed some milk plus a considerable diet

---
[5] USDA.

of substitutes and were slaughtered within four to five weeks. Today, in order to provide the consumer with a better quality of veal, most calves are strictly milk fed for as long as 12 to 14 weeks before being brought to slaughter. The decrease in the number of calves slaughtered, plus the increased cost of feeding calves, has made the price of veal so prohibitive that the tonnage sold in 30 stores today approximates what would have been sold in 3 stores 20 years ago.

Most stores today stock veal primarily for the purpose of offering the consumer a complete assortment of meat products. Unless means are found to bring this product to market at a price the customer can afford, there is little reason to believe that there will be any increase in per capita consumption.

Baby Beef

An item similar to and often confused with veal is baby beef. This is very young grass-fed cattle, weighing approximately 400 pounds, that is generally slaughtered between four and eight months of age. In the past, baby beef was priced lower than heavier beef and outsold full-grown beef in some areas of the South and Southwest. It was particularly popular in states such as Texas, but this is no longer true. The emphasis in almost all states today is on heavier, better quality beef.

Lamb

Lamb is another item that has become quite expensive in relation to beef, but it has traditionally been one of the least popular of all meat and poultry items in this country. The per capita consumption of lamb was only 4.8 pounds in 1960 and 2.6 pounds in 1973.

Many people feel the consumers' lack of interest in lamb is mainly due to the steady decline in available product which keeps prices high. In an effort to reverse this dwindling supply trend, shepherds are being brought into this country from France and Spain, because few Americans are willing to face the months of loneliness required to shepherd a flock of 800 to 1,000 sheep in the mountains. In addition, frozen lamb is being imported from New Zealand and Australia to fill the void until the domestic product is available in greater supply.

Pork

In 1971, for the first time in almost 20 years, per capita consumption of pork surpassed the 70-pound level. However, after reaching a high of 73 pounds in 1971, per capita consumption slipped back to 61.6 pounds in 1973 due to periods of short supply causing high prices. But it remains to be seen whether the downtrend in per capita consumption will continue because of higher prices or whether the short supply of this second most popular meat item is a temporary condition.

Equally significant is the fact that the nature of pork has changed considerably over the past 20 years. Today the product is leaner, has fewer calories, and is extremely rich in protein and iron. However, the consumer has not yet been fully educated to pork's higher quality and to the many varieties of cuts that are available. Most fresh pork customers buy pork chops or ham, but they are far less knowledgeable about such cuts as pork loins, country style ribs, pork steaks, and the many other items that make up the pork category.

Considering that pork typically generates a higher gross profit percentage than beef and requires lower production costs, there is very good reason for supermarkets to want to promote this product by educating the consumer to its many uses.

Poultry

Automation in poultry raising has dramatically affected both supply and consumption of the two major poultry items—chicken and turkey. Todays' poultry is mass produced in well designed housing with automated feed and water supplies, so that they no longer forage for food. Of all the items carried in the meat department chicken is the product showing the most impressive increase in consumption over the past 20 years. Per capita consumption increased from 21 pounds in 1950 to 43 pounds in 1972. Although consumption dropped slightly in 1973 to 41.4 pounds, there is every reason to believe that chicken will continue to account for a major share of meat department tonnage.

One advantage that chicken holds over other meat department items is that it produces more meat per pound of grain than either hogs or cattle. Moreover, the consumer understands chicken preparation methods better than she does methods of preparing beef, pork, or lamb and has more confidence in buying and cooking chicken than any other meat item. Also, chicken is marketed in a wide variety of forms

—frozen, fresh, whole, parts, etc.—so that it has great versatility in suiting all buying preferences.

Annual per capita consumption of turkey, which was 4 pounds in 1950, reached 8.7 pounds in 1973. The strongest impetus to turkey sales was freezing which took it out of the 1950's luxury item classification and onto the everyday table. With 80 percent of the product being sold during the holidays, production could not keep up with demand 20 years ago—hence the move to freezing. Backed by supermarket merchandising and educational efforts, freezing has resulted in turkey becoming more of a year-round demand item than it was in the past. Although turkey sales have been relatively stable during the past few years, promotional efforts to merchandise many new products, such as turkey burgers and boneless turkey roasts, indicate that turkey sales should continue to show increases in the future.

FUTURE TRENDS

While consumption of meat will undoubtedly increase in our affluent society, and tonnage sold through supermarkets will continue to rise, the distribution of meat as a percentage of total store sales will probably decrease in the future. Behind this are the trends toward: (1) larger stores housing more departments (especially non-foods), and (2) the affluent consumer buying more convenience foods and frozen dinners, as well as eating more main meals away from home.

Share of Total Store Sales

Although new products are not unknown to the meat department, they have traditionally been introduced on a very small scale compared to the explosion that has taken place in frozen, dry grocery, and non-food items.

In order for the meat department to maintain its distribution percentage over the past 20 years, in the face of burgeoning new items and new departments in other parts of the store, a very sizeable increase in dollar volume was required. This was accomplished mainly by winning shoppers over from other outlets. As testimony to the unparalleled meat merchandising capability of the supermarket industry, "more than four out of five supermarket shoppers buy 'most' fresh meats in supermarkets" today.[6] In contrast to the dominance of

---

[6] Burgoyne, Inc.

the local butcher shop 40 years ago, 85 percent of today's shoppers depend on supermarkets for fresh meats, 11 percent shop independent butcher shops, and the remaining 4 percent patronize the freezer-farm, wholesale outlets.

Although the predicted long-range increase in per capita consumption will have a positive effect on supermarket meat sales, it is expected to have more of an impact on the restaurant industry as more and more people eat meals away from home. The trend toward a more casual style of living has resulted in a tremendous increase in the number of fast food, vending machine, drive-in, and limited menu operations (i.e., hamburger stands, chicken-in-a-basket, seafood bars, barbecue stands, etc.). There is also a sizeable increase in the number of people eating meals in company and college cafeterias.

By the end of 1973, Americans were spending more than $45 billion a year eating away from home, three times more than they spent on a yearly basis the decade before. This figure is expected to at least double during the next decade.

This trend to eating out will have very little effect on the sales distribution of general merchandise and only a negligible effect on non-food departments. Although it will affect sales in other store departments to some extent, its greatest impact is expected to be felt by the meat department because the types of restaurants showing the greatest growth are those offering limited menu meat, chicken, and seafood items; and few people eat more than one such meal daily.

The combined effect of an increase in new items and departments in other parts of the store and the trend toward more people eating traditional meat department items away from home will be that the supermarket meat department will have to generate considerable additional volume (most likely through expanding its prepared, ready-to-eat food operations) to maintain its contribution to total store sales on a percentage basis. In fact, many supermarket companies have already installed barbecue and other hot, prepared-meat operations and offer specialty items such as party trays prepared by an "appetizing" department in order to capture a part of this expanding demand for ready-to-eat foods.

Cooked and Frozen Items

It is also reasonable to expect that labor rates will continue to rise, triggering a rise in retail prices and markups. For net profits to rise, a breakthrough into cooked and frozen product will have to materialize on a major scale. The industry certainly has the capabilities to produce such product, but customer acceptance is a hurdle that it has not yet been able to overcome.

The major obstacle to consumer acceptance of cooked foods is price. Such foods are understandably expensive on a per-pound basis because of the added labor cost and amount of shrinkage that takes place during the cooking process. While the customer experiences the same shrinkage when she cooks fresh product at home, she usually is not conscious of it and, for the most part, is not yet ready to accept the higher price when the cooking is done for her.

The reasons for the widespread resistance to frozen red meat are more varied. Higher price (caused by increased processing, storage, and distribution costs) is a factor, but the most important obstacles are the appearance of frozen meat (it tends to look old) and the consumer's apparent bondage to tradition when it comes to buying meat. Ironically, when she gets home the shopper herself will put 80 percent of her supermarket meat order into her own freezer. Yet, when products other than turkey, fish, meat patties, Cornish hens, and some other low-demand items are displayed in a frozen meat case, the vast majority of shoppers shy away from them, showing the greatest resistance to frozen red meat.

A number of supermarket companies have tried to merchandise frozen red meat (beef, veal, and lamb), but few have been successful. The general consensus, however, is that when economical processing methods and packaging materials are available that will enhance the appearance of the product, the acceptance of frozen meat will show a marked increase.

Consumer acceptance of frozen meat is definitely in the best interests of the supermarket owner. Its effect on controlling shrinkage and lengthening shelf life are obvious, but additional economies would accrue from having product processed centrally into retail cuts and shipped frozen, ready for the case. Conversion to frozen meat merchandising would have a positive effect on every aspect of the department's operation—ordering, receiving, displaying, sanitation, department size, payroll expense, etc.—but would require a major capital investment in display and storage equipment. For the retailer, as well as for the customer, the advantages to handling frozen product far outweigh its disadvantages.

Because frozen turkey is readily accepted by the consumer,

chicken, which is now being successfully merchandised in chill-pack form (held at 28° F.), and which does not change considerably in appearance when frozen, seems to offer the next best opportunity to penetrate consumer resistance to frozen product. An acceptance of frozen turkey and chicken could well lead to an acceptance of frozen red meat, but this will require educating the consumer to the advantages of frozen product. Despite the proven fact that frozen product is cleaner in terms of bacteria count, the discoloration of frozen red meat, as it is available today, often leads the consumer to believe that the product is old. Furthermore, she may be suspicious of the quality of the frozen product at the time of freezing.

A number of film manufacturers currently are developing wrapping materials that will greatly improve the appearance of frozen red meat. Yet, because the consumer's resistance is primarily psychological, it is difficult to predict when frozen red meat will occupy a significant place in the meat counter and contribute more than the estimated 1 to 4 percent of sales that it does today. However, it is certain that this will happen eventually because of the tremendous advantage that frozen product offers to both the consumer and the retailer.

UNIQUE QUALITIES OF THE MEAT DEPARTMENT

The major factor distinguishing the meat department from other store operations is the investment that must be made in both people and equipment.

Personnel

In terms of labor, the meat department employee requires more training and is more highly skilled than any other employee in the store. Because of the amount of processing that must be done before a meat item is ready for the display counter, it takes far longer to qualify a meat cutter to operate in the meat department than it would to qualify the same employee to work in the produce or grocery department.

To be effective, that same employee needs far more knowledge in product identification than either a grocery or produce employee. Even though the number of items carried in the grocery department is far in excess of the assortment of meat items, most grocery products are clearly labeled with regard to content and, often, method of preparation. A produce clerk certainly requires product knowledge, but compared to meat, fewer produce items present problems from the consumer's point of view. On the other hand, the meat department employee must be able to identify all the cuts, know what cooking methods are recommended for each, the cooking time required, how to store the product at home, what cuts can be substituted for others, and so on.

The average customer, young or old, is fairly knowledgeable about chicken, but she knows less about other meat items (some steaks and roasts excepted, perhaps) and is often confused when she shops the meat department. One of the biggest opportunities for expanding the horizon of the meat shopper beyond some steak and roast items lies in the hands of the knowledgeable meat department employee.

Store Equipment

In addition to its investment in people, the meat department represents a major investment in equipment.

In a 30,000-sq. ft. store, the meat department typically occupies about 10 percent of the total store space, with approximately half devoted to the backroom for processing, cooler, and freezer space, and the balance devoted to the display area, including aisles. The cost required to equip a department of this size will vary with the functions performed and the type of equipment specified. However, in a high-volume store where the use of automated scales, fully automated wrappers, multi-deck display cases, rail scales, and other such equipment is justified, the investment in equipment is considerably higher than for any other department, with the possible exception of an extensive in-store bakery operation. And although it occupies only 10 percent of the store space, the meat department contributes an average of 25 percent of the sales.

REMOVING THE MYSTERY

Many management people shy away from the meat department, feeling its operations are too complicated for non-meat personnel to grasp. But, purely and simply, the activities that take place in the meat department involve little more than common sense—common sense in ordering, displaying, merchandising, and in every other aspect of the operation.

It is only common sense to know that if an item has good movement, giving it a wider display will avoid the need for constant restocking. It takes no more than common sense to know that if an item is left out of refrigeration, at some point it will start to discolor. Observation will show that too many items stocked one on top of another will cause the bottom packages to bleed. Methods of retail cutting and trimming of fresh meats are based on common sense. And successful meat merchandising, which so many non-meat people see as an area of special mystique, is really nothing more than the use of a little creativity and ingenuity based, again, on common sense.

There is no reason for non-meat personnel to be afraid of the meat department, as so many are. The fact that a store manager does not know how to break a forequarter into primals is far less important than the contribution he can make to the successful operation of the department by applying his innate common sense, just as he does in other departments.

The purpose of this book is to do away with the mystery of the meat department by sharing with the reader the knowledge gained by the authors during their combined 85 years of experience in meat department operations.

2

Meat Department Organizational Structure

Unlike the grocery department, where lines of communication between headquarters, field, and store level people are fairly uniform throughout the retail food industry, the organizational structure of the meat department takes many shapes and forms. One reason for this is the difference in attitudes from one supermarket company to another as to how the meat department should fit into the structure of the total company and the field organization. Another factor is the variation from company to company in the titles assigned to staff positions and the responsibility that each title carries with it.

In most companies, the meat department director is responsible for buying, pricing, developing merchandising plans, and participating in advertising decisions. There are, however, many variations in the title assigned to the individual filling this position. In one company a department director may be called a department head; in other companies he may be the vice-president of meat operations, vice-president of meat sales and merchandising, meat merchandiser, meat director, head of meat operations, vice-president/meat merchandiser, or any one of several possible titles.

A district manager may be called a zone manager or a district superintendent; a meat specialist may be called a meat merchandiser or a meat supervisor. Such variations in title exist even at the store level where the meat manager in some companies is called a head meat cutter and in others a market manager.

Not only the titles but also the responsibilities and lines of authority will vary from one company to another. To some degree these variations reflect differences in company size. But more often, and particularly where responsibilities and lines of authority are concerned, variations are traceable to basic differences in the management's philosophy of organizational structure.

UPPER ECHELON ORGANIZATION

In contrast to the many variations that exist at store and field level, there is, generally, uniformity at the top of the organizational hierarchy throughout the industry. Sales and operations for the company are headed by a vice-president, to whom two or three top-level people report directly. One of these subordinates to the vice-president of sales and operations would be the director of sales and merchandising; another would be the director of operations; and the third would be the director of advertising.

Director of Sales and Merchandising

Here again there are variations in title. In some companies, the director of sales and merchandising is called the vice-president or director of sales; in others, he would be the vice-president or director of merchandising; and in still other companies, the director of buying and merchandising. However, while the title may vary from one company to another, the areas of responsibility are generally the same. The directors of the three major departments (meat, grocery, and produce) report to the director of sales and merchandising; depending on the size of the company, the size and volume of the stores, the number of stores, and the range of merchandise carried, he may also have directors of delicatessen, dairy, frozen food, and/or non foods reporting directly to him. While the sales and merchandising director most typically reports to the vice-president of sales and operations, in some companies he is directly responsible to the president.

Through his subordinates (i.e., the department directors), the director of sales and merchandising is responsible for buying products for each department, pricing the items, developing merchandising programs for each department, and determining which items are to be advertised. His is a staff function—the people working for him generally have no direct authority within the store.

Director of Operations

The director of operations, on the other hand, is responsible for operations at each of the company's stores. To him report the district managers, each of whom may supervise from 5 to 20 stores depending on the geographical spread, volume, and size of the stores. The director of operations is therefore responsible for the line operations; the people who report to him give direct instructions to store personnel on such matters as methods and systems, scheduling, labor cost control, supply cost control, and training.

Director of Advertising

In companies doing a volume in excess of $30 to $40 million annually, the vice-president of sales and operations will generally have a third person, the director of advertising, reporting to him, although some companies prefer to contract with a professional advertising firm to perform this function. The director of advertising is in a staff position in that he has no authority concerning store operations.

Generally, in a company operating 30 or 40 supermarkets, the director of advertising meets weekly, or as often as two or three times a week, with the department directors of meat, grocery, produce, etc., to establish the advertising program for the following week. With the guidance of the director of sales and merchandising, and with the very important input of each department director, the director of advertising develops a balanced program for the various departments that will put the company in a good competitive position for the following week. Very often the decisions concerning what should be advertised depend not only on past success or failure but also on what competition is doing.

Responsibility for Performance

The director of sales and merchandising and the director of operations are jointly responsible to the vice-president of sales and operations for sales and gross profits. Because of the influence that each of these departments exerts on sales and gross profits, it is not possible to hold only the operations people or only the sales and merchandising people responsible for all facets of the operation. Typically, the department directors have the responsibility for buying, developing the merchandising programs, and pricing various products. The merchandising programs that they develop, when accepted by the director of sales and merchandising, are then turned over to the operations department for implementation. Thus, both sales and merchandising, as well as operations, have a vested interest in the results produced by the buying, pricing, and implementation of the merchandising programs; and both are jointly responsible and accountable for sales and gross profits.

VARIATIONS IN ORGANIZATIONAL STRUCTURE

Variations in the organizational structure of the meat operation basically center around to whom the meat specialists in the field and the field and department managers at store level report in each company.

Chart A

Figure 2 shows one of the more conventional structures for the sales and operations end of the business in a company with from 20 to 100 stores. The main feature of this organizational structure is that the meat specialists report to the department director while the meat department managers report to their own store managers. Problems may be created if the meat specialists, who are technically staff personnel, operate in such a way that they function as line supervisors of the meat department. This can happen any time that a meat specialist issues instructions directly to the meat department manager. If the instructions contradict those issued by the district manager, who is the line supervisor of the store, or by the store manager himself, conflicts will arise and serious morale problems can be created at store level.

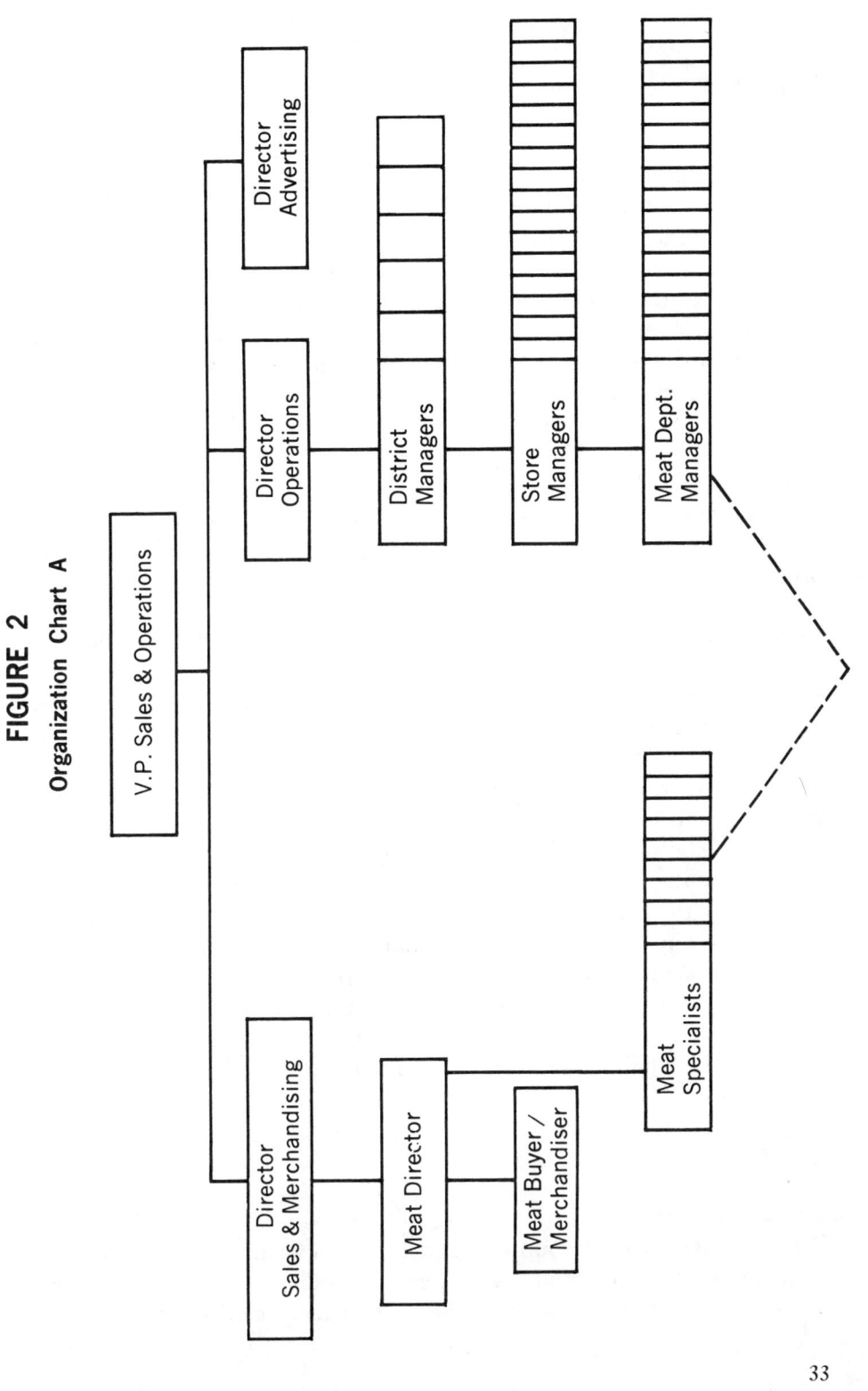

Chart B

The conflict in authority that may be created in the Chart A type of organizational structure has led many companies during the past few years to move toward the type of structure shown in Figure 3. The major difference between Charts A and B is that in Chart B the specialists report to the district manager, rather than to the meat director, and are assigned by the district manager to problem stores within the district. Here, again, conflicts will arise if the specialists, who are still technically staff personnel, act in a line capacity, bypassing the store managers and dealing directly with the department managers at store level, but they will occur at a lower level where they can be more easily controlled by the district manager who supervises both the specialists and the store managers. Chart B represents probably the most common type of organizational structure in existence today.

Chart C

Chart C (see Figure 4) is exactly the same as Chart B in that the meat specialists and the store managers report to the district manager. However, in Chart C the specialist is organized to act in a line capacity. Whereas in Chart B the meat department manager may be subject to conflicting directives from his own store manager and the meat specialist, in the Chart C structure, he is responsible to the meat specialist only for the technical aspects of his job and to the store manager only for administrative matters.

Thus, the store manager has no voice in the technical responsibilities of the meat department manager, and the specialist does not get involved in such administrative matters as employee hours, payroll and fringe benefits, and adherence to union contracts. However, the dividing line between what is technical and what is administrative is often fuzzy, particularly in areas such as ordering, inventory control, production planning, and payroll control; and conflicts can arise in these undefined areas.

Chart D

The most recent innovation in organizational structure, and one that is rapidly growing in popularity, is depicted in Chart D (see Figure 5), a variation of Charts B and C. The major differences in Chart D are: (1) there are fewer specialists, and (2) the specialists report to the

FIGURE 3

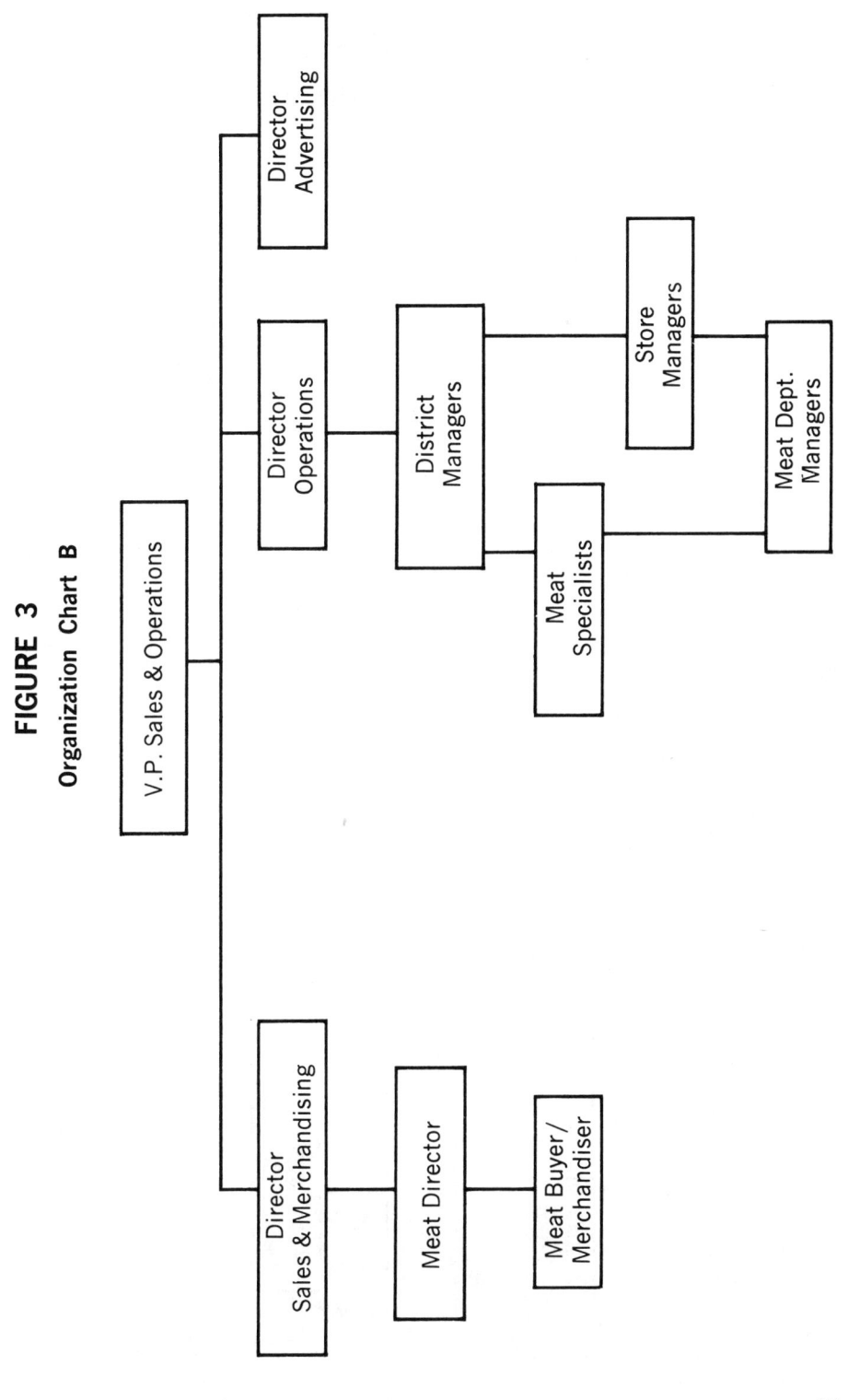

Organization Chart B

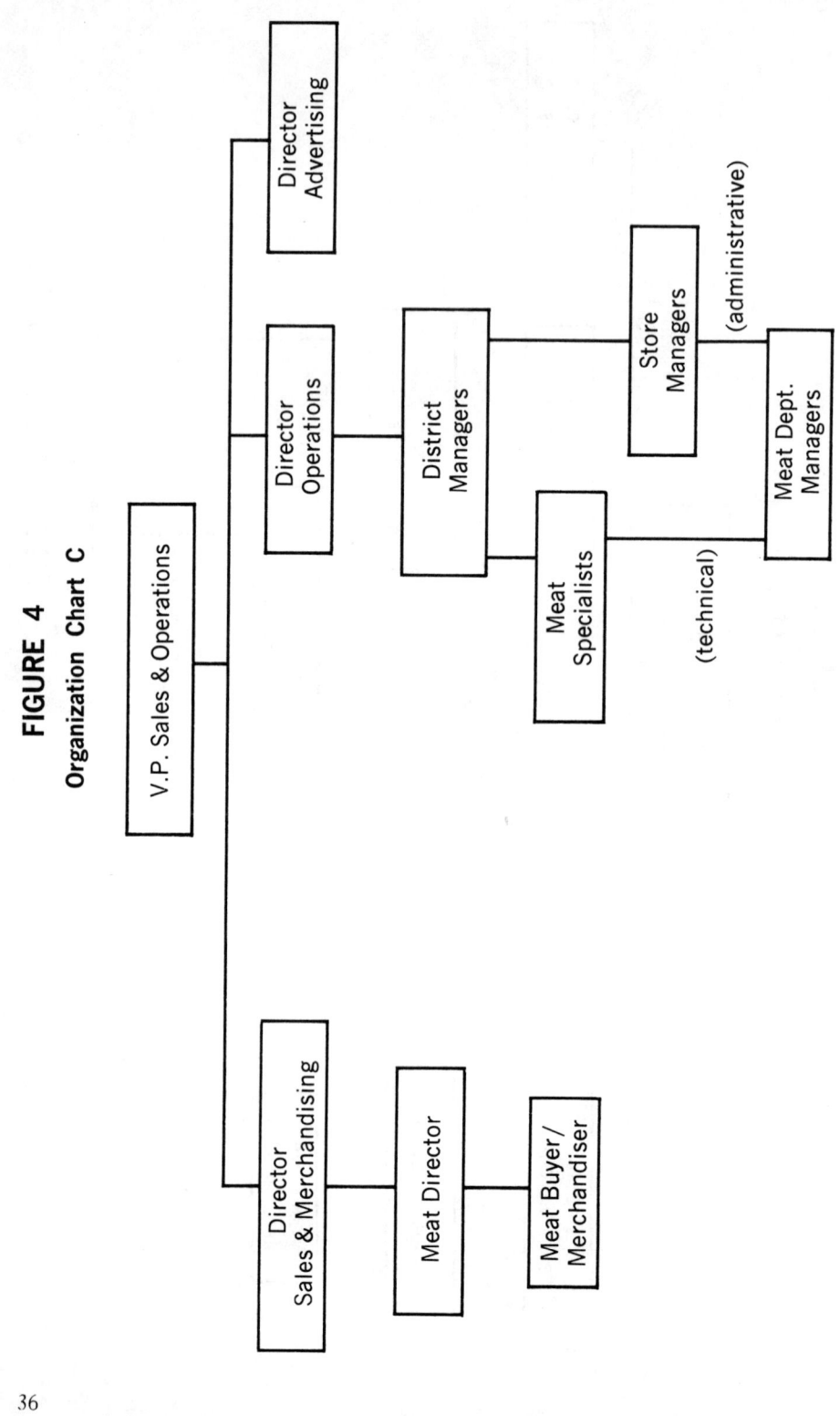

FIGURE 4
Organization Chart C

FIGURE 5

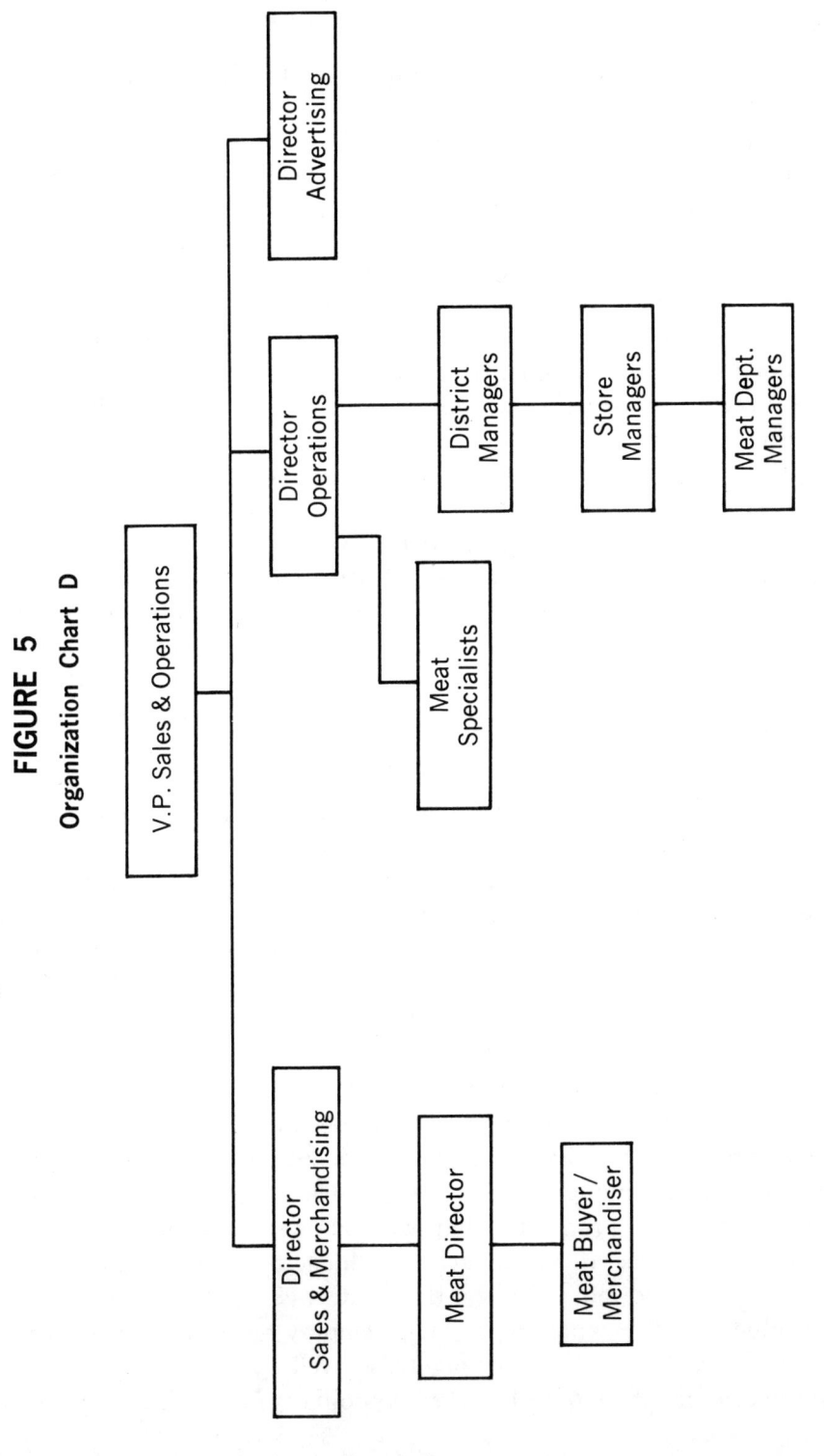

Organization Chart D

- V.P. Sales & Operations
  - Director Sales & Merchandising
    - Meat Director
      - Meat Buyer/Merchandiser
  - Director Operations
    - Meat Specialists
    - District Managers
      - Store Managers
        - Meat Dept. Managers
  - Director Advertising

director of operations rather than to the district managers. With this type of structure, a district manager can request a specialist from the director of operations to handle special problems in any of the stores in his district. The director of operations will then assign a specialist to the district manager who, in turn, assigns the specialist to the problem store. While working in that store, the specialist reports to the store manager, and the store manager is directly involved in the work of the specialist. Thus, although the specialist still acts in a line capacity when he issues instructions to the meat department manager, he does so within the line. Because the specialist reports directly to the director of operations and is only indirectly responsible to the district manager through the store manager, the possibility of conflicting directives being issued to the meat department manager at store level is minimized.

Generally, when the meat department specialist visits a store in an attempt to uncover the source of a problem, he contacts the store manager first; then they go into the department and together attempt to identify the cause of the problem. One of the major advantages of this type of structure is that the store manager is always kept up to date and knowledgeable about the causes of problems existing in his meat department; thus his technical ability in meat department operations is continually being upgraded.

This type of organizational structure tends to minimize the conflicts that arise when a store department manager is responsible to two bosses. However, it takes many, many months of intensive preparation for this type of organizational structure to become workable. The reduction in the number of specialists necessary is possible only if the district, department, and store managers are capable of functioning as real managers so that they can make decisions and handle the day-to-day, non-technical problems that are solved by the many specialists on the staffs of other companies.

The special training required to upgrade the district, store, and department managers so that they can handle the everyday problems that arise is no simple matter. Much work is required to develop the type of training programs that will qualify these people in supervisory capabilities and in meat department operations. In one company, it took two years to effect the changeover. But by accomplishing this objective, the company is able to employ fewer specialists because the department and store managers, as well as the district managers, are better qualified to solve the day-to-day, less technical problems that arise in the meat department. This enables the meat specialists to concentrate their efforts on the more technical problems, on training present and new department managers, and, equally important, on training store managers in meat department operations.

The major advantages to the Chart D type of organizational structure are: (1) the company can reduce supervisory costs due to employing fewer specialists on the staff; (2) more problems can be solved when and where they arise—at store level; and (3) perhaps most important, the number of conflicting directives issued to the meat department manager by the specialist, district manager, and store manager can be reduced substantially. Moreover, a properly trained and qualified store manager, in almost all cases, will be far more effective than a specialist who visits the store for an hour or so a few times each week. For all of these reasons, a very significant move has been taking place in the supermarket industry toward this type of organizational structure.

Another very important advantage in training store managers in meat department operations is that it provides the company with far more valuable managers. A pool of store managers, well grounded in merchandising and operating techniques in all store departments, gives a supermarket company a much better qualified group from which to select future field supervisors and company executives. Moreover, companies with this type of expertise coming from their store and district managers feel they have a distinct competitive advantage because they can react more quickly to store-level problems and solve them before they develop into serious loss situations.

Chart E

One other significant organizational structure that merits attention is shown in Figure 6. While this type of structure has been adopted by very few companies, the fact that it is being used in at least two outstanding supermarket organizations makes it worthy of serious consideration.

In this type of organizational structure the meat department is a completely separate and independent arm of the company. The meat department manager has no responsibility to his store manager; he is responsible instead to the meat specialist. The meat specialist, who supervises a number of stores, is directly responsible to an area or

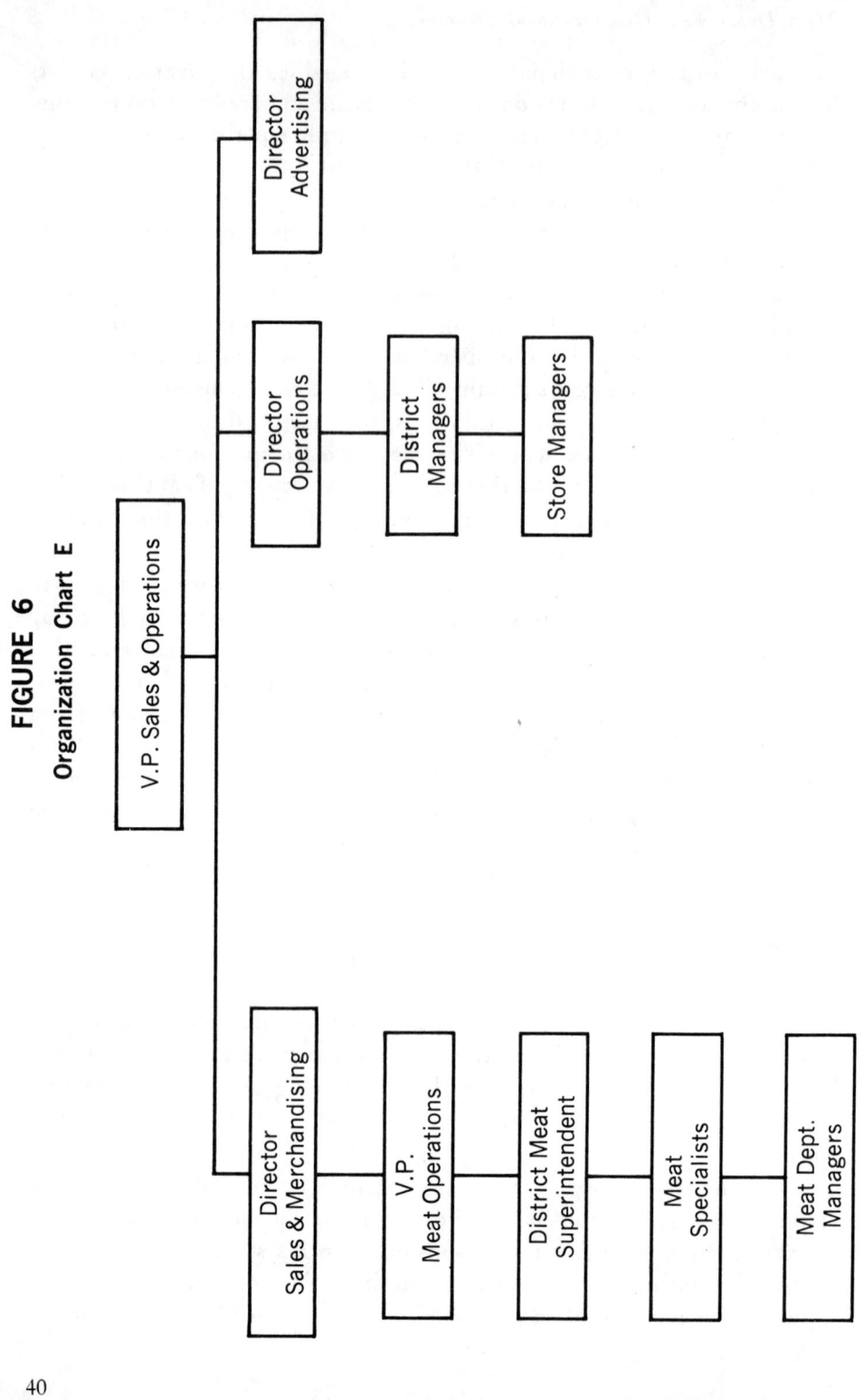

FIGURE 6
Organization Chart E

- V.P. Sales & Operations
  - Director Sales & Merchandising
    - V.P. Meat Operations
      - District Meat Superintendent
        - Meat Specialists
          - Meat Dept. Managers
  - Director Operations
    - District Managers
      - Store Managers
  - Director Advertising

district meat superintendent; the meat superintendent, in turn, is directly responsible to a vice-president of meat operations.

This organizational structure, while rare in the supermarket industry today, has the advantage of straight line supervision without the possibility of crossing lines of authority. It therefore reduces the conflict that can arise when varying directives are given to the meat manager at store level. On the other hand, several companies have found from their own experience that this type of structure limits the store manager's ability to function as a true store manager since he is essentially put into the position of being only a manager of the grocery and produce departments. Such a structure may tend to become a divisive factor as far as store unity and teamwork are concerned.

While a few companies have found this type of organizational structure to be the best solution for them, most other companies have found that the disadvantages outweigh the advantages. Such companies, which prefer the general store manager concept whereby the store manager is responsible for all departments within the store, have adopted the A, B, C, or D organizational structures described above. Of course, the organizational structure that is best for one company will not necessarily work for another company.

STORE LEVEL ORGANIZATION

In addition to the managers of the three major store departments (meat, produce, and grocery) and depending on the size of the store and the variety of merchandise carried, there may also be an assistant store manager (sometimes called a co-manager), a delicatessen manager, a bakery manager, a dairy and frozen foods manager, a nonfoods manager, and/or a checkout or front-end manager.

Even these departmental breakdowns will vary from company to company. In some companies the meat manager will be responsible for delicatessen operations (whether service or self-service) in addition to meat operations. In other companies he may be responsible for the meat operation only, with a separate delicatessen manager responsible for the service delicatessen. In some companies the delicatessen operation will include a service fresh seafood department; in others it will be part of the meat department. Here again, the variations from one company to another are based on the philosophy of management with regard to how the organization should be structured.

Generally, within each meat department there is a manager and a full-time assistant manager who is in charge of the department when the manager is not present. The assistant manager is most often the senior meat cutter in the department. The number of additional personnel in the department will vary not only with the department's dollar volume but also with the amount of packaging that is done before product gets to the store, the variety of product carried in the department, the type and amount of processing equipment used, and the layout of the department and the methods used.

Store level staff requirements are often based on the hours required for the variable and fixed functions to be performed in the department, a subject that will be covered in detail in Chapter 11.

CHOOSING THE OPTIMUM ORGANIZATIONAL STRUCTURE

In order to determine the best organizational structure which will harmonize upper echelon, field, and store level operations, a company must first make two basic decisions: (1) what is the desired authority and responsibility of the meat department manager, and (2) what is the desired authority, responsibility, and accountability of the store manager. These decisions are not easy ones, but they must be made by every company because of their far-reaching impact on personnel, the daily functioning of the meat department, and the future of the organization. It is encouraging to note that studies made over the past 10 years indicate that most companies are answering these questions in a way that leads them to the Chart C or D organizational structures which tend to straighten the lines of communication between headquarters, field, and store level personnel.

3

Knowing the Product

Practically every supermarket carries meat products that fall into the following four major categories:

1. Fresh: Includes beef, veal, lamb, pork, poultry, sausage, variety meats (offal), and fish.
2. Cured and smoked: Includes corned beef, bacon, sausage, luncheon meats, and ham.
3. Canned: Includes hams, bacon, luncheon meats, Vienna-style sausages, and main dishes such as corned beef hash.
4. Frozen: Includes any fresh or processed product that has been frozen—most typically chickens, turkeys, Cornish hens, liver, beef and other patties, luncheon meats, sausage, cooked entrees and dinners, and fish.

While fresh meats are rung on the meat department key almost without exception, there are variations from one company to another on where cured and smoked, canned, and frozen items are rung. In some companies many of these items are rung in the meat department while in other companies the department credited with the sale is determined by who handles the product and where it is displayed. For example, in one company all frozen meat and fish may be displayed in the frozen food department and credited to the grocery or frozen food department. In a second company, these frozen items may be displayed in frozen food display cases located in the meat department, and sales on frozen product are credited to the meat department. In still a third company, items such as frozen meat patties may be displayed in both the frozen food and meat departments. In such cases, if the meat department has expended the labor to process, price, and display the item, a self-adhesive price label is often attached to the package indicating to the checker that it is a meat department item.

Luncheon meat is another category subject to variations. Generally, for accountability, such sales are credited to the department handling the items. In some companies this will be the meat department; in others the delicatessen or appetizing department.

Among the items that are normally rung on the meat department key, fresh products typically capture 60 to 70 percent of the department's sales volume, with the balance of sales being generated in cured and smoked, canned, and frozen items. Typical sales ranges for fresh product as a percentage of total department sales are beef, 30 to 45 percent; pork, 7 to 18 percent; veal, $\frac{1}{2}$ to 4 percent; lamb, $\frac{1}{2}$ to 4 percent; poultry, 8 to 20 percent; and fresh fish, $\frac{1}{2}$ to 3 percent. For other items credited to the meat department, typical sales ranges would be bacon, 3 to 8 percent; smoked ham, 3 to 8 percent; canned ham, 1 to 2 percent; luncheon meat, 10 to 17 percent, and frozen items, 1 to 4 percent (See Figure 7.)

Here, too, there are considerable variations not only from one company to another but also among stores operated by the same company. These variations most often reflect customer preferences which have a marked effect on a store's product mix. These preferences also relate to income levels and geographic location. It is not unusual for a regional chain, for example, to have two stores in the same metropolitan area varying in beef distribution from a low of 30 percent to a high of 50 percent because of differences in the income, needs, and desires of the consumers shopping each store. Usually, the store that is below average in beef sales will be well above average on pork sales, as well as on items such as fresh and smoked sausages and luncheon meats.

FIGURE 7

Typical Sales Ranges by Product

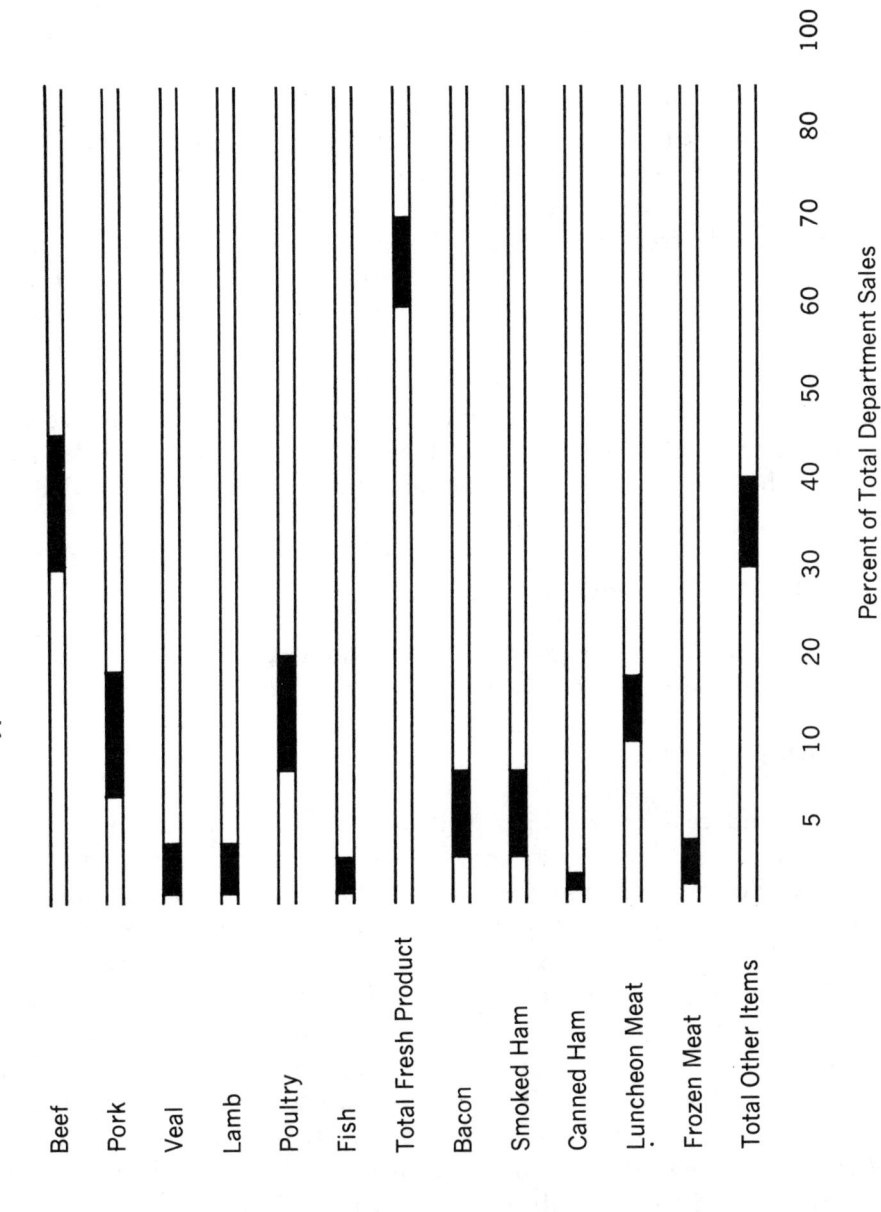

Beef
Pork
Veal
Lamb
Poultry
Fish
Total Fresh Product
Bacon
Smoked Ham
Canned Ham
Luncheon Meat
Frozen Meat
Total Other Items

Percent of Total Department Sales

Examples of variations in product mix based on geographical location would include higher than typical sales on fresh fish in coastal areas or higher poultry sales in Southern states. Income levels also affect the distribution of sales by commodity group within the meat department. For example, residents in affluent areas would be more likely to buy rib or loin steaks, as opposed to meats for stewing. In some areas, however, such preferences might also be traced to ethnic rather than economic factors.

Despite these variations in sales distribution, fresh product, particularly fresh red meats (those produced from cattle, sheep, and hogs), typically occupy the most display space and account for the largest portion of the meat department's dollar volume. Because of the tonnage moved, the perishable nature of the product, the number and variety of items stocked, and the unlimited opportunities that can be capitalized when these items are properly merchandised, fresh red meat is the most important product category in the department and the one about which personnel must be the most knowledgeable.

RED MEAT ANIMALS

In the red meat category are beef and veal, produced from cattle; lamb, produced from sheep; and pork, produced from hogs.

Cattle

Beef and veal are distinguished by the age of the cattle at the time of slaughter. Veal meat comes from a calf which is usually slaughtered between 12 and 14 weeks of age but can be as young as 5 weeks. Because of its youth, veal contains very little fat, and the lean is a light, grayish-pink in color. Baby beef is produced from slightly older cattle and is usually four to eight months old at the time of slaughter. It contains more fat than veal but less than mature beef, and its lean is more red in color. Also, the fat in baby beef is not as white as the fat in similar grades of mature beef.

What is commonly known as beef to the consumer comes from the more mature animal; most beef sold as retail cuts in supermarkets is from animals 15 to 30 months of age. Meat from cattle more than 30 months old is generally boned out and used for making processed products like frankfurters, bologna, and luncheon meats. Cattle that have grown to maturity are further identified by sex and are divided accordingly into five classes: steers (young castrated males); heifers (females that have not calved); cows (females that have had one or more calves); bulls (uncastrated, sexually mature males); and stags (males castrated after reaching sexual maturity).

Sheep

Lamb and mutton are produced from sheep and, like beef, are also distinguished by age and sex. Lamb, produced from young sheep usually less than a year old, contains lean that is pinkish-red in color. Yearling mutton is between one and two years of age, and mutton is produced from sheep more than 24 months old. The older the sheep, the redder its lean and the drier and less red its bones. Most of the sheep sold in supermarkets is marketed as lamb; only an insignificant amount of mutton is sold as fresh product. The classes of sheep according to sex are wethers (males castrated when young), rams (uncastrated males), and ewes (females).

Hogs

Pork is produced from hog barrows (young castrated males) and gilts (young females) that have been slaughtered at about five to nine months of age. The color of the lean in fresh pork ranges from grayish-pink to rose. Meat from older hogs, such as sows (females), stags (castrated males), and boars (uncastrated males) is generally boned out and used for products such as sausage meat and Canadian-style bacon.

WHOLESALE CUTS OF RED MEAT

For ease in transportation and processing, red meats are broken down in varying degrees before they reach the retailer.

Breaking Beef

The term "carcass" refers to the entire animal. After slaughtering, the beef carcass is split in half along the backbone from neck to rump. Each side is then split in half at the mid-section, producing a "forequarter" and a "hindquarter." The major subsections into which the forequarters and hindquarters are cut are known as "primal" cuts.

"Retail" cuts are made from the primals. In some cases there is an intermediary breaking stage which produces "subprimals" or "saw-ready primals."

Beef is so large and heavy it is impractical to transport it in one piece from packer to retailer. For this reason, it is cut into quarters when slaughtered. The four quarters together are referred to as a "straight" carcass, and one forequarter and a hindquarter together are referred to as a "side" of beef. The major primals cuts from the beef forequarter are the chuck (shoulder), rib, brisket, and plate; the major hindquarter primals are the loin, round, and flank. (See Figure 8.) Primals that are broken into smaller wholesale cuts are termed subprimals. For example, a loin can be divided into a short loin and a sirloin, and the tip is a subprimal taken from the round or sirloin. When subprimals are trimmed so that they are ready to be placed on the saw for retail cutting, they are called saw-ready primals.

Breaking Veal and Lamb

Veal and lamb are usually small enough to be handled without splitting and can be transported as whole carcasses, sides, saddles, or primals. The first major breakdown of a veal or lamb carcass will result in a side or a saddle, depending on how the carcass is broken. If it is cut in the same manner as beef, i.e., from neck to rump, the cutting will produce two sides. However, if it is split in half across the midsection of the animal, leaving the backbone intact, which is frequently done with smaller carcasses, the front half of the animal is called a foresaddle and the rear half a hindsaddle. When the sides, or saddles, are split in half, the resulting cuts are called forequarters and hindquarters.

The veal and lamb forequarters yield the shoulder, rib, and breast, while the hindquarters yield the loin, leg, and flank. It is from these primals that the retail cuts are made. (Figures 9 and 10.)

Breaking Pork

While pork is small enough to be transported easily in carcass form, it rarely is. Because so many pork products are processed (for example, cured and smoked hams, sausages, lard, etc.), the carcass is broken down into primal cuts at the packing plant so that the cuts to be cured, smoked, or used in manufactured meat products can be removed. The most important pork primal requiring processing in

FIGURE 8

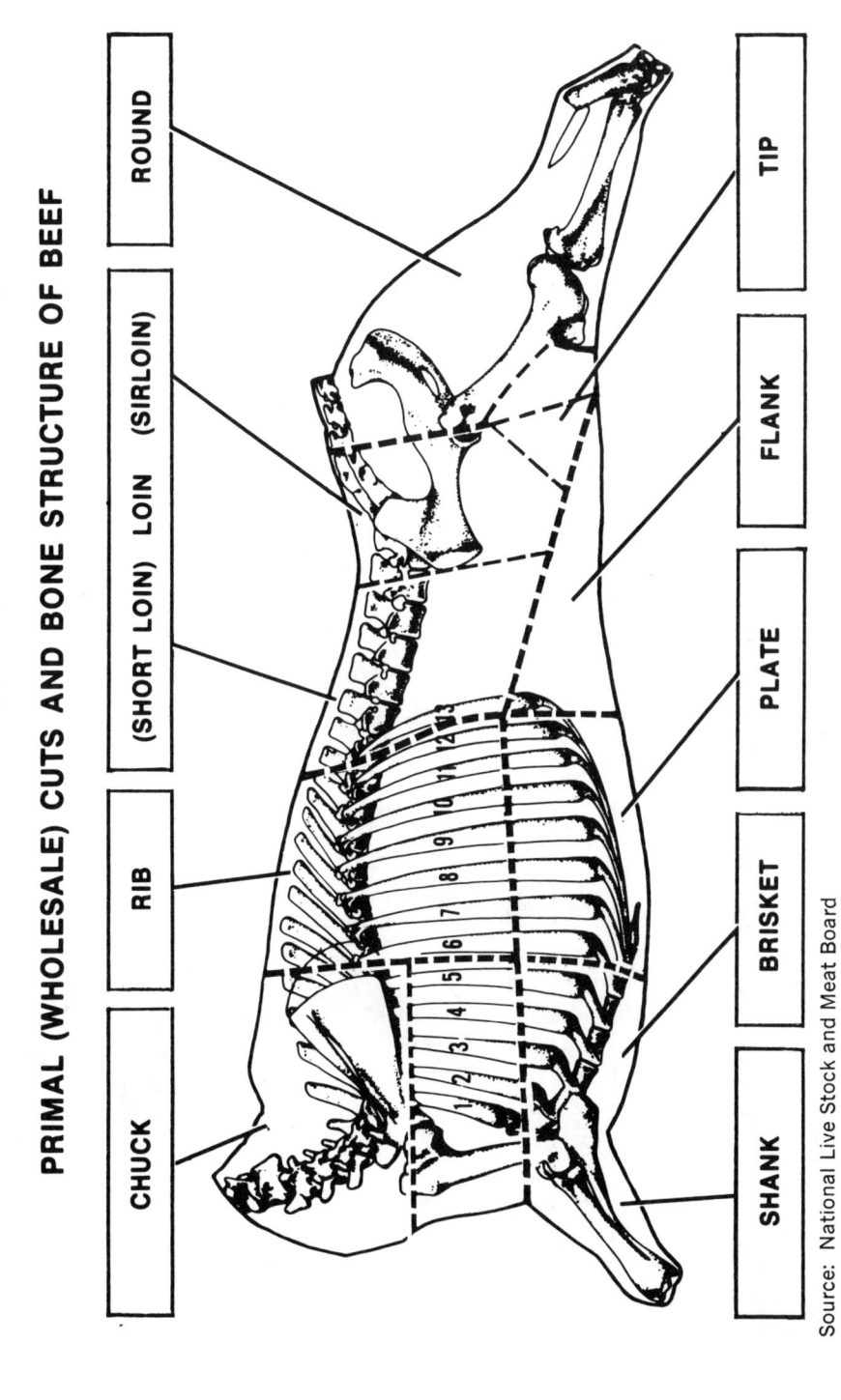

PRIMAL (WHOLESALE) CUTS AND BONE STRUCTURE OF BEEF

CHUCK | RIB | (SHORT LOIN) LOIN (SIRLOIN) | ROUND

SHANK | BRISKET | PLATE | FLANK | TIP

Source: National Live Stock and Meat Board

FIGURE 9

PRIMAL (WHOLESALE) CUTS AND BONE STRUCTURE OF VEAL

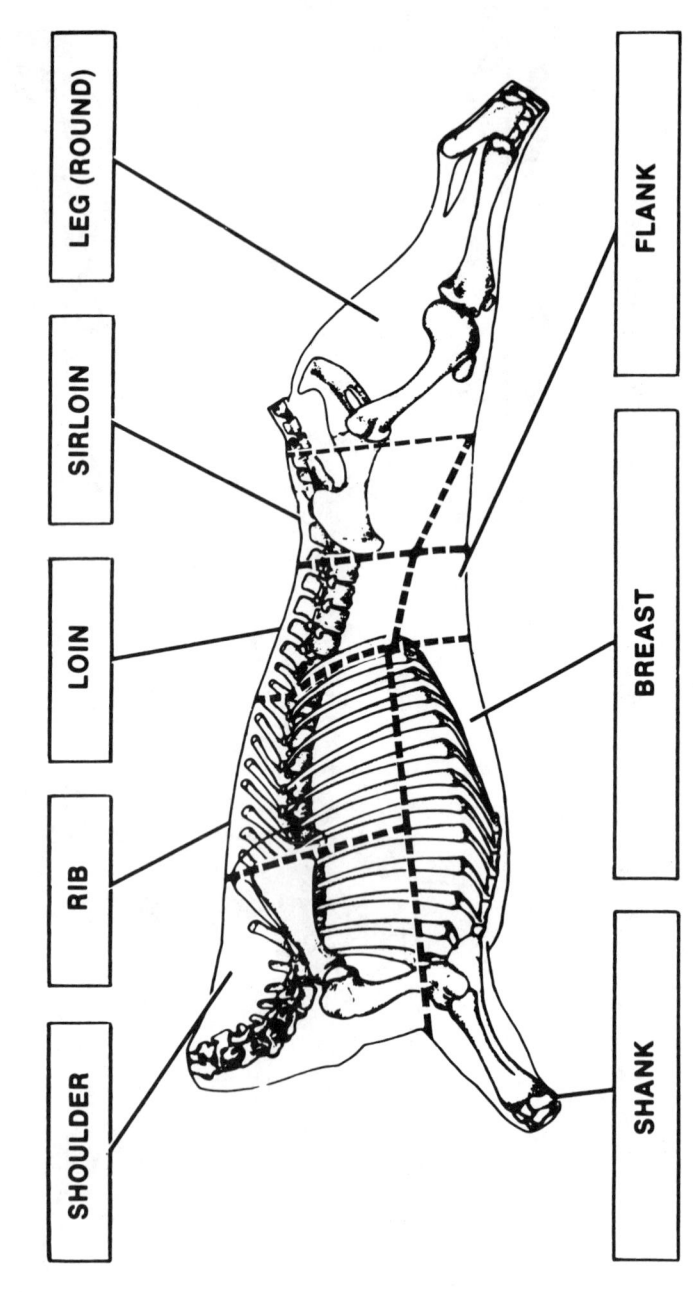

Source: National Live Stock and Meat Board

FIGURE 10

PRIMAL (WHOLESALE) CUTS AND BONE STRUCTURE OF LAMB

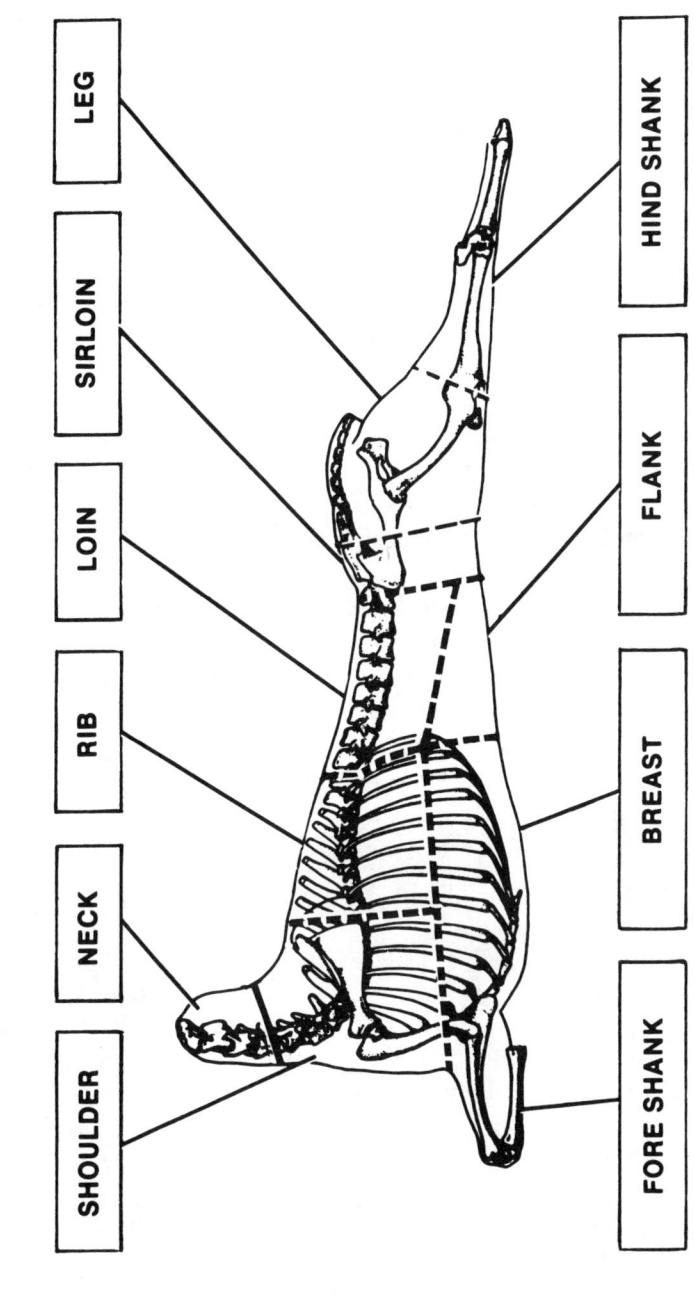

Source: National Live Stock and Meat Board

the supermarket is the pork loin, which is typically cut into chops and roasts. The balance of the animal is usually purchased from the supplier in the forms in which it will be sold, such as picnics, ham, bacon (or fresh bellies), spareribs, and blade Boston roasts (commonly called Boston butts). (See Figure 11.)

NOMENCLATURE FOR RETAIL CUTS

While no exact count has been made, probably 1,000 different names have been used to identify the 300 or so fresh cuts of beef, veal, pork, and lamb sold in supermarkets—much to the chagrin of the confused shopper. For example, the basic steaks cut from a beef sirloin are pin bone, wedge bone, round bone, flat bone, and boneless sirloin. But, depending on the store where the customer shops, a sirloin steak also may be called a hip steak, family steak, hip bone sirloin, top sirloin, rump steak, first cut sirloin, short hip steak, head loin steak, top butt steak, or one of many other variations. Similarly, roasts cut from the sirloin tip are known by several names including tip, sirloin tip, top sirloin, bottom sirloin, face rump, crescent, and veiny.

Moreover, the same name may refer to different retail cuts in different parts of the country. For example, a Delmonico steak is cut from the beef rib in some areas of the country, from the short loin in others, and from the chuck in still others. Bread and butter steaks can be bought in Minnesota, charcoal steaks in Ohio, clod steaks in Detroit, and his-and-her and family steaks in most parts of the country; but there is no general agreement on what these names mean.

The need for a standardized list of names for retail cuts has been accentuated in recent years by the mobility of the American population. The proliferation of names used by retailers and packers to merchandise meat products has made shopping difficult for the customer who can recognize retail cuts by name only.

Currently there are no federal regulations governing the names applied to retail cuts of meat, but at least three states—New York, Ohio, and Massachusetts—have enacted legislation that is aimed primarily at restricting the use of "fanciful" names (for example, Kansas City or New York steak for a beef loin, strip steak) that bear no relation to the portion of the animal from which the cut is taken. The New York State law specifically forbids the use of any fanciful names and details a list of 358 approved names for retail cuts of beef,

FIGURE 11

PRIMAL (WHOLESALE) CUTS AND BONE STRUCTURE OF PORK

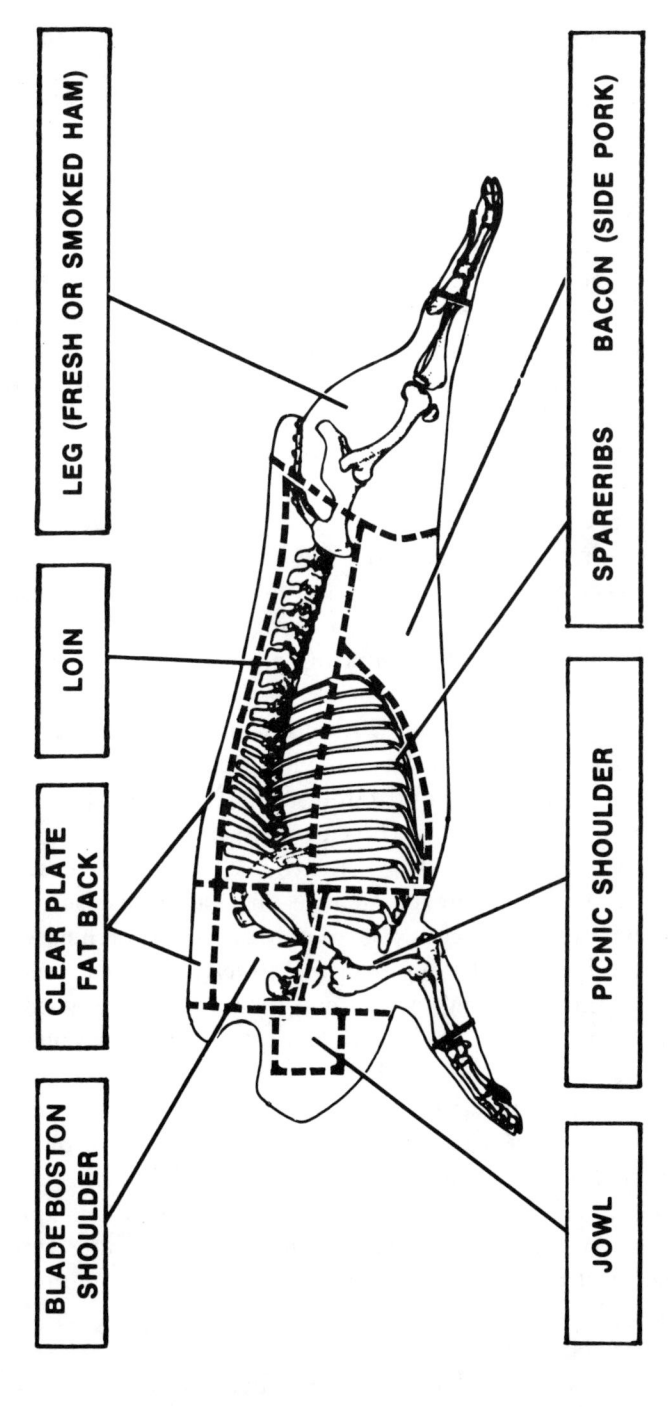

Source: National Live Stock and Meat Board

pork, veal, and lamb. The law further prescribes that the label on the retail package must indicate the name of the primal cut from which the retail cut was taken, in addition to bearing one of the 358 approved names. According to the Massachusetts and Ohio laws, fanciful names may be used in labeling; however, the approved name spelled out in the legislation must also be included.

Partly to avoid the threat of a variety of state regulations that would be impractical for interstate operators, but more so because the supermarket operator realizes that most shoppers restrict their purchases to the few cuts with which they are familiar, the meat industry has been attempting to standardize the names of retail cuts. The most impressive work to date has been accomplished by the Industrywide Cooperative Meat Identification Standards Committee (ICMISC) which was created in 1972 by the meat industry. Among the membership are executives from representative supermarket and packer/processing companies and trade associations. The Committee also has received assistance from appropriate federal, state, and municipal agencies as well as several consumer groups.

Through the coordinating efforts of the National Live Stock and Meat Board, the *Uniform Retail Meat Identity Standards* manual was published in late 1973. The manual includes, among other information, a master list of 314 recommended names for retail cuts of beef, veal, pork, and lamb. It is the most comprehensive summary on retail meat nomenclature ever assembled.

In developing the list, the Committee reviewed hundreds of names, weeding out all but the one name best suited to describe each of the 314 retail cuts. In most cases, only generic anatomical names were adopted, although a few fanciful names (such as porterhouse steak and filet mignon) were included along with their anatomical names because of their wide acceptance among consumers.

The new meat labeling standards include the species of the animal, the primal cut name, and the specific retail name taken from the master list. The species (beef, pork, lamb, or veal) is listed first on the label, followed by the primal cut (chuck, rib, etc.) which tells what part of the animal the meat comes from, and then the appropriate retail name from the master list. Some typical labels would read as follows: "Beef Chuck, Blade Roast," "Pork Shoulder, Blade Steak," Lamb Shoulder, Blade Chops," etc. (See Appendix for complete master list.)

Because the list is a comprehensive one, designed to serve stores in all marketing areas, a store in one market area will probably need to select only half of the 314 recommended names to describe its retail cuts. Moreover, a store would be able to continue to use fanciful names for merchandising purposes, as long as such names were used in addition to the basic recommended identification, assuming there were no conflicting state laws prohibiting the use of fanciful names.

A number of companies have already adopted the master list of recommended names; and there is little doubt that more will do so in the future in order to forestall a multiplicity of legal enactments governing meat labeling, which would be quite costly to both the consumer and the retailer. As meat labeling becomes more uniform and descriptive of the product, considerable consumer confusion will be eliminated. However, when shoppers can only identify meat items by name and are unable to associate the name of the cut with the proper cooking method, they will more often than not pass up cuts with unfamiliar labels.

THE BASIC RETAIL CUTS

In order for a store to merchandise as many cuts of meat as possible and get the best product mix, the retailer should help the customer learn to identify the basic meat cuts and how to cook them. This can be accomplished to some extent by making recipes available, by putting cooking information on the retail package, and by posting illustrative materials, similar to the figures shown in this chapter.

However, a more effective means is for store personnel themselvs to have extensive product knowledge, including the ability to identify by shape and appearance, rather than by name alone, the retail cuts and the primal cuts from which they originated. Because cooking methods are generally determined by the portion of the carcass from which the cut was taken, with such knowledge store personnel will have no difficulty offering advice on proper cooking procedures or suggesting substitutes when the requested item is out of stock. Customers who can take advantage of the broad selection of meat items available not only can add variety to their menus but also will be able to purchase more of the lower-priced, less-demanded items which, in turn, benefits the store.

A basic clue to identifying retail cuts is that the names of such cuts frequently reflect the names of the primal cuts or the shape or name of a bone. When the name of the retail cut reflects the name of the primal cut—for example, round steaks from the round primal—identification is obvious and simple. When this is not the case, as long as the cut contains at least part of the bone, it is still relatively easy to identify by the shape of the bone.

Bones Identifying the Basic Cuts

There are seven major groups of retail cuts. These basic cuts are identified by seven bone groups which are almost identical in beef, veal, pork, and lamb. The seven bone groups illustrated in Figure 12

FIGURE 12
Bones Identifying the Seven Groups of Retail Cuts

SHOULDER ARM CUTS	Arm Bone
SHOULDER BLADE CUTS (Cross Sections of Blade Bone)	Blade Bone (near neck), Blade Bone (center cuts), Blade Bone (near rib)
RIB CUTS	Back Bone and Rib Bone
SHORT LOIN CUTS	Back Bone (T-Shape) T-Bone
HIP (Sirloin) CUTS (Cross Sections of Hip Bone)	Pin Bone (near short loin), Flat Bone* (center cuts), Wedge Bone† (near round)
LEG OR ROUND CUTS	Leg or Round Bone
BREAST, OR BRISKET CUTS	Breast and Rib Bones

*Formerly part of "double bone" but today the back bone is usually removed leaving only the "flat bone" (sometimes called "pin bone") in the sirloin steak.

†On one side of sirloin steak, this bone may be wedge shaped while on the other side the same bone may be round.

Source: National Live Stock and Meat Board

are the key to identifying meat cuts and the only ones that must be recognized because most other bones are removed from the retail cut. Not only do bones indicate the location of a retail cut, but they are also a clue to the tenderness of the cut. Cuts from the less-used muscles along the back of the animal—the rib and loin sections—are always more tender than those from the active muscles such as the shoulder (chuck), flank, and leg (round). Consequently, the meat along the backbone is considered the most tender.

Figure 13 shows the location of the seven basic retail cuts, the wholesale cuts from which they are derived, and the names of the most important identifying bones. Note that the cuts from the breast contain the breast bone and rib bones. Arm cuts have a cross-section of arm bone, and blade cuts contain a cross-section of blade bone. Rib cuts include a rib bone except when steaks and chops are cut from between the ribs. Cuts from the short loin include a section of back bone, commonly called a T-bone because of its similarity to the letter "T." Cross-sections of hip bone are found in the cuts from the sirloin (hip). Slices from the leg contain cross-sections of leg bone. Cuts also may contain other bones, but those named are the ones most closely associated with identification.[1]

The basic cuts shown in Figure 13 are common to beef, veal, lamb, and pork; however, there is considerable variation in retail cutting methods for the breast and flank. The breast in veal and lamb, for example, is sold in one piece or it is converted into a number of retail cuts. In beef, the breast is divided into two primals, brisket and plate, which in turn are made into smaller retail cuts. Flank steaks and cubed steaks can be cut from the beef flank and the remaining lean meat processed into stew meat or ground. The veal flank is generally used for stew meat, and the lamb flank is sometimes ground. Pork is processed in a different manner. The breast and flank are left in one piece; the bones (spareribs) are removed; the boneless side (belly) is trimmed, cured, smoked, and sold as bacon or used for fresh side pork or salt pork. With these exceptions, cutting methods are fairly similar for the seven basic retail cuts of all meat.

Muscles Identifying the Basic Cuts

If the retail cut is boneless, or does not reflect the name of the wholesale cut, recognition of muscle structure becomes important. The fol-

---

[1] Portions of this chapter have been adapted from *Lessons on Meat* and *101 Meat Cuts* with permission from the National Live Stock and Meat Board.

FIGURE 13
The Seven Basic Retail Cuts of Meat *

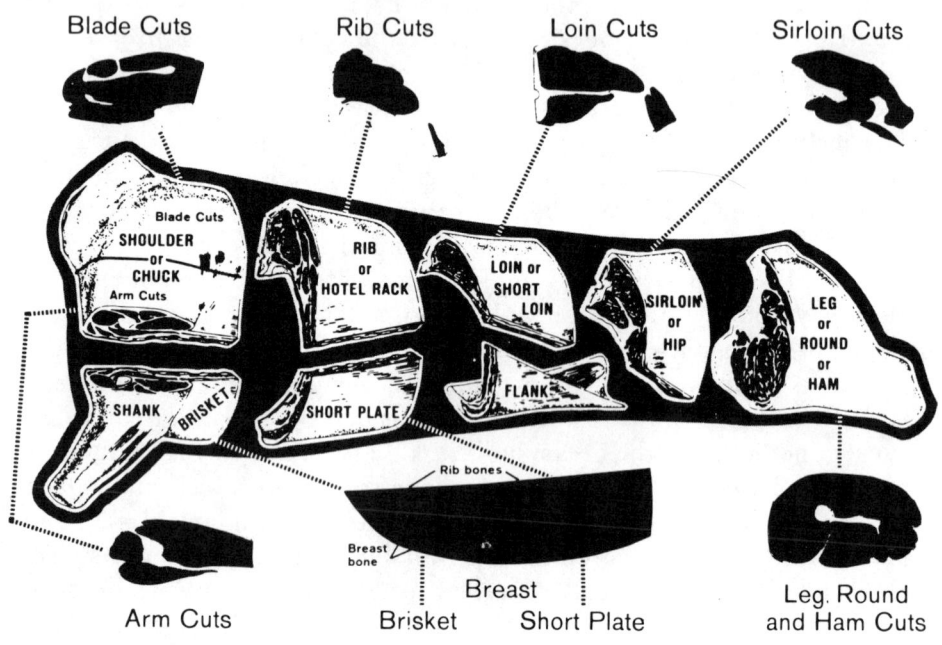

*A side of beef appears in the chart as an example. It could just as well have been veal, pork or lamb, for comparison purposes.

Source: National Live Stock and Meat Board

lowing clues are helpful in identifying all types of retail cuts. The muscles and bones, as well as the relative desirability of cuts from the various parts of all meat animals, are quite similar. In general, as mentioned earlier, cuts from along the back of the animal are the most tender and palatable. They include the rib eye or loin eye muscle, which are the two parts of the largest and most tender muscle lying along the backbone in the rib and loin.

Cuts from the short loin (the area between the hip bone and the last rib) contain two major muscles. The larger muscle is the just-mentioned loin eye and the smaller muscle is the tenderloin. These two muscles are separated by the familiar T-shaped bone. In veal, pork, and lamb this portion of the carcass usually is made into loin chops. In beef, it is nearly always used for steak. (See Figures 14-17.) If the steaks are prepared bone-in, they are referred to as T-bone, porterhouse, or club steaks (also identified as top loin steak). In porterhouse steaks, the tenderloin is large; in the T-bone, it is intermediate in size; and in club steaks, it comprises at most only a small portion of the steak.

When the bone is removed from this section, steaks from the loin eye muscle are called strip steaks, and steaks from the tenderloin muscle are called filet mignon or tenderloin steaks. A tenderloin cut to yield more than one portion has been commonly referred to as a "chateaubriand"; the label now recommended for this cut is "tenderloin roast" or steak.

Behind the short loin is the sirloin, the region containing the hip bone, with large and tender muscles. In beef, this portion usually is made into sirloin steaks. In veal, it is used for sirloin steak and sirloin roast. In lamb, it is included as part of the leg or sold as sirloin chops. And in pork, the sirloin section is made into a roast or sirloin chops.

The hind leg portion of the carcass—the round in beef, ham (or leg) in pork, and leg in veal and lamb—also contains large muscles. The main part of this primal includes only a small, round bone. In beef, the round is made into round steaks or roasts. Because of its size, the main part of the beef round frequently is separated into three major sections—the top round, the bottom round, and the round tip or knuckle.

In pork, the leg (ham) is merchandised whole, separated into rump (butt) and shank halves, or made into a center cut roast or center slices, with the remainder being sold as rump and shank portions. In lamb, the leg may be sold as one piece or made into sirloin

FIGURE 14

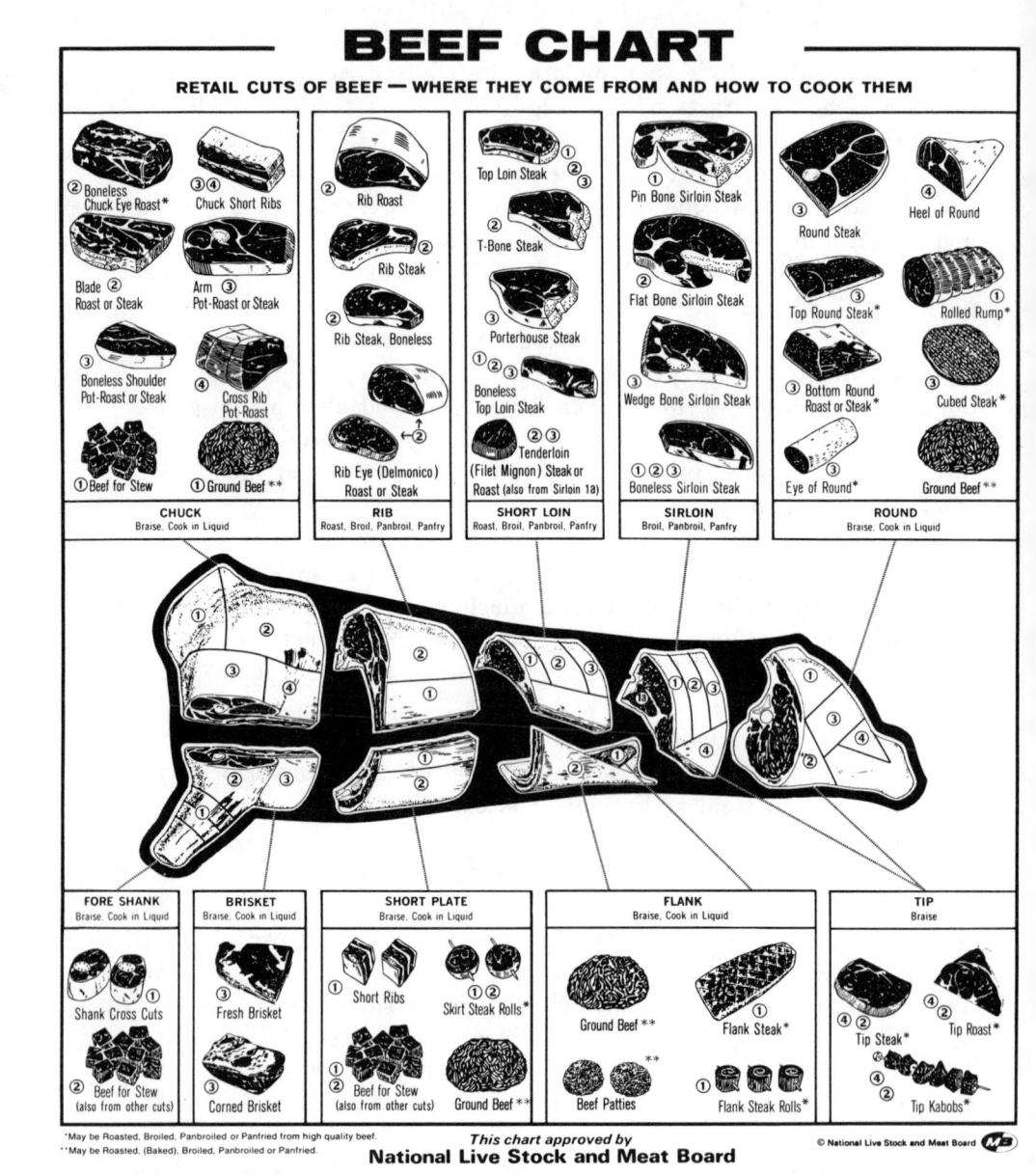

BEEF CHART
RETAIL CUTS OF BEEF — WHERE THEY COME FROM AND HOW TO COOK THEM

CHUCK — Braise, Cook in Liquid
- ② Boneless Chuck Eye Roast*
- ③④ Chuck Short Ribs
- ② Blade Roast or Steak
- ③ Arm Pot-Roast or Steak
- ③ Boneless Shoulder Pot-Roast or Steak
- ④ Cross Rib Pot-Roast
- ① Beef for Stew
- ① Ground Beef**

RIB — Roast, Broil, Panbroil, Panfry
- ② Rib Roast
- ② Rib Steak
- ② Rib Steak, Boneless
- ② Rib Eye (Delmonico) Roast or Steak

SHORT LOIN — Roast, Broil, Panbroil, Panfry
- ②③ Top Loin Steak
- ② T-Bone Steak
- ② Porterhouse Steak
- ①② Boneless Top Loin Steak
- ②③ Tenderloin (Filet Mignon) Steak or Roast (also from Sirloin 1a)

SIRLOIN — Broil, Panbroil, Panfry
- ② Pin Bone Sirloin Steak
- ② Flat Bone Sirloin Steak
- ③ Wedge Bone Sirloin Steak
- ①②③ Boneless Sirloin Steak

ROUND — Braise, Cook in Liquid
- ③ Round Steak
- ④ Heel of Round
- ③ Top Round Steak*
- ① Rolled Rump*
- ③ Bottom Round Roast or Steak*
- ③ Cubed Steak*
- ① Eye of Round*
- ① Ground Beef**

FORE SHANK — Braise, Cook in Liquid
- ① Shank Cross Cuts
- ② Beef for Stew (also from other cuts)

BRISKET — Braise, Cook in Liquid
- ③ Fresh Brisket
- ③ Corned Brisket

SHORT PLATE — Braise, Cook in Liquid
- ① Short Ribs
- ①② Skirt Steak Rolls*
- ② Beef for Stew (also from other cuts)
- ② Ground Beef**

FLANK — Braise, Cook in Liquid
- Ground Beef**
- ① Flank Steak*
- ① Beef Patties**
- ① Flank Steak Rolls*

TIP — Braise
- ④② Tip Steak*
- ④② Tip Roast*
- ④② Tip Kabobs*

*May be Roasted, Broiled, Panbroiled or Panfried from high quality beef.
**May be Roasted, (Baked), Broiled, Panbroiled or Panfried.

This chart approved by
National Live Stock and Meat Board

© National Live Stock and Meat Board

FIGURE 15

VEAL CHART

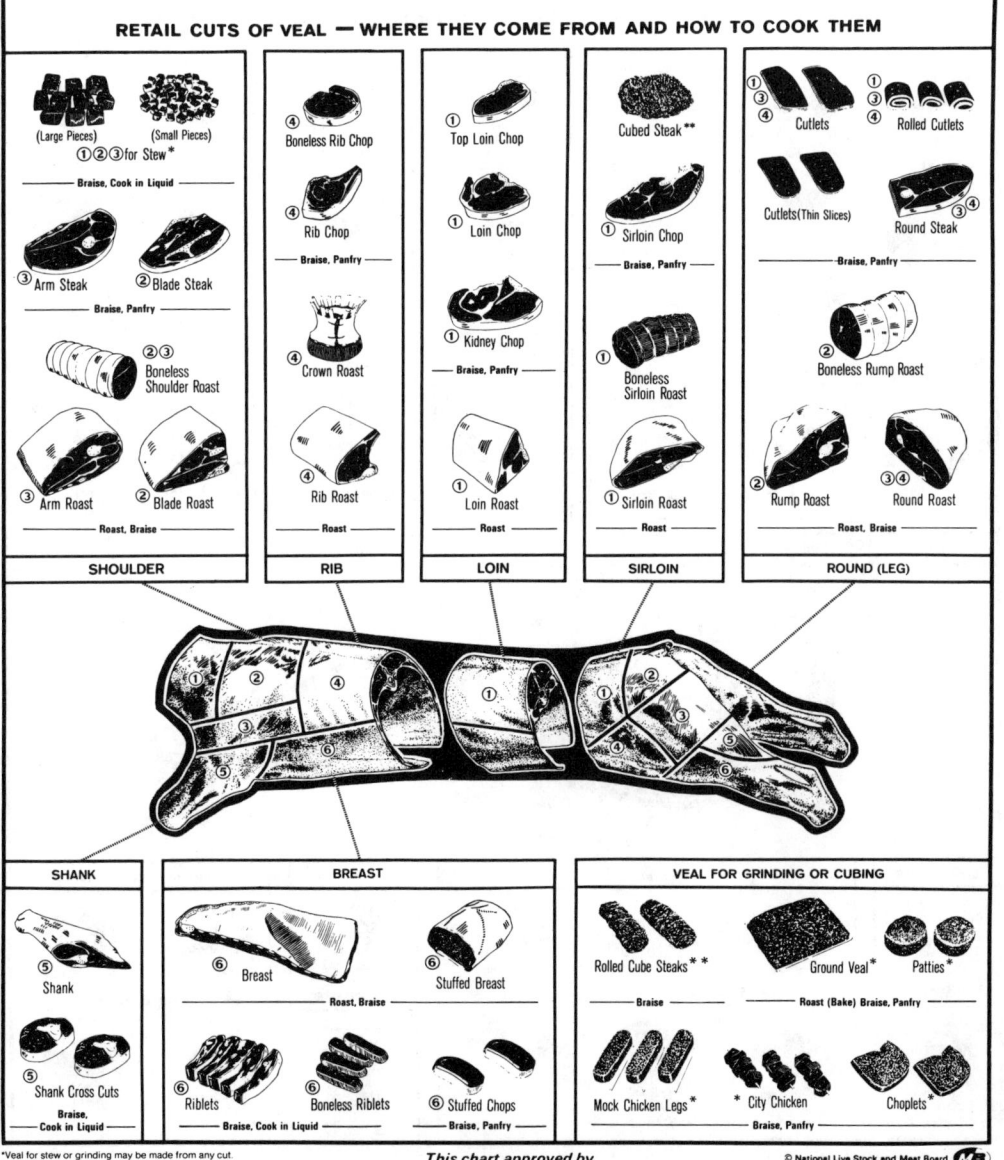

RETAIL CUTS OF VEAL — WHERE THEY COME FROM AND HOW TO COOK THEM

SHOULDER
- (Large Pieces) (Small Pieces) ①②③ for Stew*
  — Braise, Cook in Liquid —
- ③ Arm Steak / ② Blade Steak
  — Braise, Panfry —
- ②③ Boneless Shoulder Roast
- ③ Arm Roast / ② Blade Roast
  — Roast, Braise —

RIB
- ④ Boneless Rib Chop
- ④ Rib Chop
  — Braise, Panfry —
- ④ Crown Roast
- ④ Rib Roast
  — Roast —

LOIN
- ① Top Loin Chop
- ① Loin Chop
- ① Kidney Chop
  — Braise, Panfry —
- ① Loin Roast
  — Roast —

SIRLOIN
- Cubed Steak**
- ① Sirloin Chop
  — Braise, Panfry —
- ① Boneless Sirloin Roast
- ① Sirloin Roast
  — Roast —

ROUND (LEG)
- ①④ Cutlets / ①④ Rolled Cutlets
- Cutlets (Thin Slices) / ③④ Round Steak
  — Braise, Panfry —
- ② Boneless Rump Roast
- ② Rump Roast / ③④ Round Roast
  — Roast, Braise —

SHANK
- ⑤ Shank
- ⑤ Shank Cross Cuts
  — Braise, Cook in Liquid —

BREAST
- ⑥ Breast / ⑥ Stuffed Breast
  — Roast, Braise —
- ⑥ Riblets / ⑥ Boneless Riblets
  — Braise, Cook in Liquid —
- ⑥ Stuffed Chops
  — Braise, Panfry —

VEAL FOR GRINDING OR CUBING
- Rolled Cube Steaks**
  — Braise —
- Ground Veal* / Patties*
  — Roast (Bake) Braise, Panfry —
- Mock Chicken Legs* / *City Chicken / Choplets*
  — Braise, Panfry —

*Veal for stew or grinding may be made from any cut.
**Cube steaks may be made from any thick solid piece of boneless veal.

This chart approved by
National Live Stock and Meat Board

© National Live Stock and Meat Board

FIGURE 16

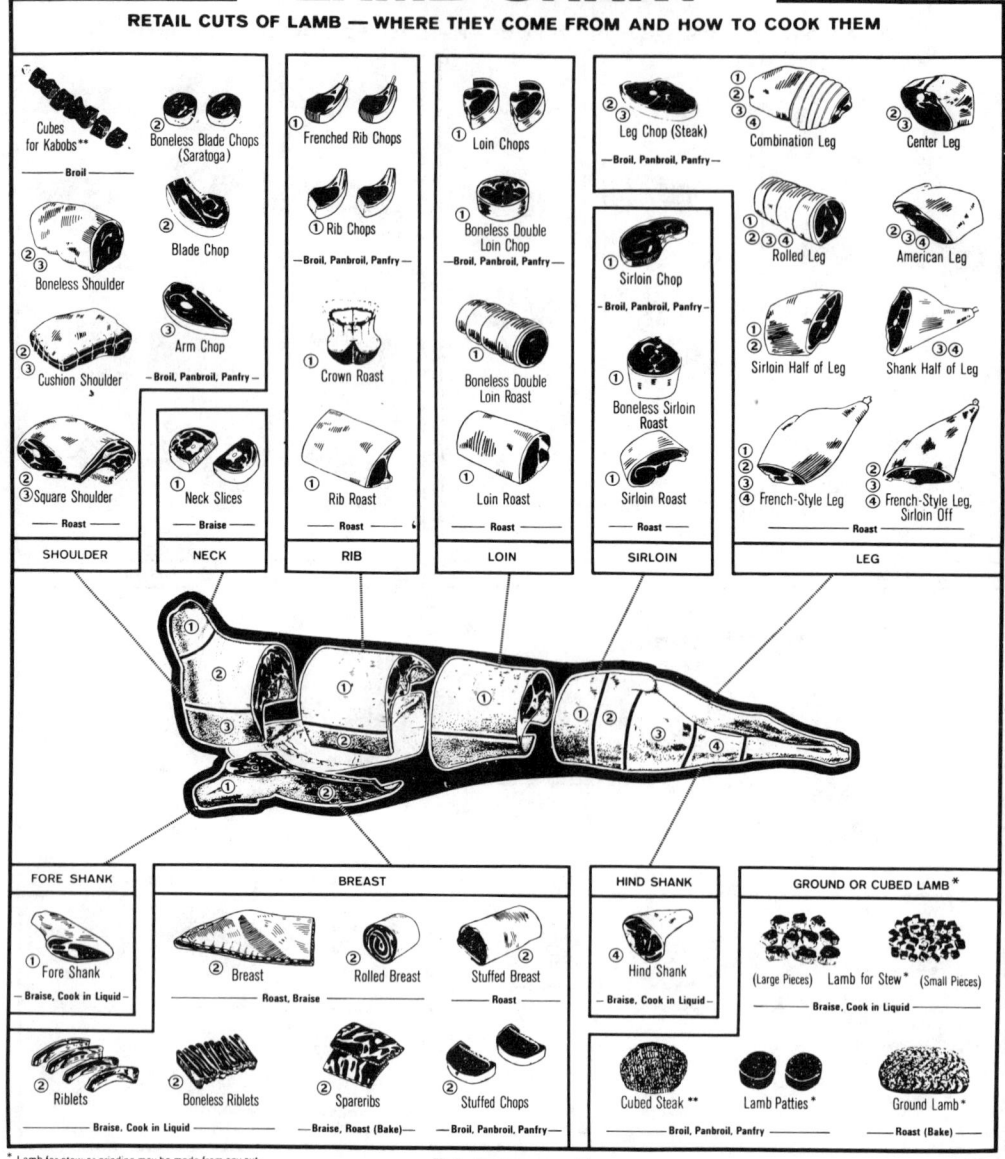

FIGURE 17

Pork Chart — Retail Cuts of Pork, Where They Come From and How to Cook Them. This chart approved by National Live Stock and Meat Board.

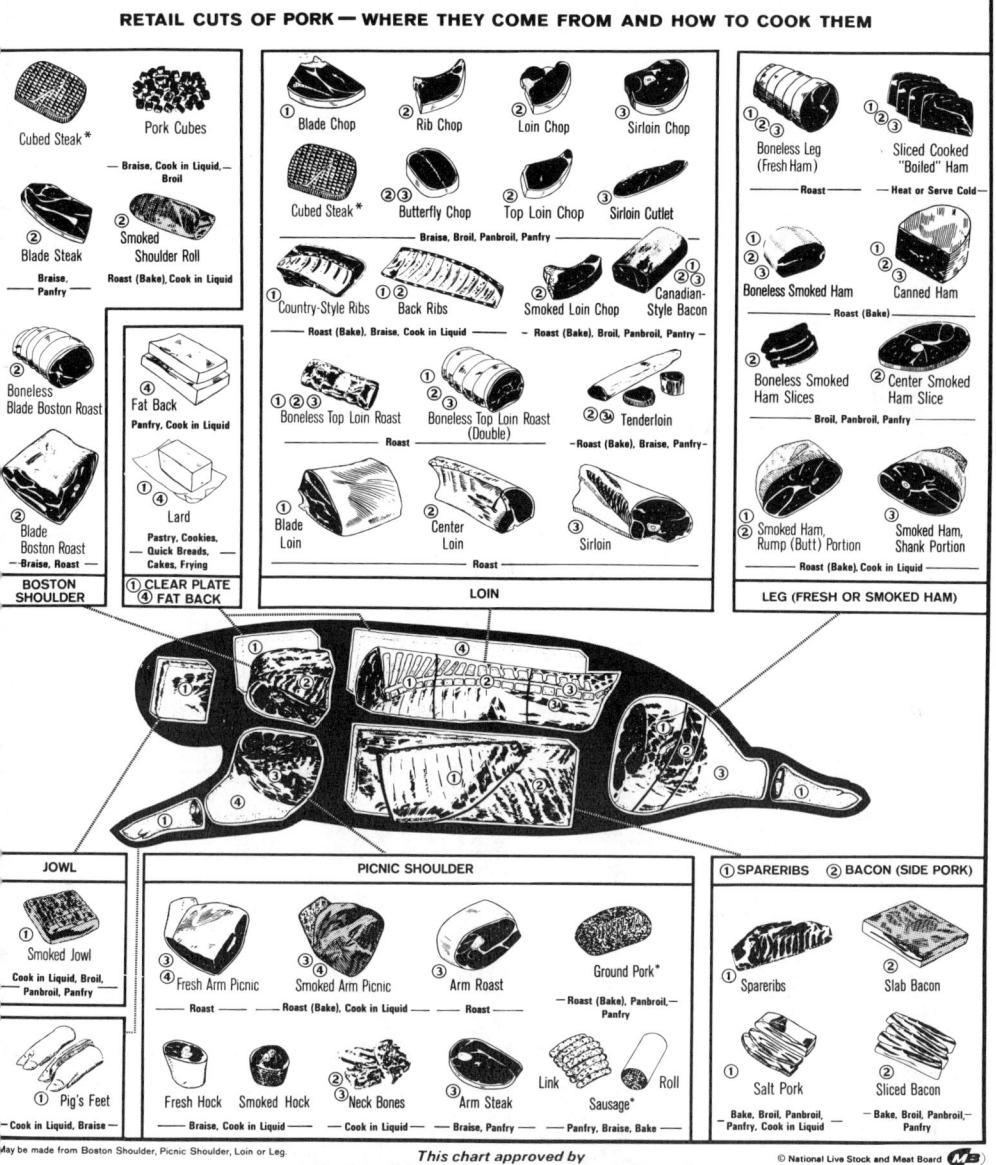

63

(butt) and shank halves. The veal leg may be cut into sirloin, round, and rump roasts, or veal cutlets.

The rib section is adjacent to the short loin, towards the front of the animal. In beef, this section is usually made into steaks or roasts. The large rib eye muscle is sometimes removed and sold as boneless rib eye (Delmonico) roasts or steaks. Roasts and steaks other than the rib eye are now recommended to be identified as "large end" (cut from the 6th to 9th ribs) or "small end" (from the 9th to 12th ribs).

In veal, lamb, and pork, this rib section usually is made into rib chops or rib roasts. When the large rib eye muscle is removed from pork and then cured and smoked, it becomes Canadian-style bacon.

The front portion of the carcass, adjacent to the rib, is the chuck in beef and the shoulder in lamb or veal. In beef and veal, the chuck, which contains the arm bone and shoulder blade towards the top of the primal and some rib and backbones towards the bottom of the section, is made into arm and blade roasts or steaks. Arm cuts resemble round steaks in shape and also usually have only a single round bone. However, the muscle structure in the arm has heavy connective tissue and is thus less palatable than the round. The muscle in the arm cuts is also usually a darker red than that found in the round. The neck portion in beef usually is made into ground beef or boneless stew meat.

In lamb, two or three blade chops and arm chops usually are removed from the shoulder; the remainder is then sold as bone-in or boneless shoulder roast. The neck may or may not be removed.

This forepart produces two major cuts in pork. The lower part is the picnic shoulder and the upper part is the blade Boston shoulder, commonly referred to as the Boston butt.

There is considerable variation in the way cuts are made from the front underside of meat animals and in the names given these cuts. In veal and lamb, the foreshank is sold as such; in beef, the shank usually is cut into portions for stewing or soup meat or is made into ground beef; and in pork the lower half is sold as pig's feet and the upper half removed by the packer for ham hocks or left on the picnic. The cuts taken from the sections behind the shank yield the less desirable cuts in all animals but pork. As indicated earlier, in pork this is where bacon and spareribs originate. In beef, these portions are made into a variety of cuts—ground beef, stew beef, short ribs, and corned beef (from the brisket), as well as flank steak from the section beneath the short loin. In lamb, these portions are normally sold as lamb breasts, for stewing, or as ground lamb.

In summary, there is a great deal of similarity in the retail cuts taken from beef, veal, lamb, and pork primals. If the name of a retail cut does not reflect the name of the primal, identification can be made by the shape of the bone or the muscle structure.

VARIETY MEATS

Variety meats, also called offal or by-products, are produced from the nonskeletal parts of beef, veal, lamb, and pork carcasses. Brains, heart, kidneys, liver, and tongue are taken from all red meat carcasses; sweetbreads from beef and veal; tripe from beef; and chitterlings from pork. Variety meats from each type of carcass vary mainly by size, with beef being the largest, then veal and pork, and lamb the smallest. Moreover, the meats from veal are more tender, finer in texture, milder in flavor, and lighter in color than those from beef.

Brains, which are most often taken from veal, are soft, very tender, and delicate in flavor. Heart, very firm and smooth-textured, is one of the less tender variety meats. Kidneys from beef and veal consist of irregular lobes and deep clefts, while pork and lamb kidneys are smooth and bean shaped. Beef kidneys are the least tender, and lamb kidneys are quite mild in flavor.

Liver is a fine-textured meat with a distinctive flavor. Beef, veal, and lamb livers have two unequal-sized lobes, while pork livers, which are somewhat coarser in texture, have three lobes of equal size. Whole liver should have a moist, smooth surface when bought, whereas the sliced surfaces of liver may appear slightly porous. Tongue is firm in texture and, like heart, is one of the less tender variety meats. Lamb and pork tongues are usually sold ready to serve, whole beef and veal tongues can be sold fresh, pickled, corned, or smoked.

Sweetbreads, the white and soft thymus glands of beef, veal, and lamb, have a very delicate flavor. Because the thymus gland disappears as the animal matures, sweetbreads are available only from veal, lamb, and young beef; however, only those from veal and young beef are generally sold in supermarkets.

Tripe consists of the smooth lining from the first beef stomach, the honeycombed lining from the second stomach, and the pocket-shaped part from the end of the second stomach. This pocket-shaped section is smooth on the outside and honeycombed inside. Honeycombed tripe is considered a great delicacy. Tripe is sold fresh, cooked, pickled, or canned.

Chitterlings are the small and large intestines of hogs that have been emptied and thoroughly cleaned. They are usually sold frozen but can also be sold fresh or cooked.

Although variety meats are highly nutritious and, except for calf liver, usually quite reasonably priced, they lack popularity among American consumers. However, Europeans consider them delicacies, and a major portion of U.S. variety meats are exported.

POULTRY

The term poultry refers to chicken, turkey, goose, guinea, and duck. Within each product group, poultry is classified by the age of the bird; the younger the bird, the more tender it will be.

Young chickens, which are ready for market in about nine weeks, are called Rock Cornish game hen, young chicken, broiler, fryer, roaster, or capon. More mature birds may be labeled hen, stewing chicken, or fowl. Broilers or fryers are the youngest birds and generally weigh $1\frac{1}{2}$ to $2\frac{1}{2}$ pounds. Roasters may be up to 14 weeks old and weigh $2\frac{1}{2}$ to $4\frac{1}{2}$ pounds. Rock Cornish game hens are very small roasters (smaller than fryers) which are produced by interbreeding Cornish and White Plymouth Rock fowl. Capons, castrated roosters about 16 weeks old, weigh 5 to 8 pounds. More mature chickens, of course, will be heavier. Young chickens are primarily produced in the Delaware, Maryland, and Virginia peninsula, as well as the Southeastern states. Mature chickens, actually by-products of the egg industry, are produced in the Southeast, the Midwest, parts of the Northeast, and in California.

Ready-to-cook chickens are easily available and sold in supermarkets as whole birds, halves, quarters, or serving pieces. Some markets also carry chickens (whole or parts), stuffed Rock Cornish game hens, and stuffed whole roasting chickens in frozen form.

Young turkeys, generally slaughtered at four or five months of age, are called young turkey, fryer-roaster, young hen, or young tom. Older birds are labeled yearling.

Whole, ready-to-cook turkeys can range in size from 4 to more than 24 pounds. Fryer-roasters are generally 4 to 8 pounds; young hens (which weigh less than young toms of the same age) run 8 pounds and up, and young toms usually weigh 12 pounds and up.

The major production areas for turkeys are the Midwest and California. Most are marketed as frozen whole birds although some supermarkets also sell fresh whole turkeys; and turkey halves, quarters, parts, and breasts are available in some sections of the country. Boneless turkey roasts and rolls are popular convenience items that are available in all white meat, all dark meat, or as a combination of both. An item that recently has been introduced is the turkey burger which is ground from the dark meat and the skin.

Young ducks, ready for market at seven to eight weeks of age are called duckling, young duckling, and roaster or barbecue duckling, while older birds are simply termed yearlings.

Ducks are produced mainly on Long Island, New York, and to a lesser degree in the Midwest, Massachusetts, and Virginia. Most ducks are sold as young birds weighing 3 to 7 pounds. About 90 percent of all ducks are sold frozen, ready-to-cook.

The least popular of the remaining poultry classes are geese and guinea hens. Geese generally are marketed young because weight gained after the first 11 weeks is mostly in the form of fat. Most geese are sold as fresh or frozen ready-to-eat young geese, weighing 6 to 12 pounds. Older geese and guineas, called "mature" or "old" are almost never sold through supermarkets.

CURED AND SMOKED MEATS

In curing, meat is treated with curing ingredients—primarily salt, sodium or potassium nitrate and/or nitrite, and sugar. Salt is used for flavor and as a preservative. However, with adequate refrigeration available today, less salt is used than in years past, and it is used more for flavor than for preservation. The nitrates convert into nitrites to protect the meat from growth of spores, which cause botulism, and combine with the meat pigments to develop the typical red color of cured meat. The sugar is added for flavor. These ingredients usually are applied to meat in a brine solution. In hams, the brine usually is distributed by being pumped into the arteries, which permits curing to be done quickly. Cuts with less density are sometimes merely soaked in the curing solution. After curing, meat is heat processed and may be smoked with a nonresinous wood for added flavor. Hickory is the most popular wood used to smoke cured meats.

Cuts of beef frequently cured are the brisket (called corned beef), the tongue, and some sausages and luncheon meats. Smoked sliced beef is made from coarsely ground beef that has been cured, cooked, and smoked after being shaped into round or square logs.

Dried beef, also called chipped beef, is made from boneless pieces of beef round which have been cured and dried. Veal tongue may be cured, but other veal cuts usually are not.

Cured and/or smoked pork products include hams, shoulder picnics, shoulder butts, Canadian-style bacon, bacon, loin, sausages, and luncheon meats. Cured pork is frequently labeled as "fully cooked" ("cooked," "ready-to-eat," "ready-to-serve," etc.) or "cook-before-eating." The fully cooked or similar label indicates that the pork has been smoked and cooked to an internal temperature of 150° F. to develop the typical color, flavor, and texture associated with thorough cooking. Cuts not so identified require cooking before serving. Moreover, some cooked products, while safe to eat, will be enhanced in flavor by additional cooking.

Pork that is cured but not smoked may also be called "pickled." Hams are sometimes long-cured with salt, then heavily smoked and aged to develop a very distinctive flavor. This product is generally produced by packers in Smithfield, Virginia. The hams are called "longcut" because they include part of the sirloin region that is normally left on the loin. They also have long shanks, and very little of the skin and fat is removed from the outside.

Normally, cured and smoked hams are also available with none, some, or all of the bones removed and with part of the skin and part or nearly all of the fat removed. During the past ten years, packers have been producing an entirely boneless, skinless, cured, and smoked ham from which substantially all of the fat has been removed. This has become one of the more popular ham items because of its convenient size, its ease of preparation and serving, and its almost complete lack of waste.

Sausages and Luncheon Meats

Sausage is one of the oldest forms of processed food and was the first processed meat product, dating back to 1,000 B.C. It originated as a means of preserving meat. Sausage gained popularity during the Middle Ages when, in towns such as Frankfurt, Vienna, and Bologna, distinctive spices were added to these products which to this day bear the name of the cities of origin.

Sausages and luncheon meats are made from beef, pork, lamb, or veal or combinations of these products which are chopped, minced, or ground to the proper consistency; seasoned with spices or condiments; then placed in casings or pans; and processed as fresh, cooked, smoked, or cured product. Loaf items are cooked in pans and then sliced and packaged. Practically all other sausage products are either canned or stuffed into casings to give them shape.

Although not technically accurate, the term luncheon meat, as used in the supermarket, generally refers to all cooked and seasoned product that is pre-sliced or can be sliced and served cold. Sausage, on the other hand, is associated with all product that requires cooking and any cooked product that is processed in link form rather than rolls. For practical purposes, the distinction between the two groups of products is secondary to knowing how the product is processed and how it is to be served.

Fresh Product

Fresh sausage is primarily made from pork that has been neither cured, cooked, nor smoked. It must be cooked thoroughly before serving and, like all fresh meat, should be refrigerated. The fresh pork (and sometimes beef) is ground and then seasoned and stuffed into casings. The most popular items in this category are fresh pork sausages, bratwurst, bockwurst, and country-style pork sausage.

Unlike fresh sausage, fresh smoked sausage may or may not have been cured, but it has been smoked. It is similar to fresh sausage in that it has not been cooked and cannot be eaten without thorough cooking. Smoked country-style pork sausage, link sausage, Mettwurst, and Roumanian sausage would fall into this category.

Ready-to-Eat Product

Cooked sausage is prepared mainly from fresh meats, although occasionally some cured meats are used. The meats are ground, seasoned, stuffed into casings, and cooked. These ready-to-eat meats include braunschweiger, liver sausage, blutwurst, and beer salami.

Cooked, smoked sausage is prepared from cured meats that have been ground, seasoned, stuffed into casings, and smoked before cooking. Although all items in this category are ready to eat, the flavor of frankfurters and smoked links is enhanced by heating. Other items in this category include bologna, knackwurst, mortadella, kielbassa, and Vienna sausage.

Dry and semi-dry sausage is the result of a complicated and carefully controlled process whereby cured meats are air dried and, in some cases, smoked before drying. The most popular items in this category include pepperoni, cappicola, cervelat, Italian salami, "summer sausage," and Lebanon bologna.

Loaf items are also fully cooked and typically available in presliced form. They include peppered, honey, meat, olive, and pickle and pimiento loaves, as well as head cheese.

There are more than 200 varieties of sausage and luncheon meats available which differ according to the meats and spices used and the processing method employed. Although it is not possible to be familiar with every item, a meat manager should at least be knowledgeable about the more popular items and should pay considerable attention to merchandising this product category which typically generates 10 to 17 percent of total department sales. Many products in this group are vacuum packed, giving them a long shelf life and a minimum of discards or other losses that fresh meats suffer. Equally important is the fact that these products generally carry the highest gross margins among all product sold in the meat department.

CANNED MEATS

The canned meat industry developed on a large scale as a response to the needs of the American Armed Forces during World War II. During the past 30 years, there has been a proliferation of canned meat products such as baby foods, meat spreads, cocktail frankfurters, meat balls, corned beef hash, luncheon meat, bacon, ham, and other products. This segment of the meat industry has shown steady growth, and all indications are that it will become increasingly important in the future.

Among those canned items usually rung at the cash register on the meat department key, canned pork items generate the largest volume. The most popular canned meat item is ham. The canned hams sold today are boneless, skinless, and usually have had a substantial amount of fat removed. They may be smoked or unsmoked and may contain added materials for flavoring. Their wide consumer acceptance can be attributed to their convenience in serving and their lack of waste, although the amount of gelatin in the can will vary from one packer to another.

Canned hams should be refrigerated unless directions on the label specify that refrigeration is not necessary. Other canned pork, lamb, beef, veal, and poultry items will retain their quality for as long as a year if stored in a cool, dry place. The product will be safe to eat during that time period if stored in completely airtight cans. Storing them at too high a temperature may cause undesirable changes in color and flavor. Once opened, canned meat products should be refrigerated and used within a few days.

FROZEN MEATS

While the entire industry is looking toward the day when meat merchandising operations will be revolutionized totally through consumer acceptance of frozen fresh meats, this product classification currently averages from 1 to 4 percent of meat department sales.

The most popular frozen items carried in supermarkets today are turkeys, roasting and stewing chickens, meat patties, and pork sausages. However, the latter product is often merchandised in the frozen food department. Some offal items, such as calf and beef liver, are bought and sold in frozen form; and in some cases frozen liver is sliced and prepackaged by the supplier. Convenience stores often carry a higher percentage of meat items sold in frozen forms than do supermarkets.

One major Midwest chain experimented with frozen meats and failed partly because of union regulations which required that product be cut, frozen, and wrapped at store level. Miniature processing plants were required at each store, rather than having one major facility at a central location. Another problem encountered was the unavailability of wrapping film that could withstand freezing temperatures without crystals of ice forming around the product, adversely affecting the bloom (the surface color of the meat). This resulted in customers rejecting product that was wholesome simply on the basis of appearance. Faced with a decrease in meat sales and a loss in distribution percentage, the chain finally abandoned the project.

There are two major obstacles to merchandising frozen product. On one hand there is the emotional roadblock created by the consumer and, on the other hand, the physical hurdles caused by a lack of adequate equipment and supplies at costs that most retailers can afford. While there is no doubt that the ingenuity of the American manufacturing community will solve the second problem, it will be the responsibility of the grower, the processor, and the retailer to mount an effective campaign aimed at changing consumer attitudes from rejection to acceptance so that fresh frozen meats can capture the share of market they deserve.

As the technology for processing frozen product advances, central cutting of case-ready product will become a very attractive alternative to store-level processing. The more surfaces of a product that are exposed, the more shrinkage takes place; therefore, retail cuts shrink more than primals, quarters, etc. However, the problem of shrinkage, which is especially serious in the retail cutting of beef, will be minimized by freezing. With consumer acceptance, frozen meat processed in meaningful quantities will most likely be less expensive than fresh product because of this lower shrinkage factor.

4

Inspecting and Grading Product

Through a compulsory inspection program, federal, state, and local governments guarantee to the retailer and to the consumer that all product leaving a processing plant is suitable for consumption. Such inspections relate to the "wholesomeness" of the product, but in no way guarantee quality, which has a direct relationship to how tasty and flavorful the product will be. However, on a voluntary basis, the United States Department of Agriculture (USDA) assigns grades which are intended to ensure uniform quality to both the retailer and the consumer. In addition, the USDA enables the retailer to more accurately control profitability on beef and lamb by assigning uniform yield grades to these products.

INSPECTING FRESH PRODUCT

According to the Federal Meat Inspection Act of 1906, all meats processed in plants that sell their products across state lines must be federally inspected for wholesomeness. Thus, all animals slaughtered and all meat, including that sold within the state by an interstate shipper, is inspected by qualified veterinarians or by trained technicians under the supervision of veterinarians.

The Federal Wholesale Meat Act of 1967 requires that each state provide inspection equal to federal inspection for plants which sell meat solely within that state.

About 80 percent of all meat sold commercially is federally inspected, with the balance being subject to state or city inspection. Meat passing inspection will carry a meat inspection stamp (federal, state, or city) which guarantees that the meat comes from healthy animals, that it has been slaughtered and processed under sanitary conditions, that it is not adulterated or contaminated when it leaves the processing plant, and that it is properly labeled and packaged. The round inspection stamp, which is placed only once on wholesale cuts, carries the words "U.S. Inspected and Passed" in abbreviated form and also the official number assigned to the processing plant. The purple or red marking fluid, which is approved by the USDA, is an edible non-toxic ink and does not have to be trimmed off. (See Figure 18.)

In addition to inspecting carcasses, inspectors often examine live cattle which are in transit from stockyards. Veterinarians assigned to railroad government shipping yards will inspect the cattle for disease before they are shipped to the slaughterer.

At the slaughter house, a veterinarian who works on the kill floor will inspect the animal's organs to ensure that they are free of disease. In some cases, nondiseased meat that is not approved for retail sale as fresh product is allowed to be boned out for cooked

FIGURE 18

Meat Inspection Stamp

sausage. Although this meat may not comply with federal standards for fresh product, it can be acceptable for sausage meat which is cooked at 212° F., a temperature high enough to destroy bacteria.

Inspectors examine not only the animal but also the meat plant itself and the delivery vehicles as well to be certain that proper conditions of refrigeration and sanitation are being maintained.

Poultry plants are subject to the same rigid inspections to ensure wholesomeness of product. While the Poultry Products Inspection Act of 1957 required federal inspection of all poultry moving in interstate commerce, a newer law, the Wholesome Poultry Products Act of 1968, goes even further. It requires inspection, at least as good as federal inspection, of all poultry regardless of whether or not it moves in interstate commerce. Under this law, if a state does not develop an adequate inspection program, all poultry processing plants within that state will come under mandatory federal inspection.

Federal inspection requires that processing plants meet strict requirements for cleanliness and that they have adequate equipment and procedures to do a good processing job. Poultry inspectors, like those who inspect meat, are either doctors of veterinary medicine or are trained specialists working under a veterinarian's supervision. They keep constant watch over the plant, the processing operation, and the birds that come through the plant.

Any birds found to be unhealthy or unfit for eating are removed immediately from the processing line and condemned for use as human food. Inspectors also make certain that the products are not adulterated and are truthfully labeled—all labels must be federally approved before they can be used. For example, if the poultry have been injected with water, oil, or other "self-basting" substances, the label must state this fact. In addition, official laboratories run continuous tests on poultry to guard against bacterial or chemical contamination.

The poultry inspection mark usually appears on either the wrapper, the wing tip, the giblet wrap, the package insert, or the label. (See Figure 19.)

Federal and local officials also inspect plants where ground meat is processed to control what goes into the product and the manner in which it is labeled. For example, according to federal regulations, unless labeled otherwise, only skeletal meat can be used in ground meats. This means that hearts, cheeks, and other portions of the

FIGURE 19
Poultry Inspection Mark

animal that do not contain bones cannot be ground. The government also prescribes labeling for ground or chopped meats; and any meat labeled "hamburger" must not contain more than 30 percent fat.

In May, 1973, the USDA proposed new regulations that would set standards for two types of patties. Those that could be called "meat patty" would have to be entirely ground meat with no more than 30 percent fat and appropriate seasonings. If labeled "beef" or "veal" patties, the meat would have to come only from those types of animals. All other meat patty products would be called "patty with meat." Such products would be required to have at least 60 percent ground or chopped meat, of which only 30 percent could be fat; but they could contain such filler ingredients as meat by-products, water, starches, poultry products, cereal, and soybean products. The added ingredients would have to be listed by their percentages.

This is only one of dozens of bills presented to Congress. Others are aimed at establishing uniform names, standardizing trimming guidelines, improving grading systems, advertising, labeling, and packaging. More and more legislative activity is also taking place at state and local levels, and it is safe to assume that pressure from consumer groups will accelerate the frequency with which new regulations are introduced and passed during the coming years. Therefore, it would be wise for every retailer to keep up to date on such changes and to establish a system for transmitting such information to staffs at store level and at central plants.

INSPECTING PROCESSED PRODUCT

A high percentage of pork is sold as processed product. This processing may include curing, smoking, cooking, and canning. Pork occasionally contains tiny parasites which can be transmitted to humans, producing a disease known as trichinosis. Therefore, in federally-inspected plants, processed pork products that might be eaten without any further cooking (e.g., luncheon meats, processed hams, and frankfurters) must be heated to an internal temperature of at least 137° F. That temperature kills any trichinae that may be present and makes the possibility of anyone contracting trichinosis extremely remote.

In curing pork, various ingredients are mixed into a brine solution and pumped into the arteries of the product. In federally-inspected plants, if the curing results in an increase in weight of up to 10 percent, the pork must be labeled with the words "water added." If the weight is increased by more than 10 percent, it is labeled "imitation." If the pork has also been smoked, the label must indicate whether artificial or natural smoke flavorings were used.

Canned cured hams and picnics may either be smoked or unsmoked and may contain added materials such as champagne or honey. At the time of canning, it is permissible for these meats to have an increase in weight of up to 8 percent over their weight before curing.

Beef brisket is the cut which is most frequently made into corned beef through a curing process. Corned briskets produced in federally-inspected plants may weigh up to 20 percent more than their uncured weight, while other corned cuts are limited to an increase in weight of 10 percent.

Federal regulations are also in force for processing sausage meats. Most sausages are made from combinations of beef, pork, lamb, and veal meat, although nonskeletal by-products—heart, tongue, liver, tripe, etc.—also are used. Federal regulations also allow sausage products to contain up to 15 percent poultry, but the label must include that information. In addition, some items include cereal or nonfat dry milk as extenders. Most sausage products processed in federally-inspected plants cannot contain more than $3\frac{1}{2}$ percent of these extenders without being labeled as imitations. However, some processed loaf items may contain more than $3\frac{1}{2}$ percent extenders, including ingredients such as pickles, olives, or macaroni. In all cases, federal meat inspection regulations require that the ingredients used in a sausage product be listed on the label in descending order of dominance.

New labeling requirements went into effect in 1973 covering frankfurters, bologna, and knockwurst. In order to use those generic names, the product must be made from skeletal meat, no more than 15 percent poultry meat, and the normal ingredients needed for processing, such as water, sweeteners, and curing substances. Moreover, the products must be labeled according to content. If all the meat is from one particular species (for example, beef), the product is a "beef frankfurter." If by-products are used in addition to skeletal meats, the label must read "frankfurter with by-products" or "franks with variety meats." If nonmeat binders such as nonfat dry milk, cereal, or dried whole milk (up to $3\frac{1}{2}$ percent) are also included, the label must say, "franks with by-products, nonfat dry milk added." In all three cases the label must list the ingredients used in order of decreasing dominance in the product.

Since February, 1973, bacon packages have been required to reveal at least 70 percent of the length of a representative strip in a window at least $1\frac{1}{2}$ inches wide. This regulation also requires that packages of bacon (and other cured meats, as well as products containing cured meats, such as frozen dinners containing ham) carry a list of all ingredients used in the curing process.

The USDA also has specified minimum meat requirements for many canned and frozen products. For example, if a product is labeled "turkey pie," it must contain at least 14 percent cooked, deboned turkey meat. Chicken dinners must contain at least 18 percent cooked, deboned chicken meat; chicken a la king, at least 20 percent chicken meat; chicken noodles or dumplings, at least 15 percent chicken meat; chilli con carne, at least 40 percent meat, and so on.

All plants that freeze or can meat or poultry products for interstate shipment must be federally inspected. Moreover, the label on such frozen and canned products must bear the common or descriptive name of the product, the net weight, the name and address of the packer or distributor, the official plant number and inspection mark, and a list of ingredients in descending order of dominance by weight. The ingredient present in the largest amount is listed first, so that a package of frozen sausages might be labeled "ingredients: pork, pork fat, salt, and spices," and a can of boned chicken, "ingredients: chicken, chicken broth, and salt." Instead of the round, abbreviated inspection mark that is stamped on fresh product, canned and frozen items carry the legend "U.S. inspected and passed by the

Department of Agriculture," together with the plant or establishment number, enclosed in a circle and printed on the package.

All imported meat items in any form must pass USDA inspections for wholesomeness. Not only processed product, but fresh product as well, must be labeled for contents. Foreign plants are visited by USDA inspectors, and products are inspected on a random basis as they arrive at the port of embarkation. Inspection stamps similar to those used domestically are applied to foreign products. A can of liver paté imported from France, for example, would carry the legend, "Inspected for Wholesomeness, France, Sanitary Agreement No. 67-09, Fab. 76." The abbreviation "Fab.", for fabricator, identifies the plant. The can also identifies the ingredients in order of importance; for example, "ingredients: pork, pork liver, goose fat, goose liver, eggs, onions, flour, salt, spices."

Thus, regardless of the form in which a customer purchases meat or meat products, she can be assured that the item is clean and safe to eat.

The Food and Drug Administration has ordered "nutrition labeling" of certain packaged foods which will indicate the calories, fats, vitamins, and related nutrients in each serving. Technically, the nutrition content labels are required of those products "fortified" with a nutrient—such as enriched flour—or which make advertising claims on labels involving such items as protein, fat, calories, diet advantages, or vitamins. However, since it is felt that products carrying such nutrition labels will have a competitive advantage, most other manufacturers will probably follow suit.

While the Food and Drug Administration order does not cover fresh meat and poultry, it is anticipated that processed foods, including meat and poultry, will soon be covered by Agriculture Department regulations which will be identical to those announced for other foods by the Food and Drug Administration.

GRADING FRESH PRODUCT

Whereas inspection is mandatory and refers to wholesomeness, grading is voluntary and identifies quality. The government meat grading program is administered by the Department of Agriculture and supported entirely by fees collected from meat packers who use the service. Government graders, who, unlike inspectors, do not have to be veterinarians, graded about 80 percent of the beef, 60 percent of the lamb, and smaller but significant quantities of the veal and calf sold at retail in the past. Currently, because of competitive pressures, there is a definite trend toward the sale of ungraded beef (which would probably be in the Good category if graded).

As a merchandising tool, many packers and retailers establish brand names which relate to USDA grades, even though the meat is generally not government graded. However, packers' and retailers' brand names, which are applied and governed solely by the company using them, do not necessarily guarantee uniform quality throughout the country or at different times of the year. Because plants located in different parts of the country will slaughter animals of different quality, meat graded "premium," for example, by two different plants owned by the same packer may not be of the same quality. It is also possible that the quality of meat in one plant will vary on a seasonal basis. If a retailer wants assurance that he is getting uniform quality from the packer, he must specify a USDA grade, such as Choice, which the packer will then relate to his appropriate brand name. Moreover, because there is such a wide range of product within the Choice grade, the buyer must also specify whether he wants high-, medium-, or low-Choice product when placing his order both with packers who use brand names and those who use USDA grades along with brand names.

USDA grades for beef, veal, lamb, and pork are shown in Figure 20. There are eight USDA quality grades for beef, six for veal, and five for lamb and pork. In actual practice, however, USDA

FIGURE 20

USDA Meat Grades

Quality	BEEF	VEAL	LAMB	PORK
	Prime	Prime	Prime	U.S. No. 1
	Choice	Choice	Choice	U.S. No. 2
	Good	Good	Good	U.S. No. 3
	Standard	Standard	Utility	U.S. No. 4
	Commercial	Utility	Cull	Utility
	Utility	Cull		
	Cutter			
	Canner			

grades are used primarily for beef and lamb. Although there are government grades for pork, they have generally not been used by retailers because pork is merchandised somewhat differently than the other meats, and many cuts of pork carry identifiable packer brands.

A considerable amount of veal is sold at retail with neither a USDA grade nor a packer brand name. This is partly due to the fact that unlike other animals, veal-producing calves are not skinned immediately after slaughter and placed in a chill box in the slaughter house where cold air is forced around the carcass to quickly remove the animal heat. Because veal has so little external fat to protect it from darkening and drying out, after slaughter it is chilled in the skin and then skinned just prior to being shipped, usually on the following morning. It is important to ship veal very quickly after it is skinned in order to maintain its quality and appearance. Because of this time element and the fact that very little veal is being sold in supermarkets today, it is usually not graded. Whatever graded veal is sold in supermarkets is usually in the Choice or Good categories.

A primary clue to the quality of a retail cut of veal that has not been graded is its color—the whiter the color, the better the quality. The color of veal is affected by the age of the calf at the time of slaughter and how it was fed. Calves that are naturally fed by the mother will have whiter meat than those fed milk substitutes or those which graze on grass.

Federal meat graders grade only carcasses or wholesale cuts because quality differences are difficult to recognize in the smaller retail cuts. When meat is graded, a shield-shaped grade mark enclosing the letters "USDA" and the appropriate grade name, such as Prime, Choice, or Good, is applied to the meat as a long ribbon-like imprint. (See Figure 21.) Thus, the grade mark which is rolled along the length of the carcass and across both shoulders will appear on many retail cuts. Like the inspection stamp, the grade stamp ink is made from edible vegetable coloring.

FIGURE 21

USDA Meat Grade Stamps

USDA Grading Standards

The standards used in grading meat for quality are: (1) conformation, (2) age, (3) marbling, and (4) color, firmness, and texture of the lean. The grade assigned to a carcass results from a combination of these four factors.

Conformation refers to the general form or shape of the animal and is a clue to the ratio of lean to bone. Good conformation implies thick backs with full loins and ribs, deep, plump rounds, thick shoulders, and short necks and shanks.

Age of the carcass is determined primarily by the characteristics of the skeleton. The bones of young beef and lamb are porous and red. The bones of older animals are white and flinty. The younger the animal, the more tender its meat will be.

Marbling refers to the intermingling of fat within the lean. Abundant marbling increases the juiciness, flavor, and tenderness of the meat. Quality grades assigned to meat are in large part based on the amount of marbling present as well as the age of the animal.

Color, firmness, and texture of the lean are often related to the age of the animal and affect the quality of the meat. Bright colored, firm, fine textured lean will be the most palatable.

Beef Grades

The *Prime* grade is applied to only 5 to 7 percent of all graded beef. Most of the Prime supply is sold to high-quality restaurants, although some supermarkets located in high-income areas offer cuts of Prime quality along with Choice meat. A supermarket carrying Prime meat exclusively would be rare, indeed. Prime grade meat is produced from young, well-fed animals. This combination of youth and feed results in high quality cuts with liberal quantities of marbling, making the meat juicy, tender, and flavorful.

Choice grade beef accounts for the highest percentage of the meat sold through retail outlets. It is preferred by customers because it is 10 to 20 percent less expensive than Prime and has less waste because it has less outside fat. While Choice beef has less marbling than Prime, it is still of very high quality.

Good grade beef, which generally costs the retailer about 2 to 4 cents per pound less than Choice, contains more lean than the higher grades and is often sold under a brand name. It is relatively tender;

but because it has less marbling, it lacks some of the juices and flavor of Choice and Prime beef.

Standard grade beef has a very thin covering of outside fat and little marbling. However, because it also comes from young animals, as do the higher quality grades, it is fairly tender but lacks the flavor and juiciness usually found in beef with more marbling. Young cattle that are grass-fed rather than corn-fed usually will lack marbling and, therefore, be graded Standard.

Supermarkets located in certain ethnic or low-income areas where customers prefer lean meat cooked in liquid will carry some cuts in this grade. Moreover, some supermarkets will carry two grades of beef—for example, Choice and Standard, in order to give the customer the opportunity to buy meat at lower prices. This practice was fairly common a few years ago when there was a meaningful price spread between Choice and Standard beef. Today, however, with the price differential narrowed, fewer supermarkets engage in this type of promotional activity.

Commercial grade beef is produced only from mature animals (the top four grades described above are restricted to young animals). It has abundant marbling but lacks tenderness unless it is cooked slowly for a long period of time with moist heat. Practically no Commercial grade meat is sold through supermarkets. Most often the better cuts (i.e., the tenderloin or the rib eye) will be removed from Commercial beef, tenderized by the packer, and sold to lower quality restaurants. The remainder of the animal will be boned out and sold either fresh or frozen to retailers for leaning up trimmings for ground meat, or sold to processors who manufacture sausages.

Utility grade meat is produced mostly from fairly old cattle and rarely, if ever, sold as fresh beef. It is either frozen and used to lean out trimmings for ground meat or boned out and sold to sausage manufacturers or to canners for items such as beef stew. Because canned meats usually are cooked for long periods of time in pressure cookers to make them tender, lower grade meat such as Utility can be used.

Cutter and *Canner* grade meat is boned out and used in processed meat products. Even though they are of a lower quality, these grades often are higher priced than Commercial beef because they have more lean and less waste.

When a USDA grader assigns a grade of Good, for example, to a carcass, that grade will apply to all the wholesale and retail cuts in that carcass. However, if the packer feels that some of the cuts in the carcass should be graded higher, he has the option to break down the carcass and have the primal cuts graded individually. Often, the traditional method of cooking a particular cut will have some effect on the grade assigned. For instance, after a Good grade carcass is broken into primal cuts, it is not uncommon for the round and chuck cuts, which are usually braised, to be graded Choice, while the rib containing the loin cuts, which are traditionally broiled and therefore require more quality, retain the Good grade. With the round and chuck making up 49 percent of the carcass, at a difference of $3 per hundredweight (cwt.) between Choice and Good grades, it is to the packer's advantage to have these cuts upgraded.

Moreover, an animal that has excellent conformation and marbling will receive a low grade if it is old because it will lack tenderness. An animal that normally would grade Choice or Good if it were young, would be graded Commercial if it has hard bones, indicating that it is from an older animal (over 30 months of age). Therefore, it is important that the animal's bones be inspected carefully if it does not carry a USDA grade.

Lamb Grades

The grading of lamb is based on a combination of the same factors that influence beef grading: conformation, age, marbling, and color, firmness and texture of the lean. Of the five grades used for indicating the quality of lamb, Prime and Choice are the grades most often sold in supermarkets. If Good lamb is sold at retail, it is seldom marked with the grade. The Utility and Cull grades are generally used in processed meat items such as frankfurters. No mutton older than yearlings can be graded higher than Choice.

Poultry Grades

Poultry is graded for conformation (overall shape and appearance), meatiness, amount of fat, and the presence or absence of defects such as torn skin, discoloration, or bruises.

The top grade for poultry, and the one most commonly sold in retail food stores, is U.S. Grade A. Grade A birds have good overall shape and appearance. They are meaty, have a well developed layer of fat in the skin, and are free from defects.

Official standards also provide for U.S. Grade B and U.S. Grade C poultry. While these birds are not as attractive as Grade A, there is

Inspecting and Grading Product 85

generally little difference in eating quality, especially between Grade A and Grade B poultry. Grade B chickens may lack the proper conformation or fat cover, but most often they have suffered bruises or skin tears. If the skin is bruised as the chicken is being slaughtered or if the skin is torn by the feather-removing equipment, the chicken is automatically labeled Grade B. Moreover, if a complete part, such as a wing or a leg is removed, the chicken is automatically labeled Grade C. Grade C chickens are used mainly for chicken parts. However, it is possible to buy Grade A chicken parts that have been cut from Grade B or even Grade C chickens because those parts of the chicken without skin tears or bruises can bear a Grade A label.

Because poultry today is quite uniform in quality, most birds are U.S. Grade A. Birds graded below U.S. Grade A are usually sold without the grademark in supermarkets or are used in processed foods where appearance is not important.

Poultry must be federally inspected for wholesomeness before it can be graded for quality. Often, the inspection mark and the grade shield are displayed together. (See Figure 22.) The grade

FIGURE 22

Poultry Inspection Mark, Grade Shield, and Class Name

INSPECTION MARK   **GRADE MARK**

shield is found on any kind of chilled or frozen ready-to-cook poultry.

The age of the bird, rather than the grade, determines how tender it will be; the younger the bird, the more tender. If the poultry is not young, the label will carry the word, "yearling," or some such similar designation.

Adjustments in Grades

USDA grade standards, which date back to 1927, are altered from time to time to reflect changes in the industry. In 1965, grades were changed to include more beef in the Choice category. In 1973, meat packers offered a proposal that would result in some beef that is now graded Choice being graded in the Prime category, as well as upgrading some Good and Standard cuts into the next higher category. The objective again is to include more beef in the high-demand Prime and Choice grades. The reasoning behind the packers' proposal is that because cattle are now marketed at younger ages than previously and are more tender because they are younger, less marbling is necessary to qualify for the higher grades. As of this writing, the government has asked meat scientists for their opinions, but no action has been taken.

YIELD GRADES

While inspection and quality grades are designed to aid the consumer and the retailer, yield grades are useful only to the retailer and processor and to the limited number of consumers who buy meat in carcass form for freezer lockers.

USDA yield grades for beef and lamb, which have been available for industry use since June, 1965, identify the amount of saleable meat that a carcass will yield. In addition to the USDA quality grades, the yield grade is an important yardstick for the retailer in determining the value of a carcass. While yield grades are based on different factors than quality grades, carcasses can be graded for quality and yield at the same time or can be graded for either factor alone. As with quality grading, the cost of yield grading is borne by the company using the service.

There are five USDA yield grades. (See Figure 23 for Yield Grade Stamp.) Yield Grade 1 carcasses (thickly muscled with little fat) have the highest yields of retail cuts and Yield Grade 5 (thinly

Inspecting and Grading Product 87

FIGURE 23
Yield Grade Stamp

USDA YIELD GRADE 2

muscled and very fat), the lowest. A beef carcass in one yield grade will yield about 4.6 percent more in retail cuts than the next lower yield grade. For lamb carcasses the average difference in yield between adjacent grades is 3.5 percent. At May, 1974 prices, the difference in retail value per cwt. of USDA Choice beef carcasses in the five adjacent yield grades was $5.90, while Choice lamb carcasses had an average difference of $5.33 between yield grades. (See Figure 24 and Appendix.)

Which yield grade is the best buy will depend on the price at which carcasses of each yield grade can be purchased. For example, if the difference in the retail value between adjacent yield grades for Choice beef carcasses is $5.90 per cwt., the higher yielding grade will be the better buy if the cost to the company, when translated into retail value, is less than $5.90 per cwt. On the other hand, if the wholesale price differential between adjacent yield grades represents more than the $5.90 retail value per cwt., it will be more advantageous to buy the lower yielding grade.

FIGURE 24
Yield and Value of Cuts from Typical Beef and Lamb Carcasses

Yield Grade	Beef % of Carcass Weight	Beef Retail Value per cwt.	Lamb % of Carcass Weight	Lamb Retail Value per cwt.
1	82.0%	$113.96	92.0%	$137.65
2	77.4	108.05	88.5	132.32
3	72.8	102.15	85.0	126.99
4	68.2	96.25	81.5	121.67
5	63.6	90.34	78.0	116.34

Yield Grade Standards for Beef

Yield grades indicate the percentage yields of boneless, closely trimmed retail cuts from the high-value parts of the beef carcass—the round, loin, rib, and chuck—which account for more than 80 percent of its value. The differences in yield from one animal to another will depend on: (1) the amount of fat that must be trimmed from the carcass in making the cuts, and (2) the thickness and fullness of the muscling. These factors are indicated by four measurements in beef:

1. *External fat.* The amount of fat over the outside of the carcass is the most important yield grade indicator. This measurement is made after the side has been separated into a forequarter and a hindquarter. Four-tenths of an inch variation in the thickness of the fat over the rib eye makes a full yield grade change.
2. *Area of rib eye.* This is part of the largest and most palatable muscle in the carcass. The muscle lies on each side of the backbone and runs the full length of the back. A cross-section of the rib eye muscle is exposed when the side is separated into a forequarter and a hindquarter. Its area is measured in square inches. Among carcasses of the same fatness and weight, an increase in the rib eye area indicates an increase in the yield of retail cuts. A change of 3 square inches in rib eye area makes a full yield grade change.
3. *Kidney, pelvic, and heart fat.* Fat deposits on the inside of the carcass around the kidney and in the pelvic and heart areas also affect yields. Since practically all of this fat is removed in trimming, an increase in this fat content decreases the yield of retail cuts. A difference of 5 percent in this fat content makes a full yield grade change.
4. *Carcass weight.* The "warm" weight (weight before chilling) is used in yield grading. When carcass weight is used in conjunction with the other three factors listed above, an increase in weight indicates a decrease in the yield of retail cuts. Weight, however, is the least important yield grade factor since it takes a difference of about 250 pounds in carcass weight to make a full yield grade change.

Yield Grade Standards for Lamb

Lamb grading is based on the following three factors which affect the yield in retail cuts from the shoulder, rack (rib), leg, and loin:

1. *External fat.* The amount of external fat is evaluated in terms of its actual thickness over the center of the rib eye muscle. As the amount of external fat increases, the percentage of retail cuts decreases. Each .05 inch change in adjusted fat thickness over the rib eye changes the yield grade by one-third of a grade.
2. *Kidney and pelvic fat.* The amount of kidney and pelvic fat considered in determining the yield grade includes the kidney knob (kidney and surrounding fat) and the lumbar and pelvic fat in the loin and leg. As the amount of kidney and pelvic fat increases as a percentage of carcass weight, the percentage of retail cuts decreases—a change of 1 percent of the carcass weight in kidney and pelvic fat changes the yield grade by one-quarter of a grade.
3. *Conformation of the legs.* Superior conformation implies a high proportion of edible meat to bone and a high proportion of the weight of the carcass in the more demanded cuts. Leg conformation is graded in terms of thirds of grades on a scale from 15 for high-Prime to 1 for low-Cull. An increase in the conformation grade of the legs increases the percentage of retail cuts—a change of one-third of a grade changes the yield grade by 5 percent of a grade.

A lamb carcass in Yield Grade 1 usually has only a thin layer of external fat over the back and loin and slight deposits of fat in the flanks and cod or udder. There is usually a very thin layer of fat over the top of the shoulders and the outside of the legs, and muscles are usually plainly visible on most areas of the carcass. In contrast, a Yield Grade 4 lamb carcass usually is completely covered with fat. There generally is a moderately thick covering of fat over the back, a slightly thick covering over the shoulder and legs, and large deposits of fat in the flanks and cod or udder.

Beef and Lamb Sales by Yield Grades

Within each USDA quality grade for beef and lamb there are five yield grades. The meat most commonly sold in supermarkets is Choice with a Yield Grade of 3 or 4. Yield Grades 1 and 2 are fairly scarce, and Yield Grade 5 normally has too much waste to enable the store to earn an acceptable gross margin. In most cases, yield grades have an inverse ratio to quality grades to some extent. For example, Prime beef, which has more waste than Choice, will rarely, if ever, have a Yield Grade 1. On the other hand, Good cattle, which is lean, will generally have a higher yield grade than Choice. Similarly, Prime lamb is in most abundant supply in Yield Grades 3, 4, and 5, whereas Good lamb is most plentiful in Yield Grades 1, 2, and 3.

With yield grades, retailers have a means of purchasing beef and lamb that ensures close control of cutability. In the absence of yield grades for veal, most retailers rely on conformation and youth of the animal to indicate yield.

GRADE STANDARDS FOR PORK

Although little grading of pork carcasses is presently being done, when pork is graded, the standards apply to: (1) class, i.e., barrows, gilts, sows, etc., and (2) grade, i.e., the quality of the pork and the yield of the four lean cuts—hams, loins, picnics, and Boston butts (shoulders). In this respect, USDA quality grades for pork are more similar to yield grades for beef and lamb than they are to the quality grades for those carcasses.

With respect to quality, pork carcasses are categorized either as acceptable or unacceptable, based on standards established for the characteristics of the lean in a major muscle, such as the loin eye. Carcasses which have characteristics indicating that the lean in the four lean cuts is of unacceptable quality, or bellies that are too thin to be suitable for bacon production, as well as carcasses which are soft and oily are graded U.S. Utility and subject to no further grading. This group accounts for about 2 percent of the graded pork carcasses.

Carcasses that have acceptable quality are further grouped, according to yield of the four lean cuts, as U.S. No. 1, 2, 3, or 4. The expected yields of the four lean cuts from carcasses in each grade are shown in Figure 25. Only 8 percent of graded pork carcasses are U.S. No. 1. The proportion of total pork carcasses graded U.S. No. 2, 3, and 4, are 42, 36, and 12 percent respectively.

FIGURE 25

Expected Yields of the Four Lean Pork Cuts Based on Chilled Carcass Weight, by Grade

Grade	Yield
U.S. No. 1	53 percent and over
U.S. No. 2	50 to 52.9 percent
U.S. No. 3	47 to 49.9 percent
U.S. No. 4	Less than 47 percent

The factors affecting the yield of cuts are the fatness of the carcass and its muscling. The actual average thickness of the fat back in relation to the carcass length or weight is used to determine the yield grade of typical pork carcasses. For example, a 30-inch carcass weighing 165 pounds with 1.3 inches fat back thickness would be graded U.S. No. 1, whereas the same carcass with 1.8 inches fat back thickness would be graded U.S. No. 3. If length in relationship to fat back thickness indicates a different grade than weight and fat back, length is used to determine the grade.

Grades for pork carcasses can be useful to the packer but are of no value to the retailer who buys pork in primal form. Any packer slaughtering hogs will produce products graded either Selection No. 1 primals (generally from barrows and gilts) or Selection No. 2 primals (generally from sows and other mature hogs). Practically all supermarkets buy Selection No. 1 primals which are meaty and tender. The yield in retail cuts from these primals will depend on the packer's standard for trimming external fat from the primal.

SUMMARY

All meat is government inspected for wholesomeness on a mandatory basis and graded for quality on a voluntary basis. Quality grades for beef and lamb are determined separately from yield grades; these carcasses can be graded for either quality or yield, or both. Yield grades are of no particular concern to the consumer who buys retail cuts which are trimmed of excess fat before being placed in the meat counter, but they can be very helpful to anyone who buys beef or lamb in carcass form. Since the value of a carcass depends chiefly on two factors—the quality of the meat and the amount of saleable meat that the carcass will yield—the retailer has the most protection when both types of government grades are used.

5

Recommended Cooking Methods

Any meat department employee who knows the grade of a retail cut and the portion of the carcass from which it was taken is in the position to offer expert advice to customers on proper cooking methods.

In the simplest terms, the higher grades of red meat are more tender than the lower grades, and the cuts from the back (rib, loin, and sirloin) are more tender than the cuts from the shoulder (chuck), flank, and round. The more tender the cut of meat, the more successfully can it be cooked with dry heat. Conversely, the less tender the cut, the greater likelihood that it will require cooking with moist heat. A Prime or high-Choice top round steak, for example, may be broiled, but lower grades of the same cut must be cooked in moist heat to be made tender unless they have been pretendered by some means prior to cooking. On the other hand, a broiled Prime top round steak may be less tender than a broiled T-bone steak of a lower grade. Thus, the secret to good cooking lies in suiting the cooking method to both the grade and the cut of meat. (See Figure 26.)

FIGURE 26

Suggested Cooking Guide for Beef by Cut and Grade

The use of an appropriate method of cooking is essential to bring out the desirable eating qualities of the specific cut and grade selected. Below is a guide suggesting the most generally accepted method of cooking retail cuts of beef of each grade.

Flank, plate, brisket, foreshank, and the heel of the round should be prepared in the same manner for all grades of beef. These less tender cuts are used for stewing, braising, or boiling, or are ground for use in meat loaves and similar dishes.

Cut	Prime	Choice	Good	Standard
Top round and tip (steaks and roasts).	Braise, broil, pan fry, or roast.	Braise, broil,* pan fry, or roast.	Braise or pan fry.	Braise or pan fry.
Bottom round (steaks and roasts).	Braise, pan fry, or roast.	Braise, pan fry, or roast.	Braise or roast.	Braise.
Rump roast.	Roast or braise.	Braise.	Braise.	Braise.
Sirloin (steaks and roasts).	Broil, pan broil, pan fry, or roast.	Broil, pan broil, pan fry, or roast.	Broil, pan fry or roast.	Broil, braise or pan fry.
Porterhouse, T-bone, top loin, and rib steaks.	Broil or pan broil.	Broil or pan broil.	Broil.	Broil, pan fry or braise.
Rib roast.	Roast.	Roast.	Roast.	Roast or braise.
Chuck, arm and blade (roasts and steaks).	Roast or braise.	Braise.	Braise.	Braise.

* High-Choice

93

COOKING METHODS FOR FRESH RED MEATS

Temperature is one of the most important factors in meat cookery. Regardless of the method used, meat shrinks (decreases) in size and weight during cooking. These cooking losses are important because they affect the appearance and the palatability of the meat as well as the amount of meat there is to serve. The higher the cooking temperature, the greater the shrinkage. Tests show that there will be less shrinkage when meat is cooked at low to moderate temperatures, regardless of the cooking method used. Moreover, meat is more tender, juicy, flavorful, and more uniformly cooked when cooked slowly. Another advantage is that there is less chance of burning fat or pans or spattering fat on racks and ovens. Also, aesthetically, meat cooked at lower temperatures will have a more even color. Thus, the customer's satisfaction will depend not only on the grade and cut of meat she has purchased but also on the method of cooking and the temperature at which the meat is cooked.

COOKING MEATS WITH DRY HEAT

There are two basic cooking methods, dry heat and moist heat. The more tender cuts of meat have a minimum amount of connective tissue (the part of the meat which is not quickly made tender) and can be cooked in dry heat at a moderate temperature. Included in dry heat cooking are the following methods:

Broiling

Broiling is cooking meat by heat from a flame, electric unit, or glowing coals. Trimming the outer edge of fat to within $\frac{1}{2}$ inch will reduce spattering and prevent the meat or drippings from catching fire unless, of course, the broiling temperature is too high. The fat edge of the meat can be slashed at intervals to prevent the meat from curling or cupping while it cooks.

The oven temperature control should be set at "broil" and the meat placed on the rack of the broiler pan 2 to 3 inches from the heat for a 1-inch thick steak or chop and 3 to 5 inches away for a 1 to 2-inch cut. The meat should be broiled with the oven door closed when using a gas range and the door ajar for an electric range.

When the meat is half done and browned (lightly browned for

cured and smoked pork), it may be seasoned if desired. Seasoning is done after browning because salt draws moisture to the meat surface which delays browning. The meat is then turned over, cooked to the desired degree of doneness as indicated by a meat thermometer inserted shortly before the estimated time for doneness (or by a cooking timetable), seasoned on the second side if desired, and served at once.

A good bed of coals is the secret to broiling over charcoal. The coals should be allowed to whiten before broiling in order to ensure a good fire. It is important not to allow the fat that drips back into the flames to char the meat. To avoid this, the grill should be placed well above the charcoal bed.

Very thick steaks or chops should be cooked more slowly than thin cuts; otherwise, the outside may char before the inside cooks. Also, large steaks take longer to reach a given degree of doneness than do small steaks with the same thickness. Broiled meat can be tested for doneness by cutting a small slit in the lean to check the color or by pressing the meat lightly with a fork to check the texture. Rare beef (140° F.) is reddish-pink, soft and pulpy; medium beef (160° F.) is light pink and slightly resistant; and well-done meat (170° F.) is light brown and quite firm.

Lamb is usually preferred medium or well-done. Medium lamb has a grayish-tan interior with a tinge of pink. Well-done lamb is grayish-tan with no trace of pink. Fresh pork (i.e., not cured and/or smoked) should be cooked long enough to allow heat to penetrate to the center of the meat; the temperature should be measured with an internal cooking thermometer. Fresh pork cooked to an internal temperature of 140° F. is safe to eat, but it will be more tender and flavorful if cooked to the higher internal temperature of 170° F. However, it should be kept in mind that as the degree of doneness increases, so does shrinkage, and that meat becomes dry and shrinks unduly when overcooked. When cooked to the correct degree of doneness, meat is juicy and flavorful and there is more to serve. Cured and smoked pork is cooked to 160° F., unless the label indicates it has been "fully-cooked," in which case it is heated to 140° F. and served hot.

Beef steaks especially suitable for broiling include tenderloin (filet mignon) in all grades, and porterhouse, T-bone, top loin, boneless top loin, sirloin, rib, and rib eye in the Prime, Choice, and Good grades. Broiling may also be used successfully for tip and top round steaks, but only in the Prime and Choice grades and served rare to medium. Ground beef patties may also be broiled.

Many cuts of lamb in the Prime and Choice grades are recommended for broiling, including leg steaks and loin, sirloin, rib, arm, and blade chops. In addition, ground lamb may be broiled.

Pork chops also may be broiled as may smoked ham slices, bacon, and Canadian-style bacon. Because veal does not have sufficient fat, broiling is not recommended for veal steaks and chops. Steaks, chops, or meat patties at least 1 inch thick and smoked ham slices at least ½ inch thick are best for broiling. Moreover, while meat can be broiled to any degree of doneness, it will be more tender and juicy if cooked only to the rare to medium stage, rather than until it is well-done.

Figure 27 shows the cuts of red meat best suited for broiling and the approximate cooking time for meats placed in the broiler at refrigerator temperature. Frozen meat, which can be broiled as

FIGURE 27

Timetable for Broiling *

Cut	Weight or Thickness	Approximate Total Cooking Time — Rare	Medium
BEEF	Pounds	Minutes	Minutes
Rib steak—1 in.	1 to 1½	15	20
1½ in.	1½ to 2	25	30
2 in.	2 to 2½	35	45
Rib eye steak—1 in.	8 to 10 ozs.	15	20
1½ in.	12 to 14 ozs.	25	30
2 in.	16 to 20 ozs.	35	45
Top loin steak—1 in.	1 to 1½	15	20
1½ in.	1½ to 2	25	30
2 in.	2 to 2½	35	45
Sirloin steak—1 in.	1½ to 3	20	25
1½ in.	2¼ to 4	30	35
2 in.	3 to 5	40	45
Porterhouse steak—			
1 in.	1¼ to 2	20	25
1½ in.	2 to 3	30	35
2 in.	2½ to 3½	40	45
Filet Mignon—			
1 in.	4 to 6 ozs.	15	20
1½ in.	6 to 8 ozs.	18	22
Ground beef patties			
1 in. thick by 3 in.	4 ozs.	15	25

Recommended Cooking Methods 97

FIGURE 27 (Continued)

Cut	Weight or Thickness	Approximate Total Cooking Time	
		Rare	Medium
PORK—SMOKED			
Ham slice—			
½ in.	¾ to 1	Always	10-12
1 in.	1½ to 2	cooked	16-20
Loin Chops—		well done	
¾ to 1 in.			15-20
Canadian-style bacon			
¼ in. slices			6-8
½ in. slices			8-10
Bacon			4-5
PORK—FRESH			
Rib or loin chops	¾ to 1 inch	Always	20-25
Shoulder steaks	½ to ¾ inch	cooked	25-30
		well done	
LAMB			
Shoulder chops			
1 in.	5 to 8 ozs.	Lamb chops	12
1½ in.	8 to 10 ozs.	are not	18
2 in.	10 to 16 ozs.	usually	22
Rib chops—1 in.	3 to 5 ozs.	served rare	12
1½ in.	4 to 7 ozs.		18
2 in.	6 to 10 ozs.		22
Loin chops—1 in.	4 to 7 ozs.		12
1½ in.	6 to 10 ozs.		18
2 in.	8 to 14 ozs.		22
Ground lamb patties			
1 in. by 3 in.	4 ozs.		18

* This timetable is based on broiling at a moderate temperature (350°F.). Rare steaks are broiled to an internal temperature of 140°F.; medium to 160°F.; well-done to 170°F. Lamb chops are broiled from 170°F. to 175°F. Ham is cooked to 160°F. The time for broiling bacon is influenced by personal preference as to crispness.

Source: National Live Stock and Meat Board

effectively as fresh meat, will require longer cooking time which will vary according to the surface area and the thickness of the meat, as well as the broiling temperature used. A good rule of thumb, however, is to allow one-third to one-half again as much time for the cooking and for the distance between the heat in the broiler and the frozen chops and steaks.

Pan Broiling

Pan broiling involves cooking meat in a heavy uncovered frying pan without liquid. No fat need be added because most meat cuts have enough fat to prevent their sticking to the pan. The meat should be cooked slowly over a moderate heat and turned occasionally. Since the meat is in contact with the hot metal of the pan, turning more than once is essential for even cooking. Excessive fat should be poured off as it accumulates during the cooking. The meat is seasoned, if desired, after it is gradually browned on both sides. Pan broiling will require about one-third to one-half of the time required for broiling. To test for doneness of bone-in steaks or chops, a small gash should be cut close to the bone near the end of the cooking time to note the color of the meat. Pan broiling is recommended for thinner cuts (1 inch or less thick) of the same tender cuts that are suitable for broiling.

Pan Frying

Pan frying differs from pan broiling in that a small amount of fat is added at the start of cooking or is allowed to accumulate during cooking. The meat is browned on both sides in a small amount of fat. Those cuts that are high in fat will cook in the fat that comes from the meat. Other cuts that are low in fat, such as cubed steaks or liver and cuts which are floured or breaded, will require additional fat to cover the surface of the frying pan and to prevent sticking. As with pan broiling, the meat should be cooked uncovered to develop crispness, cooked at a moderate temperature, and turned occasionally until done. Enough heat must be applied so that the meat will brown and crisp rather than stew in the juice. However, if the fat smokes, indicating it is burning or breaking down, the temperature is too high for the fat and also for the meat.

The object in all frying is to cook the meat through on the inside while it is browning on the outside. Occasional turning is necessary to ensure even cooking. Flouring or breading meat before frying will give it a crisp brown exterior, and chilling breaded meat before cooking will help the coating stick to the meat. Any thin piece of tender meat suitable for broiling can also be pan fried. Additionally, sausages and meat made tender by pounding, scoring, cubing, or grinding, as well as leftover meat, may also be fried—usually in less time than it takes to broil or pan broil.

Roasting

In roasting, the meat is surrounded and cooked by heated air in an oven. As with the three preceding dry heat cooking methods, no water is added, and the meat is not covered. Because salt only penetrates ¼ to ½ inch, roasts may be seasoned either before, during, or after cooking. The meat should be placed fat side up on a rack in a shallow pan. (Ham halves or quarters should be roasted cut side down.) The rack holds the roast out of the drippings while the fat on top lets the meat do its own basting. A meat thermometer should be inserted so it is centered in the largest muscle. The tip of the thermometer should touch neither fat nor bone. While some people prefer to preheat the oven, this is not absolutely necessary. Small roasts should be cooked at 350° F. and larger roasts at 300°-325° F. until the thermometer registers the desired internal temperature. Roasts allowed to sit for 15 or 20 minutes after removal from the oven will be easier to carve. However, because meat continues to cook after removal from the oven, if it is to be allowed to sit, it should be removed when the thermometer registers about 5° lower than the desired doneness.

Degree of doneness of a roast is a matter of individual preference. Rare beef has a puffy, full appearance, a brown exterior, a reddish-pink interior, and lots of clear red juice. Beef cooked to a medium degree has a light pink interior and less juice of a lighter color than rare beef. Well-done beef is light brown throughout.

Veal should be cooked well-done to make it tender and palatable. Well-done veal has a red-brown exterior and a gray interior color. Lamb is usually preferred cooked medium or well-done. Medium lamb chops have a grayish-tan interior with a tinge of pink. Well-done lamb is grayish-tan with no trace of pink.

Fresh pork should be cooked thoroughly. The recommended internal temperature for pork loin is 170° F. A good test for doneness of fresh pork is to make a small cut next to the bone and into the thicker part of the meat. If the juice is still pink, the pork is not done. "Cook-before-eating" cured hams should be heated to 160° F. and picnic shoulders to 170° F. "Ready-to-serve" cured hams may be served unheated, but heating them to 140° F. brings out a better flavor.

Roasting is recommended for Prime, Choice, and Good beef ribs, loins, sirloins, and tenderloins. In the Prime and Choice grades, the top round, eye of round, and tip can be roasted as can a Prime eye roast from the chuck. Large, blocky cuts of veal from the leg, loin, rib, and shoulder are generally roasted. Nearly all lamb cuts are tender enough for roasting, particularly those from the leg, loin, rib, and shoulder. Besides fresh and cured ham and shoulder, those pork cuts which are roasted most successfully include loin roast and spareribs.

Figure 28 shows those cuts of red meat best suited for roasting and the approximate cooking time, as it relates to the degree of doneness, for meat placed in the oven at refrigerator temperature. For frozen roasts, one-third more cooking time should be allowed.

COOKING MEATS WITH MOIST HEAT

In the less tender cuts of meat where there is more connective tissue, it is necessary to use moist heat, low temperature, and relatively long cooking time to achieve tenderness. Braising and cooking in liquid are two examples of cooking in moist heat.

FIGURE 28
Timetable for Roasting

Cut	Approx. Weight (Pounds)	Oven Temperature Constant	Interior Temperature When Removed from Oven	Approx. Cooking Time (Min. per lb.)
BEEF				
Rib *	6 to 8	300°-325°F.	140°F. (rare)	23 to 25
			160°F. (medium)	27 to 30
			170°F. (well)	32 to 35
	4 to 6	300°-325°F.	140°F. (rare)	26 to 32
			160°F. (medium)	34 to 38
			170°F. (well)	40 to 42
Rolled rib	5 to 7	300°-325°F.	140°F. (rare)	32
			160°F. (medium)	38
			170°F. (well)	48
Rib eye (Delmonico)	4 to 6	350°F.	140°F. (rare)	18 to 20
			160°F. (medium)	20 to 22
			170°F. (well)	22 to 24
Tenderloin, Whole	4 to 6	425°F.	140°F. (rare)	45 to 60 (total)
Tenderloin, Half	2 to 3	425°F.	140°F. (rare)	45 to 50 (total)
Boneless rolled rump (high quality)	4 to 6	300°-325°F.	150°-170°F.	25 to 30
Tip (high quality)	3½ to 4	300°-325°F.	150°-170°F.	35 to 40
	4 to 6	300°-325°F.	150°-170°F.	30 to 35

Recommended Cooking Methods

FIGURE 28 (Continued)

Cut	Approx. Weight (Pounds)	Oven Temperature Constant	Interior Temperature When Removed from Oven	Approx. Cooking Time (Min. per lb.)
VEAL				
Leg	5 to 8	300°-325°F.	170°F.	25 to 35
Loin	4 to 6	300°-325°F.	170°F.	30 to 35
Rib (rack)	3 to 5	300°-325°F.	170°F.	35 to 40
Boneless shoulder	4 to 6	300°-325°F.	170°F.	40 to 45
PORK, FRESH				
Loin				
Center	3 to 5	325°-350°F.	170°F.	30 to 35
Half	5 to 7	325°-350°F.	170°F.	35 to 40
Blade loin or sirloin	3 to 4	325°-350°F.	170°F.	40 to 45
Boneless double	3 to 5	325°-350°F.	170°F.	35 to 45
Arm picnic shoulder	5 to 8	325°-350°F.	170°F.	30 to 35
Boneless	3 to 5	325°-350°F.	170°F.	35 to 40
Cushion	3 to 5	325°-350°F.	170°F.	30 to 35
Blade Boston shoulder	4 to 6	325°-350°F.	170°F.	40 to 45
Leg (fresh ham)				
Whole (bone in)	12 to 16	325°-350°F.	170°F.	22 to 26
Whole (boneless)	10 to 14	325°-350°F.	170°F.	24 to 28
Half (bone in)	5 to 8	325°-350°F.	170°F.	35 to 40
Spareribs		325°-350°F.	well done	½ to 2½ (hours)
PORK, SMOKED				
Ham (cook-before-eating)				
Whole	10 to 14	300°-325°F.	160°F.	18 to 20
Half	5 to 7	300°-325°F.	160°F.	22 to 25
Shank or rump portion	3 to 4	300°-325°F.	160°F.	35 to 40
Ham (fully cooked)**				
Half	5 to 7	325°F.	140°F.	18 to 24
Arm picnic shoulder	5 to 8	300°-325°F.	170°F.	35
Shoulder roll	2 to 3	300°-325°F.	170°F.	35 to 40
Canadian-style bacon	2 to 4	325°F.	160°F.	35 to 40
LAMB				
Leg	5 to 8	300°-325°F.	175°-180°F.	30 to 35
Shoulder	4 to 6	300°-325°F.	175°-180°F.	30 to 35
Boneless	3 to 5	300°-325°F.	175°-180°F.	40 to 45
Cushion	3 to 5	300°-325°F.	175°-180°F.	30 to 35
Rib	1½ to 3	375°F.	170°-180°F.	35 to 45

* Ribs which measure 6 to 7 inches from chine bone to top of rib.
** Allow approximately 15 minutes per pound for heating whole ham to serve hot.

Source: National Live Stock and Meat Board

Braising

Braising is cooking in a covered utensil, usually with a small amount of liquid. The meat should be browned slowly on all sides in a heavy uncovered pot and the drippings poured off after browning. It is the browning that develops flavor and color. Fat is usually added to prevent the meat from sticking as it browns; however, cuts with sufficient fat require no added fat unless they are coated with flour or crumbs. The meat should be seasoned after browning unless seasoning is added to the coating. Then a small amount of liquid usually is added to less tender cuts but may be omitted when cooking tender cuts of beef or lamb, or such cuts as pork chops and pork tenderloin.

The liquid used may be water, vegetable juice, or soup; just enough should be added to keep the meat from sticking. The pan should then be covered tightly. A tight-fitting lid holds in the steam needed for softening the connective tissues and making the meat tender. The meat should then be cooked at a low temperature so that it simmers and does not boil. This can be done on top of the range or in a slow oven at 300° to 325° F. A sauce or gravy can then be made from the liquid in the pan, if desired.

Braising is recommended for less tender cuts of meat. Many beef cuts, particularly in the lower grades (Standard or Commercial) are best prepared by braising. These include sirloin, sirloin tip, round, flank, chuck, shoulder, rump, and short ribs. Braising is also good for many cuts of veal because the combination of browning and steaming tenderizes the meat and develops its flavor. The best veal cuts for braising include arm or blade steaks or chops, breast, cutlets or round steaks, and loin or rib chops. In lamb, the cuts most suited to braising are breast, shanks, shoulder chops, and cubes. All pork chops and steaks are also satisfactory when braised, as are spareribs and cured ham shanks. Two of the most popular dishes cooked by braising are pot-roast from the chuck and Swiss steak from the beef round. Figure 29 shows the recommended cooking time for braised meats.

Cooking in Liquid

Cooking in liquid is similar to braising except that the meat is entirely covered with liquid. The meat may or may not be browned on all sides; however, browning develops flavor and increases color. (The exceptions to browning are corned beef and cured and smoked pork.)

Recommended Cooking Methods

FIGURE 29

Timetable for Braising

Cut	Average Weight or Thickness	Approximate Total Cooking Time
BEEF		
Pot-Roast		
Arm or blade	3 to 4 pounds	2½-3½ hours
Boneless	3 to 5 pounds	3-4 hours
Cubes	1 to 1½ inches	1½-2½ hours
Short ribs	Pieces (2 in. x 2 in. x 4 in.)	1½-2½ hours
Round steak	¾ to 1 inch	1-1¾ hours
Stuffed steak	½ to ¾ inch	1½ hours
PORK		
Chops	¾ to 1½ inches	45-60 minutes
Spareribs	2 to 3 pounds	1½ hours
Tenderloin		
Whole	¾ to 1 pound	45-60 minutes
Filets	½ inch	30 minutes
Shoulder steaks	¾ inch	45-60 minutes
LAMB		
Breast, stuffed	2 to 3 pounds	1½-2 hours
Breast, boneless	1½ to 2 pounds	1½-2 hours
Riblets		1½-2½ hours
Neck slices	¾ inch	1 hour
Shanks	¾ to 1 pound each	1-1½ hours
Shoulder chops	¾ to 1 inch	45-60 minutes
VEAL		
Breast, stuffed	3 to 4 pounds	1½-2½ hours
Breast, boneless	2 to 3 pounds	1½-2½ hours
Riblets		2-3 hours
Chops	½ to ¾ inch	45-60 minutes
Steaks or cutlets	½ to ¾ inch	45-60 minutes
Cubes	1 to 2 inches	45-60 minutes

Source: National Live Stock and Meat Board

The meat should then be covered with either hot or cold water or stock. By entirely covering the meat with liquid, uniform cooking is assured without turning the meat. After adding appropriate seasonings, the pot should be covered and the meat simmered (not boiled) until tender. Boiling and overcooking shrink the meat and make it dry, affecting both the flavor and texture, and making it difficult to slice. If the meat is to be served cold, it should be cooled and chilled in the stock in which it was cooked. The meat is more flavorful and juicy and will shrink less if cooled in its own stock. If vegetables are to be cooked with the meat, they should be added, whole or in pieces, just long enough before the meat is tender to cook them.

When small pieces of meat are cooked in liquid, such cooking produces a stew. The meat should first be cut into uniform pieces, usually 1 to 2-inch cubes. If a brown stew is desired, the meat cubes should be browned on all sides. If the cubes have been floured, fat must be added before browning. Coating with flour often intensifies the browning; however, if a light stew is preferred, browning is omitted. Just enough water, vegetable juices, or other liquids should be added to cover the meat. If the liquid is hot rather than cold, the meat will start cooking sooner. As with larger cuts, the meat is seasoned where appropriate, the pot is covered, and the meat is allowed to simmer until it is tender. It normally will require from $1\frac{1}{2}$ to $3\frac{1}{2}$ hours to cook the stew, depending on the kind of meat and the size of the pieces. Carrots, onions, potatoes, and other vegetables can be added to the meat just long enough before serving to be cooked. When done, the meat and vegetables should be removed to a pan, platter, or casserole and kept hot. If desired, the cooking liquid can be thickened for gravy by adding 2 tablespoons flour for each cup of cooking liquid and just enough cold water to make a paste. The flour mixture should be stirred into the cooking liquid, brought to a boil, boiled for 3 minutes or until thickened, while being stirred constantly.

Cooking with liquid is the method used for making meat soups and stews, and for the large, less tender cuts of meat such as corned beef, beef shanks, smoked hams, and picnics. Figure 30 gives the recommended timetable for cooking meats in liquid.

COOKING VARIETY MEATS

As with other fresh meats, the choice of a cooking method for variety meats will depend on how tender the particular meat is. With the

Recommended Cooking Methods 105

FIGURE 30
Timetable for Cooking in Liquid

Cut	Average Weight	Approx. Time per Pound	Approx. Total Cooking Time
	Pounds	Minutes	Hours
Smoked ham (country cured)			
Large	12 to 16	20	
Small	10 to 12	25	
Half	5 to 8	30	
Smoked ham			
Shank or rump half	5 to 8	20-25	
Smoked arm picnic			
shoulder	5 to 8	45	
Fresh or corned beef	4 to 6	40-50	
Beef shank cross cuts	¾ to 1		2½ to 3½
Beef for stew			2½ to 3½
Veal for stew			2 to 3
Lamb for stew			1½ to 2

Source: National Live Stock and Meat Board

exception of liver, variety meats are generally cooked well-done, regardless of the cooking method used, and prepared for cooking by being washed in cold water first.

Liver

Lamb, baby beef, and veal liver, which are especially tender, can be broiled, pan broiled, or pan fried, while beef and pork liver are better suited to braising. To broil, slices of lamb or veal liver should be dipped in or brushed with melted butter or margarine, placed on a cold broiler rack, and broiled just long enough for the liver to lose its red color—about 3 to 4 minutes on each side. Less tender, large pieces of beef and pork liver should be coated with flour, browned in lard or bacon drippings, and braised with or without vegetables.

    Large pieces of beef or pork liver will require ½ cup liquid and about 30 minutes per pound cooking time. Sliced braised liver requires less liquid (¼ cup) and about 20 minutes cooking time depending on the thickness of the slices. For pan frying, lamb, baby beef, or veal liver should be sliced ½ to ¾ inch thick, rolled in flour, browned on both sides in a small amount of lard or drippings, and seasoned after browning. If cooked at a moderate temperature and turned occasionally, the liver will be done soon after it is browned.

Heart

After removing the coarse fibers and washing the heart, this less tender variety meat should be cooked slowly in moisture. Beef and pork hearts can be braised or cooked in liquid, simmered for 2½ to 4 hours in salted water (1 teaspoon to each quart of water), and veal and lamb hearts for about 2½ hours (See Figure 31). Beef hearts can also be cooked in a slow oven (300° or 325° F.) for 3 to 3½ hours or until tender. Hearts may be stuffed before braising.

Sweetbreads

When precooking sweetbreads, the membrane can be removed either before or after cooking. To precook sweetbreads, simmer for 20 minutes in water, allowing a teaspoon of salt and a tablespoon of vinegar or lemon juice per quart of water. The acid from the lemon and vinegar helps to firm and whiten the meat. For braising (without precooking), after the membrane is removed, the sweetbreads can be floured or rolled in crumbs, then browned in a small amount of fat, covered, and cooked slowly for about 20 minutes. Frying is done in the same manner except the pan is not covered, and the sweetbreads are turned occasionally.

Precooked sweetbreads may be broken into small pieces and scrambled with eggs or reheated in a rich cream or tomato sauce. They may be dipped in egg and crumbs and fried in a small amount of fat or in deep fat until a delicate golden brown. Sweetbreads also can be made into croquettes, used in salad, or dipped in melted butter or margarine and broiled. If sweetbreads are not to be used immediately after purchase, they should be precooked regardless of the method of cooking because they are highly perishable in the fresh state.

Brains and sweetbreads are much alike in tenderness and texture and are prepared in the same manner.

Kidney

Beef kidney, which is less tender than pork, lamb, and veal kidneys, should be cooked in liquid or braised. The other kidneys are tender enough to be broiled. Before cooking, the membrane and hard parts (inner fat and tube) should be removed, and the kidneys sliced or cut into pieces. Lamb kidneys, because of their size, are usually cut in half lengthwise or left whole. Beef kidneys cooked in liquid (usually water) will require about 1 to 1½ hours cooking time. Braised kidneys should be rolled in seasoned flour or crumbs, browned in lard or drippings, and cooked slowly for 1 to 2 hours in a tightly covered utensil to which a small amount of liquid has been added. Broiled kidneys can be marinated for 1 hour in French dressing or brushed with butter or margarine and then broiled for about 5 minutes on each side, at which point they will be browned.

Tripe

Fresh tripe is usually partially cooked when sold. However, further cooking in water is necessary before it can be eaten. To precook, tripe should be covered and simmered for 2 hours in water to which a teaspoon of salt has been added for each quart of water used. After precooking, tripe may be served with a well-seasoned tomato sauce; brushed with melted butter or margarine and broiled until lightly browned; spread with dressing and baked; dipped in fritter batter and fried in deep fat; creamed; or used as an ingredient in pepper pot soup.

Tongue

Pork and lamb tongues are usually sold ready to serve, while beef and veal tongues are usually uncooked; but any tongue can be sold fresh, pickled or corned, or smoked. Smoked or pickled tongue may require soaking for several hours before cooking. After the tongue is slowly simmered in liquid (usually water) in a tightly covered utensil and is tender, the skin is removed and the tongue is served cold or reheated, whole or sliced, often in a spicy sauce. Fresh tongue should be cooked covered with water to which a teaspoon of salt has been added for each quart of water. Spices and vegetables are sometimes added for flavor. Beef tongues require 3 to 4 hours to cook, veal tongues 2 to 3 hours, and pork and lamb tongues 1½ to 2½ hours, or until tender. Plunging the tongue into cold water after cooking helps to loosen the skin which should be removed and the roots cut away. If the tongue is to be served cold, it should be cooled in the liquid in which it was cooked; this will make it more juicy. Cooling, however, should be done under refrigeration or where there is circulation of cool air.

Cooking methods for variety meats are probably the least understood by the consumer. However, the knowledgeable store employee can do much to help move these often less popular, but highly nutritious, items. Figure 31 shows the recommended timetable and cooking method for each type of variety meat.

REAPING THE BENEFITS

Because per capita consumption is greater for fresh meat than for any other meat items, food store employees must know these products if the store is to compete successfully with others in the area. As indicated earlier, this is not a difficult task. Any employee who has knowledge of the grade of meat that is being sold and who knows whether a cut has been taken from the more tender or the less tender part of the carcass should have no difficulty providing customers with the cooking advice they so often desire. (In that connection, Figures 14-17 in Chapter 3 will serve as a very handy reference.)

By knowing how each cut should be cooked for maximum tenderness and flavor and by knowing which cuts are logical substitutes for others which may be out of stock, meat department employees will be in a position to provide an optimum level of customer service. Moreover, such knowledge will enable them to merchandise and move the less popular cuts, thereby improving the department's product mix and the company's profitability through its ability to buy whole carcasses.

COOKING POULTRY

While grades are important in determining the proper cooking methods for red meats, they have no relationship to the tenderness of poultry products. Instead, the class name (for example, fryer, capon, hen, etc.), which indicates the age of the bird and therefore its degree of tenderness, is used to determine the most suitable cooking method for poultry.

Fresh poultry requires little preparation before cooking—it merely is rinsed in cool water, drained, and patted dry. It is especially important that poultry be dried if it is to be fried, broiled, or oven browned, since this will prevent spattering. Frozen poultry usually is thawed before cooking, but whole, frozen poultry (without giblets) can be roasted, braised, or stewed without thawing. Frozen poultry parts can also be roasted, fried, braised, or stewed but will require at

Recommended Cooking Methods

FIGURE 31
Timetable for Cooking Variety Meats

Kind	Broiled	Braised	Cooked in Liquid
LIVER			
Beef			
3- to 4-pound piece		2 to 2½ hours	
Sliced		20 to 25 minutes	
Veal (Calf), sliced	8 to 10 minutes		
Pork			
Whole (3 to 3½ pounds)		1½ to 2 hours	
Sliced		20 to 25 minutes	
Lamb, sliced	8 to 10 minutes		
KIDNEY			
Beef		1½ to 2 hours	1 to 1½ hours
Veal (Calf)	10 to 12 minutes	1 to 1½ hours	¾ to 1 hour
Pork	10 to 12 minutes	1 to 1½ hours	¾ to 1 hour
Lamb	10 to 12 minutes	¾ to 1 hour	¾ to 1 hour
HEART			
Beef			
Whole		3 to 4 hours	3 to 4 hours
Sliced		1½ to 2 hours	
Veal (Calf)			
Whole		2½ to 3 hours	2½ to 3 hours
Pork		2½ to 3 hours	2½ to 3 hours
Lamb		2½ to 3 hours	2½ to 3 hours
TONGUE			
Beef			3 to 4 hours
Veal (Calf)			2 to 3 hours
Pork } usually sold			
Lamb } ready-to-serve			
TRIPE			
Beef	10 to 15 minutes [1]		1 to 1½ hours
SWEETBREADS	10 to 15 minutes [1]	20 to 25 minutes	15 to 20 minutes
BRAINS	10 to 15 minutes [1]	20 to 25 minutes	15 to 20 minutes

[1] Time required after precooking in water.
Source: National Live Stock and Meat Board

least 1½ times as long to cook as will unfrozen or thawed poultry of the same weight and shape.

There are three principal ways to thaw frozen poultry. The slowest method is to place it on a tray or platter, in its original wrap, in the refrigerator. Most poultry thawed by this method will require one or two days to become pliable; however, turkeys weighing 18 pounds or over may take three to four days to thaw. If rapid thawing is required, frozen poultry can be placed in cold water in its original wrap or a watertight plastic bag; changing the water often will hasten thawing. Poultry thawed by this method will require about an hour for small birds and up to six or eight hours for large turkeys.

Poultry can also be safely thawed in a cool room, i.e., at 70° F. or below. When this method is used, the poultry should be left in its original plastic wrapping and placed in a closed, double-wall paper bag or wrapped in newspaper and set in a corrugated box or on a tray to catch any drippings. Using this method, chickens weighing up to 4 pounds will require up to 12 hours to thaw; small turkeys will require 12 to 15 hours, and turkeys weighing 12 to 24 pounds will require from 15 to 20 hours.

Thawed poultry, which is prepared for cooking in the same way as unfrozen poultry, should be cooked promptly after thawing. It is important not to cook poultry partially one day and then complete the cooking the following day since this practice, which gives bacteria an opportunity to grow, can produce toxins and cause food poisoning.

Following are the most popular poultry cooking methods.

Roasting

All kinds of poultry—chicken, turkey, duck, and goose—can be roasted, and whole poultry can be roasted either stuffed or unstuffed. If it is to be stuffed, the whole poultry should be rinsed, drained, and patted dry; the cavity may be rubbed lightly with salt. The wishbone (neck) area should then be lightly filled with stuffing, and the neck skin fastened with a skewer. The body cavity is then stuffed lightly, and the legs are tucked under the bird, using a skewer or string, while the wings are shaped akimbo-style—that is, the wing tips are brought onto the back.

The poultry should then be placed breast side up in a shallow pan and the skin brushed with oil or melted fat if desired. If the poultry browns too early in the roasting period, the breast and drumstick should be covered lightly with aluminum foil, or a thin cloth should be moistened with fat and placed over the breast and legs to prevent overbrowning. Poultry may be basted with drippings; however, ducks, geese, and guineas have sufficient fat so that they need no basting.

At the half or two-thirds point of roasting, the string or skin should be cut to release the bird's legs. The meat is done when the temperature reaches 180° to 185° F., as measured by a meat thermometer which has been inserted into the inner thigh muscle, the slowest heating part of the bird. At the same time, the temperature of the stuffing should be at least 165° F.

Although meat thermometers can be helpful in determining the doneness of medium-size or large turkeys, they are not particularly helpful with small turkeys or chickens because the muscles are too small to hold the thermometer in place, and the chances of touching bones are too great to ensure accurate measurements. An alternate way to test for doneness is to press the fleshy part of the drumstick with protected fingers. When done, the meat will feel soft, the drumstick will move easily, and the leg joint will give readily. If the meat splits down the breast bone or on the legs, the poultry is likely to be overdone and dry. Excessive shrinkage is another sign of overdone poultry; only a small amount of shrinkage is expected in properly cooked meat. Unstuffed whole poultry is cooked in a similar manner; however, it usually requires less cooking time. Although 325° F. is the temperature generally recommended for roasting whole poultry, young whole chickens can be roasted at 400° F. The approximate cooking time for roasting young 1½ to 2-pound chickens at 400° F. is ¾ hour to an hour for unstuffed chickens and 1 to 1¼ hours for stuffed chickens.

Boneless turkey roasts should be placed on a rack in an open pan and roasted at 325° F. until the internal temperature registers 170° to 175° F.

Turkey halves, quarters, or pieces should be placed skin side up on a rack in an open pan, roasted at 325° F. and basted several times. Chicken pieces, on the other hand, should be placed in a flat pan without a rack. Although chicken will brown without the addition of fat, the skin will be more crisp if it is brushed with fat before roasting and if it is basted during roasting. Chicken pieces should be roasted at 400° F. and turned once during roasting. Pieces from 1½ or 2-pound chickens require 45 minutes to 1 hour, while pieces from larger chickens may take slightly longer.

Figure 32 gives the recommended roasting time for all types of fresh or thawed poultry. The time indicated for whole birds assumes that the poultry has been stuffed.

Braising

Basically, oven roasting is changed to braising simply by covering the poultry while it is cooking. Mature, less tender poultry often requires braising—cooking slowly in a closely covered pan with a small

FIGURE 32
Roasting Guide for Poultry

Kind	Ready-to-Cook Weight	Approximate Total Roasting Time at 325° F.	Internal Temperature of Poultry When Done
Chickens, whole:	Pounds	Hours	Degrees F.
Broilers, fryers, or roasters	1½ to 2½	1 to 2	
	2½ to 4½	2 to 3½	
Capons	5 to 8	2½ to 3½	
Ducks	4 to 6	2 to 3	
Geese	6 to 8	3 to 3½	
	8 to 12	3½ to 4½	
Turkeys:			
Whole	6 to 8	3 to 3½	180 to 185 in thigh
	8 to 12	3½ to 4½	180 to 185 in thigh
	12 to 16	4½ to 5½	180 to 185 in thigh
	16 to 20	5½ to 6½	180 to 185 in thigh
	20 to 24	6½ to 7	180 to 185 in thigh
Halves, quarters, and pieces	3 to 8	2 to 3	
	8 to 12	3 to 4	
Boneless turkey roasts	3 to 10	3 to 4	170 to 175 in center

amount of moisture—to tenderize the meat and bring out its rich flavor. Additionally, braising will cook young, tender poultry and boneless turkey roasts more quickly than will roasting.

To braise whole poultry, the oven should be preheated to 450° F. for young poultry and 325° F. for more mature birds. The poultry should be seasoned and brushed with butter or other fat and then placed on a rack in a roaster or heavy pan and covered tightly. It will be done when the leg joints move easily and the flesh on the leg is soft and pliable. If browning is desired, the pan should be uncovered for the last 30 minutes of cooking.

To braise cut-up poultry, serving-size pieces should be rolled in seasoned flour and browned well in fat in a heavy frying pan. The fat should then be drained off and one cup of hot water added, the pan covered, and the poultry cooked very slowly on top of the range or in the oven at 325° F. To prevent sticking, more water can be added, if necessary. To brown and crisp the skin, the cover should be removed during the last 30 minutes. Total cooking time should be between 1½ to 2¼ hours, depending on the size of the pieces and the maturity of the bird.

To braise a boneless turkey roast, the oven should be preheated to 400° F. The roast should be placed on a rack in a pan, a thermometer inserted in the center of the roast, and the pan covered tightly. The roast should be cooked until the thermometer registers about 170° F. (about 1½ hours for 3 pounds). If browning is desired, the pan should be uncovered during the last 20 minutes.

Broiling

Chickens are broiled more often than other kinds of poultry, but small, young turkeys, ducklings, and guineas can also be broiled satisfactorily. Young chickens or Rock Cornish game hens should be cut into halves, quarters, or meaty pieces for broiling. The pieces are brushed with melted fat or cooking oil, sprinkled with salt and seasoning, and placed on the broiler pan at a distance from the heat recommended by the range manufacturer. The poultry should be broiled 20 to 30 minutes on one side or until brown, then turned, brushed with fat or oil, and broiled until done for approximately an additional 15 to 25 minutes longer.

Small turkeys and ducklings should also be cut into halves, quarters, or meaty pieces; the wings and the leg joints should be snapped to keep them flat during broiling. Turkeys can be basted occasionally; however, ducks will not require any basting. Because turkey and duck pieces are thicker than chicken, they require longer broiling time; 60 to 75 minutes total cooking time should be allowed for this type of poultry.

Chicken is often broiled or barbecued over charcoal, and while not as popular, turkeys and ducks are also suited for outdoor cooking. When broiling over charcoal, the coals should be spaced so that no two coals touch. Moreover, the broiler rack should be 6 to 8 inches from the embers for an even heat without too much intensity. If the poultry gets too hot, the grill should be raised away from the heat since poultry tastes best when broiled over hot coals rather than in flame or smoke.

Chicken is usually halved or quartered for outdoor broiling. Small turkey quarter roasts are excellent for barbecuing, and young fryer-type turkeys weighing 6 to 8 pounds can be cut into individual servings. The poultry should be brushed with melted butter, margarine, or a barbecue sauce. It should be broiled and turned occasionally for 1 to 1½ hours, depending on the size and thickness of the pieces. Basting is optional.

Whole chickens, turkeys, ducks, geese, or large poultry pieces can be cooked on rotisserie equipment that turns the meat slowly on a rotary spit over or under direct heat. Because rotisseries vary greatly, it is best to follow directions that come with the equipment.

It is important that the whole bird or pieces be balanced and mounted before starting the rotary spit to ensure that the poultry does not slip as the spit turns. To mount a whole bird, the neck skin should be attached with a skewer to the back of the body, and the wings should be tied or skewered close to the body. The spit should then be inserted through the length of the body and the holding prongs tightened. The tail and drumsticks should be tied firmly to the rod. If properly balanced, the bird should rotate evenly when the spit is turned. More than one bird can be roasted at a time if the spit is long enough; however, it is important to be sure that the birds are mounted in opposite directions to maintain good balance on the spit. The skin should be brushed with oil or melted fat, and the manufacturer's directions for rotisserie temperature setting and time should be followed. Testing for doneness is similar to testing for doneness in roast poultry.

Frying

Young chickens, capons, Rock Cornish game hens, and small turkeys and ducklings can be pan fried, oven fried, or fried in deep fat. Poultry to be fried is usually cut into serving-size pieces. It can be fried without a coating if the pieces are thoroughly dried to prevent spattering of fat; however, coatings give a crisp surface and help retain moisture in the meat.

To pan fry poultry, about ¼ cup of fat or oil—just enough to cover the bottom of the pan—should be heated in a heavy frying pan, using moderate heat. Without crowding the pan, the pieces should be browned on one side, then turned and browned on the other side. After browning, chicken should continue to cook slowly uncovered until tender for about 30 to 45 minutes, or it can be cooked in an oven at 350° F. until tender. Turkey or duckling should be covered tightly after browning and cooked slowly for 45 to 60 minutes or until tender, and turned occasionally. Although cooking in a covered pan is not true frying, the moist temperature saves cooking time. It may be necessary

Recommended Cooking Methods

to add a small amount of water if the lid is not tight. To recrisp the skin, the pan should be uncovered for the last few minutes of cooking.

For oven frying, the oven should be preheated to 400° F. The poultry pieces should be floured and placed in a baking pan containing about $\frac{1}{8}$ inch or less hot fat, and the pieces should be turned to coat both sides with fat. Chicken should be cooked skin side down for 30 minutes, then turned, and cooked 20 to 30 minutes longer or until tender. Turkey and duck are cooked in the same manner; however, their cooking time will depend on the thickness of the pieces and their tenderness.

To fry in deep fat, the poultry pieces should be coated with a thin batter, flour, or crumbs. Fat with a high smoking point should be preheated to 365° F., and the temperature checked with a deep-fat thermometer. If the fat is not hot enough, the poultry will become fat soaked and take longer to cook. On the other hand, if the fat is too hot, the meat may scorch before it cooks through. Overheating fat also causes smoke, which gives meat undesirable flavors and makes it harder to digest. Only a few pieces should be fried at one time and then drained on paper towels after about 10 to 15 minutes of cooking time.

Simmering or Stewing

For mature, less tender poultry, simmering or stewing is an excellent cooking method. Young poultry may also be cooked by this method, but it will lack the rich full flavor of mature poultry. The poultry can be cut in halves or pieces or left whole, seasoned as desired, and placed in a pot with water to barely cover. The poultry should be simmered for $1\frac{1}{2}$ to 2 hours in a covered pan until tender when pierced with a fork. If desired, the pieces can be browned in some hot fat in a frying pan before serving. Young turkey will require only about 45 minutes to 1 hour cooking time; chicken bouillon cubes are often added to add flavor to the broth.

Cooking Giblets and Neck

To prepare the neck and giblets for cooking, they should be washed thoroughly, and any excess fat removed from the gizzard. The neck, gizzard, and heart should be covered with water and simmered until tender. Turkey giblets take $1\frac{1}{2}$ hours or more, while chicken giblets require about 1 hour cooking time. The liver can be added during the last 15 to 30 minutes of cooking and simmmered until done. If the poultry is to be roasted and broth is not needed for gravy, the giblets and neck should be salted, sealed tightly in aluminum foil and cooked in the pan with the poultry. Giblets cooked in this manner will require about the same time as the roast.

POPULARITY OF POULTRY

Poultry is high on the list of popularity in American meals. According to a recent national consumer survey of meat-buying preferences, poultry and ground beef ranked highest. When asked, "which of these meats have you served in the past 12 months?" 98 percent of the respondents said "chicken" and "ground beef." By comparison, only 82 percent answered "beef roast." The popularity of poultry is due partly to its availability. With today's modern production, processing, and marketing methods, chicken, turkey, duck, and geese are available all year for roasting, broiling, frying, stewing, or making soups, salads and other dishes. Moreover, packaged, cut-up chicken and turkey, heat-and-serve fried chicken, and the newer turkey and chicken rolls, roasts, or bars make poultry among the most versatile and easy-to-prepare dishes.

COOKING SAUSAGE

All fresh sausage and uncooked smoked sausage require cooking before eating. Cooked, smoked sausage does not require further cooking. However, some products in this category (wieners, frankfurters, and smoked links) are heated to enhance their flavor, while others are most often served cold (bologna, minced ham, and salami). Dry and semi-dry sausage and luncheon meats are fully cooked and ready to serve without heating.

Following are the most popular methods used to cook fresh sausage or uncooked smoked sausage:

Pan Frying. Sausage links or patties should be placed in a cold frying pan. About 2 to 4 tablespoons of water should be added. The pan should be covered tightly and the sausage cooked slowly for 5 to 8 minutes, depending on the size or thickness. The cover should then be removed, the sausage browned slowly, and cooked until well-done.

Oven Cooking. Sausages should be arranged in a single layer in a shallow baking pan and baked in a hot oven (400° F.) for 20 to

30 minutes, or until well done. For even browning, the sausages should be turned and the drippings poured off as they accumulate.

Frankfurters or other cooked smoked sausage links that do not require cooking may be heated by one of the following methods:

Simmering. Cooked frankfurters or sausage should be dropped into boiling water and the pan covered. The heat should then be lowered so that the water simmers rather than boils, and the meat should be heated through for about 5 to 10 minutes, depending on size.

Pan or Griddle Broiling. A small amount of fat (1 to 2 tablespoons) should be melted in a heavy frying pan or on a griddle and the meat browned by turning it slowly with tongs so as not to pierce the skin.

Oven or Barbecue Broiling. Each frankfurter or sausage should be brushed with butter, margarine, or other fat, if desired, and broiled about 3 inches from the heat. Again, the sausage should be turned to brown evenly, using tongs in order not to pierce the skin.

OTHER PROCESSES

In order to improve its flavor and/or tenderness, fresh red meat is sometimes aged or tenderized, and both fresh red meat and poultry are often marinated to improve flavor.

Aging

Only ribs and hindquarter primals of high-quality beef are usually dry aged (held for periods of from two to four weeks). These cuts are tender, and the major purpose of aging is to develop additional tenderness and characteristic flavor. To be suitable for aging, meat must have a fairly thick covering of fat to prevent discoloration of the lean and to keep evaporation at a minimum.

Meat that is dry aged is held at temperatures from 34° to 38° F. for two to four weeks. This allows enzymatic activity to break down complex proteins, which improves flavor and tenderness. There is a difference of opinion regarding the best cooler humidity. Some prefer a relatively low humidity of from 70 to 75 percent so the exposed surface of the meat will remain dry. Others, however, use humidities of up to 85 or 90 percent to reduce evaporation losses.

Meat that is fast aged is held at a much higher temperature, usually about 65° to 70° F., for two or three days in humidity ranging from 85 to 90 percent. In order to reduce the microbial growth in the aging room, ultraviolet lights are used.

Most of the dry-aged meat is used by hotels and restaurants, while fast-aged meat is normally distributed through retail outlets. However, in the normal process of moving fresh meat from packer to retailer to consumer, there is a time lapse of from 6 to 10 days, which is long enough for considerable aging to take place. Also, meat that is vacuum packaged will continue to age for two to three weeks with little weight loss or surface spoilage. However, some retailers hold beef primals for longer periods of time for customers who prefer meat that is aged for more than three weeks.

Tenderizing

Some tenderizing treatments are applied before the meat is delivered to the retailer, while others are applied by the customer at home. The two chief methods of tenderizing meat are (1) treatment with liquid, powdered, or salt-type tenderizers, and (2) mechanical treatment to cut or break connective tissues and muscle fibers.

Papain, which is derived from the papaya fruit, is the product used in most commercially prepared tenderizers. A papain enzyme solution can be injected directly into the vascular system of the live animal just prior to slaughter, or after slaughter into the less tender primals, rather than the entire carcass. If injected before slaughter, the heart's action as a pump distributes the tenderizer to all parts of the carcass. After slaughter, multiple injections are used, the amount varying in relation to the original carcass weight of the animal. The papain enzyme is activated by heat and causes a breakdown of tough muscle tissues during cooking. Meat pretendered by the processor in either manner described above is most often sold under a brand name.

There are also a number of powdered or salt-type tenderizers that can be applied by the customer to the surface of raw meat to increase its tenderness. Like seasonings, these home tenderizers penetrate only a short distance and are more effective in tenderizing thin cuts such as steaks than they are in tenderizing large cuts like roasts.

Mechanically tenderized meat can be put through a cubing machine at the supermarket that scores the surface of thin steaks such as flank, tip, or round steak. The meat is then sold as cubed steak. The consumer can tenderize these steaks herself by pounding them with a mallet or scoring them with a knife at home. Another technique is to put the primal cuts through a needle-type mechanical tenderizer at central plant or store level.

Marinating

This process, used to introduce flavor into a meat or poultry dish, can also have a tenderizing effect. Marinades usually include an acid (lemon juice, cider, or vinegar), seasonings (salt, pepper, onion, garlic, spices, or herbs), and sometimes a fat (olive or vegetable oil). Small cuts (cubes or chops) can be marinated by soaking for a few hours in enough liquid to cover them completely. Large cuts, on the other hand, should be marinated overnight or up to 24 hours in the refrigerator. Because the acid penetrates meat slowly, sufficient time should be allowed for the flavor to reach the center, and the meat should be turned several times.

STORAGE AND FREEZING

The amount of meat or poultry that the customer requires will depend on a number of factors, including the number of people to be fed, the appetites of the diners, how the product is to be prepared, the accompanying dishes to be served, whether the product is a boneless or bone-in item, whether leftovers are desired for a second meal, and the storage and freezing space available.

Storing Fresh Product at Home

Because meat and poultry are highly perishable unless frozen, for optimum quality, fresh beef, veal, lamb, and pork should be stored in the coldest part of the customer's refrigerator, at temperatures lower than 40° F., without freezing the meat, and used within two days. Ground meats, variety meats, and poultry should be similarly stored but used within 24 hours. Although fresh meat can be held safely up to four days (see Figure 33), and fresh poultry up to two days (longer if chill-packed), the shorter time periods are preferred to ensure top quality.

Prepackaged fresh meat can be stored in its original wrappings. However, meat that has not been prepackaged should be removed from the market wrapping paper and wrapped loosely in waxed paper or aluminum foil. Cured meats, cured and smoked meats, sausages, and luncheon meats should be left in their original wrappings.

Similarly, prepackaged poultry should be stored in the original wrap which controls moisture loss. Raw poultry that has been wrapped only in market paper should be unwrapped, placed on a platter or tray, covered with waxed paper, and the giblets wrapped and stored separately.

Storing Cooked Foods at Home

Leftover cooked meats should be cooled within two hours after cooking, covered or wrapped to prevent drying, and stored in the refrigerator. Meats that have been cooked in liquid should be cooled uncovered within two hours and then covered and refrigerated. The pan containing the meat and liquid can be set in cold or running water to hasten cooling. Because bacteria grow best between 60° and 120° F., the food should be taken through this temperature range as quickly as possible. It is recommended that leftover cooked meat be eaten within four days for maximum quality.

Cooked poultry should be cooled as quickly as possible, wrapped loosely, and stored in the refrigerator. Stuffing should be removed, quickly cooled, and stored separately in a covered container. Broth or gravy should be refrigerated promptly and reheated to boiling before serving. For optimum quality, it is best to use the cooked poultry, stuffing, broth, or gravy within two days.

Freezing Fresh Product at Home

For best results, fresh meat and poultry should be frozen while it is in top condition, properly wrapped, and kept at 0° F. or below.

Prepackaged items can be frozen in their original wrappers for up to two weeks. If stored for longer periods, they should be overwrapped with a moisture-proof, vapor-proof wrap or bag to seal the moisture in and the air out. The product should be wrapped tightly, pressing out as much air as possible. When air penetrates the package, moisture is drawn from the surface and "freezer burn" develops. Items to be frozen should be trimmed carefully to save freezer space, divided into meal size portions, and labeled according to type of product and date. Fresh product should not be salted since this will

Recommended Cooking Methods

shorten freezer life. Moreover, it is wise not to freeze so large a quantity at one time that it will overload the freezer and raise the freezer temperature above 0° F., which will impair the quality of the product. Refreezing defrosted product should also be avoided not only because there is some loss of juices during defrosting, but also because the product can deteriorate between the time of defrosting and refreezing.

FIGURE 33

Meat Storage Time Chart

Maximum Storage Time Recommendations for Fresh, Cooked, and Processed Meat

Meat	Refrigerator 36° to 40° F.*	Freezer 0° F. or Lower
Beef (fresh)	2 to 4 days	6 to 12 months
Veal (fresh)	2 to 4 days	6 to 9 months
Pork (fresh)	2 to 4 days	3 to 6 months
Lamb (fresh)	2 to 4 days	6 to 9 months
Ground beef, veal, and lamb	1 to 2 days	3 to 4 months
Ground pork	1 to 2 days	1 to 3 months
Variety meats	1 to 2 days	3 to 4 months
Luncheon meats	1 week	not recommended
Sausage, fresh pork	1 week	60 days
Sausage, smoked	3 to 7 days	
Sausage, dry and semi-dry (unsliced)	2 to 3 weeks	
Frankfurters	4 to 5 days	1 month
Bacon	5 to 7 days	1 month
Smoked ham, whole	1 week	2 months
Ham slices	3 to 4 days	2 months
Beef, corned	1 week	2 weeks
Leftover cooked meat	4 to 5 days	2 to 3 months
Frozen combination foods		
Meat pies (cooked)		3 months
Swiss steak (cooked)		3 months
Stews (cooked)		3 to 4 months
Prepared meat dinners		2 to 6 months

* The range in time reflects recommendations for maximum storage time from several authorities. For top quality, fresh meats should be used in 2 or 3 days, ground meat and variety meats should be used in 24 hours.

Source: National Live Stock and Meat Board

FIGURE 34
Poultry Storage Time Chart

Poultry	Freezer (at 0° F. or Lower)
Uncooked poultry:	
Chicken	
Whole	12 months
Cut-up	9 months
Giblets	3 months
Turkey	
Whole	12 months
Cut-up	6 months
Duck, whole	6 months
Goose, whole	6 months
Cooked poultry (slices or pieces):	
Covered with broth or gravy	6 months
Not covered with broth or gravy	1 month
Cooked poultry dishes	6 months
Fried chicken	4 months

The maximum length of time that frozen meat or poultry will maintain its quality depends on the condition of the product at the time of freezing, the kind of packaging used, and the storage temperature. Raw items will maintain desirable flavor and texture longer in freezer storage than will cooked leftovers. And any frozen product will be of best quality if used before the maximum recommended freezing time. (See Figures 33 and 34.)

SUMMARY

One of the most valuable meat merchandising tools that any supermarket has is a staff that knows its product and can offer advice and suggestions to customers on proper cooking methods. Such a staff not only helps to personalize a store but also helps the meat department increase volume and move high-profit items. By knowing the basic grades and cuts of meats and the cooking methods best suited to each, any store employee can become an expert in this area.

6

Product Procurement

Reliability is the cornerstone of every good buyer-supplier relationship. On the supplier's side, reliability means delivering product of consistent quality, in the proper quantity, at the right time, and at competitive prices. However, reliability is a two-way street, and the buyer must also be dependable in his loyalty to suppliers who have proved themselves to be reliable. The opportunities to be unreliable abound for both suppliers and buyers, and while there may be short-term gains for one or the other to take advantage of such situations, in the long run such practices can prove quite costly to both.

BUYER-SUPPLIER RELATIONSHIP

The *National Provisioner* (often referred to as the "Yellow Sheet") is used as a pricing guide by both suppliers and buyers. It recaps the prices at which beef, veal, pork, and lamb are sold in the major meat markets on a daily basis and, in effect, establishes a yardstick for the price at which cattle can be bought the following day. Depending on supply and demand factors and the company's purchasing power, a buyer will be able to place orders at, above, or below the price quoted in the *Provisioner,* plus freight.

In times of short supply, even the largest volume purchasers will be forced to place orders at prices above the *Provisioner*'s quote. Conversely, suppliers will be willing to sell product below the *Provisioner*'s price when they have a surplus of product on hand. In any event, many companies have arrangements with suppliers whereby they are billed in relation to the *Provisioner*'s quote on the day of shipment, regardless of when the order is placed. A beef order placed on Thursday for delivery the following Wednesday is billed at the price quoted in the *Provisioner* on Tuesday, the day of shipment. Such an arrangement, which saves considerable time for both the buyer and the supplier, works well when both parties are reliable. However, if the supplier is unscrupulous, he can delay shipping by one day if he believes the market will rise, and if the price increases by only 1 cent a pound over the 24-hour period, the company will not only pay an additional $350 for a load of beef, but it also will receive its shipment one day late. Such a situation could be critical for many companies.

By the same token, in a falling market an unreliable customer can cancel an order that was placed at a high negotiated price (i.e., without regard to the *Provisioner*), and then place the same order with another supplier at the lower current market price, thus leaving the original supplier with surplus product on hand. Such unreliability on the part of the buyer obviously encourages a reaction in kind by the supplier. Among the many retaliatory moves open to the supplier, he may simply choose not to fill an order that he accepted at a low negotiated price when the market rises or when product is in short supply.

Deciding on the Supplier

The wisest course for the buyers in any company to follow is to explore all the buying options that are available and then to buy only from those suppliers who have proved themselves to be the most reliable. Some companies prefer to deal with only one supplier, believing that if the supplier knows he is the exclusive resource, he will feel obligated always to fill the company's needs. An accompanying attitude in these companies is that, of the buying and merchandising functions, merchandising is the more important, and the buyer should be spending the most time on this activity. Other companies believe that more than one source of supply is necessary for three reasons: (1) if there is industrial strife and one supplier is closed down, another source will be available; (2) if a delivery from a distant supplier is delayed because of adverse weather conditions or other factors, an alternate source of supply is available on a "fill-in" basis; and (3) there is less risk of a supplier taking undue advantage of a buyer if the supplier knows he is competing with others for the business.

Still other companies feel that "cherry-picking" has many advantages and that they will get better overall prices if they deal with a large number of competitive suppliers. However, unless the buyer in this situation is uniquely qualified, the savings he effects on one purchase more often than not are offset by the premium he pays on another. Moreover, because of his lack of loyalty to any one supplier, he may not be able to obtain product when it is in short supply, and he has less assurance of consistency in the quality of the product delivered.

However, whether a company will want to deal with one or two or more suppliers for each commodity will depend on a number of additional factors. Foremost, of course, is the company's size and its ability to find an adequate source of supply so that it will always have sufficient quantity on hand. If a company has only four or five stores, in almost all cases one supplier will suffice. However, in a chain of 100 or more stores, it is more than likely that the company will have to depend on more than one supplier to fill its needs.

Moreover, if store-door deliveries are required, a company will probably either have to buy locally or have product trans-shipped by a local firm because most out-of-town suppliers limit the number of store drops that they will make with each trailer load. If a company does purchase product from out-of-town sources, it must evaluate the supplier's reliability with regard to maintaining delivery schedules. A company that maintains its own warehouse and can keep at least a day's supply of fresh red meat on hand can risk dealing with a supplier who ships from 1,000 miles away. But a company that cannot afford a 24-hour delay in receiving product would be wise not to depend on any supplier located more than eight hours away in traveling time; no matter how good the intentions of the supplier, adverse weather conditions, equipment failures, and other unforeseen factors will affect the supplier's ability to fulfill his commitment. Therefore, the company should be sure that the supplier is within an eight-hour delivery radius since this distance will enable him to make overnight deliveries.

Assuming that a supplier is reliable with regard to delivering the proper quantities on time and at competitive prices, the last test of reliability will be his ability to deliver product consistently according to the quality specifications that the retailer has established. If the supplier cannot consistently deliver product of the quality, yield, and weight that the company wants, all of his other capabilities will be worthless.

THE BUYING FUNCTION

A number of variations exist among supermarket companies in the meat buying operation. In a small company, the buying responsibility for all product most often falls to one person. As companies increase in size, buying is usually divided by commodity group among the buying staff. Pork and poultry are often the buying responsibility of one person with beef, veal, and lamb being bought by another individual. A third person might be solely responsible for bacon, sausages, and luncheon meats. Many other combinations of buying responsibilities exist, and while they most often are tied to the size of the company, they also reflect management's philosophy of buying, merchandising, and supervising each product line, so that even in larger companies these responsibilities might be placed in the hands of one person. Against these variations in who does the buying, there is generally more uniformity in how the buying function is actually performed.

Establishing Prices

As indicated earlier, many companies make arrangements with suppliers to be billed in relation to the price quoted in the *Provisioner* on the day of shipment. (Similarly, prices are set for poultry in relation to the quotations printed in *Urnerberry,* a publication that reports daily prices for poultry and egg products, based on government weighted averages, in nine major marketing areas.)

Whether a company will be able to buy at prices above or below the printed quotations will depend not only on its purchasing power, in terms of volume, and the available supply, but also on the additional services that the company requires. For example, a company may agree to pay 2 cents a pound more than the *Provisioner*'s quote for beef to cover shipping costs and other expenses. Or, it may agree to pay an additional ½ cent for the privilege of selecting its own cattle. A few companies also agree to pay a premium to guarantee that they will be billed for only the delivered weight of the product. However, most companies prefer to follow the U.S. Government standard which allows ½ of 1 percent in-transit shrinkage on all items, since this is usually less costly than paying the delivered-weight premium.

As compared to those companies that buy against the *Provisioner* or *Urnerberry,* other companies prefer to negotiate prices with the supplier at the time the order is placed, rather than to accept the current market price on the day the order is shipped. For example, a buyer may order a specific quantity of turkeys on July 1 for delivery at Thanksgiving at a firm price that has been established between himself and the supplier. Or, the price may be established based on the four-week average price in July, or the three-month average price in July, August, and September. In such cases, each party depends on its ability to anticipate market trends and to make the best deal for itself. However, such negotiating, which is based on supply and demand, can be dangerous for the buyer who guesses wrong. Therefore, many buyers limit their speculating to the least perishable items or use a combination of buying practices for the more perishable items.

For example, a company that uses 15 loads of beef a week may have four regular suppliers, each shipping three loads on an automatic basis for delivery on specific days, at prices established in relation to the *Provisioner*. The company would then negotiate the other three loads in the hope of getting a better price break. In other words, the company is being a reliable customer by guaranteeing to four suppliers that it will accept three loads from each every week, regardless of the market price. There is no need for the buyer even to write an order because shipments are made on an automatic basis. The company speculates on the three remaining loads but protects itself to a great degree by not speculating on the major portion of its order.

Some companies will also speculate when buying additional quantities of product for special sales. If the company using 15 loads of beef weekly is planning a chuck primal sale, for example, it will need additional chucks to meet its needs during the week of the sale. If the buyer feels that the market price will rise, he may place his order far in advance with one or more of his regular suppliers, at a price agreed upon on the day the order is placed. If the market does rise, he will have benefited from his speculating. If the market falls, as a reliable customer he will keep his commitment and suffer his loss. Or, if he does not need all of the product he has ordered, he may have to pay a penalty and request that the suppliers sell off the surplus product to other customers.

Often, when companies need extra product on an emergency basis they will turn to brokers or distributors to fill their additional requirements. Brokers, who are in a position to obtain product from a large number of processors, generally charge a 12 to 15 cent per hundredweight fee for performing this service. As compared to the broker, who does not actually take possession of the product, the distributor buys direct and often breaks down the carcasses and then sells the primal cuts to customers who have no need to buy whole carcasses. Many distributors also sell straight carcasses. However, the premium they must charge for receiving, storing, and shipping is often too high to make such purchasing realistic for a supermarket chain. Brokers and distributors are also used for buying imported products such as Polish hams, New Zealand lamb, or boneless frozen beef.

Some products lend themselves to price speculation more than others. Companies that have their own warehouses are in an excellent position to speculate on vacuum-packed product. Because such product will keep for two weeks or more without deteriorating, a buyer can speculate advantageously in a rising market by buying product in advance at the lower price and holding it in the warehouse until it is needed. Of course, there are added costs associated with buying in advance, and the buyer will have to consider factors such as the cost of storage space, the cost of capital, etc.

Buyers also will tend to speculate on the least perishable items, such as frozen and canned products. Seasonal items offer similar opportunities, and almost all buyers speculate on at least a portion of their seasonal product requirements. For example, it is not at all unusual for a buyer to place an order for turkeys or hams at a negotiated price several months in advance of delivery. Such situations test the reliability of both the customer and the supplier. In one instance, a meat buyer placed a large order for Thanksgiving turkeys in May; by November the price had dropped by 5 cents a pound, at which point he cancelled the order. Under similar circumstances, two years later, when the price advanced 7 cents over the negotiated price, the supplier simply failed to ship the product so that the company not only lost the advantage of the lower negotiated price, but also suffered a serious out-of-stock condition at Thanksgiving. In contrast, another company bought turkeys in advance, but by the time the product was delivered four months later, the price had climbed by 6 cents a pound. Because the company was a reliable customer and always honored its commitments to the supplier, the supplier filled the order even though it suffered a substantial loss on the transaction. This again points up the long-term benefits that result when the buyer-supplier relationship is built on reliability.

Buying Alternatives

As outlined in Chapter 3, fresh red meats go through a number of breaking operations before they reach the supermarket display case, and the buyer must decide the degree of breakdown desired when he places his order.

Beef is generally bought in one or more of the following forms: (1) straight carcasses which, because of their weight, are usually delivered as two forequarters and two hindquarters; (2) sides, consisting of a forequarter separated from a hindquarter; (3) primals, the major sections taken from a forequarter or a hindquarter; (4) subprimals, which result from the further breakdown of a primal; and (5) saw-ready primals (also called block-ready cuts), from which most of the fat and bone has been removed so that the cut is ready for retail processing.

Veal and lamb can be purchased as carcasses and delivered whole or in sides, but pork is always bought in primal form.

Many companies buy primals, subprimals, and saw-ready cuts vacuum packed. When a supplier vacuum packages a product, he removes the air surrounding the product and then hermetically seals the package to keep it air-tight and free from bacteria. The vacuum-packed product is then shipped in boxes to its destination. Although the process of vacuum packaging and shipping in one-way boxes is expensive, many companies have found that the greatly extended life, reduced labor cost, and lower shrinkage of such products compensate for additional cost. However, some companies that operate central meat plants have effected considerable savings by using a soft-film overwrap to deliver to high-volume stores that do not keep product on hand long enough to require the protection of vacuum packaging. In addition to the lower material and equipment costs for soft-film overwrap, product so packaged can be shipped in reusable wire baskets, whereas the boxes used for shipping vacuum-packed product must be discarded for sanitation reasons. Some companies that operate central meat cutting plants also prefer wire baskets to boxes because they allow for better circulation of refrigerated air. Moreover, the baskets can be stacked easily on dollies or pallets for delivery and occupy little space when nested empty for return.

Often, companies that buy vacuum-packed primals, or that vacuum pack primals at their own warehouse, will shift temporarily to a film overwrap on certain high-volume primals, i.e., chucks or rounds, when such items are advertised. This can be done to save packaging costs because the higher product turnover reduces the need for expensive vacuum packaging.

A number of interrelated factors must be considered by the buyer when he makes his decision concerning how far product should be broken down if the company does not have a central meat breaking plant. These factors are: (1) storage area at store level; (2) average store volume; (3) frequency of delivery; (4) distance from source of supply; and (5) labor costs.

The storage space that the meat department has available is a factor because the further a product is broken down, the less space it will occupy. The store's meat volume will influence whether it can move all the cuts that come from a carcass or whether it will be more profitable to buy primals to avoid the loss on unsold product. The frequency with which a store gets deliveries will depend on its storage area, volume, and distance from the warehouse or source of supply. The fewer the deliveries a store receives, the greater its need to buy vacuum-packed primals which can be stored in less space than whole carcasses and for longer periods of time. Labor costs must also be weighed in deciding how product should be delivered, and a company must compare the premium it pays to the supplier for processing meat with its own costs for breaking carcasses down in each store location.

A primary advantage to buying straight carcasses is that they are less expensive on a per-pound basis than primals or subsections of primals, and some companies have found that the additional store labor costs incurred in handling carcasses are generally less than the premium which the supplier charges for performing the breaking function. But labor cost is only one factor; shrinkage and yield must also be considered. Equally important is the fact that a company will generally get a better selection of beef in carcass form and will have more assurance that it is receiving what it has specified and paid for. After a carcass has been broken down into primal cuts, it is very difficult to determine its yield grade. A less desirable carcass, with poor conformation, can easily be camouflaged by removing some of the outer fat from the primal cut. When this is done, the store has no way of knowing how much internal fat there is until the primal is processed into retail cuts. If the primal contains too much fat in proportion to its lean, the department's profit will be affected adversely because the primal will have a low yield and the retail cuts will be less appealing to the customer.

Therefore, if all cuts can be sold, and labor costs, store space, shrinkage, yield, and frequency of deliveries are in line, the buyer should purchase beef in carcass form to ensure the greatest profit potential to his company. On the other hand, if these conditions cannot be met, it will be more economical to buy vacuum-packed primals or smaller vacuum-packed cuts. They will bring more profit than whole carcasses, especially in low-volume stores, because (1) there will be fewer unsold cuts; (2) the product can be held longer; (3) sanitation is more easily controlled; (4) there will be less shrinkage; and (5) delivery costs will be reduced because fewer deliveries will be required as a result of the extended shelf life, and shipments can be unitized, making loading and unloading more efficient.

The advantages of buying vacuum-packed product, however, are not limited to low-volume stores. Some companies have found this to be an economically sound buying alternative for large-volume stores that cannot balance the movement of the whole carcass because of consumer preferences for certain cuts. Moreover, even in stores where movement is balanced, during weeks when certain cuts are being heavily promoted, buying vacuum-packed (or film over-wrapped) chucks, loins, or whatever the case may be, in addition to whole carcasses, will help to provide the inventory needed for such sales.

BUYING BEEF

In most companies, beef is ordered by telephone against specifications that have been established for weight, quality, yield, and the degree of breakdown desired.

Beef carcasses fall into four weight ranges—400 to 500, 500 to 600, 600 to 700, and 700 to 800 pounds. Although the lighter carcasses are generally from younger animals and are therefore more tender, 400 to 500-pound carcasses generally have a low yield grade. Therefore, most supermarkets specify 600 to 700-pound carcasses or give the supplier an even wider weight range specification of 550 to 700 pounds. Suppliers also prefer to handle heavier carcasses because their payroll costs are on a piece-work basis, and the time required to skin a small animal is almost the same as it is for a larger one.

The buyer will specify the quality grade that he believes can be merchandised most effectively in his stores, or the company's specifications for ungraded beef. Although most supermarkets sell Choice beef, others in high-income areas may also stock some Prime cuts, and some stores in less affluent or ethnic areas may sell Good or Standard beef exclusively.

The yield grade specified is highly important because it has a direct bearing on the meat department's profits. When a company knows the number of retail cuts that come from carcasses of different yield grades and knows the price variation from one yield grade to another, it can determine the most profitable yield grade to specify.

The degree of breakdown required, as previously discussed, will depend on store volume and size, frequency of delivery, and labor costs. Many companies will specify beef in more than one form to fill their needs most economically.

A buyer in a small company generally will buy beef from a nearby source and do his own selecting. Larger companies usually will have to tap out-of-town sources to fill their needs. To ensure that they are receiving product that meets their specifications, they will hire an outside specialist to do their selecting. A Pennsylvania-based company, for example, buying beef in Iowa or Nebraska, will give its specifications to the specialist who, for a fee of approximately 25 cents per hundredweight, will provide the company with this service. The very largest volume companies are more likely to have their own full-time selectors.

The selection of beef by an expert is highly desirable for any company that does not maintain its own meat warehouse or meat processing plant. If a company receives beef carcasses at a central point, it is a simple matter to have them inspected by a qualified individual who knows the company's specifications and is in a position to reject substandard product. It is far more difficult, if not impossible, to accomplish this on store-door deliveries because few meat managers are qualified selectors, and product offered to the customer can vary greatly from one store to another in the same company.

Those companies that buy primals or subprimals in vacuum packages also buy according to weight specifications; however, they lose the advantages of selecting for yield unless they have selectors at the processing plant. If not, instead of being approved before purchase, primals and other boxed product are an unknown quantity until they are broken into retail cuts. For this reason, a company that buys boxed product will want to be very sure that it is dealing with a reliable supplier.

BUYING VEAL

Veal is bought primarily against weight and quality specifications, with Good and Choice veal weighing 100 to 120 pounds being most common. When primals and subprimals are bought, the buyer will specify that the cuts be taken from carcasses in those same weight and quality ranges, unless the company is buying heavier, formula-fed (proteins, vitamins, and minerals) Provimi veal. This veal, which would grade Prime, weighs from 200 to 250 pounds and, although slaughtered at a later age than regular veal, is of the highest quality with regard to tenderness and, therefore, is more expensive.

Before veal experienced a very steep price rise because of its short supply, it was often bought as a whole carcass either broken into quarters or as saddles. Today, however, because shrinkage can wipe out the entire profit on a carcass, more companies are buying vacuum-packed primals. Despite the fact that these primals may cost as much as 50 percent more per pound than carcasses, the reduction in shrinkage, combined with a longer shelf life, often make vacuum-packed primals a more attractive buying alternative. Many companies today buy rounds, loins, shoulder clods (boneless shoulders used for stew), and other primals that they know they can sell without difficulty.

Because a calf has little outside fat, its only protection is the wrapping paper in which it is shipped. If the product is not sold quickly, it will start drying out in the display case within two days, get dark on the outside, and generally lose its eye appeal. Therefore, because the product deteriorates so rapidly, veal should be purchased locally. If not locally available, it should be purchased from a supplier who sells vacuum-packed veal primals.

BUYING LAMB

The buying specifications for lamb are similar to beef in that they identify the weight, quality, and yield that the company desires.

Additionally, the buyer usually indicates the state of refrigeration preferred. Because lamb dries out quite rapidly in a fresh meat display case, many companies buy frozen product. Moreover, because lamb is more plentiful in countries such as New Zealand, it is often imported and purchased through distributors in a frozen state. Weight specifications are given for lamb carcasses in four ranges, with the smallest carcasses (Range 1) weighing 30 to 41 pounds and the largest (Range 4) weighing 65 to 75 pounds. Although primals can also be bought by weight, they are not as reliable an indication of the age (i.e., tenderness) of the sheep because primal cuts in each weight range do not necessarily originate from carcasses in the same weight range.

Purchasing lamb in vacuum-packed primal cuts is becoming more and more popular since it not only increases shelf life but also eliminates losses from stocking slow-moving items. Lamb preferences vary considerably from one section of the country to another. In some areas shoulder chops are in high demand, whereas stores in other sections of the country may be able to move only loin chops in significant volume. If a buyer who purchases for stores where shoulder chops are in high demand were to specify foresaddles, rather than a shoulder primal, the shipment would include 26 percent shoulder, 9 percent rib portion, 5 percent shanks, and 10 percent breast. Some 15 percent of the foresaddle would probably find its way to the bone can because few stores can merchandise lamb shanks and breasts effectively, and there might even be difficulty in selling the more expensive rib roasts and chops in areas where shoulder chops are in high demand. Stores with a high demand for loin chops will probably be in a better position to sell rib roasts and chops because the pricing structure for these cuts is more similar. The experience of most stores is that they cannot get even movement from a lamb carcass or saddle and that the best buying alternative is vacuum-packed or frozen primals.

BUYING PORK

The most important buying specifications for pork relate to weight and trim. The ordering procedure is similar to beef, veal, and lamb in that orders are telephoned to a supplier who has been given the company's specifications. However, the specifications are more numerous because pork is almost always purchased in primal cuts and each must be specified by weight with many also specified by trim allowance.

Most pork primals are identified for weight in varying pound increments. In purchasing loins, the buyer will specify 14 pounds and down, 14 to 17 pounds, or 17 to 20 pounds. The heavier loins, which usually are taken from older breeding sows and boors, are usually boned and used for sausages, Canadian bacon, and other smoked products because they are not sufficiently tender to be sold as fresh ribs, chops, or loins. Most meat buyers specify loins in the 14-pound and down range. Generally, the lower the weight of the primal, the younger the animal from which it was taken and the more tender the cut will be.

Buyers also will specify the trim desired and whether it is to be the regular trim offered by the supplier or a special trim for which the company will pay a premium, ranging from a low of 4 cents to a high of 10 cents a pound, to remove excess fat and bone. Assuming that a company pays 80 cents a pound for pork loins, and that pork fat which can be used for trimmings has a value of about 30 cents a pound, while pork fat used for lard is worth only 20 cents a pound, the cost for a 14-pound pork loin can increase significantly in relation to the amount of fat left on the loin. If a supplier leaves an extra pound of fat on a 14-pound loin, depending on the income that can be derived from the sale of the pork fat, the cost of the loin can be increased by as much as 5 cents per pound, or 70 cents per loin. Therefore, the buyer must evaluate the up-charge for special-trimmed product against the yield of a regularly-trimmed loin and determine which buying alternative will bring the most profits to the store.

Pork butts are ordered in the same manner. The buyer indicates the weight and trim desired and, if he is buying against the *Provisioner*, how much he will pay in relation to that pricing yardstick. Pork butts have a narrower weight spread than loins and are generally available in three ranges—4 to 6, 6 to 8, and 8 to 10 pounds, with those weighing between 4 and 8 pounds being specified by most supermarket buyers.

Because of the significant price spread among the four weight ranges for spareribs, a buyer will want to be sure that he is dealing with a reliable supplier who is delivering product in the weight range specified and pricing it accordingly. The smallest spareribs (2 pounds and down) come from the smallest hogs which have the highest proportion of meat to bone. These smaller ribs are the most desirable because they are more lean and tender. Moreover, the convenient unit size of the retail package is easier to merchandise to the customer. As the ribs become larger (2 to 3 pounds, 3 to 5 pounds, and over 5 pounds), they become less attractive as a retail item. Ribs weighing 5 pounds or more, which come from heavy hogs, are usually smoked in a manner similar to hams and sold as smoked briskets. Although buyers generally specify spareribs of 3 pounds or less, they usually have to accept heavier ribs because the few smaller ones that are available are generally sold to barbecue houses. Unless the supplier is reliable, $3\frac{1}{2}$-pound ribs may be shipped and the store billed for 3-pound ribs, which are approximately 10 cents per pound higher in price.

Suppliers usually ship spareribs with the brisket intact unless the buyer insists that they be removed and agrees to pay the required premium. When the brisket is left on the rib, it is common practice to split the ribs in half, leaving the entire brisket attached to only one side, so that the remaining side, which then weighs approximately 2 to $2\frac{1}{2}$ pounds, can be sold at a 10-cent per pound premium. If the brisket is removed entirely, it is cut up and sold as brisket bones or smoked and sold as smoked bones.

Fresh hams are available in fairly wide weight ranges, i.e., 14 pounds and down, 14 to 17, 17 to 20, 20 to 26, and 26 to 30 pounds. The trim is generally standard, although some suppliers offer better value by removing more of the fat and hock bone. Here again, the buyer will have to decide whether he will accept the supplier's standard trim or pay a premium to have the product trimmed according to the company's specifications. The 10 to 12-pound fresh hams are the most desirable but also the least available. Most supermarkets sell fresh hams that range in weight from 12 to 17 pounds. The highest volume in supermarkets is done not on fresh hams, but on canned hams, of which the heavier hams (20 to 22 pounds) are most popular.

Fresh picnic shoulders are specified in the same manner as fresh hams, except that their weights range from 4 to 12 pounds. Fresh and canned or smoked picnics were once quite popular, but because of the readily available market for pork trimmings, most picnic shoulders (and especially the heavier ones) are now boned and used for canned luncheon meats and processed meats such as sausages and loaves.

Although most companies have some method to select beef, pork is bought strictly on the weight, trim, and price specifications given to the supplier. The buyer seldom talks to the supplier because it is a routine process for an office clerk to telephone the order if the supplier has proved reliable and has the company's specifications. Normally, as in the case with beef, if the supplier is not local, the order is telephoned a week in advance, adjustments are made on the third or fourth day, and delivery is made six or seven days after the order is placed.

Wherever possible, most companies buy pork locally, and often at a price premium, to ensure the bloom (the color) is retained. Pork loins, for example, are wrapped individually and often packaged five to a box. Because the wrapping paper affords little protection, the pressure of one loin on another causes a loss of moisture, and within four or five days the loins begin turning gray. If the pork is purchased from an out-of-town supplier and is in transit for four or five days, it will lose most of its bloom by the time it reaches the display case. Although the quality of the product is not seriously affected, the appearance is, and without eye appeal there is often no "buy" appeal.

Currently, some suppliers are experimenting with applying a surface chill to pork that will bring the temperature down to 28° F., which will help to retain the bloom and minimize shrinkage. When this is accomplished, buyers whose stores are not located in the pork-producing centers will be able to place orders with out-of-town suppliers who, because of their volume, may offer price advantages.

BUYING PREPACKAGED PRODUCT

Luncheon meats, bacon, and other processed products are bought more by brand name than any other meat products. There is an endless variety of processed products available; often, products from different suppliers will vary considerably in quality. In addition to offering better-quality products, some suppliers have a competitive advantage because of the amount of advertising they do; some offer better or more attractive packaging; and others may depend on price to sell their products.

Only the very largest companies can specify to the supplier what they desire in their luncheon meats and, even then, the specifications must meet USDA standards. For example, regardless of what the company may desire, frankfurters may contain no more than 30 percent fat, according to USDA specifications, and all ingredients in any processed product must be identified on the package label.

As compared to buying luncheon meats primarily by brand name, bacon is bought against specifications. The buyer will specify which grade he wants, i.e., Selection No. 1, which has a high ratio of lean to fat and a uniform distribution of fat and lean layers, or Selection No. 2, which has a low ratio of lean to fat and thick fat deposits between the layers of lean. The weight of the bacon belly is also important because it determines how many slices will be yielded. Bacon bellies can weigh as little as 8 to 10 pounds and as much as 18 to 20 pounds. In terms of yield, the most desirable bellies are in the 12 to 14-pound weight range. The buyer will also specify the length of the sliced bacon and the number of slices per pound package in four-slice increments, such as 18 to 22 on the low end and 28 to 32 on the high side. If there are fewer slices per package than is standard for a particular size belly, the buyer can feel reasonably certain that a heavier belly, which is less expensive, was used.

Most buyers prefer nationally-branded bacon unless there is a local supplier available who has generated consumer acceptance through his own advertising efforts. Local suppliers are also more willing to price bacon on a sliding-scale formula. If the *Provisioner* quotes a carload of bacon bellies at 56 cents per pound, for example, a buyer can arrange to buy at, for instance, 28 cents over that price to cover the expense of curing, smoking, slicing, and packaging the bacon. If the price for bellies goes to 70 cents per pound, the premium might rise to 33 cents. National companies, on the other hand, will usually have a fixed price rather than a sliding-scale formula.

BUYING POULTRY

The specifications for poultry with regard to grade and weight (or Class name) are fairly simple to establish. Most supermarkets sell young Grade A birds and specify chicken fryers or roasters up to 4 pounds, while turkeys are most popular in the 8 to 14-pound range. The buyer will specify whether he wants whole poultry, halved or quartered poultry, or poultry parts.

The major decision that a buyer will have to make in regard to chickens in particular is the state of refrigeration that should be specified. Chicken can be shipped ice packed, chill packed, or dry ice (CO_2) packed. Each method is intended to provide sufficient humidity so that the skin does not dry out and turn brown and sufficient refrigeration to retard bacteria growth so that the product does not spoil.

Ice Packing

Ice packing is, initially, the least expensive method of purchasing chickens but eventually, according to many companies, it becomes the most costly. Ice-packed chickens are shipped in boxes in bulk without any source packaging. Some 24 whole, dressed chickens, or bags of chicken parts, are placed in a wooden box, covered with ice, and shipped immediately.

The first disadvantage to this method of shipping chickens is that the company is paying the transportation cost for the weight of the ice. Even more serious is the rapid rise in bacteria count, and therefore spoilage, as the ice melts. Although the ice-packed chickens are shipped in refrigerated trucks, the truck temperature cannot be maintained below the freezing point without also freezing the chicken. Moreover, delivery problems may be encountered because not all truckers will haul ice-packed product.

When the ice-packed chickens are received at the store, they are placed in coolers until needed. The ice continues to melt in the typical 35°F. cooler; within three or four days, if the ice is completely melted, the chicken will probably be spoiled. An equally serious problem is that the moisture from the melting ice helps to spread the bacteria from the chicken to other products in the same cooler, causing even more spoilage.

Although most stores now have separate coolers for chickens which are maintained at 28°F., boxes of ice-packed chickens cannot be placed in them because the ice and the chickens would freeze into a solid block. Ice-packed chickens also require more cooler space than chill-packed product because the shipping boxes are oversized to accommodate the ice. More space is also required in the processing area to package the chickens which have been shipped in bulk, and the working area generally will be more sloppy and less sanitary because of the water created by the melted ice, the wooden crates that must be broken down, and the solid ice that must be disposed of.

Chill Packing

Chill-packed poultry, which was introduced to the supermarket industry in the early 1960s, has already captured upwards of 40 percent of the market and will probably continue to gain an even larger share. Chill-packed chickens are slaughtered, processed, and wrapped in case-ready packages; then they are chilled to 28°F., shipped to the stores, and held at 28° to 30° F. until they are sold to the customer. Although it is preferable to have a 28° F. cooler for poultry, chill-packed chickens will safely maintain this low temperature for four or five days even in a 35° F. cooler because of the initial low temperature at which it is received. Moreover, source-packaged chill-packed poultry will not freeze into a solid block in a 28° F. cooler because it is not surrounded by ice.

The advantage of chill packing is that the consistent low temperature retards the growth of bacteria, which lengthens the shelf life of the product. Because there is little spoilage, rewrap costs for labor and materials are almost eliminated. Chill-packed chickens, which can be shipped in smaller boxes than ice-packed chickens, are especially attractive to stores with crowded conditions. Moreover, because the product is source packaged, less processing area space is required in the store, and there is less opportunity for bacteria to spread to other product in the processing area or in the cooler.

Despite the obvious advantages to chill-packed chickens, many buyers continue to specify ice-packed because of the schism between merchandising and operations people. The buyer-merchandiser's primary goal is profits; the additional costs for source processing, packaging, and pricing chill-packed chickens can result in a gross profit reduction of $\frac{1}{2}$ percent when chill-packed chickens are sold at the same price as ice-packed. However, when the merchandising and operations people work as a team, they will take into account that the additional costs for buying chill-packed chickens can be offset by the savings in labor costs at store level and reduced shrinkage due to longer shelf life. In a $20,000-weekly volume meat department, the premium for source packaged chill-packed chickens may be $400 over store packaged ice-packed chickens. In most cases, however, $400 can be saved at store level in labor hours, supply costs, and space. Even if only $300 were saved in out-of-pocket costs, the additional savings that accrue from less shrinkage, fewer rewraps, better sanitation, and better product mix usually more than make up the difference.

Because ice-packed chickens deteriorate so quickly, ordering must be done very frequently; the meat manager who over-orders will have considerable spoilage. The supplier also must handle the product on an in-and-out basis to avoid spoilage. Chill-packed chickens provide more flexibility and more of a safety cushion in ordering because they can be held for longer periods of time. The supplier is better able to plan his production run based on the inventory and orders he has on hand; and the store has a better product mix, especially on chicken parts, because it can keep a reserve inventory with less danger of spoilage.

Most companies using chill-packed poultry have standing orders with suppliers that are filled on a regular basis, and the supplier can anticipate the amount of product that will be required to fill orders. If the supplier is not in a position to provide additional quantities that are required for special promotions, the company will often supplement its inventory with ice-packed or CO_2-packed chickens unless there is another chill pack resource available.

Dry-Ice Packing

Dry ice is formed from carbon dioxide (CO_2) that has been solidified and which changes back to a gas at a temperature of $-78.5°$ C. Dry-ice and ice-packed chickens are shipped in a similar manner, i.e., the chickens are placed in a container in bulk quantities and covered with flakes of ice. The receiver must be more careful in handling dry ice which sticks to and burns the skin when touched.

Dry ice will keep temperatures down for longer periods than regular ice as long as the seal on the box is not broken. If the lid on the box forms a tight seal to prevent warmer air from entering, and the container is placed in a cooler, the dry ice will last for a number of days under most circumstances. However, dry ice will disintegrate fairly rapidly once the box is opened and it is exposed to warmer air. The advantages of dry ice over regular ice are that it releases little if any moisture as it evaporates, and it is more effective in retarding bacteria growth before the box is opened since it protects product for longer periods of time at colder temperatures. The major disadvantage to dry ice is that product is not source packaged, and bacteria will multiply fairly rapidly after the box is opened and product is exposed to warmer temperatures in either the cooler or processing area.

Turkeys

Both chickens and turkeys can be purchased either directly from the slaughterer or from a distributor, and the specifications for both are similar with regard to grade and weight. Because of the peaks and valleys in turkey sales, almost all turkeys are bought and sold in frozen form, as compared to a very small percentage of chickens handled in this form. Turkeys must also be specified with regard to sex, i.e., hens or toms. Hens generally range from 8 to 14 pounds and are usually sold at a premium because they are more tender than the 14 to 28-pound toms of the same age. Turkeys weighing over 22 pounds are generally sold for institutional use or for further processing. Few supermarkets serve customers who desire birds of that size.

Although a number of companies buy turkeys from one source against the *Urnerberry* quotes, the seasonal nature of the product lends itself to price speculation. A buyer, therefore, has the option of placing an advance order for Thanksgiving delivery, knowing that he will be billed at the *Urnerberry* price on the shipping date. Or, he can speculate by placing an order in July or August at a firm negotiated price, if he feels the price is more reasonable than it will be in November, or at an average price during a specific time interval between the day the order is placed and shipped. Normally, if a customer is reliable and is buying against the *Urnerberry* price formula, the supplier will not charge more than the *Urnerberry* quote during a time of shortage and will often charge less during a time of surplus.

RAIL VS. TRUCK DELIVERIES

The buyer must specify to the supplier how he wants product shipped. Because meat is a very bulky and heavy item, transportation costs are considerable, and the buyer must decide how the product can be shipped most economically and also guarantee that it will be received on time.

Rail delivery is less expensive than truck delivery, but it is also less reliable because of the circuitous routes that the nation's railroads follow and the lack of a direct line to most points. A rail car starting out in Iowa may be brought by one line as far east as Chicago, then sided to another line that will bring it to Cleveland, and perhaps brought onto still another two lines before it reaches its final destination on the East Coast. Because the schedules of the various rail lines are not synchronized, the danger of a delivery being a day or two late is very real. A truck, on the other hand, will have no such lay-overs and will travel on a direct line.

Although savings in the area of $\frac{1}{4}$ to $\frac{1}{2}$ cent per pound can be effected if carloads are shipped by rail, the buyer must also consider that the greater time lag will increase shrinkage (beef carcasses lose $\frac{1}{2}$ of 1 percent of their weight over a 24-hour period) and that the company is obligated to pay for that shrinkage in accordance with

Product Procurement

government regulations or prior negotiations with the supplier. Most buyers will specify truck delivery on high-volume perishable product (where day-late deliveries will create serious out-of-stock conditions) and rail delivery for less perishable product such as canned hams or frozen shank meat. The buyer will also attempt to order mixed loads, wherever possible, to make up a full rail car or full truckload.

The most common practice in shipping by rail is to use a rail-truck combination whereby two trailers are placed on a rail car. The supplier then picks up the two trailers with tractors at the end of the rail line and completes the delivery by truck. For this method of shipment to be economical, both trailers must be filled because a rail car accommodates two trailers and the company will be charged for that space whether it is full or empty. An alternative to a rail-truck combination is to have a siding at the company's warehouse where product can be unloaded from the rail car. With this method, trailers are not needed; however, carload quantities must be shipped to effect savings.

STORE-DOOR DELIVERIES

Depending on the company's facilities and the services provided by the supplier, a store will receive deliveries from the company warehouse, a cartage company, and/or the vendor. If a company operates its own meat warehouse, most, if not all, product from suppliers will be shipped to that central location and then reshipped to the stores as they order product.

If a company does not maintain its own warehouse and the supplier does not make store-door deliveries, the only alternative available to deliver product to the store is through a cartage company which acts as a trans-shipper of product owned by the company.

Most local suppliers make store-door deliveries, but few out-of-town vendors do. In the latter case, a company would buy product and have it delivered to a cartage company that would make store-door deliveries according to the distribution schedule provided by the buyer. Some out-of-town suppliers will make as many as six or eight local stops but will charge approximately $15 per delivery; and the buyer must decide whether it is more economical to pay that charge or to deliver through a cartage company.

On product such as luncheon meat, there is usually no alternative to using a cartage company if product is not bought locally and the supermarket does not have its own warehouse. It is impractical for an out-of-town supplier who delivers in huge trailers to make store deliveries that are generally no larger than a few boxes of product. Therefore, if the company is purchasing from an out-of-town source, the luncheon meats will be delivered to a cartage company which will deliver product to the stores in smaller trucks at a minimum charge ranging from $7.50 to $15 per store drop on small orders, or a minimum of 5 cents per pound on larger shipments (more than 150 pounds).

Partly in an effort to eliminate such expenses, more and more supermarket companies are evaluating the feasibility of operating their own meat distribution centers.

7

Central Distributing and Processing

As outlined in the previous discussion on making store-door deliveries, the three basic methods of delivering meat to stores are: (1) direct store deliveries from the supplier, (2) trans-shipping through a cartage company, and (3) delivering from the company's own distribution center. The particular method of distribution that a company decides upon is highly important because it has a direct bearing on costs and product availability.

If product cannot be delivered directly to the store by the supplier on an inexpensive basis (which is often the case), the supermarket company will have to choose between the alternatives of trans-shipping product through a cartage company or having product delivered to its own warehouse where it will be assembled for store delivery.

Some companies maintain their own distribution centers for the sole purpose of distributing product, while others also perform processing in varying degrees at these central locations. Distributing meat through a company's own distribution center may therefore take one or more of the following basic forms:

1. Fresh meats may be assembled from various packers and selected and shipped to meet store requirements without being processed at the distribution center. Store personnel must then break product down in much the same way as if it had been delivered directly from the packer or the cartage company.
2. Fresh meats moving through a company's meat distribution center may be broken down into primal or subprimal cuts which are shipped to stores for further processing into retail cuts. (A combination of these first two methods is employed by most companies operating their own distribution centers.)
3. A very limited number of supermarket companies have central meat plants in which fresh meats are processed into retail cuts and prepackaged and price-marked for shipment to the stores, where they are placed on sale without further processing.

DETERMINING THE NEED FOR A MEAT DISTRIBUTION CENTER

In addition to the costs involved in building or leasing and maintaining a meat distribution center, there are four major factors that will influence a company's decision to operate its own central facility: (1) product availability, (2) quality control, (3) shrinkage control, and (4) total meat volume.

A distribution system that supplies the stores with an adequate inventory of the desired product specifications at the time that it is needed can be considered to be fulfilling its responsibility to the stores. Two interrelated factors make the achievement of this goal more difficult today without a central facility. One is that there are fewer but larger packers, and the second is that the larger packers generally do not make store drops.

Because of competition in the meat packing industry, the smaller meat packers, who were once scattered throughout the country and in a position to make local deliveries, have all but disappeared. The major livestock producing areas are now located west of the Mississippi River Valley where feed is more plentiful. The larger packers are also concentrated in those areas to minimize the cost of shipping live animals from the grower to the packer's plant. The small packers, which are located at great distances from these sources of supply, work at a disadvantage because the longer the shipping route is, the more expensive it is to ship the live animal. Live cattle occupy more space than dressed cattle so that space in trailer-trucks and rail cars is better utilized when slaughtered cattle are shipped. When a live 1,000-pound steer or heifer is shipped, a minimum of 400 pounds of by-product is being paid for in transportation costs.

Equally important is the fact that the further live cattle are hauled, the more weight shrinkage will occur. Although there are federal requirements that animals be given water while in transit, there is no requirement that they be fed. An animal can shrink by as much as 40 to 50 pounds while in transit due to the lack of food or activity, the movement of the vehicles, and other factors. Moreover, if cattle are held for any length of time at the slaughter house, they will shrink further because there are usually no feeding facilities available. Therefore, the large packer who is located close to the source of supply has a definite competitive advantage with regard to shipping costs and shrinkage. The large packer also will use more automated equipment to reduce labor costs and will be in a better position to sell the animal by-products, recovering about $15 more per head (about 3 cents per pound), which further offsets his costs and enables him to offer product at lower prices than can the small packer.

These factors have resulted in a greatly diminished number of small, local packers, which in turn has created a need among supermarket companies to rely more heavily on having product shipped from distant sources to a central point and then trans-shipped to the stores. However, most medium or large supermarket companies are hard pressed to locate a sufficient number of cartage companies with refrigerated facilities to unload tractor-trailers or rail cars or to receive product in all commodity groups and in the quantities that the company requires.

Another difficulty that arises in trans-shipping through a cartage company is the control of delivery time. In most cases, a cartage company will be receiving product from a number of packers and delivering to stores of more than one supermarket company. Thus, the supermarkets often have limited control over when deliveries will be made. It is not unusual for a delivery scheduled for the morning to arrive after the meat department clerks have finished their working day. Or, the delivery may not be made until the following day, causing out-of-stock conditions.

Meat department managers tend to over-order when delivery schedules fluctuate. When a meat manager knows within an hour of when a delivery will be made, as is usually the case with shipments from a company's own distribution center, he is more confident of his in-stock position and has less need for a large safety cushion. Without this assurance of on-time deliveries, the manager may be reluctant to risk running out of product and often will over-order to compensate for the possibility of a late delivery. Product, therefore, is held in the cooler for longer periods of time than it need be, which results in unnecessary shrinkage. Unless the product is vacuum packaged, it loses weight through the normal loss of moisture while it is in the cooler, and additional losses result from the need to face (slice off) thicker surfaces of darkened products.

In addition to the advantage of maintaining a schedule tailored to fit store needs, fewer deliveries are required when a company operates its own distribution facility. By consolidating orders and shipping mixed loads of different meat products, when necessary to make up a full truckload, the number of deliveries to each store can be reduced dramatically. This is advantageous in maintaining temperature control because the fewer stops a delivery truck makes, the less exposure to outside air as the truck door is opened at each stop. Moreover, when a company uses its own delivery vehicles, there is more opportunity for the receiving and delivery equipment to be compatible. Ideally, when meat is purchased and delivered in carcass form, receiving rails should be installed at the store which connect with the rails on the refrigerated truck. Air seals should connect the truck interior and the store loading dock so that product can be moved from the refrigerated truck into the store cooler with the least amount of exposure to warmer air.

An additional advantage to limiting the number of store-door deliveries relates to pilferage control. When a store receives between 20 and 40 deliveries a week from packers, local suppliers, and cartage companies, there is considerable opportunity for theft by drivers. The further problem of employee-vendor collusion is minimized when all product is delivered to a central facility and trans-shipped by company employees. Similarly, the opportunity for vendor's representatives to have access to pilferable items in the back room or in the cooler is eliminated. Additional losses may occur when a number of deliveries arrive at the same time, causing confusion for the receiving clerk and a weakening of company controls on checking in product. Unless product is carefully weighed and checked against the receiving document, the company will suffer additional shrinkage by paying for product that it has not received. A further advantage to fewer deliveries is the labor savings for receiving personnel and the ability to better schedule work assignments.

In addition to a cartage company lacking the facilities to handle high-volume items in large quantities, low-volume items may also present difficulties. For example, if a store requires 20 pounds of a slow-moving item on a single delivery, it is often not economically feasible for the store to receive the product from the supplier or for the supplier to deliver it. Delivering in such small quantities is extremely costly in terms of the driver's salary (about $9 per hour including fringe benefits) and the cost of owning and operating the vehicle (approximately 75 cents per mile). But shipping in such small quantities can be equally costly through a cartage company (unless mixed loads are delivered) where there is often a minimum charge of approximately $10 per store drop. On a 20-pound order, this would add about 50 cents per pound to the cost of the product. However, if a company operates its own distribution center, by consolidating orders from all stores for slow-moving items it is able to buy at a discount, receive product centrally, and distribute it on an economic basis by shipping mixed loads of meat products.

Distributing through a company-owned facility is especially advantageous where item movement varies considerably from store to store. A 30-store chain may sell 3,000 pounds of a particular item weekly, but one store may sell 300 pounds and another less than 50. The supplier would probably not deliver to the lower-volume stores, and the cartage company's cost for delivery to such stores would make it unprofitable for those stores to handle the item. However, by placing one order to be delivered centrally, the company can not only buy at a lower cost, but it also can make product available to both high and low-volume stores by delivering it on its own trucks.

Another advantage to the company operating its own distribution center is that a cartage company functions as a distribution point, rather than as a storage or holding area. Products are bought and shipped to a cartage company against current store orders. With a distribution center, less perishable product can be held for varying periods of time, thus affording the company a greater degree of flexibility in both buying and merchandising. Because meat is a perishable commodity, for which supply and demand fluctuates, suppliers will have surplus product on hand from time to time. When such situations arise, the supplier, or a broker or distributor, will often call the buyer, offering to sell the surplus at below-market prices in order to dispose of the product quickly. If the company operates its own warehouse and is set up to merchandise and move the item, it can effect considerable savings and offer its stores a competitive promotional advantage. If the company only uses the facilities of a cartage company, in most cases the cartage company would not be equipped to receive and store the extra product.

By having the necessary holding capacity, a company also has greater assurance that any product it buys will meet its specifications. If a company has at least one day's supply of beef on hand, it can reject an incoming shipment that does not meet its specifications without causing out-of-stock conditions in the stores. Or, if product is in short supply and what is available does not meet the company's standards, a safety cushion of product in the warehouse will give the company the flexibility to delay its purchase until satisfactory product is available. It is also far easier to enforce specification standards at a central point because the company can afford to employ a highly qualified meat inspector.

Discounts offered for purchasing large-volume quantities that are to be delivered to a distribution center typically range from 1 to 5 cents per pound of product. A savings of 3 cents per pound is generally used as a yardstick to determine the feasibility of a meat warehouse that will be used solely for distribution purposes. Yet, depending on land and construction (or lease) costs, labor costs, the distance from the source of supply, the dispersion of stores, the availability of product, and other factors, a company with a low volume may be better able to justify the need for a distribution center than a high-volume company with different characteristics.

Although a company's meat volume is an important consideration in determining the need for a distribution center, it must be evaluated in terms of the entire distribution function. A dollar volume that will make one distribution center economically feasible may not be an acceptable criterion for another.

One Texas-based supermarket company with a total weekly beef tonnage of 150,000 pounds found it feasible to operate its own distribution center, while most companies with that volume would not. A contributing factor to the viability of their operation is that the company's stores are dispersed over a 150-mile radius, making store-door delivery costs excesssive. By operating its own distribution center, the company is able to ship mixed loads in full truckload quantities, providing better product availability to the stores with fewer deliveries and at lower costs.

On the other hand, a Chicago-based company with total weekly beef tonnage in excess of two million pounds does not operate its own distribution center because of union restrictions on the activities that their employees can perform centrally. Nevertheless, they run a very successful meat operation and are able to service their stores without a distribution center because of the proximity to their source of supply, plus their ability to buy from reliable suppliers who deliver product in the right quantity and on time.

In contrast, another Midwest company operated successfully for many years without a distribution center but found that it could not fulfill its expansion plans without a central facility to guarantee product availability to additional stores. The company sells more than 700,000 pounds of beef weekly in 30 stores. To have product available that meets its specifications, 10 suppliers are used, and none is located nearby. The lack of a central storage facility caused day-late deliveries to become a critical factor, particularly during the winter months when snow and ice storms delayed truck deliveries. The problem was compounded when the late deliveries reached the cartage company on the same day as other scheduled deliveries. The cartage company was not only incapable of receiving such large quantities of product, but it also did not have sufficient trucks to deliver the product to the stores.

The company was also receiving a major portion of its chickens, canned hams, bacon, and luncheon meats from one distributor who also supplied other companies in the area. Because of the distributor's overloaded schedule, rather than delivering all product that the stores required on Monday, he would make partial deliveries and return to the same stores on Tuesday to fill the balance of the orders. Although the stores had adequate receiving facilities, they were short of product on Monday and had to duplicate the receiving function because the distributor lacked the facilities to serve these stores and his other customers as well.

Moreover, this was the only local distributor with adequate facilities to handle the chain's volume. Because the owner of the distributing company was advancing in years, the supermarket company would be in an extremely vulnerable position if the distributor were to retire.

With four new stores on the drawing board, the company had to seriously consider setting up its own distribution facility. The company realized that it could not expect any substantial increase in the purchasing discount it was currently earning because its stores, with their very high volume (100 percent above the national average), were already benefiting from volume discounts. Although many companies require a 3 cents per pound saving to justify distributing meat centrally, the actual discount earned when the company opened its distribution center was only 1½ cents per pound of product purchased, which represented the suppliers' savings in delivery costs. Nevertheless, because the stores were clustered together and the number of deliveries could be greatly reduced, the company found that it could receive, store, and deliver at less than 1½ cents per pound, making the distribution center economically feasible.

THE PROS AND CONS OF OPERATING A DISTRIBUTION CENTER

Some advantages of delivery through a company's own distribution center, as opposed to other distribution methods, are:

1. All the varieties of meat needed by a store may be consolidated and shipped on a single truck or trailer. The number of weekly deliveries per store can be reduced greatly, in contrast to the more than 30 that are required when deliveries are made directly by the packer. When shipments are concentrated in fewer deliveries, time spent in receiving at the store is also reduced considerably.[1]
2. When a truck travels from the distribution center directly to one, two, or three stores, delivery schedules can be better timed than if product is received from a supplier who makes 15 or more stops a day. Moreover, product will have longer shelf life when it has less exposure to outside air along the delivery route, especially in warm climates.
3. Man-hours for the receiving function can be reduced, and the meat manager can more efficiently schedule department labor when fewer deliveries are made. When a large number of deliveries are made on an erratic time schedule by a number

---

[1] S.O. Kaylin, *Understanding Today's Food Warehouse* (New York: Chain Store Publishing Corp., 1968), p. 138.

Central Distributing and Processing

of suppliers who deliver different products, employees are continually interrupted as they perform other duties.
4. When a store receives meat from its own distribution center, it has the assurance that fresh product has passed a rigorous quality inspection because the inspection of the meat is centralized and performed by highly skilled personnel whose cost can be justified centrally but not at individual stores.
5. Stores receiving shipments from their own central warehouses have the assurance of receiving proper weight and therefore spend much less time for weight checks than when they receive direct deliveries.
6. Shipping directly from a central facility reduces the opportunity for pilferage.
7. Store bookkeeping chores are reduced when deliveries are consolidated and come from a single central distribution facility, and data processing equipment can be better utilized to analyze meat movement and department performance.

Some disadvantages of delivery through a company's own food distribution center are:[2]

1. A company owns the meat when it is received at the central facility and thus directly absorbs any losses due to shrinkage, spoilage, or deterioration while it is held there or during the process of distribution to the individual stores.
2. A substantial investment must be made in warehouse space, equipment, trucks, and personnel.

The fact that 70 percent of the top 100 supermarket chains operate their own distribution centers tends to support the premise that the advantages far outweigh the disadvantages of maintaining a central facility.

OPERATING A CENTRAL PROCESSING PLANT

There has been a marked trend in recent years towards moving the beef breaking operation out of the stores and into a central facility. Some companies rely on the packer to perform the breaking operation,

---
[2] Kaylin, p. 139.

but many others feel that substantial profit opportunities exist when a company can afford to operate a central facility not only as a distribution center, but for performing certain processing operations as well.

Most companies that process meat centrally limit their operations to the production of primal, subprimal, and saw-ready cuts; however, a few also do some retail cutting. With a central cutting plant, a company can purchase whole carcasses (in quarters), break them down, and ship to the stores only those portions of the carcass that they order.

This works advantageously for both low and high-volume stores that cannot get even movement from a whole carcass. The loin, for example, represents 17 percent of the cuts in a beef carcass, and the round 23 percent. If a store has heavy demand for steaks from the loin, but cannot effectively merchandise the steaks and roasts from the round, considerable profit will be lost if the store must accept a whole hindquarter to get the loin cuts it needs. With a central processing operation, whole carcasses can be broken down and primals, subprimals, and even retail cuts shipped to the stores in the quantities needed. This also allows the stores to have slow-moving items available which a supplier would probably not want to ship direct because of the small quantities involved. Moreover, quality is better controlled when a company buys meat in carcass form, rather than in primals from the packer.

Obviously, additional labor is required at the plant when processing is added on to the distribution center's function. However, on balance, the labor added is usually less than the labor that then can be removed from each store. Productivity is increased as a result of assembly-line production where a handful of people become expert by performing repeated segments of a specific breaking operation. At the store, the meat cutter may be breaking beef for an hour or two, cutting up chickens, checking the display case, handling special orders, and performing other functions that make it difficult for him to attain the skill and speed that is possible when an employee processes product on an uninterrupted basis at a central plant.

Productivity is also enhanced by the use of more automated equipment at the breaking plant, conveyors to move the meat to the cutters, specialized work stations, and other equipment which makes the work easier than it is in the stores. Central breaking also provides for more standardized cutting methods and better control over miscuts. Although companies establish standards for cutting methods that are to be used at the stores, variations do occur in both cutting and trimming practices. At a central plant, it is more feasible to produce primal cuts that are consistently uniform.

Moreover, breaking and shipping centrally facilitates the gathering of information and the application of data processing techniques to evaluate scientifically the store's profitability. An analysis of what was shipped to the stores will indicate whether the store has the best product mix, whether certain high-profit items are being overlooked, whether there is excessive shrinkage, and whether labor costs are in line with the amount of processing required on each commodity line. By having a precise picture of what was shipped to the store, the company is better able to evaluate the profit that should be returned.

In addition, because fewer functions are performed at store level, meat department employees can be more quickly and effectively trained. A further advantage to processing at the distribution center is that shipping costs are reduced because central breaking involves the trimming away of waste, which reduces the volume of weight transported to the stores.

Processing

Most of the activity in central processing plants today involves the breaking of beef into primals and subprimals and, to a much lesser extent, the processing of lamb and veal. Another important activity involves the processing of trimmings into ground meats. Some companies also package rough cuts, such as short ribs, at the central plant. Pork, which is purchased in primal form, and poultry are normally shipped to the stores without any further central processing.

In a typical operation, the beef quarters, which come into the plant on rails in refrigerated trucks, are shunted on to matching rails in the plant and are weighed, inspected for quality, and checked for internal temperature. If acceptable, the quarters are then moved into the holding cooler on a powered rail. The forequarters and hindquarters are usually directed to different areas of the cooler by the employee at the control panel who also is responsible for proper rotation.

In some companies, the quarters are processed the day they are received; in others, they are held for 24 hours to ensure that the internal temperature has been lowered to 32°F. The 24-hour holding time also provides the company with a safety cushion on inventory.

When ready for processing, the quarters are moved by rail to the breaking area, dropped on the power saw platform, and the hook removed. In some companies, the saw-breaking operation is performed by one man using one saw; in other companies, one man makes the preliminary cuts and a second man completes the cutting on a second saw.

After the final cuts are made on the power saw, the product is moved on to a conveyor which feeds the primal cutters. Here the primals are trimmed, broken down into subprimals, and conveyorized to the packaging area. The bones are placed on the conveyor, dropped into containers, and held in the cooler until sold. The cod fat above the flank portion, which contains no lean, is carried away on another conveyor, placed in lugs or huge tubs, and stored in the cooler until it is shipped to a rendering plant. The trimmings, which are used for ground meat, are placed on a third conveyor and are unloaded into huge tubs which are transported to the grinding area or placed in the cooler until needed.

Processing Beef Trimmings

The central production of ground beef, as a by-product of the central breaking of beef into primal cuts, is not only a profitable and practical operation, but it also extends shelf life because rigid temperature and sanitation standards can be enforced centrally. Moreover, the advantages of assembly line operations make it more efficient to grind meat centrally than at individual stores.

Even without central grinding, there are advantages if trimmings are accumulated centrally. In some companies, the trimmings from the plates, flank, and other cuts, which result from the primal cutting operation and which are subject to rapid deterioration, are removed at the breaking plant and shipped to the stores in the freshest state possible. Although meat deteriorates rapidly after it is ground (unless it is vacuum packed), trimmings can be held safely for $1\frac{1}{2}$ days and up to 3 or 4 days if they are properly stored and refrigerated. Without central processing, the normal procedure is for the trimmings that accumulate at the store to be placed in plastic lugs and stacked in racks until needed. The problem is especially acute after a beef sale when a store has accumulated trimmings far in excess of its ground meat volume. If the trimmings are left in the cooler, rather than being frozen, they probably will have deteriorated by the time they are needed for grinding. By accumulating trimmings centrally under sanitary conditions, maintaining proper temperature control, freezing surplus product, and shipping to the stores only the quantities they need, there are fewer trimmings at the store and therefore less shrinkage.

Other companies coarse-grind trimmings centrally into vacuum-packed keeper casings in varying sizes (usually 10 or 20 pounds) and ship the keeper casing packages to the stores where they are opened as needed, ground one more time, and wrapped in retail packages.

The advantages to shipping keeper casings over shipping trimmings are: (1) the trimmings are ground centrally in a fresher state and with more highly automated equipment than can be used at the store; (2) a central location can afford the installation of sophisticated testing equipment which would be prohibitive on an individual store basis, and the fat-lean ratio is better controlled and more uniform because it is easier to supervise two or three people centrally than employees at 50 or 60 stores; and (3) the vacuum-packed coarse-ground trimmings have a longer shelf life.

Another alternative, which is currently operational in several large companies, is to final-grind trimmings and centrally package them into case-ready vacuum chub packs in 1, 3, and 5-pound quantities. Companies that use these opaque, roll-type chub packages usually do so only for hamburger. The more expensive trimmings from the chuck and round are ground at the store as needed. This allows the store to use up the more expensive trimmings that accumulate when the subprimals are broken into retail cuts at the store and to supplement their needs for the lower-priced ground meats with keeper casings or trimmings shipped from the central plant.

Chub packs offer all the advantages of keeper casings. In addition, this method of processing ground meat requires the least amount of time because the meat is fully ground with automated machinery at the central plant and requires no further processing, packaging, or weighing at the store. And, because the retail package is vacuum packed under optimum temperatures and in the most sanitary environment, shelf life can be extended to 10 days.

The only disadvantage to chub packs is that the customer cannot see the product because of the opacity of the packaging material. However, as long as companies maintain product of consistent quality, it is realistic to believe that the customer's resistance to buying fresh product that she cannot see will be overcome.

There are other ways in which the by-products of the beef-breaking operation can be capitalized. Some companies make beef patties from the plate and brisket trimmings and sell them either through their own stores or to institutions. When there is insufficient demand for fresh briskets, which is often the situation, stores generally convert briskets to braising or stewing beef, both of which have lower retail prices. However, companies with central breaking plants can corn the briskets that cannot be sold in sufficient quantities in the fresh state and sell them to institutions or through their own meat or delicatessen departments as vacuum-packed corned beef. The objective in all cases is to move enough of the trimmings and rough cuts to make feasible the purchase of whole carcasses with the minimum amount of waste and at an acceptable gross margin percentage.

PACKAGING PRIMAL CUTS

Vacuum packing has made a tremendous impact on the retail meat industry in recent years. Although the process was perfected some 20 years ago, the first experiments in vacuum packing meat were conducted by wholesalers supplying restaurants and hotels in the late 1960s; and it has only been during very recent years that meat has been vacuum packed for supermarket distribution in meaningful quantities.

As discussed in Chapter 6, meat shipped as primals or subprimals is generally either soft-film wrapped or vacuum packed. When product must be kept for more than a few days, either because of delivery cycles or slow-item movement, it should be vacuum packed to prevent shrinkage from the loss of moisture, discoloration from exposure to air and deterioration from bacteria accumulation. Vacuum packing, which accomplishes these goals, has made it possible for suppliers to ship saw-ready primals.

Although many companies quickly took advantage of buying vacuum-packed product from the supplier, there has been somewhat of a reversal in this trend as companies have learned to do their own vacuum packing economically. Most suppliers charge 3 cents per pound to vacuum pack product. This covers the cost of the vacuum bag, the box in which the saw-ready primals are shipped, and the labor involved in the breaking and trimming function. These costs are expected to balance out against the amount of labor that can be removed from the stores and the savings in shipping costs that result from less weight being shipped due to the trimming away of excess bone and fat. However, some supermarket companies with central breaking plants have found that they can vacuum pack saw-ready primals at lower costs than buying them in that form from a supplier.

The first decision that a company must make is whether it wants product vacuum packed or whether the less expensive soft-film overwrap will be adequate for its needs. If a company decides that vacuum packing is the best shipping method, then it must determine whether it is more feasible to buy vacuum-packed product from the supplier or whether to perform the vacuum packing operation itself.

Vacuum Pack

Small companies with low-volume stores will often have too much waste to buy whole carcasses. The needs of such companies would be best served by buying saw-ready vacuum-packed primals of the cuts that they need. In addition to the reduction of losses from unsold product, there will be less shrinkage because of the longer shelf life that vacuum packing affords, and all of the savings that result from fewer deliveries (which are possible because vacuum-packed product can be held longer) will be realized.

Larger companies may prefer vacuum-packed product for a variety of reasons, but they may, in some cases, find it more feasible to buy whole carcasses and vacuum pack product themselves. If a company vacuum packs its own beef, for example, it is ensured of better control over quality and aging. By buying whole carcasses, it is able to select beef against its own specifications. The quarters can then be broken into saw-ready primals and vacuum packed and aged with less shrinkage than if product were soft-film overwrapped. While the beef ages, the vacuum package retards the growth of bacteria and also reduces shrinkage caused by discoloration of exposed surfaces.

An additional benefit to a company doing its own vacuum packing is that trimmings can be removed when the carcass is received and used immediately, while the primals can be vacuum packed and held until needed. Such a procedure is important in improving the quality and shelf life of ground meat.

In other circumstances, heavy-volume companies may find it preferable to buy vacuum-packed product from the supplier. For example, a company may want more rounds than it can cut from a whole carcass for a special sale; and to ensure that product is on hand when it is needed, the order will be placed for vacuum-packed rounds which can be held up to three weeks. Or, a company that normally vacuum packs its own cuts may want to take advantage of a special offer from a supplier who has vacuum-packed product available at a reasonable price.

Although beef offers a number of alternatives, i.e., soft-film overwrap, vacuum packing, or a combination of both, some companies prefer to buy vacuum-packed veal primals when they are available rather than whole carcasses primarily because veal is so expensive and has such slow movement. Purchasing vacuum-packed veal primals will minimize the shrinkage and discoloration that takes place while the product is in transit from the supplier to the central plant. Moreover, the vacuum-packed primals can be held longer and opened at the store as they are needed.

Many companies buy some lamb in carcass form and supplement their needs for high-turnover items with vacuum-packed primals or saw-ready primals. Some companies will only buy lamb in vacuum packages because (1) they are unable to move the whole carcass, and (2) they do not generate enough volume on this product to vacuum pack it more economically than it can be done by the supplier. Moreover, there are few by-products from either the lamb or veal-breaking operation that can be used or sold in any great volume.

Pork is almost always bought as a saw-ready primal. It generates less volume than beef, but has longer shelf life and very rarely requires vacuum packaging.

Soft-Film Overwrap

Companies with high-volume stores which receive frequent deliveries will save considerable money if they ship beef primals or saw-ready primals overwrapped in soft film. If high-volume stores receive five deliveries a week, there is no need to vacuum pack because the product will neither shrink excessively nor discolor for up to five days under proper temperature and sanitation conditions.

Often, nearby high-volume stores receive only soft-film overwrapped product while distant stores in the same company, doing the same dollar volume, will receive vacuum-packed product in addition to soft-film overwrapped product because they are on a less frequent delivery schedule and must hold more reserve inventory in the cooler.

Some companies will soft-film wrap certain cuts and vacuum pack others. For example, boneless cuts such as sirloin tips and rounds are vacuum packed because they bleed and discolor faster than bone-in cuts.

CO_2

A more recent development involves shipping beef primals and saw-ready cuts in plastic lined boxes to which about 5 pounds of CO_2 (dry ice) pellets or "snow" has been added. According to suppliers using this packaging method, the pellets help the meat resist bacterial growth, and the beef can be held for as long as 7 to 10 days. Here, again, the company must decide whether it is more economical when the supplier performs the various functions that are involved or whether the company should do its own breaking into primals or subprimals and packaging them using CO_2.

PROS AND CONS OF OPERATING A CENTRAL PROCESSING PLANT

The central production of primal or saw-ready cuts has the following advantages:

1. Central breaking into primal cuts involves the trimming away of waste, thus reducing the volume of weight transported to the stores.
2. The stores can be shipped the cuts of meat that they demand so that waste is reduced, markdowns are better controlled, and out-of stock conditions are minimized.
3. Plant-manufactured ground beef is produced under strict supervision and according to rigid standards. This results in a uniform, high-quality product being made available at low cost. Trimmings from rough cuts, plates, and shanks can be fully utilized.
4. Plates and briskets may be processed or sold to processors for conversion to pastrami and corned beef.
5. The number of man-hours required to break a given number of carcasses are less in a central plant than at many decentralized store locations.
6. Equipment in use many hours a day repays the investment made in it faster than equipment in use for only a short time each day. Highly specialized or high-volume produc-

tion machines that are not economical in a retail store are well adapted to use in a central plant.
7. A central facility can produce primal cuts that are consistently uniform with regard to breaking and trimming standards. The cost of supervision of decentralized meat cutters, to make sure standard methods are followed, is greater, per pound of meat processed, than the cost of supervising centralized meat cutters.
8. Because a central plant is under government inspection, fat trimmings can be sold as edible fats, which command a higher price than inedible fats. The same is true for edible bones.
9. Some of the equipment used in a central plant need not be duplicated in the individual stores, and less cooler space is required for storing boxed product than for hanging rail stock. Costly receiving and cooler rails for hanging stock are no longer required at store level.
10. Less physical labor is required at store level to handle boxed product than carcass meat.
11. Fewer hours are required for receiving, processing, and cleaning at store level, allowing for more productive use of man-hours in merchandising the department.

The disadvantages that apply to a central breaking facility are the same as those that apply to a center that is used solely for distributing product. Additionally, when meat is broken down from a carcass or a quarter to a primal or saw-ready cut, the number of surfaces exposed to air increases, thus accelerating shrinkage. Therefore, the control of temperature, humidity, and sanitation is extremely critical in a central plant.

OPERATING A CENTRAL PACKAGING PLANT

Although central processing of carcasses into primals and subprimals has shown steady and significant growth among packers and supermarket operators, central packaging of retail cuts has gained only limited acceptance to date, and many observers feel that there will be no widespread use until frozen product is accepted by the consumer.

Beef, which is the highest tonnage meat item, is also the most perishable meat product. When retail cuts are made, the number of exposed surfaces increases drastically, greatly shortening the shelf life of the product unless it is frozen or vacuum packaged. Because of consumer resistance to frozen product and the high cost of vacuum packaging, most retailers currently carry beef in its most perishable form, i.e., fresh and wrapped in see-through film. When beef is packaged in retail cuts, accuracy in ordering at store level becomes critical and is far more difficult to attain than when retail cutting is performed at the store, where case inventory can be closely monitored and cutting can be done closer to the time of sale.

In addition, the production of retail cuts at a central plant, which operates on an assembly-line basis, cannot always be balanced against demand, and at times more product may have to be processed than can be absorbed by the stores. Or, the sizes of portions may be too standardized, and some stores may not receive packages best suited to their customers' needs.

The acute need for ordering accuracy on highly perishable steaks and roasts has resulted in many companies limiting their central packaging of beef to the less perishable rough cuts, such as short ribs, flank steaks, stew meat, etc., which are cut from the primals.

Pork, which does not discolor as quickly as beef, is better suited to central cutting, packaging, and pricing. A few companies have experimented successfully with a special knife cutter that allows pork to be sliced, rather than sawed, if the internal temperature is lowered to 28° F. to make the product firm. Such companies claim that this procedure, which is too expensive to employ at store level, saves labor, provides for better uniformity of case-ready product, minimizes bacteria, eliminates the bone and fat smear across the face of the product which results from traditional sawing, and extends case life significantly. The central processing of pork has the additional advantage of allowing the company with sufficient pork trimmings to produce sausages which retail at approximately 70 to 90 cents per pound more than the trimmings would generate. Some companies also vacuum package ham slices and smoked meats, but few slice and package bacon centrally because of the operating cost and the waste that results from the end slices which cannot easily be sold.

Veal presents a special problem because it discolors quickly, and its slow movement makes a longer primal life necessary. Moreover, few trimmings are generated from processing veal to make central grinding worthwhile. Therefore, for better product appearance and shrinkage control, there are advantages to having veal delivered to the stores as vacuum-packaged primals so that the stores can open the primals as they are needed, sell the rough cuts, such as the veal breasts, and use the few trimmings that are generated for meat loaf.

Lamb, which is less expensive than veal, also produces a minimum of trimmings so that the advantages of central grinding, which is such an important by-product of central beef packaging are, to a great extent, lost. Moreover, because lamb preferences vary considerably (negating the advantage of buying straight carcasses), and tonnage is usually low, most companies see little advantage to retail packaging at a central source with its attendant shelf-life problems.

There is little doubt that automated and sophisticated equipment, the diminished need for skilled personnel at store level, uniformity of cuts, better control of sanitation and temperature, and all of the other advantages that accrue to a centralized operation make central packaging of retail cuts an attractive alternative which many supermarket companies will want to pursue. Although only a handful of companies are currently engaged in retail cutting, packaging, and price marking, many more have indicated that they will have such plants in operation within the next few years. And, should frozen red meats gain universal acceptance, central processing of retail cuts will become more widespread.

8

Store Ordering and Receiving

Accuracy in store ordering is the starting point of any profitable meat department. A manager who is incapable of predicting with a degree of certainty how much product he will sell during the coming week will either under-order or over-order. If he under-orders, he will not only lose sales but also will have disappointed customers who may not return to the store if the department is frequently out of stock. Moreover, when the department runs out of an item, extra product has to be added to the next order which affects the workload of the staff and its ability to process all the items needed for the display case. Over-ordering is equally serious in that it causes excessive rewraps, markdowns, and shrinkage, and leads to dissatisfied customers when they are not sold product in as fresh a state as possible.

WRITING THE ORDER

The first step in writing an intelligent order is to take an inventory of the amount of product on hand and to review the amount of product still in transit to the store. An inventory of all product in the cooler is taken before the order is placed. In many companies, the inventory does not include product in the display case, which serves as a cushion against late deliveries or unanticipated heavy sales.

Knowing how much product is on hand and how much is still scheduled for delivery serves two purposes: (1) it helps the manager determine how much product he will need for the following week, and (2) it indicates the adjustments he should make on the product that is still to be delivered on the current week's order.

This inventory should not be confused with the period-ending inventory, which is taken for gross profit measurement, rather than for ordering purposes. In some companies, a period covers four weeks, whereas others take weekly or bi-weekly period inventories. Often, companies taking four-week or two-week period-ending inventories will take additional weekly inventories in problem stores. The meat manager is almost always responsible for taking the period inventory, whereas the ordering inventories, which are taken between the period inventories, can be delegated to qualified subordinates in the department.

The period inventory is a complete inventory of all product in the cooler and in the display case. When taking a period inventory, the conventional method is to take the case inventory at retail value and the cooler inventory at cost. The case inventory is converted back to cost by deducting the markup percentage. This conversion is often computed by headquarters personnel. If the store does not have access to cost figures, the cooler inventory is indicated by piece weight and the accounting office converts the quantities to dollars.

After the manager has determined his in-stock and on-order position, he reviews his historical movement records which will tell him how much product he ordered, how much was sold, and how much was left over during each preceding week. His records should also indicate which were holiday weeks, which weeks included paydays, what were the advertised items and at what retail price, whether he had to add to or delete from his order, the activities of his competitors, the weather, the season, and any other circumstances that affected sales during that week.

In order to project his tonnage requirements for the coming week, he reviews his movement records and looks for weeks with similar characteristics. He may have to use a combination of the previous week and the same week a year ago, or a week with bad

Store Ordering and Receiving

weather conditions, or local industrial strikes, or similar advertised items, etc. He must also keep in mind trends that have developed and changes in volume that may have taken place since the earlier weeks.

The manager also will take into consideration the merchandising information he has received that week from headquarters. He will review the items to be promoted and determine how effective he believes the sale prices will be in his store. Headquarters may bulletin him that sales for the previous Fourth of July week on frankfurters were three times normal movement. Although these figures reflect total company performance, they are another guideline and input into his ordering decision. Finally, he must be sure that his order will have the right product mix to reach his projected gross profit.

After projecting his total weekly requirements, the manager must indicate how much product he needs on each delivery. If he gets beef deliveries on Monday, Wednesday, Thursday, and Friday, for example, and 15 percent of the total weekly beef volume is done on Monday and Tuesday, he will want 15 percent of his order delivered on Monday, plus a 5 percent cushion to ensure that he will have product on hand until the truck arrives on Wednesday morning. The cushion, plus product in the display case which he did not inventory, should be adequate for this purpose. Some companies provide order breakdown charts to assist the manager in determining the quantities needed for each product or commodity on each delivery. (Figure 35 shows such a chart for a company whose stores are open seven days a week, where deliveries are made before noon). However, the chart only serves as a guideline because the manager must also take into consideration the holding capacity of his cooler, the amount of processing that must be done on each commodity, and the labor available to do the processing on any one day.

Beef shipped in carcass form will require more processing time than boxed beef, and a store may prefer to receive 75 percent of its carcass beef by Wednesday or Thursday, in order to have product ready for sale on Friday and Saturday, the heaviest volume days. However, if the store has limited cooler facilities, it may be forced to receive a considerable amount of product on Friday and, perhaps, an additional shipment on Saturday. Even where cooler facilities are adequate, some companies prefer that as much product as possible be shipped later in the week to minimize shrinkage. Although additional labor hours are required to have product ready for sale on Friday and Saturday, and often at overtime rates, the longer shelf life, and im-

FIGURE 35
Order Breakdown Chart
Beef—Pork

Pcs/bxs per Week	20% Mon	18% Wed	24% Th	38% Fri	Pcs/bxs per Week	20% Mon	18% Wed	24% Th	38% Fri
1	1				27	5	5	7	10
2	1			1	28	6	5	7	10
3	1		1	1	29	6	5	7	11
4	1	1	1	1	30	6	6	7	11
5	1	1	1	2	31	6	6	7	12
6	1	1	2	2	32	6	6	8	12
7	1	1	2	3	33	7	6	9	13
8	2	1	2	3	34	7	6	8	13
9	2	2	2	3	35	7	6	9	13
10	2	2	2	4	36	7	6	9	14
11	2	2	3	4	37	7	7	9	14
12	2	2	3	5	38	8	7	9	14
13	3	2	3	5	39	8	7	9	15
14	3	3	3	5	40	8	7	10	15
15	3	3	3	6	41	8	7	10	16
16	3	3	4	6	42	8	8	10	16
17	4	3	4	6	43	9	8	10	16
18	4	3	4	7	44	9	8	10	17
19	4	3	5	7	45	9	8	11	17
20	4	4	5	7	46	9	8	11	18
21	4	4	5	8	47	9	9	11	18
22	5	4	5	8	48	10	9	11	18
23	5	4	5	9	49	10	9	12	18
24	5	4	6	9	50	10	9	12	19
25	5	5	6	9	51	10	9	12	20
26	5	5	6	10	52	10	9	13	20

Store Ordering and Receiving 169

FIGURE 35 (Continued)

Psc/bxs per Week	20% Mon	18% Wed	24% Th	38% Fri
53	11	9	13	20
54	11	10	13	20
55	11	10	13	21
56	11	10	14	21
57	11	10	14	22
58	12	10	14	22
59	12	11	14	22
60	12	11	14	23
61	12	11	15	23
62	12	11	15	24
63	13	11	15	24
64	13	12	15	24
65	13	12	15	25
66	13	12	16	25
67	14	12	16	25
68	14	12	16	26
69	14	12	17	26
70	14	13	17	26
71	14	13	17	27
72	15	13	17	27
73	15	13	17	28
74	15	13	18	28
75	15	14	18	29
76	15	14	18	29
77	16	14	18	29
78	16	14	19	29

Pcs/bxs per Week	20% Mon	18% Wed	24% Th	38% Fri
79	16	14	19	30
80	16	15	19	30
81	16	15	19	31
82	16	15	20	31
83	17	15	20	31
84	17	15	20	32
85	17	15	21	32
86	17	15	21	33
87	17	16	21	33
88	18	16	21	33
89	18	16	21	34
90	18	16	22	34
91	18	16	22	35
92	18	17	22	35
93	19	17	22	35
94	19	17	22	36
95	19	17	23	36
96	19	17	23	37
97	20	17	23	37
98	20	18	23	37
99	20	18	24	37
100	20	18	24	38
200	40	36	48	76
300	60	54	72	114
400	80	72	96	152

proved product appearance are important factors in offsetting the added labor expense.

Obviously, there are many sensitive factors that enter into the ordering decision when perishable product is involved. Although the manager has considerable historical data to rely on and guidelines to follow, they only serve as a tool to which sound judgment must be added.

TRANSMITTING THE ORDER

An unaffiliated independent or one not served by a wholesaler with a meat facility would have many salesmen calling on his store. Each salesman would come to the store to pick up his order and then submit it to the company that he represents. Because a store must have a reliable source of supply, even one with a low volume may have to deal with a number of suppliers to protect itself against late deliveries and shortages. The meat manager may have a weekly standing beef order with an out-of-town supplier and fill the balance of his requirements with one or more local suppliers, who he feels offer price advantages. The number of deliveries that he receives each week and the number of salesmen who call on him to take orders will depend on the variety of product that he stocks and the number of suppliers that he deals with.

Chain and affiliated stores that are served through a central meat distribution facility may also have salesmen calling on them to take orders, or the salesmen may telephone the meat manager each week for the orders. However, many companies feel that having salesmen call on the stores creates pilferage problems. Some companies have also done away with salesmen telephoning for orders, which they feel is a distraction to the meat manager. The policy in such companies is for the meat manager to write the order, which, depending on the available facilities, is then either mailed, telephoned, or teletyped to the central buying office. The central buying office then places the order with the supplier. The most sophisticated systems enable the store to transmit its order over regular telephone lines directly to the data processing department, where it is printed out separately for each store, and consolidated for all stores for buying purposes.

Such stores may still have a limited number of salesmen calling on them, representing luncheon meat or specialty item suppliers. The

Store Ordering and Receiving 171

salesmen remove damaged or out-of-date guaranteed sale items, monitor the display space allocated to their lines, and check on how the items are being merchandised by the store. As such, they function much like rack jobbers who perform a service function and may or may not take orders.

ORDERING PROCEDURES

In most companies, meat orders are written once or twice a week. The orders are broken down to indicate the quantity of each item to be included on each delivery; however, the meat manager usually can make adjustments in the quantities ordered a day or so in advance of delivery. In a typical large company, the procedure might be for all store orders to be teletyped to the central buying office by 3:30 on Wednesday afternoon, for the week beginning the following Monday. The store orders are consolidated at headquarters, broken down by commodity group and delivery day, and telephoned to the supplier on Thursday. If the company does not operate its own distribution center, the supplier will be instructed to which cartage company it should deliver and the cartage company, in turn, will be given store delivery instructions.

For example, a buyer may have placed orders with eight packers for a total of ten carloads of beef to be delivered to four different distribution points. The buyer will know how much product will be at each distribution point each day, and his staff personnel will assign deliveries to the stores based on that information. Unless the buyer does not want a particular supplier's product in a specific store, an attempt will be made to have product delivered to each store from the closest distributor. However, the amount of product available at each distribution point will vary according to the cartage company's facilities. If one cartage company requires two days to receive a carload of beef and stage the orders, while others have greater capacity, a store getting three deliveries a week may be getting product from three different distribution points.

The number of deliveries to each store will vary according to the location of the store, the store's volume and cooler capacity, the perishability of the product, and the transportation equipment available. The company will try to limit deliveries to distant stores, but may have to make extra deliveries to high-volume stores with limited cooler capacity regardless of where they are located. Some companies have solved these problems, and reduced their deliveries on products such as beef from four to two or three a week, by purchasing vacuum-packed primals which have a longer shelf life and occupy less storage space than does rail stock.

Pork primals may be delivered as often as four times a week and ice-packed chickens, because of their perishable nature, on a daily basis. On the other hand, stores receiving chill-packed chickens may need only three deliveries a week to handle the same sales volume.

It is typical for a store to receive less perishable items (vacuum-packaged luncheon meats, bacon, canned hams, etc.) once or twice a week and most often on a low-volume day, such as Monday, Tuesday, or Wednesday. Should a high-volume store require two deliveries on bacon, for example, about 40 percent of the week's order would be shipped Monday and 60 percent Thursday to parallel the store's sales volume. Also, mixed loads would be shipped when feasible to reduce the number of deliveries to any one store and to better utilize the transportation equipment.

Some high-volume stores receive deliveries every day of the week; however, a number of companies discourage any deliveries on the manager's day off because of the importance of the receiving function.

Because supermarket sales are not evenly balanced on a daily basis, transportation equipment is heavily taxed as the weekend nears. Therefore, although a store may request that a certain percentage of the weekly order be delivered on specific days, the transportation department may have to adjust schedules to ensure that all stores have adequate supplies on hand.

Adjustments and Transfers

Despite the care with which a manager may write his order, he may find himself in an overstocked or understocked position because of unforeseen circumstances. The weather is one factor that has an important influence on sales. During the summer months, if the weather is good, outdoor cooking items will sell well; however, if there are four or five rainy days during the week, the store will be hard pressed to move such items. In northern climates, severe winter storms will drastically affect volume. Moreover, competitive activity, for the most part, is not known to the meat manager when he writes his order for the coming week. If competition features some similar items at considerably higher or lower prices, this will affect sales.

For these and other reasons, most companies allow their stores to make adjustments on ordering quantities, usually up to the day prior to delivery. Assuming the manager wrote his week's order on the previous Wednesday for product that will be delivered on Monday, Thursday, and Saturday, he can telephone the buying office on Saturday to adjust the Monday delivery, or on Wednesday to adjust Thursday's delivery, and so on. The buyer, in turn, when possible, adjusts the order that he has placed with the supplier.

An exception to this procedure is on product that the buyer has to order with considerable lead time because of the distance from the source of supply. Luncheon meats and bacon, which have long shelf life, often fall into this category. For example, a company may prefer a specific brand of bacon because of customer demand for the manufacturer's item. It may be necessary, however, for the company to place its order a week or 10 days in advance of delivery, and it may also receive only one delivery a week. In such cases, the buyer would not be able to adjust his order and, therefore, the stores could not do so either. In some circumstances, the stores can adjust their orders upward, but cannot delete. If, for example, bacon orders from all stores in the company total 400 cases and the buyer feels the price is especially attractive, he may increase the order by about 10 percent, which would allow the stores to add on to their orders during the week. If the stores do not absorb the 40 cases, they are held at the distribution center or cartage company; by the code-dates applied by the packer, the meat manager will know that those are the first cases to be used when the bacon order is shipped on the next delivery. Similar inflexibility in adjusting orders can occur on short-life product, such as beef quarters, when they are received from a distant packer or cartage company.

An alternate means of adjusting quantities on hand is through store transfers, whereby product from an overstocked store will be transferred to a store that is running short. In most cases, the transfer is made by the supervisor covering the stores in a district. Many companies disapprove of this procedure because it becomes a crutch for the meat manager who no longer feels the need to order accurately. Additionally, instead of supervising and helping the stores, the supervisor can be downgraded to a messenger. Transfers can also create security problems and losses due to spoilage when product is transferred in a non-refrigerated car.

RECEIVING PRODUCT

The perishability of meat and poultry means that the condition of these products will not improve after they are received and that they are in the best condition that they will ever be at store level at the moment they are removed from the truck. It is, therefore, imperative that every company establish receiving procedures that will facilitate moving product as quickly as possible from the receiving door to the cooler.

The initial step in maintaining quality is to be sure that the cooler has been readied for each delivery. This means that it has been cleaned and sanitized according to schedule, that old stock has been brought forward for proper rotation, that specific areas have been assigned to each commodity, and that there is ample space available in the cooler for the new merchandise.

In some companies, the practice is to date beef, veal, or lamb carcasses with a grease pencil mark on a card which is attached to the quarter or carcass. Other companies do not mark the carcass, but instead rely on the product being moved to the front of the cooler to ensure rotation. Boxed product should always be marked to show when it was received. The most direct method is to write the date of receipt on the package. However, when a considerable number of packages are delivered at one time, this can be a very time-consuming activity. Therefore, in many companies, the procedure followed is to draw a line across any box that is in the cooler when the new shipment arrives, indicating that those packages are to be used first. However, all boxed products should be checked for the code date applied by the processor to ensure that the product received has a more recent code date than any product on hand. By having the cooler ready, the amount of time product is away from refrigeration will be greatly reduced.

COMPANY SPECIFICATIONS

When a store receives meat from its own distribution center, considerable time can be saved in the receiving operation at store level because product has already been rigorously inspected centrally by a qualified receiver for temperature, quality, grade, and yield.

The central inspector knows that the optimum internal temperature for fresh meat is 32° F. He will generally accept frozen product if it is firm when delivered. He prefers to have smoked meats delivered at 35° F. and knows that shelf life will be limited if the temperature on arrival is above 40° F. On poultry, which is highly perishable, he looks for an internal temperature of between 28° and 30° F.

Because steers are more expensive than heifers, the inspector will check the sex on beef. He will check weights on all commodities, knowing that there are price and/or quality differences in relation to weight ranges. At certain times of the year, 400 to 500-pound cattle are less expensive than heavier carcasses. Generally, pork loins weighing less than 14 pounds are the most expensive, but also the most desirable for their eating quality. The inspector will know if he is to reject spareribs weighing more than $3\frac{1}{4}$ pounds, hams weighing more than 17 pounds, fryers weighing more than 2 pounds, 12 ounces, etc. He also will know if the company has paid a premium for special-trimmed loins and if product with more than $\frac{1}{4}$ inch surface fat should be rejected. The inspector will also be aware of the allowable in-transit shrinkage or whether the company is paying for net weight on delivery.

The receiver will know the quality grades that the company buys; if the meat is ungraded, he will know whether it meets company specifications. He also will know the yield grade standards on beef and lamb and will check incoming carcasses to be sure they are free from faults or discoloration. He will reject smeared pork (i.e., product with an oily film) or veal which is dehydrated on the outer surface. In short, the receiver will check against all the specifications that the buyer has given to the supplier and will inspect incoming product to be sure that it meets the company's standards.

RECEIVING AT THE STORE

Although the receiving operation is simplified to a great extent when the store receives product that has been inspected at the company distribution center, there is still a need for experienced personnel at store level if the receiving function is to be properly handled.

Each store should have two or three people authorized to receive deliveries; they should be trained in the company's specifications on quality, weight, and temperature. These receivers should also be qualified to check invoices against delivered product and must be alert to the need for maintaining security in the receiving operation.

Store level receivers should be able to detect whether the product is wholesome and whether it meets company specifications on quality. Although this is especially important on direct deliveries from suppliers, the burden is not altogether removed when product is delivered through a central company-owned facility. In many cases, the central inspector is spot checking, and product that is atypical may slip by and be shipped to the stores. Or, there may be a problem in the rotation system centrally, which results in old product being shipped.

Carcasses that have been centrally inspected might also have unwanted characteristics that do not show up until they are broken down at store level. Some beef, for example, cuts dark and is therefore unsaleable not because of quality or taste but because of negative customer attitudes towards dark-colored meat. Usually a "dark cutter" is weeded out by the selector when quarters or primals appear in that condition. It is possible, however, for primals not to start dark cutting until they are broken into subprimals or retail cuts at the store.

Many theories have been advanced as to what causes a dark cutter, but no one knows definitely. Some believe it reflects a high sugar level, but that has not been proven conclusively. It was once theorized that dark cutters resulted from cattle being too excited just prior to slaughter. That theory was disproven after an experiment that involved chasing the animals, waving flags at them and using other means to increase their level of excitement; however, the experiment did not produce any dark cutters. Some have felt that it is caused by the animals' drinking water. But, when animals were shipped to areas where dark cutters were more prevalent and fed the local drinking water, there was no effect on them. Although there are more dark cutters from some parts of the country than others, the condition does not appear to be traceable to climate. The only fact that most meat scientists seem to agree upon is that there are more dark cutters in July and August than at other times of the year.

If only a portion of a round or chuck, for example, is a dark cutter, it is usually converted to the next best item where customer acceptance does not depend on color. If a significant portion of the primal is a dark cutter, it is usually returned to the packer who can sell it easily to a hotel, restaurant, or any establishment selling cooked meat. The meat has the quality, flavor, and tenderness of any similar cut and the same color as any other product when cooked.

Because the less obvious quality characteristics of beef are more difficult to evaluate at store level, some companies who employ their own selectors do not allow their stores to reject beef shipments. The cattle are stamped by the selector or buyer, and the store must accept any beef carcasses carrying the stamp. However, if the store feels that the quality of the shipment is questionable, the buyer or merchandiser can be summoned to the store to inspect the product. If the company does not employ a selector, or if the beef is not centrally inspected, then store level personnel must be qualified to inspect carcass beef for quality and condition.

In all cases, any product shipped in carcass form or as quarters or saddles should be inspected for freshness and surface flaws when it is received at the store. Vacuum-packed primals should be spot checked for leaking packages, weight specifications, and color.

Primals or smaller cuts that are not vacuum packed should be random sampled for freshness, quality, weight, and trim specifications. Luncheon meats should be spot checked for code dates and to ensure that the label indentification on the box agrees with the contents.

What constitutes an adequate sample will depend on how reliable the supplier is. Obviously, a new supplier should be closely monitored. Moreover, although the policy may be to spot check one of every six boxes of pork loins, every box may be inspected if the random sample shows discrepancies from the invoice or that the product is of poor quality.

Specifications on what is acceptable and what product should or can be refused will vary from one company to another. In some instances, the receiver can automatically reject product that does not meet company specifications. Product that is old or out of the company's weight specifications would fall into this category. In other situations, the procedure is for the receiver (if he is not the meat manager) to confer with the manager who will, in turn, contact his supervisor if he cannot resolve the problem. The supervisor may contact the meat buyer or merchandiser for a final decision. Regardless of where the decision is made, however, it is the responsibility of the receiver to identify the problem; to do so he must know the company's standards.

APPROVING THE INVOICE

It is the receiving clerk's responsibility to see that the company is receiving the product for which it is being billed. Because of the considerable profit drain that could take place, all companies make efforts to exert tight control on this aspect of the receiving operation.

One device used is to have a signature card filled out by each person who is authorized to receive deliveries at the store. The accounting department maintains the file of signature cards and verifies the signature on each invoice with the signature on the card. Such systems are intended to circumvent any attempt by an unauthorized receiver to approve invoices for product that was not delivered.

Most companies also require that the invoice be stamped with the store's identifying number. This allows for tracing a delivery that has been shipped or billed to the wrong store. The receiver dates, stamps, signs the invoice, and also writes down the weight or number of pieces delivered. No invoices are paid unless they bear the store stamp. If the invoice is stamped but not signed, it is processed for payment and the supervisor contacted to follow up on enforcing company policy.

Product that is not shipped through the company's distribution center should either be weighed and/or piece counted. The recommended procedure is to weigh all rail stock and other merchandise received on a catch-weight (i.e., variable weight) basis direct from the supplier, to random sample the weight of primals, poultry, or any other catch-weight product shipped from the company distribution center, and to case count smoked meats or any other product shipped in even weights.

Some companies that operate their own distribution centers feel there is sufficient control if the stores simply piece count rail stock. However, because beef, lamb, and veal carcasses vary so much in weight and shrink in transit, the majority of companies require that each such rail stock piece be weighed. The deliveryman brings the product from the truck to the rail scale and, in most cases, the receiver can weigh four beef or veal quarters or four lamb carcasses at one time. Unless the scale has an automatic printer, the receiver writes the weight from each scale reading on the back of the invoice (or in any other space provided for this purpose) and checks the total against the amount indicated on the face of the invoice. A careful scale reading is important in controlling costs, especially on direct deliveries. Either the company has made an agreement to pay for only the delivered weight, or it will be credited for in-transit shrinkage that exceeds $\frac{1}{2}$ of 1 percent.

Although it is more accurate to weigh all product shipped on a catch-weight basis, it is sometimes impractical to do so. A high-volume store may receive 30 boxes of ice-packed chickens, 15 boxes of pork loins, plus boxes of spareribs and other pork primals all at one time. Weighing so many boxes while the driver is waiting would place a burden on the receiver who would have to stop all other activities and lift each box to the scale for weighing in the presence of the driver. In such situations, it is common practice for the receiver to count the number of boxes delivered, compare the total weight indicated on the boxes with the weight indicated on the invoice, and then spot check every third box, or perhaps every fifth box, depending on the product and the reliability of the supplier. If the receiver weighs 6 of 30 boxes of chickens and finds each box short by one pound, he indicates the weight of each of the 6 boxes that have been checked on the back of the invoice and claims a credit for 30 pounds on the assumption that the 6 boxes selected at random are typical of the entire shipment.

The weight stamped on even-weight boxes is checked against the invoice and then multiplied by the number of boxes received. Because there is a considerable difference in the prices of, for example, bologna and boiled ham, it is also important to check the invoice to see that the product billed and the product delivered are the same.

When bone and fat are sold, they should be weighed separately because fat usually commands twice as much income per pound as bone. The receiving clerk should also get a signed receipt from whoever picks up the fat or bone.

Invoices accompanying store deliveries usually consist of an original and two copies. The driver retains the original, and the store and accounting office each get a copy. The receiver signs the top copy of the carbon set, and his signature therefore appears on the copies. Because items can be added to the duplicate copies, it is important that the receiver check all three copies before he signs the invoice. He should also check the name, address, store number, and date on the invoice to be sure that he is receiving the correct order.

As an added control, in some companies neither the driver nor the receiver can make any changes on the face of the invoice. The receiver indicates the weight or number of boxes delivered on the back of the invoice and uses a separate form to show any discrepancies. He writes the supplier's name, invoice number, and the amount of the claim on the form which the driver must sign. The driver receives one copy; the receiver sends the original to the accounting office and retains one copy for his own records.

If the invoice indicates prices, the receiver (in some companies) is required to check the extensions to see that they are correct. When price information is not shared with store employees, the usual procedure is for the buyer to send a copy of his purchase order to the accounting department so that prices can be checked against the supplier's statement. The accounting office will also compare the invoice that accompanies the supplier's statement with the signed copy of the invoice that the store receiver submitted to be sure that they agree.

BACKROOM SECURITY

It is a sound practice to keep the receiving door locked at all times, except when a delivery is being made. This not only will stem the flow of products disappearing out the back door, but it also will help to maintain backroom temperatures and keep flies, insects, and other bacteria-causing agents out.

Usually, only one person is assigned to the receiving operation at any one time. Therefore, the store should never receive two orders at one time and the receiver should remain with the deliveryman until he leaves the store. Moreover, to control pilferage and shrinkage, no deliveries should be received while bone and fat are being weighed and picked up.

Although there are demurrage charges at a warehouse for keeping delivery trucks waiting to unload, this is not the case at store level where unloading can be done fairly rapidly. Suppliers' deliveries should be handled one at a time at the store on a first-in, first-out basis. If the company is also shipping product in its own trucks, a supplier may be asked to wait if the company-delivered product can be quickly unloaded, piece counted, and placed in the cooler.

After rail stock has been weighed on the rail scale and even-weight items have been piece counted, they should be placed immediately by the receiver in the cooler. Items to be spot checked for weight should be left at the receiver's platform scale.

The receiver is often tempted to take the short cut of having the deliveryman place product directly in the cooler, rather than leaving it at the scale. When this happens, there is little to prevent the deliveryman from removing items from the cooler or taking cases of dry groceries or other items from backroom storage areas unless he is under constant surveillance. Even if there were no pilferage problems, outside people should not be allowed in the cooler area because of the bacteria carried on their clothing. An additional precaution is to keep items such as store stamps in a locked drawer to prevent any unauthorized person from approving an invoice.

The receiving clerk can contribute significantly to the success of the meat department. He is the first line of control against losses caused by pilferage and shrinkage and an important link in enforcing quality standards and building customer confidence and satisfaction.

9

Pricing and Merchandising for Maximum Profit

One broad definition of merchandising is: "to promote the sale of goods." The techniques available to accomplish that goal are numerous, but inherent in any promotional activity aimed at moving goods is the need also to earn a profit. Pricing, therefore, is an integral part of any merchandising program; and the successful merchandiser will know at what level his prices are low enough to draw traffic to the store, yet high enough to meet profit projections.

SETTING PROFIT GOALS

Every company must establish profit goals for the entire store and determine what contribution each department will make toward reaching those goals.

For example, a company might determine from historical data that it requires $19.37 in total gross profit dollars from every $100 in sales to cover its fixed and variable expenses and earn a profit. It knows that 67 percent of sales will come from the grocery department, the meat department will contribute 25 percent, and the produce department will account for the remaining 8 percent of sales.

Analyzing past performance, the firm knows that the grocery department can cover its handling and merchandising costs and make a contribution to profits if it operates at a 16-percent gross profit. However, produce and meat will have to carry higher gross margins to cover their relatively high shrinkage, labor, equipment, and supply costs. The meat department requires more processing and packaging than does the produce department, but its direct expenses as a percentage of sales are lower because it has a higher sales volume and makes more efficient use of labor and equipment; therefore, gross margins for the meat department can be set at a lower level than for the produce department. On that basis, the company determines that the produce department will operate on a 30-percent gross margin and the meat department on a 25-percent gross margin.

By multiplying the percentage of sales that each department will generate by its gross margin percent, the company can project the profit dollars that each department will contribute. Of the $19.37 profit required, the grocery department will contribute $10.72 or 55.3 percent of the total, the meat department will contribute $6.25 or 32.3 percent, and the produce department, with its lower sales volume, will account for $2.40 or 12.4 percent of the total gross profit dollars. The meat department is projected to contribute a higher percentage of gross margin dollars (32.3 percent) than of store sales (25 percent) because of its relatively high gross margin percentage, and the same is true for produce. (See Figure 36.)

FIGURE 36

Contribution to Total Sales and Gross Margin Dollars by Department

	Percent of Total Sales	Percent Gross Margin	Contribution to Total Store Gross Margin	Percent of Total Store Gross Margin
Grocery	67.0	16	$10.72	55.3
Meat	25.0	25	6.25	32.3
Produce	8.0	30	2.40	12.4
Total	100.0		$19.37	100.0

Establishing Prices

In the simplest terms, the meat department will meet the company's projections if it adds the correct profit to the cost of the item, either on a percentage or cents-per-pound basis. On a percentage basis, the selling price is arrived at by dividing the cost of the product by the difference between 100 percent and the desired gross profit. If an item costs 50 cents per pound, and the desired gross profit is 25 percent, the selling price will be 67 cents:

$$\begin{aligned}\text{Selling price} &= \frac{\text{Cost of product}}{100\% - \text{Gross profit desired}} \\ &= \frac{.50}{100\% - 25\%} \\ &= \frac{.50}{.75} \\ &= .666 \text{ or } 67 \text{ cents}\end{aligned}$$

Priced at 67 cents on a percentage basis, the item will contribute 17 cents to the department's gross profit dollars for every pound sold.

During an inflationary period, the merchandiser will also want to set prices on a cents-per-pound basis to ensure that the company's prices are competitive. If the cost of the 50-cent item climbs to 60 cents, it will be priced at 80 cents at a 25-percent gross margin (.60÷.75=.80), and contribute 20 cents per pound sold to the department's gross profit dollars. However, at 80 cents the price may not be competitive. Moreover, if no expenses other than the product cost have increased, 17 cents should still be an adequate contribution to gross profit dollars so that the item can be priced at 77 cents.

Using either percentages or dollars alone will be misleading. For example, if Delmonico steaks cost $2.30 per pound and retail at $2.80, the gross profit return will be 18 percent. In contrast, if pigs feet cost 20 cents and retail at 35 cents, the gross profit return will be 43 percent. However, pound for pound, the steaks return 50 cents in gross profit dollars, while the pigs feet bring in only 15 cents. To use another example, adding 20 cents to an item that costs 40 cents will result in a 33-percent gross profit, whereas adding 20 cents to a $1 item returns only 17-percent gross profit; yet both items contribute the same gross profit dollars. Or if bacon, priced at 70 cents per pound to return a 28.6-percent gross profit, experiences a cost increase of from 50 to 80 cents per pound, the retail price will be increased from 70 cents to $1.10 to maintain the same margin percentage. However, not only may $1.10 be too high a price competitively, but if there are no additional expenses involved, the gross margin can be lowered to 24 percent and the bacon priced at $1.05. Even though the margin is lower, the contribution in gross profit dollars is higher, i.e., 25 cents (.80−$1.05) instead of 20 cents (.50−.70).

Both gross profit percentages and gross profit dollars are important, and prices must be set so that both goals are reached. The profit goals for the meat department take into account the cost of operating the department. If volume declines, the fixed expenses as a percentage of sales will increase. Conversely, if dollar volume increases, the fixed expenses decrease and lower margins can be set to attain the same net profit. The cents-per-pound formula ensures that prices will be competitive in an inflationary market and focuses on the gross profit dollars that are required to meet profit projections. The gross profit percentage formula usually results in prices being set at a higher level during an inflationary period. Because expenses are indicated as a percentage of sales on the operating statement, the gross profit percentage is a useful measure of the department's performance. For these and other reasons, most companies use a combination of percentage and cents-per-pound formulas to establish prices. They are closely interrelated, and both must be used in setting prices.

Pricing to Meet Profit Goals

If each product in the meat department had the same handling costs, shrinkage, demand, and so on, pricing would be a simple matter of building the same gross profit into the price of each item. Since that is not the case, each retail cut must be priced separately and in such a manner that the high and low-profit items balance each other out and result in an acceptable profit performance for the department as a whole.

The first step in pricing a product is to determine the actual cost per pound. If a chuck primal that is purchased at 50 cents per pound contains 30 percent fat and bone, which have little resale value, the chuck will yield about 70 pounds of saleable product for each 100 pounds of product purchased. This has the effect of raising the cost price from 50 cents to approximately 70 cents per pound. The amount of processing that an item requires also must be considered as part of its cost and reflected in the gross margin. Obviously, it is more profitable to earn 15 cents on a luncheon meat item that requires only pricing and stocking than to earn 20 cents on a beef item that requires processing, wrapping, labeling, etc. Some companies also will include a shrinkage factor to account for loss in weight that occurs while the product is in the display case, plus costs for rewraps and pilferage. By taking all of these factors into account, a gross profit percentage can be set to cover adequately the purchase price, waste, labor expense, shrinkage loss, and any other direct expenses involved in handling product.

Once the gross margin has been determined for a primal, the retail cuts must be priced. Because of customer demand and competition, some cuts will carry high gross margins while others may have to be sold at or below cost; but the average return from all of the cuts should be such that the primal generates the desired gross profit.

Assuming the desired gross profit on a beef round is 22.4 percent and the cost is 90 cents per pound, the overall return from the sale of all cuts taken from the round will have to average $1.16 per pound (.90 ÷ .776 = $1.16) or $116.00 per 100 pounds of product.

In order to price the various retail cuts, a series of cutting tests are performed to establish the typical yield of a round. The round is weighed, the cuts made, and then the weight of all of the product, including fat and bones, is totaled. The total will be slightly less than the original weight because of weight losses that result from the cutting action of the power saw blade.

The weight of each cut is entered on a cutting test form. (See Figure 37.) Then, by dividing the weight of each cut by the total weight, the percentage that each cut represents is calculated. For example, Figure 37 shows the results of a cutting test on two saw-ready rounds. The 11.99 pounds of bone-in steak represent 14.8 percent of the total weight of the rounds. Based on experience and a knowledge of what competition is doing, the bone-in steaks are priced at $1.48 per pound. This represents a 39-percent gross profit, which is necessary to cover the cutting loss, and the soup bones, other bones, fat, and trimmings which will be sold at a loss. Family steak,[1] a fanciful name for a cut for which consumers are willing to pay more, is priced to return a 49-percent gross profit to help offset the loss from waste and the less desirable cuts. Boneless stew meat, which is less attractive, can only carry a 35-percent gross margin, and so on.

---

[1] In some parts of the country, this fanciful label is used for cuts from other primals than the round.

Pricing and Merchandising for Maximum Profit 187

FIGURE 37
Saw-Ready Round Cutting Test

Date: 9\5\74

Taken by:		Weight	% of Whole	Selling Price	Sales Value*
2 pieces Saw-Ready Round Total Wgt: 81# Cost: 90¢ Per lb.	BONE-IN STEAK	11.99	14.80	1.48	21.90
	BONELESS STEAK	11.93	14.73	1.68	24.75
	FAMILY STEAK	6.13	7.57	1.78	13.47
	CUBED STEAK	1.52	1.88	1.68	3.16
	BONELESS RUMP ROAST	13.90	17.16	1.58	27.11
	BONELESS STEW	2.78	3.43	1.38	4.73
	HEEL ROUND	5.38	6.64	1.48	9.83
	SOUP BONES	2.00	2.47	.19	.47
	BONES	6.06	7.48	.03	.22
	FAT	4.64	5.73	.06	.34
	CUTTING LOSS	.95	1.17		
	TRIMMINGS	13.72	16.94	.88	14.91
	TOTAL WEIGHT:	81#	100%		120.89
−4% Shrink				−	4.84
					116.05
	Average Price per Pound Return				$1.16
	Gross Profit %				22.4%

*Per 100 lbs. of product processed

By multiplying the retail price by the percentage that the product represents, the sales value per 100 pounds of product processed is determined. For example, bone-in steaks, which represent 14.8 percent of the whole and are priced at $1.48, will generate $21.90 per 100 pounds of rounds processed.

All of the remaining cuts are priced in a similar manner and their sales values totaled. If 4 percent is allowed for shrinkage, the sales value will be $116.05 per 100 pounds of product processed or $1.16 per pound, the average price per pound return required to achieve the gross profit goal established at 22.4 percent.

The conversion of pounds of product to percentages is extremely useful in planning merchandising strategies in that the effect of a price increase or reduction on total performance can be easily determined. For example, if the family steaks, which represent 7.57 percent of the round, are featured at a 10-cent reduction, the average price per pound return from the round will be only $1.15 per pound, if all other prices remain the same:

Original average price per pound return	$1.1600
10¢ reduction × 7.57%	.0076
New average price per pound return	$1.1524

Lowering the price of family steaks by 10 cents per pound also has the effect of lowering the gross profit to 21.7 percent, which means the gross profit will have to be increased on another item to reach the desired gross profit goal of 22.4 percent. On the other hand, reducing the price of family steaks by 10 cents per pound will have less of an impact on gross profit than reducing the price of the rump roasts. A 10-cent reduction on rump roasts, which account for more than 17 percent of the product, will lower the average price per pound return to $1.14 and the gross profit to 21.1 percent.

In selecting advertised items, the merchandiser must keep in mind the total profit that the round is projected to earn, the percentage of sales that each retail cut represents, and the effect that a price change on any particular cut will have on the total gross profit return of the round.

Based on the desired gross profit, the selling price is determined for each cut from a primal in a similar manner. In addition to the retail cuts from any one primal not carrying the same gross margin, not all primals are necessarily priced to return the same gross profit. A company that purchases whole carcasses may decide to price the chuck cuts, if they are not selling well, very low in order to get even movement from the carcass, and to make up the lost gross profit on cuts from the rib or loin. In another situation, a company may be losing thousands of dollars a week on a high-volume item because of competitive pressures. Because there is a limit to how high any one item can be marked up, the company probably will compensate for the loss by marking up a few items with higher than average gross profits. What is important is that the total product mix return the desired profit.

Margins also vary seasonally. Seasonal items, such as turkeys and hams, generally return a lower gross profit when they are heavily promoted for holiday sales. Some merchandisers lower margins during July and August in an effort to generate sales which often decline during vacation periods, and then attempt to compensate for the loss during the fall months when store volume is higher and costs are lower because product is more plentiful. Gross profits often decline during the summer months, even when prices are not lowered, because of an increase in shrinkage during the warm weather. With less shrinkage during the colder months, gross profits will improve without increasing the retail price.

Competition is probably the most important factor in establishing prices and is the reason why many products are sold either at a loss or far below the average gross profit. Even so, the astute merchandiser will be able to offer the stores a sales-generating, profitable product mix by knowing which cuts sell best at what prices and, using the information from the cutting tests, knowing how to adjust prices to meet the desired profit goals.

Evaluating Performance

The meat department's performance is evaluated in terms of gross profit dollars and percent by determining the cost of goods sold and sales rung on the register. The actual gross profit can be measured only after a period-ending inventory has been taken. If the period-ending inventory is taken bi-weekly or every four weeks, a "book" or theoretical gross profit is calculated for weeks between inventories.

The cost of goods sold is arrived at by adding together the beginning inventory and the new purchases and deducting from that sum the value of the ending inventory. (All figures are usually taken at cost.) Once the cost of goods sold and the dollar sales for the week are known, the gross profit dollars can be determined by subtracting the cost of goods sold from the dollar sales. If a meat department had sales of $20,000 and a $15,000 product cost, the gross profit dollars would be $5,000:

$$\begin{aligned}\text{Gross profit \$} &= \text{Sales} - \text{Cost of goods sold}\\ &= \$20{,}000 - \$15{,}000\\ &= \$5{,}000\end{aligned}$$

The gross profit percent is calculated by dividing the gross profit dollars by the weekly sales and multiplying by 100:

$$\begin{aligned}\text{Gross profit \%} &= \frac{\text{Gross profit \$}}{\text{Sales}} \times 100\\ &= \frac{\$5{,}000}{\$20{,}000} \times 100\\ &= 25\%\end{aligned}$$

The gross profit indicates the dollar amount or the percentage of the selling price that remains after the cost of the product has been deducted. In other words, it indicates the amount of money remaining after the merchandise sold has been paid for—that is, the amount available to cover the operating expenses and net profit.

ADVERTISING

Pricing and advertising are closely interrelated and have a direct effect on how profitable and successful the company's merchandising program will be.

The goal of any advertising campaign is to attract people to the store, and to do so requires an eye-catching ad. Common sense dictates that the ad layout should be designed to highlight the best values and to relegate items of less value to a secondary position. In their ads, most companies highlight seasonal items as well as demand items which are attractively priced in relation to competition.

In some companies, the policy is to have a "red-hot" sale drastically reducing the retail price on two, three, or four items. Another approach is to advertise 10 or 12 items at a less dramatic but still low gross profit, which has the effect of spreading the same total markdown over a larger number of advertised items. For example, instead of cutting the price on a round steak by 40 cents, the price may be reduced by 15 cents and the remaining markdown dollars spread over chicken parts, bacon, a luncheon meat item, etc., to create a total low-price image.

Although the first approach may be more dramatic, it runs the risk of limiting the traffic draw. When 10 or more items are featured, there is a better guarantee that at least some of the items will appeal to every customer. Nevertheless, both methods are used and both appear to be successful in individual companies.

Sale periods also vary. Some companies run only early week specials, some run one-day features, some run ads for a full week beginning on Monday, and others run their ads for a full week that starts on Wednesday and ends on Tuesday. Although the practice differs from one company to another, running early week specials or one-day features is likely to be irritating to the loyal cutomer who cannot shop on those days.

Some companies use recipes in their ads, relating to the advertised feature. Those who give trading stamps may offer bonus stamps with the purchase of a specific cut. Some stores use coupons, but more often on bacon and sausage items than on fresh meat. Some do tie-in advertising on a limited basis with the produce department— for example, corned beef with cabbage, steak with mushrooms, roast beef with potatoes, and so on.

If a meat department carries 300 items, a typical ad might feature 30 items in a two-page spread, with perhaps 10 of the items reflecting very significant price reductions. The advertised fresh meat items are often grouped by commodity (e.g., all beef items together, all pork together, etc.) and items such as bacon, canned ham, and luncheon meat, combined in a separate grouping.

In deciding on the items to be advertised, attention must be given to the amount of labor that will be required to process each item. Beef, for example, requires a considerable amount of store labor as does pork. Therefore, it is more practical to feature chill-pack chickens, bacon, frankfurters, canned hams, or other items that require little store labor when a beef feature is run, rather than to advertise beef and pork together. By the same token, it would be unwise to feature cuts from both the beef forequarter and hindquarter during the same week because of the labor requirements involved. It is preferable to offer a few cuts from the chuck primal (steaks, roasts, ground meat, short ribs, etc.) and to feature in the same ad items that require a minimum of processing.

If it is necessary to advertise cuts from the forequarter and hindquarter to get more even movement from a whole carcass, cuts from the chuck might be offered at a very attractive sale price while those from the round are advertised at a lesser reduction. It is often preferable, however, to buy extra chucks in primal form to supplement those taken from the whole carcass for the chuck sale. This not only does away with the problem of balancing movement on the hindquarters plus the heavy labor requirements, but the ad will have broader appeal if a non-beef feature is substituted for items from the round.

The pulling power of any ad depends not on how many loss leaders are featured, but whether or not the customer has been offered a true value. A company can afford to offer any number of loss leaders if the items have slow movement. However, such items would not draw traffic, which is the purpose of advertising. On the other hand, if a high-demand item such as chickens were offered below cost, volume could multiply eightfold and create such a significant profit drain that no other loss leader could be afforded that week. The optimum situation is to offer a popular, staple item at a reduced yet competitive price, and to do so at a profit, however small, rather than at a loss. Such a feature would offer a true value to the customer and create the most traffic.

Basically, the decision on what items to advertise and at what price depends on the number of markdown dollars that are available (i.e., the gross profit goal for the department), the labor required to process each item, and the demand for the item. But, in the last analysis, the choice and price of an advertised special will be affected as much or more by what competition is doing than by any other factor.

PRODUCT PLACEMENT

If the purpose of advertising is to draw people into the store, the test of a good merchandising effort is how much the customer buys after he or she has entered the store.

In addition to the attractiveness of a display, the location of the product in the case can have an effect on what the customer will buy. Basically, there are two ways to lay out a case: (1) by commodity, and (2) by cooking method. Both approaches are based on philosophies regarding the customer's shopping habits and both methods have strong proponents.

The commodity theory assumes the customer is interested in purchasing either lamb or beef or another commodity; therefore, all the items in one commodity (for example, all the lamb chops, roasts, shoulders, etc.) are grouped together. The cooking approach assumes the customer shops according to how the meat will be prepared, in which case all the beef, lamb, pork, and veal roasts are grouped together, then all the quick-fry items, etc.

One major advantage to the placement of product by cooking method is that if the store is out of stock on a veal roast, for example, the customer will immediately be exposed to three alternate roast substitutes. Another advantage is that this type of arrangement lends itself to a more attractive display. Display heights are more even and the case looks better stocked when lamb chops, for example, are displayed with other chops rather than appearing lost when placed next to large lamb roasts. Moreover, when products are placed by commodity, there is less of an opportunity to convert the traditional beef customer, who may only shop the beef section of the case, to higher profit items.

Multi-deck cases allow the store to combine both of these merchandising methods by placing items horizontally by cooking method and vertically by commodity group. All the roasts, for example, are placed on the bottom shelf, the pork chops are placed above the pork roasts, the lamb chops above the lamb roasts, etc. More product can be displayed in fewer linear feet. One major disadvantage to the multi-deck case is that the initial cost is more than double that of a single-deck case.

Both the cooking and commodity grouping methods are aimed at accomplishing the same objective, i.e., to draw the customer through the entire department and to expose her to the more profitable items. Generally, high-profit items, such as luncheon meats, are placed first in the customer's traffic pattern so that she is exposed to them before she commits her available shopping dollars to others items. Low-profit, high-demand items, such as poultry, are placed at the end of the display case to pull traffic through the entire department and to increase the opportunity for the customer to shop the case from beginning to end.

Because they are highly perishable and must be sold quickly to avoid shrinkage, ground meats usually occupy the center of the case, the location that generally draws the most traffic. Although most companies offer ground meats in three price categories—hamburger, ground chuck, and ground round—it is customary not to display them side by side because doing so might injure the sales of the higher priced ground chuck and ground round. Since few stores can justify the expense of sophisticated equipment to test fat-lean content ratios, there is considerable guesswork involved and it is sometimes difficult to discern the difference between product in adjacent price categories. Or, there may be a significant difference in the fat content of the hamburger and the ground chuck, but the hamburger can have a better appearance in the late afternoon if a second batch has been ground and the chuck is from the morning's grind. Therefore, in order not to discourage sales of the higher priced, more profitable products, ground meats are placed centrally in the display case, but separated by stew meat, short ribs, or other items; and the most expensive ground meat is placed first. In companies that merchandise according to cooking methods, ground meats are often the divider between chops and steaks on one side and roasts on the other.

Although some merchandisers feel that the regular customer will be confused by changes in case layout, many companies spot advertise items throughout the case to draw traffic. Advertised items are often placed in more than one location, with high-profit items placed next to them. Ethnic items are also used strategically, with the higher profit items placed in an immediately available position and the lower profit items placed so that the customer will shop the entire case.

The objective is always to place the most profitable items first and the high-turnover, low-profit items last. An advertised steak item would be placed last in the steak section after the higher priced steaks; a profit-generating boneless beef roast would be placed before the lower profit chuck roast, and so on, to draw the customer through the department. One exception is to place offal at the end of the traffic pattern, not because it draws traffic but because offal products rarely create an attractive display.

It is a common practice to reset cases twice a year, especially among stores located in areas where there are significant seasonal temperature changes. The week of Memorial Day usually signals the time to place roasts before chops because the demand for roasts falls off in warm weather, or to move spareribs further back because the demand increases, etc. In the cured and smoked meat section, more space is devoted to summer items such as frankfurters and luncheon meats. Outdoor cooking sections are often set up where pork chops, spareribs, half broilers, quartered chickens, thick-cut steaks, higher priced ground meats, and other barbecue items are grouped together and displayed, usually in addition to their regular display in the case. The barbecue meat section, with its high demand items, is usually placed last in the fresh meat line-up until Labor Day, after which it is dismantled and the store returns to its fall counter layout.

Point-of-sale signs are often used in and above the meat cases. These are most effective when they are not overdone; otherwise, the signs compete with each other and lose their impact. Signs are often used to direct a customer to a particular item where increased sales are desired, or they may be used to create a price image or to create an atmosphere supporting a merchandising theme. Signs are usually evenly spotted throughout the case to promote both advertised and regularly priced items. In addition to limiting the number of signs, signs must also be policed to be sure that last week's signs, which have probably become soiled and tattered, have been removed and are not an eyesore in the department.

Regardless of whether product is arranged by commodity or cooking method, there will be a better opportunity to reach the desired profit objective if: (1) there is always a sufficient quantity of advertised items on display so that even late shoppers will have a selection from which to choose, (2) the display space for high-profit items (in either high or low demand) is widened to promote sales, and (3) the display space for high-demand, low-profit items is narrowed so as not to draw customers away from the higher profit items, while still having a sufficient quantity on hand to satisfy the customer's needs without frequent restocking.

RESPONDING TO CUSTOMER PREFERENCES

The customer's buying habits will be conditioned by many factors including age, health, income level, ethnic background, etc. The buying public is never homogeneous, and individual preferences must be catered to.

It is understandable that a meat manager will be inclined to focus his attention on the highest profit items and to ignore, or perhaps not even stock, products that carry the lowest gross margins. This is shortsighted because a meat department must have a variety of product on display to draw customers. If the meat department fails to stock low-profit items for which there is some demand, it will lose customers not only for its own department, but for the entire store as well.

When a meat manager decides, for example, that veal can be eliminated because it accounts for only 2 percent of sales and the price has risen too steeply for it to be a profitable item, he is forgetting how many other items the veal customer is buying not only in the meat department but also in the rest of the store. As long as there is a demand for veal, it should be on display and priced according to a cents-per-pound formula. It is unwise to maintain a traditional margin because the retail price would be so high that the number of people who could afford to buy the product would be severely limited. In the long run, it will be more profitable to sell the product at a lower gross profit because more product will be sold and there will be less shrinkage.

In addition to having a full variety of product on display, it is also important to have a sufficient variety of package sizes and cuts. Thin-cut chops and steaks, for example, will appeal not only to elderly customers who may have dietary problems, but also to those customers who prefer fast-cooking items or to those who are cost-conscious. For many customers, a package of six $\frac{1}{2}$-inch pork chops will be more attractive than a package of four $\frac{3}{4}$-inch chops at the same price. Having both thick and thin cuts on display also will reduce requests for special orders which increase labor costs. Having prepackaged product on display can also increase dollar volume. Although a customer might order one thin-cut strip steak if there were none in the case, she would be more than likely to buy two prepackaged strip steaks, if they were on display.

Special orders for roasts also can be minimized by having a variety of package sizes on display. In most cases, a customer who desires a $3\frac{1}{2}$-pound roast will readily buy a 4-pound roast if it is in the display case. However, if the only roasts on display average $2\frac{1}{2}$ pounds, they will not fill her needs and she will either ask for a special order or pass up the item. Because of variations in family size, beef and pork roasts, legs of lamb, hams, and other large cuts should be offered in a variety of weights.

The meat manager also must know customer preferences with regard to boneless and bone-in cuts and have product available accordingly. Although boneless cuts are more expensive, they appeal to younger homemakers and others who prefer easy-to-cook items. But the meat manager should avoid the temptation of preparing too many boned-out cuts, which generally have a higher gross profit, and running the risk of not having product available for customers who prefer a bone-in cut.

Another pitfall to avoid is merchandising too many similar cuts with fanciful names. The lure, of course, is that a "fanciful" cut can generally command a higher gross when merchandised as a new item. However, carried to extremes, this type of overmerchandising can be self-defeating if it confuses the customer or if it results in basic items not being available. It is far more important to concentrate on the basics and to build the merchandising program around that.

After a decision has been made on the variety and types of cuts to offer, there is a packaging question to be answered: Best side up or best side down? Despite the fact that there are fewer customer complaints if the most attractive surface of the cut is hidden from view, it can be a risky merchandising approach unless every store in the trading area follows the same procedure. Some companies have had the courage to place product best side down and have successfully promoted the concept to their customers. Most, however, are unwilling to risk the lost sales that generally result until the customer is educated to the idea and has confidence in it. More often than not, product is placed best side up in the package.

Getting Customer Reaction

Some companies conduct surveys to keep in touch with their customers' preferences and changing needs. In addition to checking attitudes on package size, type of cuts, etc., much useful information can be obtained regarding the company's competitive position by asking questions such as: What store carries the best meat? Who has the lowest prices? Who provides the best service? Who has the best display? Where do you shop? What do you like about the store? What are your dislikes?

A company can either conduct its own survey, without identifying itself, or hire an outside firm for the purpose. One successful approach is to telephone about 500 people in a trading area and then to follow up the same interviewees a few months later to see if their attitudes about the company or their product preferences have shifted.

Some companies depend on consumer panels for their feedback. Both the store's regular customers and those who shop competition are invited to air their views at a half or full-day meeting. In addition to showing the customer that the company really cares, much useful merchandising information can be gathered. One company that was heavily promoting its Choice beef learned that customers had little interest in grades and made their selection based on the appearance of the package, particularly the amount of lean and marbling. Rather than relying on government grades of meat, customer confidence was placed in the store and the clerk behind the counter. As a result, the company changed to an ungraded beef that met the customer's demand and offered a better profit opportunity. The same panel exposed how little customers knew about meat and the importance of offering cooking aids as a merchandising tool. This reassessment of the customer's knowledgeability also gave the company a better insight into how to handle customer complaints.

The panel also made the company aware of additional profit opportunities by uncovering the facts that (1) a significant number of potential customers were purchasing meat in quarters from companies that specialized in product for the home freezer market, and (2) some 30 percent said they patronized local butcher shops because they preferred the quality, service, and product assortment. Armed with such information, the supermarket company was able to make inroads into competitive areas that it formerly had not considered important.

Regardless of the technique used, it is important to determine accurately the customer's needs and to merchandise the most profitable product mix that will satisfy those needs.

BUILDING IMPULSE SALES

Although customers know in a general sense what they want to purchase before they enter a store and many use shopping lists, studies show that between 50 and 85 percent of the purchases made by supermarket shoppers are done on an impulse basis. Impulse buying is therefore a major factor in the success of any meat department and the number of impulse purchases that can be created are a direct reflection on the meat manager's merchandising skills.

In its broadest sense, impulse buying refers to any unplanned customer purchase. While almost any item can be an impulse item, some are more so than others. A small turkey, for example, will have more impulse appeal than a large turkey because, despite outstanding merchandising efforts, the desire to buy on impulse is limited by the ability of the customer to pay for, as well as to consume, the item.

A fairly staple item, such as bacon, would be considered less of an impulse item. The customer who regularly includes bacon on her shopping list, in much the same way that she includes milk or orange juice, is not likely to be encouraged to make additional purchases of bacon on an impulse basis because there is just so much she can use. But, there are many customers for whom bacon is not a staple, and the promotion-minded manager will direct his energies towards them. He may place bacon in the dairy department next to eggs, or create an entire breakfast department in the meat case, featuring ham, sausage, and bacon. While the customer may have overlooked bacon when displayed in its home position in the meat department, she is much less likely to do so when it is presented as part of a special meal display. The seasonal appeal of bacon also can be capitalized by featuring canned bacon during the hunting, camping, or fishing season.

Most merchandisers feel that appearance is the most important factor in boosting impulse sales—not simply the appearance of the featured item, but also the appearance of the entire department. Therefore, in addition to broadening a display for impact and placing certain items in the first part of the counter, they will also make sure that those items have good eye appeal through quality control, good lighting, and effective signing and display techniques.

Such efforts will boost sales volume by motivating the ground beef customer to buy, instead, a loin roast with good eye appeal; or, the typical "sandwich for lunch" customer to purchase an easily prepared heat-and-eat item; or, the "casserole" customer to buy some fancy cuts for entertaining purposes—all of which build profits.

While a beef roast is a staple item in a poorly merchandised department, it becomes an impulse item when it is lean and has a nice trim and good color. Even if the roast is fairly large and the customer feels it is a little more than she needs, if it has the proper eye appeal she will be more likely to buy it for a main meal and plan to use the remainder for sandwiches another day. Large canned hams similarly can become impulse items by using good signing and having recipes available that will give the customer numerous ideas for using ham as the main dish, as well as for such budget-stretching meals as salads, casseroles, sandwiches, fillings, etc.

The same principles apply to merchandising pork roasts, or for that matter, almost any meat item. There are some merchandisers who take the narrow view that the more expensive steaks (T-bone, for example) are best suited to impulse sales, and they concentrate their promotional efforts on such items. This is not only far from true, but it is also an impractical approach to merchandising. Because there are a limited number of T-bone steaks in a primal, selling too many will create out-of-stocks and an imbalance in the other cuts that come from the primal or subprimal or, if the store receives beef in carcass form, from the entire hindquarter.

Generally, selling straight carcasses offers a better profit and merchandising opportunity because the cost of the product is lower than it would be if trimmed quarters or primal cuts or subprimals were purchased from a packer. However, the advantage of purchasing at a lower price will be lost unless all cuts from the carcass can be moved. Therefore, if there is high demand for T-bones, one or two rows should be displayed to avoid frequent restocking and to satisfy the demands of the customer. Cubed steaks, on the other hand, should be merchandised heavily because they can be cut from any primal and from some trimmings and are therefore more plentiful. Often two displays are given to these boneless, tenderized steaks to create impulse sales and balance the carcass movement without resorting to grinding higher priced cuts.

Interdepartment Merchandising

Such staples as corned beef are readily turned into impulse sales by merchandising them along with tie-in items. The obvious approach is to display corned beef with cabbage in the meat department. An equally effective approach is to display the two items in the produce department as well, for double exposure. While not all meat items can be displayed out of the department because of refrigeration problems, unless the produce department has refrigerated cases or portable cases are available, vacuum-packed corned beef creates no such problems. By taking advantage of its seasonal appeal, one promotion-minded chain moved a carload of corned beef one St. Patrick's Day by implementing this simple interdepartment merchandising technique.

Some companies use dump displays of tie-in items, either as an end display in an aisle across from or close to the meat department or in a completely separate department. Seasonal dump displays of frankfurters with mustard, sauerkraut, beans, or other tie-in items in a portable refrigerated case are highly effective. Or, the same tie-in display can be merchandised in the meat case and highlighted by widening the display, putting colorful streamers above the display, and using any other decorations or signing that will attract attention.

Interdepartment merchandising definitely creates impulse sales because when a shopper makes a meat purchase, she is actually planning an entire meal. Lamb usually means mint jelly, ham means pineapple, ham hocks go with dried beans, chicken with rice, and so on. However, there must be some evaluation as to how much space the meat department can give to other departments. For example, one successful chain regularly sets up a soup section in its meat cases during the cold weather season and displays soup bones, soup chuck, short ribs, beef shank, and other items. The display usually is placed next to the ground meat, the area of the counter that generates the highest traffic in the stores. When chickens are low priced, chicken wings and other parts are included in the soup display. However, there is a policy of not tying in related produce items, the feeling being that to make an impact with produce at least 4 or 5 feet of display space is required. To make produce meaningful as a merchandising aid requires a mass display, not just one row. And, space in the meat department is just too valuable so that often only a few out-of-department items find their way into this company's meat case displays. One solution is an even trade of tie-in merchandising displays between departments to help the sales and profits of both departments.

Sub-departments

Barbecued items are almost always bought on impulse, even by regular customers. Because this is not usually a planned purchase, unless the department is creatively merchandised, most customers will pass barbecued products by.

Many companies feel they lack the volume necessary to sustain a barbecue department. However, when one considers that there are countless numbers of free-standing barbecue stands that offer no other items, it is obvious that a supermarket, with its greater traffic draw and item assortment, should be capable of competing successfully and more profitably. This is especially true for any store located near high density or resort areas, regardless of its volume.

Barbecued items are highly profitable, even with the 30 percent shrinkage that is encountered in barbecuing a chicken. With many stores earning between 0 and 10 percent gross profit on fresh chickens, the 30 to 35 percent profit generated by barbecued chicken is quite attractive.

It is true that in many low-volume stores, barbecuing often cannot be justified during the early part of the week. There is a feeling in some such stores that rather than disappoint the early week shopper and risk poor customer relations, it is better to have no department at all. However, there are sound alternatives available when the department is properly merchandised. If the department is originally set up to barbecue only on Thursdays, Fridays, and Saturdays, and effective signing is used to reinforce that information, the shopper will not expect to have product available on other days and will not be disappointed. Other alternatives are to barbecue and freeze the surplus product, or to barbecue a few spareribs each day to keep the department open, or to establish a barbecue "special order" operation, using prominent signing telling the customer to "call in advance and we'll have your order ready." Thus, the justification for a barbecue department depends less on store volume than it does on the ability of the store to properly merchandise the department.

The principles for successfully merchandising such high impulse items as party trays are similar. Too often, customers are unaware that the store offers such items because they cannot be displayed. But, it is a very simple task to have a dummy tray of luncheon meats and salads displayed in the meat and appetizing departments.

For convenience, many people entertain outside of the home at a cost for snacks of approximately $5 per person. Therefore, the cost of only $2 per person for a party tray affords the supermarket some very basic merchandising opportunities. If the economy, attractiveness, and convenience of these "prepared-to-order" party trays are properly stressed, considerable volume can be generated from filling orders for office parties and at-home entertainment. Considering the 35 to 40 percent profit that is built into these items, they deserve the best in merchandising support.

Store-wide Promotions

Store-wide promotions can build impulse sales not only for the meat department but for other departments as well. When each department ties into a central merchandising theme, there is greater impact and the promotion generally has a longer life. Since the customer thinks in terms of a total meal, so should the store.

As an example, one company successfully promoted a warm weather, store-wide "Leave the Cooking to Us" promotion, which was heavily backed by ad copy, window signs, and point-of-sale material.

Much of the signing and banners was supplied by manufacturers.[2] The major items promoted were barbecued chickens and spareribs from the meat department; party trays from the appetizing department; paper plates, napkins, plastic spoons and forks, paper cups, etc. from the non-foods department; a wide array of such prepared items as salad dressings, sauces, yogurt, frozen dinners, canned meats, etc. from other departments, as well as beer, soda, and other beverages. The promotion enhanced the store's image as an enjoyable place to shop and also boosted sales on many high-profit items.

If the product has good eye appeal, the opportunities for building impulse sales are endless and are limited only by the imagination of the meat manager.

MERCHANDISING HARD-TO-SELL ITEMS

Moving the slower selling, lower demand items really puts the creative talents of the meat manager to the test. It requires not only attractive, carefully positioned displays, but also innovation in product preparation.

Cutting Techniques

Many companies have boosted sales on hard-to-sell items by discovering new ways to cut and package them. Obviously, the last resort to moving a hard-to-sell item is to grind it because ground meats usually return the lowest profits, and rapid deterioration is a serious problem after meat has been ground.

Some items offer few alternatives. Plate beef, for example, rarely lends itself to an attractive display. Because it contains a considerable amount of fat, it does not offer a value to the customer even at a very low price and, therefore, should be ground. Fresh brisket, on the other hand, is an item subject to ethnic preferences and, despite its value, is often ground in stores with low demand. However, the item can take on a new look and return a much higher profit if it is boned and rolled, cut and sold as stew meat, or tenderized and sold as cubed steak.

---

[2] Point-of-sale materials are also available, either free or at a nominal cost, from such organizations as the National Live Stock and Meat Board (Chicago), American Meat Institute (Chicago), American Lamb Council (Denver), National Turkey Federation (Mt. Morris, Ill.), National Broiler Council (Richmond, Va.), and other associations.

Most companies experience lower sales on roasts during warm weather periods. This can be a significant profit drain in companies that buy whole beef carcasses because the cuts from the chuck, which represent half of the forequarter and 26 percent of the forequarter and hindquarter combined, are generally prepared as roasts.

Compounding the problem, blade roasts traditionally have been in less demand than those cut from the arm section of the chuck and a number of meat managers cut back on the arm roasts, hoping the customer will buy a blade roast if that is all that is available. Many companies have solved this problem by cutting more steaks from the chuck in the summer months and have gained consumer acceptance through promotional and educational efforts. If the customer knows that chuck steaks can be made more palatable if they are tenderized or marinated, the economy of the cut is an important merchandising plus to customers who cannot afford porterhouse or sirloin steaks.

If a company buys beef in carcass form, there obviously will be as many forequarters as hindquarters to sell. In the winter months, fewer steaks and more roasts are cut from the forequarter. The hindquarter, which represents 48 percent of the carcass and yields the most steaks, generally presents no problem during the summer when demand for steaks is high. When demand sloughs off in the winter months, the most common approach is to price beef steaks more attractively to generate volume. Additionally, more of the cuts from the hindquarter that are traditionally sold as steaks are prepared as roasts.

Because pork is not bought in carcass form, the pressure to move all cuts evenly is somewhat alleviated. For example, if beef is bought in carcass form, the low-demand brisket and short plate will have to be moved to avoid a profit drain. In pork, this part of the carcass provides the spareribs, which can be bought as needed, so that the store is not burdened with an oversupply when demand is low. Although the spareribs taken from hogs slaughtered in the wintertime far exceed the demand, producers freeze them until the summer months when customer demand is high and the overproduction can be absorbed easily.

Nevertheless, a store will not meet its profit projections unless pork, which represents the most profitable fresh meat commodity, is heavily merchandised and sales are maintained at acceptable levels year round.

As with beef, pork roasts are less in demand during the summer months and some do not sell well in the cold weather, but many companies have recaptured profits by varying their cutting methods. Some companies that have difficulty selling the sirloin end of the pork loin as a bone-in roast remove the tenderloin, which is sold as a separate item, and the back bones to create a more easily merchandised boneless loin roast. Others convert the roast to boneless or bone-in chops and boneless cutlets.

The rib end of the loin traditionally has been a slow seller because it is so difficult to carve at home. In some companies it is priced far below ground beef; in others it has been upgraded to a high-profit item with substantially increased sales, simply by changing the retail package.

Some companies merchandise the rib end as a roast, separating the ribs from the backbone. By sawing across the ribs, close to the bottom of the backbone, and then turning the roast over and removing the blade bone, the backbone will come off easily after cooking and the roast can easily be carved. Some companies bone and roll the roast and merchandise it as a boneless top loin roast. The ribs are then cut in half, about one inch above the backbone. The bottom half, which contains the backbone, is the most desirable even though it has more bone because it also has more lean meat. This portion is merchandised as country-style ribs which are meatier and more tender than spareribs and command a higher price. The top portion, merchandised as back ribs, has less bone but also more fat. In other companies the ribs are left intact, but the meat is cut into strips of two or three ribs for ease in cooking and serving. Still other companies cut various types of thick and thin chops from the rib end of the loin.

Considerable profit is earned on ham slices, which have customer appeal because they are easy to prepare and serve. There are two traditional ways to merchandise them. The pork leg can be divided into three sections—butt, (rump), center, and shank—and the ham slices can be cut from the center. Or, ham slices can be purchased from the packer, and the ham sold whole or split into a rump and shank half. One advantage to buying ham slices separately is that if they are vacuum packaged, the color and shelf life are improved. Of equal importance is the fact that when an excessive number of ham slices are cut from the pork leg, there is usually not enough meat left on the shank portion for it to be a value to the customer, even at a lower price. Therefore it is often easier to merchandise a whole ham when the center slices have not been removed because few customers will be satisfied with the shank portion if it contains so much bone.

Many cuts can be improved and sales on slow selling items increased by changing cutting techniques. The meat manager should look at his slow movers, analyze why they are not generating sales, and give some creative thought to how they can be converted to faster moving, profitable items.

Discolored Product

The most difficult items to sell are those that have lost their eye appeal. Because meat is perishable, it is impossible to eliminate the problem completely, but it is possible to limit the loss by reacting quickly.

The least loss will be suffered on a discolored but wholesome roast if a thin slice of the discolored surface is faced off. The roast should then be repackaged, reweighed, relabeled, and returned to the display case immediately. Another alternative is to convert the roast to steaks after it has been faced off. In no event should the discolored roast be turned over to hide the discolored surface because it will blacken within a short time and result in a much more serious loss when it is returned by a dissatisfied customer.

Some companies mark down wholesome discolored product that cannot be faced off and return the item to its regular location, merchandising it with a special sticker as a manager's special. If the customer has confidence in the store, she will know that only the appearance of the product has been affected, and that the marked down item represents a good value.

There are also some companies that merchandise such products in a special section of their frozen food cases. However, this is rarely an effective solution because when discolored fresh meat is placed in a freezer, it quickly turns black.

Nor should discolored product be converted to a higher priced item without the discoloration being removed. A discolored bone-in steak, for example, should not be boned out and repackaged as a higher priced cubed steak because there is nothing that can be done to a discolored product that has not been faced off to improve its eye appeal. As a discolored cubed steak, the item will more than likely sit in the display case until it has to be discarded. If the steak is too thin to be faced off, it should be reduced in price.

Timing is the most important factor in merchandising product that has lost its eye appeal. This requires policing the display case on a regular basis, removing product as soon as it starts to discolor, rewrapping product after it has been faced off or converted to another item, and returning it quickly to the display case so that it can be available for purchase. If the meat manager does not believe the product will sell at a reduced price or after it has been converted to another item, it should be faced off and ground as quickly as possible and returned to the display case.

If ground meat is made only from fresh trimmings, it will not discolor as quickly and the last batch ground each day usually can be carried overnight and sold the following morning. It is also necessary to control carefully the quantity of meat ground so that only a minimum of product is carried over to the next day. In some companies, production is scheduled so that the store will run out of the lowest priced ground meat toward the end of the day, and customers are offered the next highest priced ground meat at the lower price. It is felt that this loss is less than the loss that would be suffered if surplus product were to discolor and have to be discarded.

Some companies keep their beef, veal, and pork trimmings moving by mixing them and merchandising them as a meat loaf item. Others shape beef trimmings into patties and sell them at a premium to customers who are willing to pay for the convenience. Some merchandise the patties as frozen product to extend shelf life.

Restaurants are another outlet for surplus ground meat and a practical solution if a company grinds meat centrally. However, restaurant sales are not as easy to handle when grinding is done at store level, and in many companies such sales are assigned to one store for better control. One disadvantage to institutional sales is that product is sold at a generous discount and although this may be acceptable on ground meat, where a ready sales outlet is beneficial, a restaurant may also demand unrealistic discounts on other items, which would make the items unprofitable. Moreover, there is usually a need for portion control on items such as steaks, which increases costs and can adversely affect customer service. Most important of all is the need for the store to serve its regular customers, who also buy dry groceries and shop the entire store, and to place the customer's needs before that of a restaurant or any other institutional outlet. Institutional sales are extremely attractive and should be sought by the one-store operator. However, a chain that does not grind meat centrally should be sure that it can effectively control the operation so that service to the store's regular customers is not jeopardized.

New Items

New items come under the hard-to-sell category because they require expert merchandising skills to ensure their successful introduction and acceptance. For the most part, new meat department items are variations of traditional cuts—for example, steaks cut from the chuck or the addition of texturized vegetable product to ground meat. Such product introductions can be successful if the customer is educated to their value and use; however, less familiar new items require considerably more fanfare.

Recently, a new item, called a turkey burger, was created in an effort to get better movement on the dark meat portions of the turkey hindquarter, and considerable effort went into promoting it. The product was introduced with heavy print and television advertising, window signs, and point-of-sale material, including recipes. The advertising was aimed at two broad categories of customers; those on diets and those with limited budgets. The copy stressed that the product was lean, high in protein, low in calories, inexpensive, and that it could be prepared as simply as any other ground meat.

Prior to its introduction, meat buyers held meetings with the meat supervisors who were given the opportunity to sample the product. The meat supervisors were then asked to visit each store, cook the product, and allow the employees to taste it so that they could answer customers' questions. The product was placed with ground meat, not only because of the similarity between the items, but because the ground meat section would draw the greatest traffic. When demonstrators were used, sales were reported to be excellent.

No amount of merchandising will ensure the success of a new product unless the product has appeal. But a product with eye appeal will also fail unless it is promoted in such a manner that the customer (1) knows it is there, (2) understands its value, and (3) knows what to do with it.

MERCHANDISING SUPPORTS

Three common techniques used to promote sales on both new and old items are demonstrators, cooking aids, and contests.

Demonstrators

The in-store demonstration is an example of hard-sell merchandising techniques that are especially effective in building impulse sales. Cooking odors, especially the spicy odors of fried sausage or grilled hot dogs, help to stimulate the appetite and build sales. The customer tastes a sample and hopefully says she'll take a pound. Demonstrations create an impulse for the item at the time the customer is shopping, but even more important, create the opportunity for a repeat sale, which is the objective.

To get the maximum impact from demonstrations, experienced demonstrators should be employed. Often suppliers will provide this service, but the company should be sure not to have too many demonstrations taking place at one time as this can create a carnival atmosphere which may boomerang and actually interfere with sales. Also, the merchandiser must have a feeling for what will sell in his stores. One merchandiser was convinced by an overzealous supplier to allow the supplier to demonstrate a canned ham that retailed at 30 cents more per pound than similar products. The basic difference in the items was a slice of pineapple on the more expensive canned ham. The demonstrator was given space in the high-volume meat department, and over a two-day weekend sold only six cans of the item.

Space is expensive, and space devoted to one item takes space away from another. A good merchandiser knows that he cannot create a desire in the customer's mind for an item that is too far removed from her normal buying practices. He also realizes that when he devotes space to or attempts to attract attention to one item, that item is competing with all other items in the case. Before using a demonstrator the manager should be sold on the product to be demonstrated, regardless of who is paying the bill, so that valuable time and effort is not being wasted on products that have little sales potential.

Some companies employ their own demonstrators at a cost of more than $30 per day. The common practice is for the demonstrators to work two days a week on the highest traffic days. Some companies use demonstrators on an irregular basis to promote items, while others have traveling demonstrators on a year-round basis who visit each store about three times a year. It is not unusual for sales to triple on a demonstrated item and to be maintained at a 10 percent higher than average level for months thereafter. Most companies are satisfied if the increased sales during the demonstration simply cover the demonstrator's expenses because the real goal is to get the product into the customer's shopping cart and to make the profit on the repeat sale.

Cooking Aids

Because she does not want to appear unintelligent, a shopper is often reluctant to ask questions of store employees about meat preparation. This is particularly true for the new homemaker who, lacking experience in the preparation of fresh meats, will often solve her dilemma by purchasing frozen dinners. The fact is that the more the shopper knows, the more dishes and items she will try—and buy. Thus, many meat merchandisers now furnish such information without waiting for the customer to ask for it. Some chains use signs over the meat counter to describe the various cuts of meat and their uses. Some have booklets available on special display racks answering such questions as: What cuts are best for broiling? How is meat kept from curling while broiling? How is broiling done in a range? Over charcoal? How do you pan broil? Pan fry? What cuts are best suited to roasting? How do you roast? How do you braise?

One chain runs a combination recipe-promotion-merchandising program for consumers. Each week certain preselected cuts of meat are singled out for prominent display in the case, surrounded with a variety of supporting point-of-sale material, plus a set of recipes showing how to prepare and cook the meat.

Another chain has a consumer cooking school taught by a home economist. Sessions are held in each of the chain's meeting rooms. Although the home economist teaches all phases of cooking, the emphasis is on meat and how to buy it, prepare it, and serve it. In one three-day period, 3,000 people attended the classes, and future classes had to be scheduled six months in advance to accommodate the crowds.

Still another chain runs a combination cooking school and instruction seminar. The course attempts to give the consumer an overview of the meat she buys—how it gets to the store, and what to do with it once it has been bought. Chain meat merchandisers explain how meat is procured. Meat managers show how it's cut, wrapped, and merchandised. The consumer also gets a tour of backroom facilities, a variety of specially prepared recipes, and sees a motion picture supplied by the American Meat Institute. Says a company spokesman, "When it comes to meat, the customer wants to know everything."

Recipes can be a potent merchandising force in introducing new items. One chain recently introduced a thick-cut steak from the round. It was a new type of cut for the stores, and it was obvious that sales would be minimal unless the customers were given instructions on how to prepare it. Through testing, it was determined that the meat should first be marinated and then barbecued. The chain was supplied with recipes by a major spice manufacturer, and the recipes were included in each package. After the recipes were added, the item started generating excellent sales. It has been a steady mover in that company ever since.

Recipes are a simple but effective merchandising tool not only for promoting new items, but for winning over inexperienced young homemakers and new customers as well. According to various studies, 5 percent of the people shopping a store each week are new customers. In some areas, the figure is considerably higher. The customer who has moved, for example, from the East to the West Coast, is going to be confronted with meat cuts and names with which she is unfamiliar, unless standard nomenclature is used. The meat manager and department employees should remember that she wants help, even though she may be embarrassed to ask for it, and with all other things being equal, she will shop the store that provides it.

Contests

Contests are a viable means of motivating store employees to build sales. Competition may be between districts or stores or departments, but the most important factor in the success of any contest is to ensure that everyone has a fairly good chance to win. It is obvious that if the contest is structured so that one store is so far ahead at the end of the first week that it cannot be overtaken, all other stores will lose interest and the contest will not have served its purpose to encourage store employees to build sales volume.

Contests can be run either on single items or on several items. In each case, however, awards should be made on the basis of a percentage of increase, rather than on a pound-for-pound basis. If a contest is being run on sausage sales, for example, the company should have available a sales history for each meat department showing the tonnage sold in relation to total department sales. The winner of that contest would be the department showing the greatest percentage increase in sausage sales in relation to total volume. In this way, the opportunities for small and large stores to win are equalized.

The rewards, of course, must be commensurate in both dollar and prestige value with the returns that the company hopes to get. One company recently held a six-week contest measuring the following factors: sales on two items, department gross and net profit, distribution percent (ratio of meat sales to total store sales), and housekeeping. The prizes included a mink stole, a color T.V., and a number of less expensive awards for the runners-up. In addition, all meat department employees in the winning district and their spouses were invited to an elaborate dinner. It was apparent that the increased volume and profits that resulted from the employees' efforts to merchandise the department with vigor compensated for the cost of the prizes many times over.

According to the meat merchandiser who set up the contest, "There is no question that the department doing the worst job generally has the best opportunity to show improvement and, therefore, to win. That may be a disadvantage to the other departments that are competing, but it has some real advantages to the company. For one thing, if that department starts falling off after the contest, you can go back to the manager and confront him with what he has shown himself capable of accomplishing. Also, when a contest runs six to eight weeks, habits are established—to run a clean department, to have fresh displays, etc.—and hopefully those habits will be maintained. We included housekeeping in this particular contest because we wanted to get everyone enthused about its importance. We established a point rating system and an inspection check list against which points were awarded. While housekeeping was not the most important part of the contest, the stores could earn extra points for maintaining good practices. We supported the contest with newspaper advertising but gave fewer points to the two meat items in the contest than we did to gross and net profit and distribution percent because what we really wanted was total department improvement. And, we got it."

The duration and frequency of a contest should be determined on the basis of the nature of the competition. Contests based on meat items only can be run for three weeks and as often as six times a year. It is not unusual to have a dollar trade-off on directly competitive items when "item only" contests are held. For example, if the contest is based on sales increases for Brand X sausage, sales on Brand Y usually fall off. Interestingly, however, overall department sausage sales will increase in a well designed and well managed contest.

Some companies run quarterly contests based on increases in dollar volume, customer count, and payroll. More elaborate contests, such as the one described earlier, should be held only once a year, or at the most twice. Moreover, to keep employees interested, they should not run longer than six to eight weeks. Because it generally takes at least two weeks for a store to get the feel of what it can sell, the meat items included should remain the same during the duration of the contest. The experience of most companies has been that improvements in sales and ordering accuracy are usually seen in the third week.

The success of any contest rests on employee commitment and how motivated the employee is to merchandise the department to the customer. In order to get employees behind a contest, the factors measured must be realistic, each participant must have an opportunity to win, and the rewards must be meaningful.

CUSTOMER RELATIONS

Customer relations is the backbone of any successful merchandising program, and it begins with having friendly store employees who have sufficient product knowledge to answer questions and handle complaints. Many companies have consumer relations departments which not only handle complaints but also serve as a feedback mechanism for customer attitudes on store employees, items that should be carried, cleanliness, etc. Often they handle matters that should not reach headquarters and would not if they were handled properly at store level. However, many customers are shy and would prefer to write a letter or telephone their opinion or complaint rather than face a store employee.

Customers can be encouraged to communicate directly with store personnel if the meat department employees create the impression of being friendly, courteous, and helpful. Rather than saying, "At the end of the counter, lady," when a customer asks where the chicken livers are, the employee should seize upon the opportunity to chat briefly with the customer and to direct her to the product she is seeking. The employee can also befriend the customer by suggesting substitute items, instead of barking, "We're out of it, lady."

The proper handling of a customer complaint is another important aspect of customer relations because many customers are timid about returning merchandise, even when the justification is obvious. Rather than risk alienating a customer who spends upwards of $2,500 a year in the store, many companies have a standard guideline that the customer is always right—even if she is wrong.

Store employees are encouraged to let the customer talk out her complaints. If she complains that an item is not fresh and the label clearly indicates that she purchased it two weeks ago, her money is refunded—cheerfully. If it is clear that the item was purchased at a competitor's store, in many companies the money is also refunded. In some cases, the manager will let the customer know that he is aware that the purchase was made elsewhere, but that he will save her a trip to the other store and send for the refund himself. In similar situations where the customer is obviously wrong, many companies feel that the few dollars spent in making a friend of a customer who has the potential to spend thousands more in the store is a very worthwhile investment.

One exception is with chronic offenders whose complaints are not justified. Most companies agree that they would rather lose such customers to competition. To discourage customers from repeatedly making unjustified returns, many companies ask the customer to sign a complaint slip when a refund is made. The store manager, meat supervisor, and meat merchandiser receive a copy of each complaint, telling how it was handled and whether it was handled to the customer's satisfaction.

An attempt should always be made to handle the problem at the lowest possible level, but in some cases the solution is not clear cut and the supervisor or merchandiser has to make the decision. As an example, if a valued customer who spends $3,000 a year in the store complains that the chicken she purchased for Sunday night's dinner was inedible, the meat manager will not hesitate to refund her money. If, however, she says she had nothing else in her refrigerator and she and her husband had to go to a restaurant, and she demands to be reimbursed for a $10 restaurant bill, the manager may be on the fence as to how to handle the problem. But, if she says that the turkey she purchased for Thanksgiving dinner was so tough that it couldn't be sliced and she had to take her 15 guests to dinner, and threatens never to return to the store unless the $145 bill is paid by the store, obviously the manager cannot make the decision and should honestly tell her so. He should listen to her, being certain that he does not act in any way that will further agitate her, and then contact his supervisor for advice.

Most complaints are less complicated and more easily handled. If a customer returns an item, she is generally given a credit, refund, or replacement. If she telephones her complaint, in many companies the store manager or supervisor will deliver a replacement to her home and collect the unsavory item. In some companies, if the customer has used the item, a replacement will be provided; in others, a nominal gift certificate and letter of apology will be mailed.

Although supervisory personnel are in general agreement as to how to develop good customer relations, there is often a need to impress the importance more strongly on store employees. The meat manager should be responsible for indoctrinating his people and for setting the proper example for them to follow.

If there were similar agreement as to other aspects of meat merchandising, every meat department would look the same, every company would use the same advertising layouts, there would be no variation from one store to another in the products carried, and they would all be placed in the same location in the display case. However, unlike customer relations, there is no one best way to merchandise the department. The challenge is to experiment continually in search of the optimum, keeping in mind that what works well in one store may not be successful in another.

10

Sanitation and Safety

All retailers operate under sanitation and safety codes of one type or another, which vary according to where their stores are located. Although regulations affecting retail establishments, distribution centers, and processing plants are currently in a state of flux, there is little doubt that they will become more stringent and complicated as the Environmental Protection Agency (EPA), the Food and Drug Administration (FDA), the Occupational Safety and Health Administration (OSHA), as well as other national and local regulatory agencies issue new standards.

Until recently, scant attention was paid to formalized sanitation and safety programs because the rewards had not been clearly documented. However, a number of research studies conducted in the 1960s and 1970s proving the value of such programs, plus the government's increasing involvement in wholesale and retail food operations, have made sanitation and safety high priority items. Many companies have hired consultants to assist them in developing effective sanitation programs, and most insurance carriers have been useful resources in customizing safety programs for their retail clients. Additionally, quality assurance and safety departments are now part of the organization chart in many companies, with the greatest concentration of effort being placed on the meat department because of the potential hazards that exist due to the nature of the product and the equipment used.

THE ECONOMICS OF SANITATION

The similarity between an effective sanitation program and an effective merchandising program is that the results of both efforts are often measured in terms of profits. Effective sanitation has an enormous impact on the profit picture by reducing spoilage and providing a longer shelf life. It also helps to maintain the bloom that makes meat more attractive and leads to more sales as well as saving time and labor costs by reducing the number of rewraps. Good sanitation provides a healthy, clean environment that upgrades the image and reputation of the entire store and provides a better atmosphere for customers and employees.

Various research studies conducted at universities throughout the country have pinpointed the benefits in quantitative terms. A 1964 study conducted at the University of Missouri awakened the entire industry to the fact that good sanitation practices could double the shelf life of fresh meat. "A shelf life of one week is possible with proper sanitation plus temperatures that will hold the meat below 32° F. after packaging."[1] A seven-day shelf life would have a beneficial effect on smoothing out processing peaks and valleys to meet weekend sales requirements. It would reduce the number of deliveries and reserve inventory and make central processing far more feasible. The study also concluded that doubling the shelf life would "reduce rewraps or reprocessing of discolored prepackaged meat by at least 50 percent."[2]

In 1967, several researchers at the University of New Mexico undertook a study to determine whether the sanitation and temperature practices recommended by the University of Missouri could be

---
[1] H. D. Naumann, W. C. Stringer, and P. F. Gould, *Guidelines for Handling Prepackaged Meat in Retail Stores,* Cooperative Extension Service, University of Missouri, Manual 64, May, 1965, p. 4.
[2] Naumann, et. al., p. 14.

economically justified—whether the additional costs exceeded the added returns. Their test confirmed the University of Missouri findings that shelf life could be increased significantly as a result of improved sanitation management. Because resources were limited, they could not evaluate the cost of product loss, rewraps, etc. for the entire department. The meat manager suggested that cubed steaks represented one of the most difficult items to merchandise and that he had experienced loss of product. The researchers used this product, which has a relatively high gross margin but short case life, for their analysis.

Using a three-week base period, they determined that product loss decreased from 11.02 to 0.81 as a percent of the total value and resulted in an annual savings of $501.18 for cubed steaks alone. For each dollar invested in detergents, sanitizers, etc., "an average of $8 of product was saved and an average of nearly $46 in net value of cubed steaks sold was gained every three weeks."[3]

The additional benefits resulting from the changed sanitation practices are equally significant:

> "Because of the increase in case life realized for cubed steaks, the department manager displayed more cubed steaks without fear of loss of quality. He used several rows of cubed steaks in different places in the fresh meat case with the result that sales were increased by an average of 63 percent.
>
> "During the monitoring period of this study, 36 linear feet of the existing refrigerated meat case was used for fresh meat display. Following the testing period, the longer case life made possible the increase of fresh meat display from 36 to 48 linear feet. [Product that had occupied that space was moved elsewhere.]
>
> "Meat sales as a percentage of store sales increased nearly 2 percent over the previous year.
>
> "The increased case life also provided more merchandising flexibility for fresh meats.
>
> "The departmental personnel became more aware of the need for following good sanitation management practices as a result of the study.
>
> "The authors determined subjectively that departmental pride

---

[3] Ruth Sneed, Ann R. Stasch, and William J. Vastine, *Costs and Returns of Improved Sanitation Management in a Retail Meat Market,* New Mexico State University, Cooperative Extension Service Circular 416, November, 1968, p. 8.

and morale increased above its already high level. Management's recognition of the improved financial operations of the department undoubtedly contributed to their pride and morale." [4]

Under a USDA contract, the University of Missouri meat scientists conducted a follow-up to their 1964 study and showed that one store realized a saving of $184.57 weekly or $9,597.64 annually by implementing planned programs for sanitation and temperature control. A Midwest chain, conducting its own sanitation program, projected a one-store annual savings of $2,100. If the store operated at a 1 percent net profit, it would take an additional $210,000 in sales to generate such a profit.

Other research studies duplicated these findings and have proved conclusively that compliance with government health and sanitation codes is only a secondary reason for training employees in proper sanitation practices. The primary reason is that not doing so will result in a formidable profit drain.

BLOOM AND DISCOLORATION

Through the landmark research efforts of the University of Missouri meat scientists, much has been learned about the effects of temperature and sanitation on product appearance and how to extend shelf life by maintaining the bloom of product.

According to their report, "The characteristic colors of meat (both desirable and undesirable) are due to changes that take place in the meat pigment, myoglobin. The color of freshly cut meat is purplish-red. After it is cut, meat 'blooms' by absorbing oxygen from the air. The meat pigment is than called oxymyoglobin and is responsible for the normal, bright red color of meat." [5] This is the optimum appearance which consumers associate with freshness. However, prolonged exposure to air, which dehydrates the product, and/or microbial (bacteria) populations in abundant numbers, which deplete the oxygen and attack the meat fibers, cause the pigment to change to brownish-red or grayish-red, called metmyoglobin.

The length of time between blooming and discoloring (i.e., the shelf life) can be controlled to a great extent. Today's wrapping

---
[4] Sneed, et. al., p. 8.
[5] Naumann, et. al., p. 3.

films provide the proper environment for blooming by allowing the oxygen to enter the package and preventing moisture from being drawn out. The major cause of discoloration, then, is the action of bacteria growing on the cut surface; and how quickly bacteria will multiply depends largely on the temperature at which the meat is held. Although the bacteria are not generally harmful to human health (because they are destroyed in the cooking process), they cause discoloration and an unpleasant aroma. This greatly shortens the shelf life of the product which must be pulled from the case and reprocessed or, if totally unattractive or unwholesome, discarded.

Bacteria and Temperature

The bacteria that attack meat grow and reproduce rapidly at poor refrigeration temperatures. Their growth is greatly retarded at the freezing point of meat (between 28° and 29° F.). Bacteria cannot be seen with the naked eye. Four hundred million would occupy space the size of one grain of sugar; and a single microbe can multiply to 250,000 within six hours.

Bacteria thrive best on moist, high protein foods, such as meat, in warm temperatures. The greatly extended shelf life of frozen meat results from the fact that the solidified moisture cannot sustain rapid bacterial growth. A high concentration of salt in the moisture will also prevent bacterial growth since bacteria need moisture to absorb nutrients. Salt in heavy concentration has the effect of reversing the absorption process so that instead of nutrients flowing out of the product, moisture is drawn out of the bacteria, which dehydrate and die. It is for this reason that salt has been used as a preservative since biblical times.

Today, temperature is one of the most effective means of controlling the growth of bacteria in meat departments. The University of Missouri study showed that when temperatures are increased from 32° to 40° F., bacteria grow three times faster. If held at 32° F., steaks with 100 bacteria per inch will have only 800 bacteria per inch after $2\frac{1}{2}$ days, as compared to more than 50,000 if held at 40° F. Bacteria commonly found on meat take 20 hours to double at 32° F., but only $6\frac{3}{4}$ hours at 40° F.

Bacteria and Sanitation

Temperature alone is not the answer. "Temperature control must be combined with good sanitation to control, effectively, initial contamination of the product during processing and to control growth of these contaminants during processing and display." [6]

Summarizing the observations of the University of Missouri scientists, the muscle, fat, and bone in an animal are practically free of microbes, and much of the contamination takes place during slaughtering, processing, and delivering to the stores. Therefore, there is a need for better temperature and sanitation control before the product reaches the store because bacterial contamination from the surface of the quarter or primal contaminates the retail cut during the cutting process. Absolutely clean equipment becomes soiled immediately upon contact with contaminated meat and, in turn, contaminates the inner surfaces of the meat. There must, therefore, be a concerted effort at store level to control the bacteria that already exist and to minimize any additional contamination that can occur during store handling and processing.

The primary source of contamination of meat at store level is equipment that is not properly cleaned on a frequent basis. Equipment quickly attains a certain level of contamination during use and maintains that level through the work period. Moreover, when dirty equipment is not in use, a rapid build-up of bacteria occurs and results in severe contamination of meat cuts when the equipment is re-used. If proper attention is not given to the use of clean equipment and the level of contamination of the cuts going into the retail package, the meat will discolor very rapidly despite good temperature control.

PRODUCT AND SANITATION

To eliminate the entry of airborne bacteria, flies, vermin, and insects to as great a degree as possible, the store's receiving door should be open only when absolutely necessary. And, because delivery personnel carry bacteria on their bodies and clothing, their activities should be contained within the receiving area. Meat should be removed from the delivery vehicle quickly and inspected in accordance with the company's standards for receiving product. Any bloody ends or discolored meat should be trimmed off as soon as possible to prevent further spoilage. Rail stock should be hung on clean hooks; vacuum-packaged boxed meat should be spot checked for leakers and the boxes stored on racks or shelves in the cooler.

---

[6] Naumann, et. al., p. 6.

Simply placing meat in a 30° F. cooler will not ensure that product is being maintained at the proper temperature. Meat can be spoiled in a cooler unless it is spaced so that the air circulates freely around it. Therefore, rail stock should not be touching, and no product should be placed on the floor or against a wall. Placing meat in a cooler that is set at too low a temperature can also spoil meat. When meat is placed in a 24° F. cooler, moisture is drawn out of the product as the animal heat is removed, which causes surface freezing. This surface freezing will close the outside pores, and the internal meat will spoil if it has not been sufficiently cooled before the cold air is prevented from penetrating.

The optimum temperature for the receiving area is 30° to 32° F. and 29° to 30° F. for the cooler, with a relative humidity of 80 to 85 percent in the cooler. Realistically, maintaining such temperatures is difficult because of opening and closing of doors, defrost cycles, etc. However, because few bacteria found in a meat department grow at 32° F., maintaining a constant temperature as close to 32° F. as possible will greatly extend shelf life.

As much processing as possible should be done in the cooler where constant low temperatures are easiest to maintain; this includes grinding meat and breaking quarters. The more perishable cuts, such as flanks, kidneys, necks, skirts, and so on should be removed first and quickly processed. To avoid cross contamination, only one type of commodity should be processed at a time at one work station. Moreover, trimmings should be worked up as they accumulate so that they are not out from under refrigeration for any length of time.

The recommended temperature for the processing and wrapping area is below 40° F. At higher temperatures, not only will bacteria multiply on the retail cut, but it also will be further contaminated by the bacteria growing on the cutting equipment and cutting tables.

Because few supermarkets maintain cutting, processing, and wrapping room temperatures at below 40° F., it is important that product be quickly processed, packaged, and placed in a refrigerated display case or holding cooler. One complication is that the time required to process different types of product varies considerably; and, therefore, it is not possible to balance precisely the workload of the cutters and wrappers. For efficiency, it is necessary to have product available for the wrappers to work on while the cutters are involved in the more difficult and time-consuming processing operations. Also, there must be product ready on the wrapping line for the wrappers while the cutters are at lunch. On the other hand, product will accumulate on the wrapping line while the wrappers are at lunch. However, if the production is properly planned and controlled, and lunch hours and breaks are staggered and set for optimum times, there will be a minimum of product out from under refrigeration on the wrapping line at any one time.

Meat should be wrapped snugly, keeping the packaging film in contact with the meat surface to allow for uniform bloom. Packages should not be stacked immediately after packaging (or package surfaces should be inverted on alternate layers) because the heat from the sealing operation will warm the top surface of the lower level packages and create discoloration.

Optimally, retail packages should be placed in a display case maintained at 29° to 32° F., and the internal temperature of the product should be maintained as close to 32° F. as possible. However, the lighting that is commonly used in supermarkets warms up the product, and the height to which product is stacked interferes with free air circulation. Although the temperature gauge in the case measures 32° F., the product on top, if stacked above the load limit, can have a temperature of over 50° F. Keeping the top packages at 29° to 32° F. requires an inflow of air much below 29° F., which would freeze the meat on the bottom layer. It is therefore imperative that product never be placed above the load line. Overloading not only leaves product out from under adequate refrigeration but it also tends to draw warm room air into the case, thereby diminishing the efficiency of the equipment by causing a heavy build-up of frost on the coils, which results in increased operating costs. Drafts have the same effect in that they displace the refrigerated air with warm room air and add moisture to the case, adversely affecting the equipment and creating frost on the product.

When single-deck cases are used, the shelf should be adjusted so that product is always within the refrigerated area and so that the weight of the top packages does not crush those beneath and result in a moisture loss. On high-volume days, the shelf should be lowered to ensure that there is adequate product on display and that it is placed within the refrigerated zone of the case. At the same time, if an item should not be stacked more than three high—for example, a boneless round steak—the appearance of an even, in-depth display can be accomplished by raising the display shelf.

Some of these problems have been overcome with newly designed multi-deck cases. With these cases, the height to which any product can be stocked is limited to the space available between the shelves, and refrigeration is considered to be more effective. Defrosting, however, can be a problem with any refrigerated equipment, but is more so with single-deck cases. Generally, when cases are on the defrost cycle, rising temperatures have an adverse effect on the product. However, unless refrigeration units are defrosted regularly, they will not function properly. When a build-up of frost closes the space between the coil fins, less air can pass over the coil surfaces, which reduces the cooling capability of the equipment.

It is generally recommended that refrigerated units be defrosted when the store is closed. Whether or not this can be accomplished will depend on the hours that the store is open, the efficiency of the equipment in use, and, perhaps most important, the temperature of the sales area in the store. When the temperature in the sales area is about 72° F., it is often necessary to have three defrost cycles every 24 hours to keep the equipment functioning properly.

Although refrigerated cases are equipped with thermometers, the temperature of product in the case can vary, depending on how and where the items are placed and on the temperature of the retail cut before it is placed in the case. Also, temperature gauges are often placed at the back of the display case, so that the reading may not be accurate for product displayed in the front of the case which is normally warmer. Therefore, the thermometer should be checked regularly, and the packages should also be inspected. Flowing juices are a positive sign that the temperature is too high.

The sooner that meat can be sold after being placed in the display case, the better for all concerned. The consumer gets a higher quality piece of meat with better color, less weight loss, and lower bacteria count, while the retailer has fewer rewrap problems and the attendant product, labor, and material costs. Therefore, assuming that the refrigerated equipment is functioning properly, the best control on shelf life and rewraps is the ability of the meat manager to estimate customer demand accurately and to order, process, and display product to match sales velocity. If that is successfully done, there will be a minimum of product carried over from day to day or over the weekend. If the store is closed on Sunday, any unsold fresh meat product should be removed from the display case and stored in the cooler until Monday morning. On a day-to-day basis, product does not have to be returned to the cooler, but display lights, which hasten discoloration, should be turned off.

EQUIPMENT AND SANITATION

In addition to maintaining proper temperatures, cleaning and sanitizing are required to control the growth of bacteria. A detergent will clean, but will not kill bacteria; a sanitizer will destroy microbes with which it comes in contact, but surface soil prevents the sanitizer from penetrating. Therefore, microbial control is accomplished only when *sanitizers* are applied to *clean* surfaces.

The soil to be removed in a meat department is mostly protein and fat. Some of the fat can be removed by rinsing with hot water, but the residual fat requires a detergent that will make the fat soluble in water. Proteins are far more difficult to remove. Detergents containing alkaline are recommended for removing both fat and protein soils.

Sanitizers are produced by many companies in varying strengths; those sold in interstate commerce must be approved by the EPA. They consist of rather complex chemical compounds, and their level of toxicity is important when they are applied to surfaces that come in contact with food. Twice yearly, the USDA revises and publishes the "List of Chemical Compounds" indicating those which have been approved for use where meat is processed. The effect of the sanitizer on the worker, the cost, the service provided by the supplier, and local restrictions are other considerations in choosing a sanitizer.

Household detergents and bleaches are far too expensive when used in the concentration required to be effective cleaners and sanitizers in a meat department. Products prepared for commercial use will be far more economical and although they vary in effectiveness, they will do an adequate job if the manufacturer's directions are followed. If not used in the proper proportion of chemical to water, they can corrode equipment and cause skin rashes. Combination cleaners/sanitizers which, by performing both functions with one application, reduce the time to clean and sanitize, are readily available. However, some local health codes require that cleaning and sanitizing be performed in separate operations. Many companies offer either high or low-pressure spray equipment that also automatically mixes the cleaners and sanitizers (or the combined product) with the proper amount of water at proper temperatures.

How difficult and effective the sanitizing program is will depend not only on whether the work is being done with a pail and brush, as opposed to a sophisticated power sprayer, but also on the nature of the equipment to be cleaned. Because bacteria need moisture to survive, a porous wooden surface will be more difficult to sanitize than equipment with moisture-proof stainless steel or fiberglass surfaces. Removing soil and bacteria from square case corners or around screwheads is difficult and time-consuming with a brush, but requires little effort or time with a power sprayer. Accessibility to drains and grease traps, the ease with which equipment can be dismantled, and whether or not equipment is watertight or electrically shielded all have a bearing on the ease with which the equipment can be cleaned and how effective the sanitizing efforts will be.

The Cleaning Schedule

There are few hard and fast rules with regard to sanitizing that will hold for all stores. The requirements for each store must be evaluated on an individual basis, and cleaning and sanitizing scheduled in the same manner as any other important store function. Obviously, equipment in most frequent use and most easily contaminated such as a power saw will need attention more often than shelving in the cooler. However, depending on the workload and the product being processed, the saw may have to be cleaned and sanitized every four hours in one store, but only once daily in another unit. The temperature of the working area is also an important factor. It may be sufficient to clean a saw used exclusively for beef only once a day if the processing area temperature is maintained at 40° F., whereas the same saw, used in an air-conditioned or uncooled work area, may need sanitizing every four hours. The only sure way to measure the need for cleaning and sanitizing is to take bacteria counts on a regular basis. Either a bacteriologist can be brought to the store to take swabs, or company personnel can collect swabs and have counts made by a laboratory. Some companies, especially those engaged in private label manufacturing, have quality control laboratories with microbiology sections which perform bacteria counts as part of the company's store sanitation program. Based on their findings, cleaning and sanitizing schedules are adjusted for each individual store.

Processing Room Floors

Sawdust, a notorious breeding place for bacteria, also has a dusting quality which causes air-borne bacteria. Sawdust is usually contaminated before it is used and becomes increasingly so with use.

In addition, personnel have a tendency to leave dropped pieces of meat, fat, and debris on the floor when they are hidden by the sawdust, something they would not be likely to do on an exposed floor.

With the elimination of sawdust, retailers have been hard pressed to find a substitute that will keep processing room floors dry and slip-proof. Some companies are using crack-resistant tiles joined by cement, and some are experimenting with epoxy materials which are troweled on like cement; but the search continues for an inexpensive, moisture-proof flooring material with abrasive qualities to resist slipping.

Processing room floors should be tightly sealed where they meet the wall to eliminate entry of bugs and other pests and to avoid a damp breeding place for bacteria to grow. It is preferable to have the flooring material extend up the wall a foot or more. Drains should be positioned in accordance with the requirements of local building codes, and the slope of the floor should be such that water flows into or is easily swept to the drain. The drain pipes should be sloped properly to empty into a grease trap. The grease trap should be in an accessible place and should be cleaned and sanitized once a week while the drain itself should be flushed out about once every three months. An adequate floor drainage system will permit flushing and hosing of large equipment and will facilitate the cleaning and sanitizing of floors.

In some companies, processing room floors are cleaned and sanitized at the end of the day; in others, cleaning and sanitizing is done before the cutters break for lunch and again at the end of the day.

The water temperature for all cleaning must always be above 140° F.; when a combination cleaner/sanitizer is used, the manufacturer's directions for water temperature should be followed. Regardless of whether a floor, a wall, or a piece of equipment is being treated, if the cleaning is performed in a separate operation, obvious loose soil should be removed first by rough cleaning. Then a hot water rinse should be applied to loosen residual soil, after which the cleaning solution is applied and the area is scrubbed with a stiff bristle brush. The detergent is then washed away by rinsing with hot water, and excess water is removed. The sanitizer is then applied for the recommended time. A final rinse may or may not be required.

If a combination cleaner/sanitizer is used on the processing room floor, loose particles should be scraped up and the floor swept.

The floor would then be mopped or scrubbed with the detergent/sanitizer solution and then rinsed. Excess water would be either mopped up, pushed to the floor drain with a squeegee, or vacuumed off.

The Processing Area

Other than the walls, which are cleaned and sanitized weekly at a minimum, and the ceiling, which is cleaned and sanitized at least monthly in some companies and weekly in others, all other equipment in the processing area should be cleaned and sanitized at least daily, and far more often if needed.

Any tool that drops on the floor should be cleaned and sanitized immediately. Any time production changes from poultry to smoked hams to beef or to any other items where cross-contamination is likely to occur, the knives, saws, cutting blocks, etc. must be cleaned and sanitized before the next item is processed. Smoked pork, which probably creates the greatest problem, can discolor beef within hours. Cross-contamination from poultry to meat can shorten case life by as much as 24 hours.

Small equipment, such as knives and scrapers, should be cleaned, thoroughly rinsed, dipped into a sanitizing solution, and rinsed again often during the day. Lugs should be cleaned and sanitized each time they are emptied.

Whether or not a cutting board will have to be cleaned and sanitized every four hours or only daily will depend on how it is used—how quickly it becomes contaminated. It is best to use removable synthetic cutting boards which fit into the tops of stainless steel frame tables. Replaceable tops are advantageous because the tops become a major source of contamination when the surface becomes marred. The cutting boards should be no longer than three feet so that they can be removed easily by one person for cleaning and sanitizing. Neither boxes nor crates which have come in contact with floor surfaces should be placed on cutting blocks or tables for unpacking since they are highly contaminated.

Power tools should be unplugged and dismantled as far as their construction will allow. Removable parts should soak in a detergent/sanitizer solution and then be scrubbed and rinsed, while the equipment frames should be scraped and scrubbed with the solution and then rinsed. If drying is necessary, it should be done with a disposable towel.

Sanitation and Safety 229

How frequently to clean and sanitize power tools and equipment during the day depends on their use. Grinders, however, should be washed and sanitized at least daily as well as immediately following the grinding of fresh or cured pork.

It is recommended that all power equipment and tools meet all safety standards. Electrical parts, bearings, switches, and connections should be moisture-proof. Dismantling and reassembling should be easily done. The finish on power equipment should have as much stainless steel as possible to ensure longer wear; and, where appropriate, legs or stands should be adjustable so that the height of the equipment can be regulated for different employees.

Sinks for cleaning equipment should be constructed of stainless steel with three basins so that washing, rinsing and sanitizing are easily done. Drain boards should also be provided.

Employee hand sinks in the processing area should be made of stainless steel, with foot pedals to control the water supply and equipment for dispensing disinfectant soap for hand washing. Disposable paper towels should be supplied. The liquid hand soap used must be approved by the USDA and EPA as a safe and effective sanitizer. Sinks should be cleaned and sanitized daily. Waste cans should have plastic liners and be emptied regularly, and no food should be stored near them.

Because equipment that comes into direct contact with meat contributes much more to contamination than any other sources, effective sanitation in the processing area will be highly instrumental in extending the bloom period on perishable product.

The Cooler

In most companies, the cooler floor is treated at least once a week, and in some companies it is cleaned and sanitized daily. Overloading the cooler can retard proper air circulation and hinder cleaning, especially when there is rail stock. Obviously, if there is little walking room in the cooler, employees will wait until the cooler inventory is worked down and cleaning can be done more conveniently. Receiving saw-ready product that can be stored on mobile equipment in the cooler will greatly facilitate cleaning the cooler; moreover, there is less soil with saw-ready product, especially if it is vacuum packaged.

Cooler accessories must also be cleaned and sanitized on a regular basis. Racks and shelves should be treated at least once a week.

Racks should be placed 6 inches off the floor, and shelves should be purchased in sizes that will facilitate handling for cleaning purposes. Both should be constructed of rust-proof metal.

Trees and hooks (used for hanging primals and quarters) should be constructed of stainless steel for ease in cleaning and sanitizing and to avoid rusting. Both should be cleaned and sanitized after each use. The rails should be cleaned and sanitized weekly and treated with edible oil once a month.

Cooler walls should be cleaned and sanitized weekly or more often if necessary. Ideally, coolers should be equipped with brackets designed to keep all product 2 to 3 inches away from the cooler wall. This is not only important for sanitation purposes but also for proper circulation of refrigerated air around product in the cooler. Although the meat will not normally come into contact with the walls in such coolers, the walls serve as a source of contamination to hands, clothes, and the air, which in turn contaminates the meat.

The Display Area

Having a clean display case is important not only for sanitary reasons but also because of the impression it creates. The care taken in the cooler and processing areas will have little beneficial effect on sales if product is displayed in a soiled case.

Both the outside and inside of the display case should be wiped daily, using a clean cloth and a general alkaline cleaner. Any blood or moisture in the case should be wiped up with a clean cloth as observed during the day.

In many companies, the removable parts inside the case are washed and sanitized on Monday morning, before product has been returned to the case from the cooler. If a combination cleaner/sanitizer is not used, the racks and shelves in the case should be rinsed with hot water, washed with a brush in a detergent solution, rinsed again in hot water, sanitized, and then rinsed again.

Drain lines should be flushed out and coils and other concealed parts cleaned according to the manufacturer's directions. A properly cleaned case will maintain lower temperatures more consistently, which will enhance the shelf life of the product. In addition, electricity costs will be lower when refrigerated equipment functions properly, and maintenance costs also will be reduced.

PEOPLE AND SANITATION

Having an effective sanitation program requires an investment on management's part in the facilities, equipment, and materials that are necessary to do the job. Management, then, must be committed to high standards of sanitation and must provide the training and follow-through needed to ensure that the program is implemented at store level.

Unless employees are thoroughly indoctrinated with the concept of cleanliness and wholesomeness, they can be a major source of bacterial contamination. When a meat cutter receives a forequarter from a bacteria-laden truck, carries it against his dirty apron, hangs it on an unsanitized hook in the cooler, then removes a pork loin for processing, carrying it against the same apron, rests the pork loin on a box of ice-packed chickens while he bends down to recover a pencil he has dropped on the floor, retrieves the pencil from the dirty floor, and starts processing the loin, all without ever stopping to wash his hands, he has contaminated a considerable amount of product along the way, often without even being aware of the effect of his performance on product shelf life.

When an employee enters the store, he should place his coat and other personal possessions in a separate area away from the preparation area. Employees should don clean uniforms and wear hats or hair nets and masks if they have beards. They should wash their hands and arms every time they re-enter the department—when they start work, after a break, after lunch, after visiting the restroom, smoking a cigarette, etc.—using a medicated liquid soap or a nonmedicated soap followed by a sanitizer. They should also wash and sanitize their hands every time they pick up an item that has fallen on the floor and every time they begin work on a new commodity. For example, if a meat cutter has been slicing liver, he should wash and sanitize his hands, tools, and cutting surface before he changes to another commodity. Similarly, someone who handles the traying function should wash arms and hands when the product on the line-up changes. Scale operators, who generally do not touch the product, will not have to wash as frequently. Once an employee understands the nature of bacteria and how product becomes contaminated, the need for washing should become second nature.

The same principle applies to aprons, coats, or other linens. The frequency with which they should be changed during the day depends very much on the function the employee performs. An employee who grinds beef or slices liver will have a soiled apron before an employee who stocks the case. Employees who process heavy pieces of product, like breaking beef in the cooler, will normally accumulate considerable bacteria on their clothes and should change often. If an impression of cleanliness is to be created, any employee who comes in contact with the customer should change linens if they become soiled. It is shortsighted to save pennies on linens and to lose dollars on discolored product and dissatisfied customers.

Mesh gloves should be cleaned and sanitized at least three times daily, regardless of whether the cutter is changing from one commodity to another, because the construction of the gloves permits bacteria to accumulate. Of course, they must be cleaned and sanitized each time there is a change in the commodity being handled.

Standards for personal hygiene should be enforced. An employee should wear clean clothes and shoes and have clean hair, face, and fingernails. Obviously, there should be no spitting on floors or sneezing or coughing on product. When an employee does not cover a cough, it can be propelled at the force of 200 miles an hour and spread bacteria as far as 14 feet. An employee with a boil or open infection should not be allowed in the processing area or in any way be allowed to come into contact with product. Smoking and eating should be restricted to designated areas outside the department, and except for supervisors and management people, nonmeat department personnel should be prohibited from entering the department. Unsightly and unsanitary practices such as scratching the head, placing fingers in or about the mouth or nose, etc., should be prohibited.

The employee rest room should contain a sink, preferably with foot pedals to control the water flow, and a liquid, sanitized soap dispenser, a fingernail brush, and paper towels or a blower for drying hands. The rest room should be cleaned and sanitized daily, at a minimum.

Traditionally, when departments are short of labor dollars, sanitation is the first activity to suffer. However, this will not happen in companies that indoctrinate their supervisory and store level people in the concepts of wholesomeness and the profits that a sanitation program can bring. Manuals, slides, films, and workshops are important in getting the training done; but without regular inspections and follow-up, there will be considerable backsliding. The need for follow-up cannot be overemphasized. According to the head of meat operations of a major chain, "People need supervision in housekeeping and sanitation more than in any other part of the operation."

SAFETY

The need for adequate safety training programs has been given tremendous impetus since the passage of the Occupational Safety and Health Act of 1970. However, enlightened retailers have long understood the benefits of creating a safe environment for employees. A good safety program reduces absenteeism, cuts the cost of training replacements for injured workers, lowers workmen's compensation insurance premiums as well as premiums for other company-paid insurance benefits, and improves morale and productivity which suffer when the working atmosphere is poor and the accident rate is high. It also eliminates the risk of fines for occupational hazards for which retailers have been liable since 1971.

OSHA and NIOSH

OSHA, which stands for Occupational Health and Safety Administration, was created by the Williams-Steiger Occupational Safety and Health Act of 1970, which was signed in December, 1970, and became effective on April 28, 1971. The purpose of this landmark legislation is to assure safe and healthful working conditions for the nation's wage earners.

NIOSH, which stands for National Institute for Occupational Safety and Health, conducts the research to establish the standards enforced by OSHA. The administration and enforcement of the act are vested primarily in the Secretary of Labor through OSHA; research and related functions are vested in the Secretary of Health, Education and Welfare through NIOSH.

The law provides that each employer has the basic duty to furnish his employees jobs and a place of employment which are free from recognized hazards that are causes of or are likely to cause death or serious physical harm. The original act had extremely broad coverage in that it included "every business affecting commerce which has employees," except railroads and mining, which have their own federal safety and health laws. In 1974, however, due to a shortage of funds, inspection of firms with 25 or fewer employees, accounting for about 20 million workers, was temporarily eliminated.

The lack of adequate funding is one of the reasons federal inspectors have spent only 3 percent of their time inspecting retail firms. With fewer than 800 inspectors in the field to monitor more than five million businesses, the concentration has been on large industrial plants where the potential for hazardous conditions is greater. However, "meat and meat products" is included in OSHA's priority list of target industries.

Moreover, the act allows each state to administer the OSHA law. To qualify as administrator, a state must submit an approved plan to the Secretary of Labor, which, among other requirements, "must be at least as effective as the counterpart federal standards in providing safe and healthful employment."

Both management and labor have been critical of state plans, but for different reasons. Labor unions fear that the state plans will not adequately protect the employees. The Labor Department has reinforced management's concern by admitting that the spread of state plans presents "real operational problems for multi-state employers" who must comply with a variety of regulations. Despite these objections and the fact that only 16 states are currently operating federally-approved job safety and health plans, OSHA expects between 2,500 and 3,000 inspectors to be added during the next few years through the state programs, which will dramatically increase the number of inspections.

OSHA Requirements

On May 29, 1971, the 248-page book of OSHA standards was printed in the *Federal Register*. Although some standards are fairly simple to interpret—for example, "Aisles and passageways shall be kept clear and in good repair, with no obstruction across or in aisles that could create a hazard"—most are extremely complicated and subject to varying interpretations.

When the standards were first issued most retailers were at a loss to understand what they had to do to comply. Moreover, OSHA refused to conduct on-site educational inspections so that corrections could be made before formal inspection. OSHA inspectors had to issue citations and propose fines once they entered a work site and found violations, even though the request for an inspection was made by a retailer who wanted to comply.

OSHA's safety and health standards, which filled 325 pages in the *Federal Register* when recently republished, are still highly technical and sometimes impossible to decipher without expert help. In 1974, however, a proposal was approved by the House of Representatives creating a new class of OSHA employees called "consultants" who are permitted to visit work places and point out violations without issuing citations.

There are some provisions of the act which are quite clear. The first is, "Any employees who believe that a violation of a job safety or health standard exists may request an inspection by sending a signed, written notice to the Department of Labor." Moreover, "Within a reasonable time after issuance of a citation for a job safety or health violation, the Labor Department shall notify the employer by certified mail of the penalty, if any, which is proposed to be assessed. The employer then has 15 working days within which to notify the Department that he wishes to contest the citation or proposed assessment of penalty." If the employer takes no action within the 15-day period, the citation and assessment become final. If the employer files an objection, a hearing is provided before the Occupational Safety and Health Review Commission, whose findings are final if not appealed within 30 days. If an employer objects to the findings of the Commission, he can ask for a review in the United States Court of Appeals.

In addition to being liable to fines, employers must also correct violations within a "reasonable time." The time limit may be contested by either the employer or the employees within 15 days after a citation is issued, whereupon the review procedures begin anew.

"Willful or repeated violations of the act's requirements by employers may incur monetary penalties of up to $10,000 for each violation.... Any employer who fails to correct a violation for which a citation has been issued within the period prescribed therein may be penalized up to $1,000 each day the violation persists. A willful violation by an employer which results in the death of any employee is punishable by a fine of up to $10,000 or imprisonment for up to six months. A second conviction doubles these criminal penalties."

Inspectors have the authority to appear unannounced at a work place; however, the employer and employee have the right to accompany the inspector or to have their representatives do so.

Record-keeping is also an important part of compliance. The

basic forms to be maintained are identified as OSHA No. 100, 101, and 102.

Form No. 100 is the Log of Occupational Injuries and Illnesses on which each recordable occupational injury or illness must be entered within two working days after the injury or illness occurs. (See Figure 38.) The log must be kept current and retained for five years following the end of the calendar year to which the entries relate. Although OSHA sets no standard assessment fees, failure to maintain the log has resulted in a $100 fine (which cannot be appealed) in some areas of the country.

Form No. 101 is the Supplementary Record of Occupational Injuries and Illnesses and details the specifics on each incident entered on Form 100. (See Figure 39.) Under some circumstances, workmen's compensation, insurance, or other similar reports are acceptable in lieu of Form 101. The information must be available in the work place within six days of receipt of information that a recordable injury or illness occurred, and the records must be maintained for at least five years.

Form No. 102 (See Figure 40) is the annual Summary of Occupational Injuries and Illnesses. This is actually a summary of the information contained in Form No. 100. Form No. 102 must be posted in each establishment in a place accessible to all employees for 30 days, within one month following the end of the year, i.e., on February 1. Failure to complete Form No. 102 and/or failure to post the Form has resulted in $100 fines.

Any citation issued by an OSHA inspector will include the time allowed for correcting the violation. The citation must be posted until the violation is corrected or for three working days, whichever is the later date. Failure to post a citation at the work site for employees to see can result in a $500 fine.

Retailers must also post in a prominent place the official "Safety and Health Protection on the Job" poster furnished by OSHA. (See Figure 41.) This poster fills the requirement that "employees be informed of the job safety and health protection provided under the act." The poster briefly states the intent and coverage of the law and the responsibilities of employers and employees to maintain safe and healthful working conditions. Failure to post this notice can result in a $50 fine.

OSHA penalties for a first violation range from a few dollars up to $10,000, and have averaged about $25. While this is a relatively

FIGURE 38

safety and health protection on the job

The Williams-Steiger Occupational Safety and Health Act of 1970 provides job safety and health protection for workers through the promotion of safe and healthful working conditions throughout the Nation. Requirements of the Act include the following:

Employers: Each employer shall furnish to each of his employees employment and a place of employment free from recognized hazards that are causing or are likely to cause death or serious harm to his employees; and shall comply with occupational safety and health standards issued under the Act.

Employees: Each employee shall comply with all occupational safety and health standards, rules, regulations and orders issued under the Act that apply to his own actions and conduct on the job.

The Occupational Safety and Health Administration (OSHA) of the Department of Labor has the primary responsibility for administering the Act. OSHA issues occupational safety and health standards, and its Compliance Safety and Health Officers conduct jobsite inspections to ensure compliance with the Act.

Inspection: The Act requires that a representative of the employer and a representative authorized by the employees be given an opportunity to accompany the OSHA inspector for the purpose of aiding the inspection.

Where there is no authorized employee representative, the OSHA Compliance Officer must consult with a reasonable number of employees concerning safety and health conditions in the workplace.

Complaint: Employees or their representatives have the right to file a complaint with the nearest OSHA office requesting an inspection if they believe unsafe or unhealthful conditions exist in their workplace. OSHA will withhold names of employees complaining on request.

The Act provides that employees may not be discharged or discriminated against in any way for filing safety and health complaints or otherwise exercising their rights under the Act.

An employee who believes he has been discriminated against may file a complaint with the nearest OSHA office within 30 days of the alleged discrimination.

Citation: If upon inspection OSHA believes an employer has violated the Act, a citation alleging such violations will be issued to the employer. Each citation will specify a time period within which the alleged violation must be corrected.

The OSHA citation must be prominently displayed at or near the place of alleged violation for three days, or until it is corrected, whichever is later, to warn employees of dangers that may exist there.

Proposed Penalty: The Act provides for mandatory penalties against employers of up to $1,000 for each serious violation and for optional penalties of up to $1,000 for each nonserious violation. Penalties of up to $1,000 per day may be proposed for failure to correct violations within the proposed time period. Also, any employer who willfully or repeatedly violates the Act may be assessed penalties of up to $10,000 for each such violation.

Criminal penalties are also provided for in the Act. Any willful violation resulting in death of an employee, upon conviction, is punishable by a fine of not more than $10,000 or by imprisonment for not more than six months, or by both. Conviction of an employer after a first conviction doubles these maximum penalties.

Voluntary Activity: While providing penalties for violations, the Act also encourages efforts by labor and management, before an OSHA inspection, to reduce injuries and illnesses arising out of employment.

The Department of Labor encourages employers and employees to reduce workplace hazards voluntarily and to develop and improve safety and health programs in all workplaces and industries.

Such cooperative action would initially focus on the identification and elimination of hazards that could cause death, injury, or illness to employees and supervisors. There are many public and private organizations that can provide information and assistance in this effort, if requested.

More Information: Additional information and copies of the Act, specific OSHA safety and health standards, and other applicable regulations may be obtained from the nearest OSHA Regional Office in the following locations:

Atlanta, Georgia
Boston, Massachusetts
Chicago, Illinois
Dallas, Texas
Denver, Colorado
Kansas City, Missouri
New York, New York
Philadelphia, Pennsylvania
San Francisco, California
Seattle, Washington

Telephone numbers for these offices, and additional Area Office locations, are listed in the telephone directory under the United States Department of Labor in the United States Government listing.

Washington, D.C.
1973
OSHA 2003

Peter J. Brennan
Secretary of Labor

U. S. Department of Labor
Occupational Safety and Health Administration

FIGURE 39

OSHA No. 101　　　　　　　　　　　　　　　　　　　　　　　　　　　Form approved
Case or File No. _____　　　　　　　　　　　　　　　　　　　　OMB No. 44R 1453

Supplementary Record of Occupational Injuries and Illnesses

EMPLOYER

1. Name _____
2. Mail address _____
　　　　　　(No. and street)　　　　　(City or town)　　　　　(State)
3. Location, if different from mail address _____

INJURED OR ILL EMPLOYEE

4. Name _____ Social Security No. _____
　　(First name)　　(Middle name)　　(Last name)
5. Home address _____
　　　　　　(No. and street)　　　　　(City or town)　　　　　(State)
6. Age _____　　7. Sex: Male_____ Female_____ (Check one)
8. Occupation _____
　　(Enter regular job title, *not* the specific activity he was performing at time of injury.)
9. Department _____
　　(Enter name of department or division in which the injured person is regularly employed, even though he may have been temporarily working in another department at the time of injury.)

THE ACCIDENT OR EXPOSURE TO OCCUPATIONAL ILLNESS

10. Place of accident or exposure _____
　　　　　　(No. and street)　　　　　(City or town)　　　　　(State)
　　If accident or exposure occurred on employer's premises, give address of plant or establishment in which it occurred. Do not indicate department or division within the plant or establishment. If accident occurred outside employer's premises at an identifiable address, give that address. If it occurred on a public highway or at any other place which cannot be identified by number and street, please provide place references locating the place of injury as accurately as possible.
11. Was place of accident or exposure on employer's premises? _____ (Yes or No)
12. What was the employee doing when injured? _____
　　　　　　(Be specific. If he was using tools or equipment or handling material, name them and tell what he was doing with them.)
_____
13. How did the accident occur? _____
　　(Describe fully the events which resulted in the injury or occupational illness. Tell what happened and how it happened. Name any objects or substances involved and tell how they were involved. Give full details on all factors which led or contributed to the accident. Use separate sheet for additional space.)

OCCUPATIONAL INJURY OR OCCUPATIONAL ILLNESS

14. Describe the injury or illness in detail and indicate the part of body affected. _____
　　　　　　　　　　　　　　　　　　　　　　　(e.g.: amputation of right index finger at second joint; fracture of ribs; lead poisoning; dermatitis of left hand, etc.).
15. Name the object or substance which directly injured the employee. (For example, the machine or thing he struck against or which struck him; the vapor or poison he inhaled or swallowed; the chemical or radiation which irritated his skin; or in cases of strains, hernias, etc., the thing he was lifting, pulling, etc.)
_____
16. Date of injury or initial diagnosis of occupational illness _____
　　　　　　　　　　　　　　　　　　　　　　　(Date)
17. Did employee die? _____ (Yes or No)

OTHER

18. Name and address of physician _____
19. If hospitalized, name and address of hospital _____
_____
　　Date of report _____ Prepared by _____
　　Official position _____

FIGURE 40

OSHA No. 102

Form Approved
OMB No. 44R 1453

Summary

Occupational Injuries and Illnesses

Establishment Name and Address:

			Lost Workday Cases			Nonfatal Cases Without Lost Workdays*	
Injury and Illness Category		Fatalities	Number of Cases	Number of Cases Involving Permanent Transfer to Another Job or Termination of Employment	Number of Lost Workdays	Number of Cases	Number of Cases Involving Transfer to Another Job or Termination of Employment
Code 1	Category 2	3	4	5	6	7	8
10	Occupational Injuries						
	Occupational Illnesses						
21	Occupational Skin Diseases or Disorders						
22	Dust diseases of the lungs (pneumoconioses)						
23	Respiratory conditions due to toxic agents						
24	Poisoning (systemic effects of toxic materials)						
25	Disorders due to physical agents (other than toxic materials)						
26	Disorders due to repeated trauma						
29	All other occupational illnesses						
	Total—occupational illnesses (21-29)						
	Total—occupational injuries and illnesses						

*Nonfatal Cases Without Lost Workdays—Cases resulting in: Medical treatment beyond first aid, diagnosis of occupational illness, loss of consciousness, restriction of work or motion, or transfer to another job (without lost workdays).

FIGURE 41

small average, within a three-year period OSHA compliance officers made more than 159,000 inspections, issued 106,000 citations alleging over 549,000 violations, and proposed penalties totaling $13.7 million.

Between July, 1972 and June, 1973 alone, OSHA compliance officers conducted more than 2,500 inspections of wholesale and retail operations. Nearly 9,000 violations were cited, 63 percent involving machinery and machinery guarding, 21 percent for walking-working surfaces, 16 percent for electrical appliances, and 12 percent for fire protection violations. Machinery citations usually resulted from exposed fan blades and the lack of protection from hazards at the point of operation of a machine. Walking-working surface violations, such as the lack of orderly and clean work areas, were common to both retail and wholesale operations; however, wholesalers were often cited for lack of guarding on open-sided platforms and for improper stairway railings and guards. Electrical equipment is almost as common in stores and warehouses as in factories; and there were many citations for improper use, most often involving lack of grounding, installation in hazardous areas, frayed wiring, and exposed circuits and plugs. Improper position, marking, and maintenance of fire extinguishers brought other violations. (Extinguishers weighing less than 40 pounds must be installed so that the top of the extinguisher is not more than 5 feet above the floor. If an extinguisher weighs more than 40 pounds, the top cannot be more than $3\frac{1}{2}$ feet above the ground.)

Citations have also been issued for failure to have an interior door release mechanism in a cooler to prevent the possibility of anyone being accidentally locked in, and for the following: improperly guarded fans, failure to provide a covered receptacle in a lunch room or in a rest room used by women, the lack of an adequately trained person to administer first aid, pallet truck operators not wearing safety-toed shoes, vending machines not being grounded, keys not removed from switches of unattended industrial trucks, carrying loads on broken pallets, compressed air used for cleaning exceeding the allowable pressure, portable ladders with broken rungs, uncovered floor openings, exits narrower than 44 inches in width or locked exits without panic devices, failure to have a guard over the saw blade of a table saw, absence of grounds on electrical power tools, failure to provide guards on foot-controlled machines to prevent accidental tripping, failure to show evidence of efforts to properly train and educate workers in safety and health practices in relation to their jobs.

MEAT DEPARTMENT SAFETY

There is little doubt that the need for controlling meat department injuries remains great. Whereas 1 out of every 10 U.S. workers experienced job-related injury or illness, food stores had 12.1 injuries for 100 workers during 1972, according to figures released by the Bureau of Labor Statistics. Other retailers fared much better; 8.3 injuries for general merchandise stores, 5.5 injuries for furniture and home furnishing stores, and 2 injuries per 100 workers for apparel and accessory stores.

According to OSHA, the reason supermarkets have a relatively high accident rate is primarily the meat department with its machines, cutting equipment, and slippery floors. The problem is compounded by the weight of the product and the equipment necessary to move it, as well as the equipment needed for cutting, packaging, and pricing.

Some of the more frequently reported injuries result from the following, according to NIOSH:

1. Improper use of knives and saws when cutting meat.
   (a) Failure to adjust guard on band meat saw to proper height for a particular cut of meat.
   (b) Being careless with hand knives.
   (c) Knives not replaced in holders in back or on the side of the cutting table.

NIOSH requirements specify that "all machines and saws must be adequately fitted with proper machine guarding devices. Any attempt to bypass these guards is prohibited. All employees using this equipment should be thoroughly trained in its safe operation."

2. Improper lifting techniques.
   (a) Over-exerting oneself.
   (b) Failure to use materials-handling equipment.
   (c) Not using the proper muscles or having the proper weight distribution.
   (d) Stretching and being in an awkward position while lifting.

When lifting an object, it is recommended that the employee stand close to the load with feet spread for good balance. Then, bending the knees but keeping the back straight, the load should be gripped with both hands, and lifted slowly, letting the legs and not the back carry the weight. If it is necessary to turn with the load, the feet should be shifted first to avoid twisting the back.

Many companies now have their own safety inspectors visiting the stores, pointing out violations and ways they should be corrected. Checklists are also used to train the employee in safety procedures. A typical checklist might include the following precautions:

1. Store meat knives in racks when not in use.
2. Keep knives (and other cutting tools or equipment) sharpened. Dull blades require more pressure and increase the potential for an accident to occur.
3. Keep hands and handles of all tools dry and free from grease.
4. Hold tools with a firm grip.
5. Do not grab for a falling knife; move away and allow it to fall.
6. Carry tools at the side of the body, point facing downward.
7. Never lay a piece of meat over a knife or in any other way conceal the knife from view.
8. Wash, sanitize, and dry knives one at a time, with the sharp edge facing away from the hand.
9. Always cut down and away from the body.
10. Wear steel, mesh gloves when cutting with a knife.
11. Keep cutting table tops free from defects, excess tools, etc.
12. Do not operate any machinery unless guards are in place.
13. Properly guard all points of power transmission (e.g., belts and pulleys).
14. Be sure all fixed machinery (trimmers, meat saws, wrappers, etc.) are secure to prevent movement.
15. Do not allow hands and arms to cross when operating a slicing machine.
16. Use tamper when feeding product into the grinder.
17. Unplug power tools (saws, grinders, cubers, etc.) and observe safety precautions in dismantling for cleaning and sanitizing.

18. Turn off power saws and other equipment when not in use.
19. Periodically inspect hazardous pieces of equipment (tenderizers, slicing machines, grinders, bandsaws, knives, etc.) to ensure that the safety interlocks, guards, and electrical connections are in good working order.
20. Properly ground all electrical receptacles.
21. Cover and label all electrical control boxes and individual switches if their functions are not evident.
22. Store empty meat hooks safely in a remote place away from work and walking areas.
23. Align rail segments or joints and repair loose rails or switches or missing stops.
24. Keep the hot wire on the wrapping machine taut and maintain the roller so that the wrapping film is kept tight to provide a quick, clean cut with the least amount of fumes.
25. Keep wrapping and sealing equipment free of worn or frayed cords and turned off when not in use.
26. Do not reach into the exit end of a wrapper to grasp a package—the pusher will amputate fingers.
27. Turn off wrapping equipment before attempting to adjust a malfunction or to free a lodged package.
28. Do not wear ties (other than bow ties) or jewelry that can get caught in machinery; wear short sleeves or protect sleeves with elastic to prevent their being caught in machinery.
29. Keep floors free of holes and tripping hazards.
30. Keep floors clean and dry to prevent slipping.
31. Pick up any fallen object or product immediately and then wash and sanitize hands and arms.
32. Have adequate and properly protected lighting in work areas and cooler.
33. Carry large pieces of meat with flesh side against body to avoid skin cuts and scratches from bone splinters.
34. Lift heavy merchandise with emphasis on legs, not back.
35. Guard portable fans that are less than 7 feet from the floor with grille or mesh, limiting the openings to not more than $\frac{1}{2}$ inch.
36. Have first aid supplies available and kept in a sanitary manner.

37. Be sure that exit paths are maintained unobstructed, i.e., that there are no meat racks, broken-down cardboard boxes, or shopping carts accumulated in the path of egress.

Safety and sanitation go hand in hand. With proper safety precautions there will be fewer accidents, and those that do occur will result in fewer infections if the work area is kept clean and sanitary. Among companies that have effective programs, there has been a 10 percent decrease in absenteeism due to infections and virus-caused illnesses such as colds. As with sanitation, government pressure is the least important reason for maintaining an effective safety program. The rewards are immeasurable in terms of profits and morale.

11

Principles of Retail Operations

No company can measure successfully or control store level performance without establishing standards that spell out the firm's policies and procedures for operating the meat department. In most cases, the standards will represent those procedures which the company has found over the years to be most effective for turning a profit for the meat department. In other cases, the standards also encompass mandatory government regulations.

A major benefit derived from establishing standards is that it does away with variations in practices from one store to another, thus giving management greater overall control and facilitating the transfer of personnel to different stores within the company as they are needed.

Each company must establish its own standards, based on its own individual circumstances, for each area of meat department operations. Standards should certainly be set for areas such as receiving, temperature, sanitation and safety, production scheduling, retail cutting and trimming, trimmings for ground meat, ground meat, rehandling product, packaging materials, weighing and pricing, code-dating and shelf life, product availability, display height and width, special orders, customer service, inventory control, controllable expenses, and legal compliance.

RECEIVING

The basic standards for receiving involve following proper unloading procedures, checking the product for quality and condition against company specifications, checking the quantity delivered against the invoice, placing the product under refrigeration, and maintaining a product rotation system in the cooler.

The responsibility of the receiver should include getting the product off the truck as quickly as possible so that warm air does not enter the truck and so that the truck can move on to its next stop without undue delay. This is especially true when a company delivers in its own vehicles. Rapid unloading is also desirable from the standpoint of maintaining proper internal temperatures of product by reducing the exposure, particularly during the warmer months, to outside air. In southern climates, this is a year-round problem and care should be given to rapid unloading, checking the product, and placing it under refrigeration in the store cooler as quickly as possible.

Each company should establish standards for the acceptable temperature of the product when it is received, and the receiving clerk should have an internal thermometer available for that purpose. Standards for receiving temperatures are important because, more often than not, fresh products are delivered at higher than the ideal internal temperature of 32° F. It is not unusual for a beef supplier, for example, to make as few as 6 or as many as 12 stops on a delivery route. In warmer weather especially, each time the truck door is opened the product picks up some of the outside heat so that by the last stop the internal temperature of the product could be as high as 50° F. The buyer can, of course, pressure the supplier to make fewer stops or to deliver in refrigerated trucks with air curtains covering the doors. However, the company should establish standards so that the receiving clerk will know whether to accept or reject a shipment.

The weights of all product shipped direct by a supplier should be carefully verified, while product received from a company's own distribution center should be spot checked for weight, counted, and checked against the receiving document. It is best to weigh all rail stock, even when the company operates a distribution center.

Product should go directly from the truck to the cooler and not remain in the receiving area except for the time required for weighing. The cooler should be made ready for receiving before the order is delivered. Space should be cleared in the area of the cooler where the product is to be stored, and merchandise should be code-dated when it is received to ensure proper rotation. When boxed product of any type is received, the date of receipt should be written on the outside of the container. As far as hanging stock is concerned (beef, veal, and lamb), the product should be so positioned on the rails that rotation is guaranteed.

TEMPERATURE

If separate coolers are used, cooler temperatures should be maintained as close to 32° F. as possible for all fresh meats and at 40° F. for smoked and luncheon meats. Although 32° F. is acceptable for holding chicken, a more ideal temperature is 28° F. If all product is stored in one cooler, the temperature should be held as close to 32° F. as possible. At lower temperatures beef and veal, in particular, will harden and become difficult to cut. Higher temperatures will increase the growth rate of bacteria and cause discoloration and shrinkage, which can be very costly. Therefore, it is in the interest of every profit-minded company to maintain cooler temperatures at between 30° and 32° F. Additionally, relative humidity should be maintained at 80 to 85 percent; at lower humidity levels the refrigeration will draw moisture from the product, drying it out and thereby creating shrinkage and discoloration.

There are many differences of opinion regarding the ideal standard for temperatures in the store processing area. In relatively few companies, the processing area is maintained at 32° to 35° F., or the processing is actually performed in the cooler with the packaging being done outside. If concern for the product were the sole determinant, 32° to 35° F. would be an ideal temperature for the processing area. Practically, however, operators must also take into account the increased labor costs (in some companies union contracts require higher labor rates to be paid at any temperature below 50° F.) as well as the higher absenteeism due to illness and the lower productivity that results from working in such cold temperatures and high humidity.

At the other extreme are those companies that operate the processing area at room temperature, around 70° F. The surface temperature of retail cuts and trimmings left exposed to such temperatures for more than an hour can pick up as much as 10° to 15° of the room temperature, depending on how the product is being worked. For example, if the trimmings being worked up from the breaking operation are few, and they are scattered over a large trimming table, they will pick up more of the room temperature than if the trimmings are plentiful and piled on top of each other. This is so because the density of the product in the latter case will insulate it against the room temperature, lessening the exposure to the heat. But the surface temperature of such product, left out for even a half hour, will probably pick up 4° or 5°. The most serious effect of higher temperatures on all product, but especially on trimmings which are highly perishable, is the rapid increase in bacteria growth and discoloration.

According to the study conducted by the University of Missouri Extension Division in cooperation with the U. S. Department of Agriculture, "Cutting, processing, and wrapping-room temperatures should be maintained below 40° F., if possible. Relative humidities of 60-70 percent will help maintain worker comfort at these temperatures."[1] But even at a temperature of 40° F., the appearance of the product is enhanced, shelf life is lengthened, and rewraps and shrinkage are less than if processed at higher temperatures. Moreover, some companies report that productivity is higher at the 40° F. temperature range than at 32° F. This is especially true when forced-air refrigeration is used. In order to operate at 32° F. (or even at 40° F.) and maintain acceptable productivity levels, gravity coil refrigeration should be used to eliminate the worker discomfort that results from drafts caused by forced-air refrigeration.

Processing can be performed at up to 50° F. if the operation is properly controlled, i.e., if the product is processed quickly and then returned immediately to the display case or the cooler. This means that only a minimum amount of product should be brought into a 50° F. processing area—that amount of meat that can be processed within a short period of time. Production requirements should be

---
[1] Naumann, et. al., p. 13.

determined and quarters broken into primals to fill one day's needs. Ideally, if 15 chuck primals are needed for processing into retail cuts, the beef quarters should be broken into primals on the rail in the 32° F. cooler for proper temperature control and for ease in handling (whole quarters generally weigh more than 150 pounds). The chuck primals should be brought to the power saw operation two or three at a time on tree hooks. If only a limited number of saw-ready primals are processed into retail cuts on the power saw and trimmed with a knife in the 50° F. processing area, the product temperature should rise by no more than 2° or 3° before being returned to the display case or cooler, which is acceptable. If exposed to 50° F. or warmer temperatures for longer periods of time, the danger of spoilage and shrinkage increases rapidly.

Store coolers are engineered to hold internal temperatures, but not to bring them down. Over a 24-hour period, a hindquarter with an internal temperature of 50° F., placed in a 32° F. cooler, will have its temperature reduced by only 1° or 2°. Because of the density of the product, the internal temperature is lowered very slowly. While the temperature of a retail cut, because it has less density, should be capable of being brought down more readily than the temperature of a forequarter or a hindquarter, this does not always occur. If there is insulation on the product, such as packaging materials, or if the packages are stacked on top of one another, it will take longer to bring the temperature down, or it may not be possible to reduce the temperature at all. Thus, it is imperative that product be returned quickly to the cooler or display case if processing areas are maintained at 50° F. or higher.

The secret to the success of any beef operation is to receive product at the proper internal temperature of 32° to 40° F. and not to leave it exposed to higher temperatures for any considerable length of time. Display cases for fresh meat should be set so that product is held at about 32° to 35° F., or just above freezing level. Lower temperatures will cause freezing because of the thinness of some retail cuts, while higher temperatures will have an adverse effect on shelf life. Except for chickens, this temperature is ideal for all non-frozen product. The recommended temperature for chickens is 28° to 30° F. This lower temperature may cause an ice crust to form over the chicken, but it will not cause discoloration.

Although 32° F. is also ideal for luncheon meats, a temperature of 35° or 36° F. is acceptable if the product is vacuum packaged.

Frozen product, on the other hand, should be held in cases maintained at 0° to −10° F. Most cases available today are engineered with sufficient coiling, coiling surface, and refrigerant to operate at 0° or −10° F. without ice crystals forming on the product.

SANITATION AND SAFETY

There is ample reason to believe that in this era of environmental concern and consumerism, stringent government standards covering sanitation conditions in retail meat operations are not far off. However, any company that awaits such regulations before establishing its own effective sanitation program will long since have lost far more in profit dollars than such a program would cost.

While some companies use outside services for cleaning sales areas, it is more typical for meat department personnel to perform the work required to clean and sanitize the department, with the manager being responsible for seeing that the work gets done properly.

Because cleaning and sanitizing schedules will vary from one store to another, depending on the processing functions performed, physical layout, equipment, etc., they must be set for each store on an individual basis. Safety standards, on the other hand, are subject to fewer variations. For recommended sanitation and safety standards see Chapter 10.

PRODUCTION SCHEDULING

For maximum efficiency, each company must make available to its meat cutters (and especially new employees) its standards covering the amount of product to be processed in any given production run and the sequence in which various types of product are to be processed.

It is not unusual for a department to be out of stock on one or several items when the store opens. This could be caused by poor forecasting and scheduling the previous day, by a late delivery, or perhaps by an unusually good response to an advertised item. The tendency will be to fill in that product immediately.

However, the first item to be processed in the production run is ground meat, regardless of the status of the rest of the display case. Ground meat is the one item on which there is rarely sufficient saleable product carried over from the day before. Since it is one of the highest turnover items, no store should be out of stock on freshly ground meat when the doors open.

If there is only one person available in the department to process product, the rewraps should be handled after the ground meat requirements are filled because the number of rewraps may affect the day's production requirements. Moreover, rewraps should be put back on display as soon as possible to facilitate their sale. Ideally, rewraps should be pulled and processed throughout each day so that there are few in the case in the morning.

Rewraps that are on hand in the morning should be handled immediately after the ground meats because if they are left in the backroom out of refrigeration until other processing is completed, they will further discolor. Moreover, if they are placed in the cooler, there is a possibility that they will be forgotten and not worked on at all and eventually will have to be discarded.

After the ground meat requirements and rewraps are completed, the meat cutter should then do the processing required to fill the case needs for those items that are out of stock. For example, a store may have had an exceptionally good sale on pork the previous day and consequently be out of stock on pork, but have enough beef cuts prepared to meet the demand for a couple of hours. Under those circumstances, what is needed for the counter should be processed first, but not the full production run to fill the total requirements for the day. Those pork items that are needed to fill the counter should be run and then the rest of the processing of the pork primal handled in its logical sequence in the production run later in the day. A sufficient quantity of the out-of-stock item should be processed to allow the department to have product available up until the regularly scheduled time for processing that product.

When a department opens with two cutters, one man should process the ground meat while the second man handles the rewraps, giving the first man those rewrap conversions that will go into ground meat. If there are third or fourth men in the department, they should simultaneously be handling the out-of-stock items.

When the counter is adequately stocked on all items, those products that can be processed the quickest should be handled next. Veal and lamb would fall into this category. Since very little of those items are needed, they should be processed very early in the day and gotten out of the way. If they are not, chances are that once the meat cutters get into the more time-consuming items, they will never get back to processing the lamb and veal.

After the veal and lamb cutting is completed, the amount of product needed to meet the day's needs should be processed on each item, with trimmings being handled at the same time. For example, the manager should know how many beef loins he will need for the day, and all the loins should be processed at one time. The same procedure would be followed on ribs and on each of the other products. Trimmings normally accumulate as primals are broken down into retail cuts. These trimmings should be prepared for further processing as the primal is broken down; i.e., dark surfaces should be removed and discarded and lean meat should be segregated for later conversion to cubed steaks, stew meat, or ground meat. Because there are more trimmings from the chuck than from any other beef primal, it is advisable to process the chucks last to minimize the length of time that these trimmings are left out of refrigeration.

The amount of product that accumulates at the wrapping station will fluctuate from time to time during each day because the workloads for retail cutting and for wrapping and pricing vary from one type of product to another. A balance must be struck so that there is sufficient product to keep the wrappers and pricers busy while those stations are manned, but not so much that product is left exposed to warm temperatures for too long a period of time.

The meat manager should write down on his production schedule or cutting list the exact number of rounds, ribs, loins, chucks, and so on that are to be processed, and in so doing should take into account the lunch hours of the cutters and wrappers. The cutters should always go to lunch before the wrappers so that the meat is not left in the processing area any longer than necessary. The production line should be full when the cutters go to lunch, and the cut product should be wrapped, priced, and placed under refrigeration by the wrappers by the time the cutters return and the wrappers go to lunch. The ideal condition every meat department should strive for is never to have any product out from under refrigeration unless it is being worked on.

RETAIL CUTTING AND TRIMMING

Standards relating to the acceptable fat and bone trim on retail cuts will vary from company to company depending on what the customer demands and what the company can afford, profit-wise, in relation to its competition.

In some companies, no more than ¼ inch of surface fat is allowed on beef, pork, and lamb; in other companies, the allowance is ⅜ or ½ inch. Some companies also set standards for internal fat whereby if the fat content is more than ½ inch on any one facing, the fat is cut out if it can be removed without cutting into the meat. Additionally, there are standards for removing certain bones. For example, in order to give the customer better value, those companies that do a good trim job on sirloins will have as part of their standard the removal of one of the two flat bones and the in-between seam. Most companies establish policies on the length of the tail on steaks such as T-bone and porterhouse; similar policies are established for veal and lamb chops. Because of the objectionable appearance of glands, many companies will set as a standard removing the glands from various retail cuts (for example, from a leg of lamb or from certain pork cuts) in which the gland is exposed. These glands must be removed when retail cuts are made because to do so earlier would gouge the primal, making it difficult to cut and causing more shrinkage.

While proper training will reduce the number of miscuts (i.e. cuts that do not meet company standards), realistically they cannot be eliminated completely. For example, even a highly skilled cutter, working on a bone-in round roast, will not be able to tell exactly, within ¼ inch, where the bone will start changing shape. As he gets further down into the round primal, the bone gets larger and the cutter finds himself with a roast that has a small bone on one side and a large bone on the other side.

In some meat departments, attempts are made to camouflage such miscuts by placing the large-bone side of the meat down, thus hiding it from the customer. Such practices are really shortsighted because the customer will be disappointed when she opens the package at home. Companies or stores that engage in such misrepresentation can do the industry considerable harm.

Each company should set standards for the size and shape of each cut and policies for disposing of miscuts. In the case of the roast described above, the first standard should be that a bone-in round

Principles of Retail Operations

roast (or steak) must have a round bone. If the bone loses its round shape, the cutter has cut too deeply and the result is a miscut. Practical standards would be to (1) convert the roast to another cut, or (2) remove the bone entirely and sell it as a boneless cut.

Another typical example of a miscut is a steak that is cut thin at one end and thick at the other, making it impossible for the customer to broil it to an even degree of doneness. The company should set standards for the allowable thickness and uniformity of such cuts.

The method of processing cuts should also be standardized. For example, if the chine bone on a loin is discolored, the discolored portion of the bone should be removed. The proper procedure is to face the bone on the saw and to set the guide, which controls the thickness of the cut, to ensure that only the discoloration on the bone is removed. However, in order to save time, a meat cutter will often face the chine bone on the saw without setting the guide. He then usually saws off both meat and bone because he cannot properly run the whole primal through the saw if the guide is not set. With porterhouse and T-bone steaks retailing at 12 to 15 cents an ounce, such miscuts can be quite costly. They can be minimized if the company enforces the standard of facing bones on the saw with the guide in place.

If a miscut does occur, it should be worked up into the next best cut that will bring the most profit; for example, beef steaks should be converted into cubed steaks or stew beef. The most important factor in handling miscuts is to be sure that they are corrected before they are placed in the display case. Not only will offering them for sale cause customer dissatisfaction, but more often than not, they will be passed over by the customer, start to discolor, and result in unnecessary shrinkage and loss of product.

If a miscut does get into the display case, a meat manager who is functioning properly will spot it immediately and remove it from the case before it becomes too discolored to salvage any profit from it. If the miscut is allowed to remain in the case to the point where it becomes badly discolored, it may have to be discarded, which will thereby represent a total loss to the company.

Some companies set up a special display section of reduced price items. Because such sections are unattractive and detract from the image and appearance of the department, this policy is not recommended. If a steak, for example, becomes discolored and cannot be faced off, it should be rewrapped, reduced in price, perhaps by 20 percent, and placed back in the case in the regular steak section.

There is an adage among meat merchandisers that "the first loss is the best loss." Managers who adhere to this line of thinking realize that it is far better to take a loss (either through a markdown or converting the product) while an item is still saleable, than to try to wait until an unsuspecting customer picks it up at its regular price. What happens is that the item eventually has to be converted or discarded. Even worse, if the item is sold at its regular price, this can lead to a disappointed customer who will shop elsewhere the next time.

Overtrimming and undertrimming refer to the amount of fat or waste that remains on the product when it is placed in the display case. If a T-bone that retails at $1.89 a pound is overtrimmed by 1 ounce, the loss to the company will be close to 12 cents, far more than the net profit on the item. When that figure is multiplied by the number of T-bones sold throughout the company's stores, the loss is substantial. Trimming with a knife will reduce the possibilities of overtrimming. Any experienced meat supervisor should be able to tell, simply by looking at the product, whether it has been trimmed according to the company's standards. And if properly trained, as he should be, the store manager would have the same ability.

When meat departments show poor profits, overtrimming and undertrimming are often the culprits. Overtrimming reduces the weight of the product and thus the profit, while undertrimming affects sales velocity through customer rejection of items with too much fat or waste.

Trim standards are often abused by overzealous, profit-minded managers. Those showing low profits will be especially inclined to leave more fat on a lamb chop or more tail on a steak in an attempt to improve their bottom-line figures. Undertrimming is always tempting, e.g., most companies try to balance the movement of cuts by establishing pricing practices that encourage the movement of items in low demand. Nevertheless, because of variations in customer preferences, the percentage of each type of cut sold in each store will vary. When a store has an unbalanced movement, there is a temptation to vary trim practices to get balanced movement. For example, a meat manager will leave extra fat or bone on the fastest moving cuts.

There is also a tendency for meat personnel to change trim standards on advertised items. This is not only dishonest to the customer, but it also sabotages the company's advertising efforts and eventually affects sales because the customer is not easily fooled. Shipping primals and subprimals has eliminated some of the problems that relate to miscuts in the breaking operation at store level; however, miscuts that occur at store level can only be controlled by proper supervision. Thus, it is to management's benefit not only to set standards, but also to see that they are enforced rigidly in all stores regardless of variations in profits among the stores.

TRIMMINGS FOR GROUND MEAT

The most important standard to follow on trimmings is to be sure that they are clean and fresh. Trimmings will be clean if all discolored portions of the meat have been trimmed off and discarded and if proper attention has been given to rotation and to temperature and sanitation controls. Trimmings for ground meat should be lean, with as much excess fat (i.e., in excess of the fat-lean ratio desired) trimmed off as possible.

The sales volume that a company can generate on ground meat will govern how lean the trimmings should be. When ground meat sales are greater than the amount of product that can be generated from the trimmings, more fat can be left in the trimmings. When this is done, frozen lean meat must be added to bring the trimmings up to the desired fat-lean ratio. Conversely, if ground meat volume is low, compared to total beef sales, rather than buying extra lean meat, the trimmings are made leaner by discarding the excess fat which cannot be used up in the trimmings. In either case, the minimum standards for the ratio of fat to lean must be maintained. In addition, by trimming meat lean, a company with sufficient ground meat volume that buys beef in carcass form can buy a higher percentage of straight carcasses.

Many companies have difficulty moving such cuts as briskets and plates from the straight carcass and therefore purchase the other cuts that they can move in primal form, as they are needed. However, by trimming the briskets and plates lean, these cuts can be used up as trimmings for ground meat, enabling the store to move the whole carcass and to buy fewer primals, thereby reducing product cost and improving gross margins.

Those trimmings that can be converted into more expensive items should be worked up first. Trimmings should be separated as they are being worked on so that regular trimmings are reserved for the lowest priced ground meat (commonly labeled "hamburger") and the leaner trimmings are used for the more expensive ground meats (usually labeled "ground chuck" or "ground round"). Every company should set standards on how to trim so that stew beef or cubed steak materials are taken from the trimmings first. When the lowest priced ground meat sells at 89 cents a pound, against $1.58 for cubed steak or $1.24 for stew meat, it is obvious that considerable profits will be lost if such cuts find their way into ground meat trimmings. This is one of the most critical sources of lost profits in the typical meat department. Because of the additional processing required and because some companies place undue emphasis on controlling labor costs, meat managers often neglect these high-profit items, with the result that they are not presented for sale and gross profits are lower than they should be. For those companies, this is an area that offers excellent opportunities for improving profits.

Excess fat is generally sold in either of two ways: (1) through the display counter in retail packages at approximately 19 to 29 cents per pound, or (2) to a renderer at considerably less. Although there is only a limited amount of fat that is saleable as a retail product, obviously the more that can be sold to the customer, rather than to the renderer, the greater the profit opportunity. Fat, as well as bones for soup, should be packaged immediately if they are to be sold to the retail customer, and some should be kept on display at all times. Fat and bones sold to a renderer should be separated as they accumulate in the trimming operation, because they are sold at different prices, and kept under refrigeration until picked up by the renderer. Any fat that is not to be sold should be discarded immediately.

In the winter months particularly, ground suet can be sold through the retail counter at a higher price than the renderer offers. Many customers use it to make suet puddings or bird balls. The latter are made by sprinkling bird seed into the suet, rolling it into balls, and running a string through the ball which can be tied to a tree to feed birds. Moreover, a number of people buy suet as a substitute for fats and oils, and certain ethnic groups purchase it in meaningful quantities.

The ideal way to keep trimmings fresh is constantly to have a minimum on hand—that is, to be constantly in need of trimmings. If trimmings are not moving well, they should be placed in containers, such as plastics lugs or clean cardboard boxes, with a maximum of 60 pounds per lug, covered with freezer paper, and frozen until they are needed. If more than 60 pounds of trimmings are placed in one lug, there is a possibility that those in the interior will sour before the meat hardens and freezes. Moreover, when the frozen trimmings are needed, they should be processed in the same manner as frozen lean meat; the frozen block should be cut on the saw without being thawed. Frozen blocks weighing more than 60 pounds will create difficulties in handling. Trimmings that are not thoroughly covered with freezer paper will suffer freezer burn and discoloration.

Some companies set a standard of not having more than a day and a half's supply of trimmings in the cooler at any time. This is an ideal inventory. Often, a considerable amount of trimmings will accumulate from a beef item sale. If, for example, the company has a sale on chucks, it is unlikely that the need for trimmings for ground meat will keep pace with the amount of trimmings available from the forequarters or chucks. If those trimmings are placed in the cooler, by the time they are needed they might well be old and still more trimmings will have accumulated so that the store will always be using old trimmings. Therefore, it is wise not to have more than a day and a half's supply on hand and to freeze all excess trimmings.

GROUND MEAT

Because ground meat is a major traffic draw, it is the heart of any meat operation; but it is also the most perishable fresh meat item carried in the department. For these reasons, there should be clear-cut standards that spell out the company's policies on discoloration, fat-lean ratios, and regrinding.

While ground meats could have a shelf life of up to 48 hours under ideal sanitation and refrigeration conditions, such conditions do not exist in most supermarkets today, and ground meats start to discolor within 6 to 8 hours in most stores. Much, of course, depends on the condition of the trimmings that go into the ground meats. In stores that carefully control the quality of their trimmings, as well as their sanitation and refrigeration, ground meats will usually not discolor in less than 24 hours.

To guard against discoloration, it is wise to grind meat a minimum of twice daily. The last grind is the most important grind. It should be small in quantity but sufficient to ensure that there will be some product available to the last customer, in at least one of the three price ranges.

Because ground meat is so vital to the success of the store, most companies have a policy that it must never be sold out when the store closes. If the product is properly handled and ground late in the afternoon, it will be saleable the next morning. Therefore, planning the last grind so that it results in a minimum carry-over will ensure that the store will not be out of stock at closing time or when the store opens in the morning.

When product is not properly handled, packaged ground meat inventory carried over from one day to the next will usually show some discoloration, depending on the sanitation, refrigeration, and trimming controls. Some companies have a policy of regrinding such carried-over ground meat with the first batch ground in the morning. The ideal standard is never to regrind meat, but rather to handle it properly at the beginning so that it does not discolor. If, despite all efforts, it does discolor, a standard should be set for disposing of it. If it is no longer wholesome, it should be discarded. If it merely lacks eye appeal, in some companies it will be discarded and in others it will be reduced in price by, for instance, one-third and returned to its regular location in the display case. Other companies will sell discolored ground meat to outlets such as restaurants or drastically reduce the price and sell it as pet food. How best to dispose of the product will depend on the degree of discoloration. Because this is a matter of judgment, close and careful supervision is required.

The standard to never regrind meat is one of the most difficult policies to control in the meat department because it creates a conflict in objectives for the meat manager. On the one hand he is under pressure to build profits, and on the other hand he is instructed never to offer the customer less than optimum quality. To achieve one of these goals means the other will suffer. But this very common problem can be solved easily by following the prescribed methods for handling and processing ground meat so that there is no need to regrind.

The eye appeal of ground meat is also affected by its fat-lean ratio. While it is a government regulation to have a minimum of 70 percent lean in any meat labeled ground meat or hamburger, each company must set its own standard to suit the needs of its customers. In some areas, 70 percent lean hamburger will be too fat to merchandise effectively, and the company will set a standard of 72 or 75 percent lean and 28 or 25 percent fat. Some companies set a standard of 80 percent lean for meat labeled ground chuck and 90 percent lean for meat labeled ground round. Originally the various names used for ground meats reflected the sections of the carcass from which they were cut and, hence, their value. Ground meat from the round is the leanest because meat from this section of the carcass contains the least fat. Ground chuck is fatter than ground round and ground sirloin falls between the round and the chuck in fat content but traditionally carries a higher price because it comes from the loin-sirloin section, ordinarily highest in value. However, in an attempt to utilize trimmings and keep costs and prices down, over the years most retailers have balanced the content of their specifically-labeled ground beef with trimmings from other parts of the carcass. Thus, meat labeled ground round will often contain trimmings from the chuck or loin.

Most experts believe that the most important factor in ground beef is the lean-to-fat ratio, not the point of origin. The Meat Identification Standards Committee has, therefore, recommended the use of the singular, all-inclusive "ground beef" name, with the lean-to-fat ratio indicated on the label as "not less than X percent lean." In those companies where the descriptive "ground round" or "ground chuck," etc. have merchandising impact, it is recommended that the package be labeled, "ground beef round, not less than 90 percent lean," or "ground beef chuck, not less than 80 percent lean," etc., depending on the lean-to-fat standard that the company has established.

It is therefore recommended that the actual lean content be maintained at a level higher than shown on the label to allow for a margin of error. The mixture of trimmings is usually a judgmental decision based on visual observation. In making hamburger, for example, the man grinding the meat "guesses" at how much fat and lean to grind to produce a 70-30 ratio.

Some companies use color charts as a guide for meat managers to compare fat-lean ratios, using one for hamburger, another for ground chuck, one for ground round, etc. A color chart is a far better control method than using past experience and judgment alone. However, whether the hamburger contains 70 percent lean is still a matter of judgment unless sample tests are made of each batch ground to ensure the proper ratio. Some allowance should therefore be made to account for errors in judgment. For this reason, many companies establish a standard of 72 or 75 percent lean as a minimum for hamburger. Moreover, such a standard gives the customer a better quality product and less shrinkage when the ground meat is cooked. The standards for the higher priced ground meats are also set above the minimum acceptable levels to allow for errors. What is most important is that there is a difference in lean content that corresponds with the price differences among the types of ground meat offered for sale. The most expensive ground meats should not only look leaner, but the customer also should be assured that she is getting the value promised in the higher priced item.

REHANDLING PRODUCT

The amount of product requiring rehandling can have a major impact on department profitability. A study on rewraps in five stores showed that the average number of rehandled packages ranged from 12.6 to 28 percent of new packages of meat wrapped—an average of 21.8 percent. Typically, 218 of every 1,000 packages wrapped required rehandling, and 80 percent resulted from the packages being out of date. The second major cause for rewraps was discolored product, followed by bloody or torn packages. Of the rehandled items, 3.6 percent were disposed of as trash, 7.5 percent suffered price reductions, and 24.3 percent were converted to ground meat.

In another study on rewraps, 17 percent of the packages required rehandling and 98 percent of them were out-of-date packages. Of 10,370 rehandled packages, 14.3 percent had to be disposed of as trash, 17.5 percent were put into ground meats, and 11.2 percent were reduced in price. In both studies, the remaining packages were rewrapped and returned to the case at the same price per pound.

The percent of product requiring rehandling is usually shocking to the managements of those firms that have measured this factor. The one out of five packages requiring rehandling in the first study is an extremely high figure; however, it is due in part to the fact that these are low-volume stores, i.e., doing less than $15,000 weekly meat volume. In higher-volume stores, the rehandling ratio is usually much lower. In one major regional chain in which the average weekly meat volume exceeds $30,000 per store, rehandled packages run less than 5 percent.

Rehandling costs are divided into two major categories. The first, and by far the most serious, is loss in value of the product requiring rehandling. The other significant cost of rehandling product relates to the labor and materials usually required. If not properly controlled, the combined losses will cause a serious profit drain.

Thus, a manager who is skillful in ordering prepackaged product in the proper quantity, who properly schedules product requiring processing through the cutting and packaging operation to meet anticipated customer demand, who enforces company standards on cutting techniques, wrapping practices, and sanitation and temperature control, and who insists on proper rotation of all items will keep to a minimum the serious losses that occur when rehandled packages are marked down, converted to ground beef or to other lower priced items, or thrown in the trash barrel. He will effectively control not only the dollar losses in package value, but also the increased supply and labor costs that rehandling entails.

PACKAGING MATERIALS

In order to control costs, reduce rewraps, and guarantee optimum appearance of the retail package, standards should be set so that the type and size of the film and trays used in each store are uniform and so that the size of both packaging materials properly match the size of the product being packaged. Using film that is too small for the tray or trays that are too small for the product increases the need for rewraps. For example, when a rump roast is placed in a smaller than optimum-sized tray, blood and drippings will seep down the sides of the film and underneath the package, affecting not only that item but also adjacent items and those beneath the leaking package, as well as the cleanliness of the display case.

Ideally, the company should set standards that detail which type or size of tray and film are to be used for each cut. Such standards of uniformity are especially valuable when there are a number of people performing the traying and wrapping functions in the department and this information should, therefore, be carried at each traying and wrapping station.

If a store is equipped with a shrink tunnel, it will use shrink film, but the film in most popular use today is stretch film. Here, too, the company should limit the number of film sizes that can be used and should set guidelines for the film width to be used on each package.

In some areas, see-through plastic trays are mandatory; however, when given the option, most companies will specify foam trays because they enhance the appearance of the product. This is especially true for cuts that have a tendency to bleed, such as boneless roasts or round steaks. When foam trays are used, "soakers" can be placed under the product to absorb the blood. When plastic trays are used, the blood is allowed to accumulate in the bottom of the tray because using soakers would be even more unsightly. Additionally, when products such as pork chops are shingled or overlapped in the tray, little more than bone and fat are visible on the underside, again making for an unattractive package in a plastic tray. Many companies feel that there is a lower incidence of discolored product when foam trays are used and that the visibility that plastic trays are intended to provide is considerably diminished after the film has been heat sealed to the tray. Yet, there are other companies that have had excellent results using see-through trays. When given the option, each company should set its standards based on its own experience with different packaging materials.

Any company that operates a dry grocery warehouse should carry an inventory of packaging materials from which the meat manager can draw according to his needs. If that is not possible and the manager orders directly from a supplier, the company's requirements should be given to the supplier, specifying the authorized types and sizes of trays and films that may be purchased.

WEIGHING AND PRICING

One area of government inspection that is diligently policed is that of weights and measures. Government inspectors (city, county, state, and/or federal) regularly spot check retail packages to be sure that the weight indicated on the label is the same as the weight of the product.

Since the customer may not be charged for the packaging materials, standards are set indicating the "tare" allowance for each size tray and film used. The scale is set so that it automatically computes the net product weight shown on the package label.

Furthermore, all fresh meat items lose weight after being packaged as retail cuts. The weight is lost in the form of moisture (through evaporation or the flow of juices) which can escape through the film, cling to the inside of the film, be absorbed by the tray, or accumulate in the tray. In some states, the law prescribes that product and label weight must agree at the time of packaging; in other states, the regulation covers the weight of the contents of the package when it is sold.

When regulations cover the weight of the product at the time of sale, an allowance must be made for the natural loss of weight of the product from the time it is packaged until the time it is rung up at the register. The shrinkage allowance should be set based on the number of days the company allows a product to remain in the display case. For example, it is wise to allow for three days' shrinkage if all items must be removed from the case, rewrapped, and relabeled (reweighed) after three days. Even though the customer who buys the item the day it is put on display will get more net weight than she is paying for, in the long run this is the safest procedure to follow.

Since products lose weight at varying rates, different shrinkage allowances should be set for each product and added on to the tare weight (in those states where it is required). Tare and shrinkage allowances should be given to the pricing clerk as two separate figures, rather than as a combined total. This disallows for errors in weighing and pricing the package if the wrapper does not use the tray size that has been standardized for the product. Thus, a clerk should be instructed to allow, say, .03 pounds tare for a number 8S tray and film and .06 pounds shrinkage for a chuck steak, for example, rather than a total of .09 pounds.

While pricing policies vary from company to company, they should be uniform among the stores operated by any one company within a specific geographical area. In some companies, price lists are issued and each store adheres to those prices regardless of any local conditions. Other companies also establish prices at headquarters level, but do so on a zone basis so that there is a variation in price from one marketing area to another among stores of the same chain.

Other companies allow store personnel to adjust prices, within certain specified limits, according to how well the item is moving. The manager can raise the price of an item that is doing exceptionally well; conversely, he has the authority to reduce the price of a slow-moving item. Giving store personnel such wide latitude in pricing can be dangerous. Any manager faced with gross profit problems thinks of higher prices as the most immediate solution. However, since he is more likely than not to raise the price on the wrong item, and since he is not in a position to know what all competition is doing, he runs the risk of outpricing himself and even running the store out of business. Moreover, from a customer relations standpoint, it is poor policy to have the same item merchandised at different prices in stores within one trading area.

Since managers must be given the flexibility to react to local conditions and to make decisions on the spot, the most practical solution is to allow a manager to decrease a price, but never to increase one. However, the company should go one step further and establish guidelines as to the maximum reduction that is allowed. This approach gives a certain amount of pricing freedom to the manager but still affords management the control it needs.

CODE-DATING AND SHELF LIFE

Many companies view open code-dating primarily as a response to consumerism and fail to appreciate the value of the discipline it exerts at store level with regard to ordering, rotating, and maintaining inventories at proper levels.

All product labeled at the store should be code-dated, indicating the shelf life of the item. Any item that is in the display case beyond its indicated shelf life should be pulled and rewrapped or converted to a less expensive cut.

Code-dates may be open so that they are easily understood by the customer, or the date may be indicated by a series of numbers or letters that are decipherable only by store personnel. A number of states have passed legislation that requires the open code-dating of some highly perishable dairy and meat items, and such regulations may eventually be extended to other meat products as well.

Some code-dates are applied by the supplier. Packaged luncheon meats, for example, are usually purchased with an expiration date printed on the label and most often it is an open code-date.

Store personnel apply the code-date on all items that are processed and labeled at the store. The code-date reflects the acceptable shelf life that management has decided upon for each type of product. Some typical standards would be one day for ground meat and three days for all other fresh meat, with the exception of rolled and tied boneless roasts. Because the physical pressure (caused by tying) on these particular items is such that shrinkage is considerable, some companies require that these items be pulled from the case daily and be rewrapped and reweighed. Since there could be a tenth of a pound loss in weight due to weepage in a 24-hour period, it is less expensive to pull the item, rewrap and reweigh it, than to allow for a three-day shelf life. Other typical standards are two days for ice-packed chicken and five days for chill-packed. In all cases, the code-date is applied to each retail package, enabling store personnel easily to identify and remove any item that has reached its expiration date.

In some companies, a $2\frac{1}{2}$-day shelf life is set for certain product even though three days is acceptable. This means that the product will be pulled in the early afternoon, rewrapped, and placed back on display the same afternoon before there is any further discoloration. Allowing a three-day shelf life in reality means postponing rewrapping for almost 20 hours, because instead of product being pulled at noon, it is more often removed from the case at the end of the day and not worked on until the next morning. This not only causes additional shrinkage but it also increases the number of rewraps to be handled the following morning. In a high-volume store, it is fairly certain that there is something wrong with a package that has not been sold in $2\frac{1}{2}$ days, i.e., it has either not been wrapped tightly enough, it contains too much fat, it is cut too thick, etc. Such product should be removed from the case and reworked and rewrapped at the earliest opportunity since it is obviously not saleable in its present form.

PRODUCT AVAILABILITY

It is not uncommon for a large-volume store to carry as many as 120 fresh meat items in the display case and for sales on some of those items to vary considerably from one store to another within a company.

In order to control gross profit and to get even movement on all cuts taken from a loin, for example, (including strip steaks, T-bones, porterhouse, and sirloin), the company must establish standards as to the variety of product that each store must carry on display. By setting minimum standards, the company will give the stores the flexibility they need to meet local demands.

For example, a company may set a standard that each store must carry a minimum of one or more rows of either porterhouse or T-bone steaks, depending on store volume. Allowing the store to display either one or the other is based on the fact that the two are so similar (the T-bone contains less of the tenderloin than does the porterhouse) that a customer will often purchase them interchangeably.

Moreover, since the company wants to move the whole loin evenly, and since there are more sirloin and strip steaks than there are porterhouse and T-bones in a loin, the company will set higher minimum requirements for the more plentiful cuts. If the experience in most stores is that the T-bone and porterhouse steaks are moving too quickly in relation to the other cuts, the company should adjust prices to keep the movement in balance. But it is not only the price of the retail cut that keeps the movement in balance; it is also the merchandising proficiency of the manager of that department.

The same principle would apply to pork (and to veal and lamb as well). The company might establish a standard that each store must display one row of pork loin chops, one row of center cut chops, and one row of shoulder (blade) chops. Depending on its volume, a store could display two or three rows of each type of pork chop; but it could not carry less than one row, and there should be a reasonable relationship between the quantity of loin, shoulder, and center cut chops offered to get even movement from the pork loin.

Setting minimum standards is especially important on items that have local appeal. In certain ethnic areas, for example, such items as neck bones might sell up to 200 pounds a week, whereas stores with the same total meat volume in other locations in the same city might sell only 30 pounds a week. To set the same display standard for both stores, based on average movement for the company, would require constant restocking for the heavier neck-bone volume store and too much space for the other store. Therefore, the company should set the same minimum standards for all stores on basic items, but make exceptions where they are warranted on items with unusually high movement. In this particular case, an acceptable standard might be for stores with a low volume on neck bones always

Principles of Retail Operations 269

to have some available, and for the high-volume neck bone store to display as many rows as necessary.

While it is true that minimum standards on product availability are more easily set for high-volume stores, they can and should be set for all stores. Similarly, companies that operate stores in more than one state, or in trading areas that show marked differences with regard to consumer buying habits, will have to adjust their standards from one area to the next.

In addition to the variety of items that should be made available, the company also should set minimum standards with regard to package size. Again, by setting minimum standards, the company gives the stores the opportunity to merchandise according to local preferences. For example, a company might insist that no T-bone steak be cut thinner than $\frac{3}{4}$ inch, or that a boneless sirloin steak must weigh a minimum of one pound, or a chuck roast must weigh at least two pounds. These are the minimums that must be followed, but it should be left to the manager's discretion how much thicker or heavier an item to package to best fill the needs of his customers.

DISPLAY HEIGHT AND WIDTH

Both maximum and minimum standards should be set for display heights so that the meat manager has a range within which to work. Obviously, all product must be displayed within the refrigeration area (i.e., not above the load limit), and the number of products that can be placed one on top of another should be limited so that the bottom layer products are not crushed. When high-priced or soft items, such as boneless cuts and cuts that have high bleeding possibilities, are stacked on top of one another in the case, the pressure that is put on the lower packages forces moisture out of the meat, causing additional shrinkage and more discoloration. Therefore, the display height on such items as boneless rounds should be no more than three packages even in a high-volume store that is having a sale on the item. Instead, the item should be stocked more often to guard against excessive shrinkage and discoloration.

Additionally, however, one display standard should be prescribed for the early part of the week and another standard should be set for the weekend. The manager should know both the minimum and maximum display heights that are allowed.

While minimum standards should be set on display widths, the maximum allowances should be quite flexible. If a manager has excess inventory on a particular item, he should be allowed to make his own decision as to how far he should go in widening the display in order to move the product. More display space tends to sell more of a given item, but there are limitations. Often it is more effective to set up two displays of one item than to spread the item out in one location in the display case.

The company should provide the manager with guidelines as to how to stock the counter—that is, the height of the display and the minimum quantity to display. However, he should be allowed to increase the width of a display or to set up two displays of one item as the need arises.

SPECIAL ORDERS

A meat department that follows company standards on product availability should have a very small number of special orders to fill. If the proper variety of product is available in the proper package sizes, and if the company has built customer confidence through freshness and quality control on such items as ground chuck or round, requests for special orders should be minimal.

The need to fill special orders is most likely to occur at the end of the day when the product has been sold down (but this will not happen with effective production planning and control). Too often, if there is only one man on duty and he is busy with other chores, he will tell the customer that he is out of the product when he is not. The standard to be followed is that if the product is in the cooler, it should be made available to the customer.

CUSTOMER SERVICE

In addition to making available to the customer any product that is in the cooler, every attempt should be made to satisfy the customer when she requests an item that is not on hand. The manager should talk to the customer and tell her that he will try to have the product for her the next day or suggest an alternate item. If she is really quite dissatisfied, the manager should obtain her name and offer to have the item delivered to her.

Additionally, if the customer is dissatisfied with an item she has bought, it should be accepted for return without causing the customer any discomfort or embarrassment. In most cases, such returns are legitimate and the customer should be reimbursed for the full cost of the purchase. On the other hand, there are some customers who repeatedly return items, and policies must be set so that decisions can be made with regard to how such customers should be handled. But the frequency with which a customer returns an item should not be the sole determinant in deciding whether the customer is a chronic complainer. During certain seasons when product is highly susceptible to spoilage or discoloration, a customer could have a legitimate reason to return items as often as twice a month. Conversely, during other seasons two complaints a month might indicate a "problem" customer. Therefore, while the manager should maintain and refer to a refund slip file before issuing a refund, he should use sound judgment in making his decision and give the customer every benefit of the doubt.

No customer who comes to purchase an advertised item should ever be deprived of the opportunity because the store is out of stock on the sale day. In such a case, some substitute should be offered the customer. For example, if a private label bacon product that is on sale is not available, the company can offer her the more expensive national brand as a replacement. Or, if the more expensive national brand has been advertised and is out of stock, the company should offer the customer a rain check that is good on any other day.

While every attempt should be made by store personnel to satisfy customers, there are some services that some managements discourage. One such service is telephone orders for certain items or under certain conditions. Stores that have a large number of orders placed by telephone will have higher than average labor costs because of the time involved in taking and processing such orders. Of equal importance is the fact that when a meat manager spends too much of his time in that manner, he has little time left to manage the department.

The standard among some companies is never to accept a telephone order for any item that is regularly on display. Rather, the manager is instructed to tell the customer that the item will be available in the display case when she comes to shop. Or, if a customer calls to order an item cut in a special way, as long as the product is in the cooler she is told that it will be cut for her when she comes to the store.

On the other hand, telephone orders are often accepted for items that the department does not usually have on hand. For example, a customer may want to purchase a whole beef tenderloin, or 25 canned hams. The manager should take such an order and advise the customer when it will be available. Because of its promotional impact, some stores also encourage customers with home freezers to call in large orders for such items as whole loins or whole hindquarters, which they offer to process and cut up in advance of the customer's arrival.

The best type of service, and the one most appreciated by customers, is having knowledgeable people in the department to help the customer. Trained people should be available to help the customer identify cuts of meat, as well as to recommend the best cooking methods for various cuts of meat. This is not only a service that the customer genuinely values, but it also helps the store to move a variety of items and to cut down on the need for filling special orders by suggesting similar cuts that may be easily substituted for those that are not available in the display case.

INVENTORY CONTROL

The main purpose of inventory control is to ensure product availability for the customer without carrying excess product in the cooler or the display cases.

Managers should order so that they have sufficient product on hand to carry them through to the next delivery, plus an adequate safety cushion. The safety cushion is determined in part by the store's meat volume, the frequency of delivery, and the type of item. The most highly perishable items should have the least amount of cushion and the less perishable items the most. Another factor in determining the amount of cushion to be planned is whether or not the item is to be promoted.

The standard for weekend inventory is often expressed as a percentage of total weekly sales in dollars. For example, some companies ask their stores to have product equal to one-third of their weekly dollar volume in the cooler and cases on Saturday night. A $10,000 weekly meat volume store that is open six days a week should therefore be carrying a total meat inventory of approximately $3,300 on Saturday night in order to have sufficient product available for Monday sale, assuming the next order arrives on Monday. A small inventory would be carried on the more perishable items and a larger inventory on less perishable product such as bacon, luncheon meat, and canned hams; but the total carry-over inventory would average out to approximately one-third of the week's volume. In a high-volume store, the percentage of inventory carry-over to weekly sales should be less than in a low-volume store.

When inventory levels are properly controlled, the amount of excess inventory carried is eliminated. This, in turn, reduces shrinkage and the amount of money tied up in inventory, while guaranteeing that an adequate supply is on hand for the customer.

CONTROLLABLE EXPENSES

The three major controllable expense areas, in order of importance, are labor, supplies, and linens.

Some companies establish their labor standards solely on the basis of sales per man-hour and even use national averages as their guidelines. A typical yardstick used in such companies in 1972 was $50 sales per man-hour per week. Thus, in a meat department with a weekly sales volume of $15,000, the amount of time scheduled for the department manager, assistant manager, meat cutters or apprentices, wrapper and pricer, and display clerk totaled 300 hours a week. However, because man-hours required are related directly to the amount of processing required and because significant variations will occur from week to week, such a standard is often meaningless. For example, receiving chill-pack poultry (i.e., prepackaged and priced at the plant where slaughtered) normally saves about five man-hours per 1,000 pounds of poultry processed, and beef received in saw-ready primals saves in the neighborhood of $1\frac{1}{2}$ hours per 1,000 pounds of beef processed. Therefore, in a store where poultry is received chill-packed, the store may show a 20 percent increase in its sales per man-hour productivity level during a week when poultry is heavily advertised. On the other hand, during a chuck or round sale, if the store receives beef in carcass form, the productivity level may drop significantly.

Even within a company, the sales per man-hour can vary greatly from store to store depending on the product mix. A store that does a high volume on products that require a great deal of processing should be expected to have a lower sales per man-hour rate than a store that is able to take the bulk of its product from the cooler to the display case with a minimum of processing. Moreover, sales per man-hour will also vary because of the fluctuations in price per pound of product sold from week to week. For example, the average sales per man-hour was estimated at $70 in 1973, as compared to the $50 figure used in 1972, and see-sawed as prices decreased and then increased in 1974. Therefore, to use a dollar sales per man-hour figure to establish standards for performance is hazardous unless the company can identify the form in which each product is received, the percentage of each type of product processed at the store, and the average price per pound of product sold.

Payroll cost (i.e., labor dollars as a percentage of meat sales) is another index used by some companies to set labor standards. However, because labor rates vary from time to time, and because the average price per pound of product sold is not constant, payroll cost is as equally ineffective a yardstick as sales per man-hour.

The only valid unit of measurement for meat department productivity in any company is volume expressed in pounds per man-hour for each major commodity group. As with sales per man-hour, pounds per man-hour will vary from store to store, even within the same company, and from week to week within the same store, as the product mix changes. Therefore, labor standards should be established on an individual store basis, by forecasting the amount of product that will be processed in each product category each week and allowing labor hours for that amount of processing based on the equipment the store has available.

Some companies have refined this concept further by setting standards for the fixed and variable functions that must be performed in the department each week. A standard is set for the number of hours it should take to perform certain fixed functions such as writing orders, receiving, cleaning and sanitizing, and so on. These are functions that must be performed whether the department is doing a small or large volume. The fixed hours are the same from week to week.

Standards in hours per 100 or 1,000 pounds of product are established for each of the variable functions that must be performed (for example, breaking, cutting, grinding, displaying, and so on). These are the functions for which man-hour requirements vary ac-

Principles of Retail Operations 275

cording to the tonnage sold. Through time studies or work sampling methods, the company determines how many man-hours are required to process 100 pounds of product for each meat commodity group (beef, veal, lamb, pork, poultry, luncheon meats, and so on) and allows the store a specific number of man-hours for these variable functions in direct relation to the tonnage expected to be processed on each product.

Figure 42 shows the man-hour requirements for fixed functions, while Figure 43 shows a sample form that can be used to indicate the forecast of tonnage to be processed and the man-hours required for that processing. Note that in Figure 43 the required man-hours per 100 pounds of product to be processed has been entered, based on the work sampling studies that have been conducted. Each week the meat department manager fills out columns X and Y in Figure 43. The number of pounds of each commodity group to be sold during the coming week are forecast and entered in column X. The number of pounds forecast are then multiplied by the man-hours required per 100 pounds for each commodity group and the total is entered in column Y. After the department manager has filled in columns X and Y, in duplicate, he mails the original to the meat office by no later than Thursday of each week for the following

FIGURE 42

Man-Hour Requirements for Fixed Functions

Fixed Functions	Man-Hours Required per Week in Each Store *
1. Cleaning	19.5
2. Handling Supplies	2.1
3. Taking Inventory	2.4
4. Ordering	.9
5. Policing Case	9.0
6. Changing Prices	3.0
7. Receiving	4.2
8. Preparing Reports	4.8
9. Handling Salvage	4.0
10. Supervising	5.7
11. Traveling	22.0
12. Others	2.4
Total Fixed Functions	80.0

* For stores with similar layouts and equipment.

FIGURE 43

Meat Department Tonnage and Man-Hour Forecast [2]

Store Number _____   Week Ending _____

Commodity Group	Pounds Sold			Required Man-Hours	
	Forecast (X)	Actual	± Variance	Per 100 lbs.	Forecast (Y)	Actual
A. Variable Functions						
Beef				1.32		
Veal				1.06		
Lamb				1.16		
Pork Loins				1.29		
All Other Pork				.87		
Variety Meats				1.29		
Smoked Hams				.60		
All Other Smoked Meats				.93		
Table-Ready Meats and Sausages				.30		
Sliced Bacon				.21		
Canned Meats				.67		
Poultry (ice packed)				.80		
Sea Foods				1.06		
Frozen Meats				.30		
B. Total						
C. Fixed Functions					80.0 *	80.0 *
D. Barbecue Allowance (maximum of 4.2 hours)						
E. Customer Relations Allowance (maximum of 6.5 hours)						
F. Subtotal of Variable and Fixed Functions (sum of B, C, D, and E)						
G. Add 7.5 Percent of F for Personal Time and Breaks						
H. Total Weekly Man-Hours Required Based on Tonnage Forecast (sum of F and G)						
I. Total Weekly Man-Hours Scheduled						
J. Total Weekly Man-Hours Required Based on Actual Tonnage (I adjusted to H)						
K. Weekly Man-Hours Paid-Actual						
L. ± Variance (difference between J and K)						

* See Figure 42

[2] NOTE: Man-hours required for fixed and variable functions relate only to the company's operation used in this illustration. Function man-hour requirements are not transferable, as they vary considerably from one company to another.

week. The meat office then computes figures in all columns other than X and Y on the forecast form and returns the completed copy to the meat department manager, the store manager, and the supervisor no later than Wednesday night following the week in question so that they can compare the forecast to the department's actual needs.

In forecasting meat tonnage for each commodity group, certain factors should be taken into account. For any items to be advertised in the coming week, reference should be made to several past weekly promotion records in which the same items were advertised. Any factors which have been shown to influence the sale of advertised items should be considered—for example, the season of the year, the advertised price, recent or current competitive ads, etc. How much tonnage was moved and how the sales affected the movement of other commodity groups should also be noted.

In addition, special in-store promotions will affect the movement of the items promoted and of other items as well, and this must be considered in projecting tonnage figures. Store-wide special promotions, such as anniversary sales and store manager sales, also can influence movement of various commodity groups. The past weekly movement in pounds of each commodity group of all nonadvertised items should also be reviewed along with the amount of case-ready product on hand; and, on the basis of sound judgment and reasoning, a projection should be made of the number of pounds of product that probably will be processed during the coming week.

Once the pounds are forecasted and the man-hours required are determined for each commodity group, the man-hours forecast in column Y are added to find the total variable man-hours required (B). In this particular example, a requirement of 80.0 man-hours has been established for fixed functions (C); an allowance of up to 4.2 man-hours has been made for a barbecue operation (D); and an extra allowance of up to 6.5 hours for customer relations (E), if the supervisor feels that this is warranted. These figures (B,C,D, E) are added to obtain a subtotal of variable and fixed man-hours required (F). Then, 7.5 percent of this figure (G) is added to F to obtain the total man-hours required for the coming week (H).

Once total man-hour requirements have been established, daily schedules for each employee are developed, keeping in mind the activities that must be performed each day and the scheduling principles that the company has established with regard to people and product. To adjust man-hours scheduled from week to week, at least one part-timer is needed to provide scheduling flexibility. A part-timer may be employed and trained in some of the less technical areas of work such as sanitation, grinding, cubing, cutting fryers, pricing, and displaying table-ready meats. With the approval of the store manager and where union agreements permit, an employee from another department in the store may be used to perform non-technical work in the meat department on a part-time basis; or a meat employee may be assigned to another department, to match the forecast requirements.

If it becomes evident during the course of any week that department sales will not meet expectations, efforts are made to reduce the part-time employee schedule for the balance of the week to ensure that no more man-hours are used than are necessary to cover the functions to be performed. On the other hand, if it becomes evident that department sales will considerably exceed expectations, part-time hours are increased to make sure that all variable functions are covered. Figure 44 shows a forecasting and scheduling system for three stores in one company. Note that while each store has been allowed 80.0 hours for fixed functions, the hours allowed to perform variable functions varies considerably because of the differences in product mix and the number of man-hours required to process different product in the three stores.

While the optimum labor requirements for each store must be determined on an individual basis, standards for supply costs are more uniform nationally, and typically run between .8 and 1.25 percent of meat sales. As the volume of product bought prepackaged increases, supply costs decrease. Supply costs can be controlled somewhat through minimizing waste that is caused by using the wrong size tray or film, by minimizing loss that occurs from damage when film or trays are not properly stored, and by reducing the number of rewraps in the department.

Linen costs generally run in the area of .1 percent of sales. How much they vary from that average will depend on working habits of the meat department employees and on the guidelines that the company establishes with respect to how often coats or uniforms are to be changed, how many aprons are to be used within a week, whether or not hats are to be worn, and so on. But overemphasis on controlling linen costs can be more than offset by the

Principles of Retail Operations 279

FIGURE 44
Forecasting and Scheduling System

Commodity Group	Hrs. Required per 100 Pounds	Man-Hours Required Based on Forecast of Tonnage To Be Processed During Week		
		Store A	Store B	Store C
Total Weekly Meat Volume Forecast		$15,300	$14,500	$13,550
A. Variable Functions				
Beef	1.32 hours	103.0 hours	89.4 hours	45.6 hours
Veal	1.06	1.4	4.8	—
Lamb	1.16	1.6	1.2	—
Pork Loins	1.29	32.9	16.0	30.1
All Other Pork	.87	3.7	.8	13.1
Variety Meats	1.29	2.0	1.6	4.3
Smoked Hams	.60	5.6	20.4	5.6
All Other Smoked Meats	.93	4.4	4.4	6.4
Table-Ready Meats and Sausages	.30	7.0	3.0	5.4
Sliced Bacon	.21	2.8	4.0	4.3
Canned Meats	.67	.4	—	—
Poultry (ice packed)	.80	26.8	23.0	30.4
Sea Foods	1.06	1.4	.2	1.0
Frozen Meats	.30	2.2	1.0	1.4
B. Total		195.2	169.8	147.6
C. Fixed Functions		80.0	80.0	80.0
D. Barbecue Allowance (maximum of 4.2 hrs)		4.2	.8	4.2
E. Customer Relations Allowance (maximum of 6.5 hours)		0.0	6.5	1.6
F. Subtotal of Variable and Fixed Functions (sum of B, C, D and E)		279.4	257.1	233.4
G. Add 7.5 Percent of F for Breaks and Personal Time		21.0	19.3	17.5
H. Total Weekly Man-Hours Required Based on Tonnage Forecast (sum of F and G)		300.4	276.4	250.9

product shrinkage that will result from increased bacteria, caused by infrequent cleaning.

LEGAL COMPLIANCE

There are various government statutes regulating the employees and the conditions of employment in the meat department to which each company must adhere, depending on where its stores are located.

Some examples are that minors may not operate power equipment; employees working in food establishments must take physical examinations and have health cards; women must wear hair nets; bearded men must wear masks, etc.

As far as sanitation is concerned, comfort stations must be maintained for employees, areas must be set aside for soiled linens, and separate sinks must be provided for washing hands and washing utensils.

The number of licenses required vary. For example, in some areas local boards of health require a general license to operate the department; another license is required for grinding meat; while still another is prescribed for making such products as sausage. However, currently there are attempts being made to combine these licenses so that all functions that are normally performed in the meat department come under one license.

While every operator is affected by federal codes and regulations, each must be sure that he is also staying within the dictates of the law with regard to both state and local requirements which can vary considerably even between communities within the same state.

12

Training Meat Department Employees

A few short years ago, a small but very progressive supermarket chain decided it was time to stop talking and to start acting with regard to training store employees. Its first action was to make a thorough analysis of store level training needs. In order to determine those needs, the chain conducted surveys, gathered statistics, and evaluated such factors as its current productivity, gross profits, shrinkage, accidents, grievances, morale, customer complaints, turnover, and absenteeism. The company compared its various performance indicators with general industry averages and with those of other supermarket chains.

The conclusion drawn from these studies clearly pointed out that the training of clerk level employees in the meat department was the area of greatest need. Within the meat department, the training of apprentices was identified as the job requiring immediate action.

The company operated in a highly competitive market and during recent years its productivity had not kept up with increases in wage rates. With gross profit being held constant, due to competitive pressures, profits had slipped precariously. Morale among meat cutters was low, as indicated by the number of grievances, turnover, absenteeism, and tardiness, all of which were at a higher level than in other departments in the company. Skilled meat cutters were becoming increasingly difficult to find, and it was almost impossible to recruit and to hold competent young men to train as apprentices during the long training period.

Top management decided that, for the first time in its history, the company would take a professional approach to training. They hired an experienced trainer from another industry to head up the new training department. They brought into the department a bright young meat manager from one of their stores to develop and implement the meat apprentice training program under the direction of the training director.

The results produced by the new training director and the new meat trainer shocked the entire company from the president all the way down to the meat cutters in the stores. The net result was that within a year the company was producing skilled meat cutters in a 13-week training period. After 13 weeks, the trainees had acquired the skills required to perform each task without hesitation or false movement and without making mistakes, but not with a high degree of speed. They were similar to typist-trainees who have learned the keyboard, but need practice to develop speed. After three months of experience following their training, during which time they achieved 95 percent of their final speed potential, their performance was equal to that of meat cutters trained for 24 to 30 months by conventional training methods. At the end of a year, they reached their full speed potential, a feat not normally accomplished under conventional training methods in less than two or three years.

At the same time, various performance indicators in the meat department improved significantly; productivity and gross profits went up while turnover and absenteeism went down. Employee attitudes were rejuvenated in meat departments throughout the company, and the meat department became the store leader in sales and profit rather than the follower it had been for too many years.

Of course, not every trainee learns at the same rate; this depends on the ability and attitude of the trainee and the trainer. However, several highly progressive supermarket chains have duplicated the effort and have attained similar results to those outlined above. Because of traditional attitudes, skepticism to this story remains, but the bare fact is that this kind of training can be and is being accomplished in supermarket companies every day.

THE MANPOWER SHORTAGE

Almost since the inception of self-service meats, most supermarket companies have found meat department employees, particularly men, the most difficult of all store employees to attract and to keep on the payroll. Unfortunately, all indicators point to a worsening of this situation in the years ahead.

In attempting to solve this problem, some of the larger companies have moved toward partial fabrication of some meat products at central plants. Although this action somewhat reduces the need for certain skills in meat cutters at store level, the need for retail cutting skills remains.

A number of supermarket companies have turned to raiding competition for experienced people, using various devices to lure them away: higher-than-union wage rates, guaranteed overtime, better fringe benefits, opportunities for more rapid advancement, and so forth; but these companies find their competition using the same tactics on them. This dog-eat-dog cycle is becoming vicious in some metropolitan areas, and sky-rocketing costs are the inevitable result.

One major cause of the meat employee shortage the industry faces today can be traced to the rise in educational level of young people. In 1910 the typical retail food clerk was 12 years old and had three years of formal education; in 1935 the typical clerk was 15 years old and had six years of schooling. Today the typical clerk is 19 years old and is a high school graduate, and tomorrow the average new supermarket employee will have at least some college education.

One successful West Coast company profiled its typical new meat apprentice as follows: He is a high school graduate, 18 to 28 years of age. He has the mentality to go to college, but due to economics or an early marriage he has postponed further education. When he is interviewed and screened, he is given the same battery of tests as other employees, but the results are gauged according to the specific requirements of his job.

The company standards are that he must: (1) be in the upper third percentile in learning ability because he must quickly master the techniques of his craft; (2) score moderate-to-high on intellectual achievement tests because he must have supervisory potential; (3) have the temperament to get along with other people, but he must also show vitality and leadership traits; (4) have a good high school scholastic record, thus indicating ability to complete the required training; and (5) show evidence of physical coordination and strength and be able to work in below-normal temperatures.

Whether it is desirable or not, the educational level of employees in the supermarket industry will continue to rise each year. The importance of this trend is that the supply of people available for manual jobs is shrinking faster than the demand. Unless the industry is willing to make major revisions in the techniques it uses to recruit, select, and train meat personnel, the drop-outs and the dregs of the labor market will soon be the only source of available manpower. The educated employee simply will not tolerate the tortuous, lengthy, and boring type of apprenticeship training that is common in the industry today.

As a step in this direction, the aforementioned company insists that the apprentice be given all-around training, not just be assigned menial tasks; and their meat department managers and meat supervisors are responsible for seeing that this is done. There are other encouraging and solid indications that the use of proper recruitment programs and modern training techniques can overcome manpower shortage problems in any area of the country.

Sources of New Employees

Several companies have learned that the best source of meat trainees lies right under their noses—the part-time and full-time employees who are already on the payroll in other departments of the store. In some areas, interdepartment transfers are limited by union restrictions. But wherever possible, present employees in other departments should be given careful consideration as prospective meat trainees for the obvious reasons that they have demonstrated their ability to be productive employees, and they are less likely to be lost through turnover.

It is interesting to note that 60 to 80 percent of all full-time supermarket employees were originally hired as part-timers. Most part-timers begin their employment at the front end or as grocery or produce clerks and when they become full-timers, seldom change departments. Yet, several chains have been able to satisfy all their requirements for meat cutter trainees by aggressively selling the advantages and opportunities of meat cutter training to full-time employees in other departments. Other companies have also learned that a major portion of its meat trainee needs can be filled from this source.

The second best source of meat trainees are the local high schools and junior colleges. It is really amazing what some companies have been able to accomplish by establishing close relationships with local school administrators and counselors. In most areas these education officials are more than willing to cooperate. They will often recruit, interview, evaluate, test, and recommend talented students who are in the graduating class, or do the same for 18-year-old students (minimum age for meat cutters) who may be a term away from graduation. There are many varied techniques for establishing close and cordial relationships with local school officials and for motivating them to cooperate and participate in a company's recruiting efforts. One vital ingredient in any such association is for the chain to provide the school administrator and counselor with information outlining the advantages and opportunities within the company for new employees.

The rapidly expanding field of distributive education is another important contact for the supermarket recruiter. Several large regional chains have found DE students to be an excellent source of dependable and productive meat department employees.

The Female Trainee

The question of training women to be meat cutters is often raised but seldom answered with one definitive statement. Since the legal restrictions were eliminated in many states on the allowable weight a female could lift and the equipment she could use, some companies have started to employ females to perform a limited number of cutting jobs. This is especially true for those companies that are using block-ready beef or vacuum-packaged product, which considerably reduces the weight of the item being handled.

While it is true that women can perform certain functions equally as well as men (for example, cutting fryers on a saw, grinding meat, etc.), the real problem created by hiring female meat cutters is the resulting loss in flexibility in scheduling employees for certain tasks, and the resentment of male employees who are asked to perform all tasks in the department. For example, some boxed product, weighing 80 to 90 pounds, is usually unloaded from delivery trucks by store personnel. Since few women can lift such heavy loads without risk of injury, in a department employing both female and male meat cutters, this task would fall to the males. Often, the attitude of a male employee in that situation is that if the female is to earn equal pay, she should be expected to perform equal work. A female's inability to lift heavy product would be an especially serious handicap in a small store employing only two or three people in the meat department. In such a case, one man might have to do all the heavy work, a situation to which he would rightfully object.

Thus, while the legal restrictions have been removed, there are still practical obstacles to employing females as meat cutters at store level. The greatest opportunities for female meat cutters appear to exist at central plants where product is moved to the meat cutter by mechanized equipment and where it is practical to assign cutters a limited number of tasks on an assembly-line basis. But such opportunities rarely exist at store level where there is a greater need for flexibility among meat department personnel.

Problems in Holding New Recruits

No matter how successful a company is in developing effective recruiting and selection techniques, without an effective training program all its efforts will be in vain. Most supermarket companies use an archaic, inadequate, and inefficient apprenticeship system to train its meat cutters. This holdover from the old craft system used in the pre-industrial revolution era of the eighteenth century hardly meets today's training needs.

For example, the typical approach used in the supermarket industry to train meat cutters is simply to place the new trainee in a meat department. His first assignment invariably is to do the dirty work in the market—the jobs no one else wants to do—like grinding beef in the cooler, cutting up fryers, and cleaning up the department. He is likely to be on these jobs for three or four months before he learns any other part of the operation. By the time he becomes skilled in all manual jobs in the department, as many as two or three years can expire. He learns by osmosis and emulation, being overtrained on some tasks and undertrained on others. It is not surprising that he becomes thoroughly bored and disenchanted with the meat business and with the company, which explains why the industry loses 7 out of every 10 trainees before they complete their training.

Some supermarket companies have reduced the training time of apprentice meat cutters to 12 months through a program of planned rotation from one job in the department to another at specified time intervals. Under this plan, the trainee may spend only two months grinding beef, cutting up fryers, and cleaning the department. He may spend another two months in the wrapping and pricing operations, a month on the display case, two months on the power saw, and so on.

Some people commend this planned rotation system of training and call it progress, but it is really nothing more than accelerated osmosis training. The trainee still learns by emulation in a totally unstructured way. His overtraining is reduced but not eliminated. He still becomes bored and disenchanted because he is not allowed to progress according to his capabilities.

DEVELOPING A TRAINING PROGRAM

The development of a professionally designed program for training meat department employees is no simple task. It is time-consuming and expensive and requires a total commitment on the part of top management and the involvement of the top meat executive, the district managers, meat specialists, store managers, and meat department managers. But those supermarket companies that have developed such training programs have evidence that the results are worth the efforts.

The six steps required to build an effective, structured training program are as follows:

1. Determine the method of training
2. Select the meat trainer
3. Qualify the meat trainer in training principles and techniques
4. Develop a meat department standard practices manual
5. Install standard practices in all meat departments in the company
6. Develop a meat instructor's manual

Determining the Method of Training

The method of training is usually classified according to where the training takes place. The primary options are:

1. On-the-job training
2. Central or off-the-job training
3. Model department training

The great majority of meat employees learn on the job. A few companies do give the new apprentice meat cutter some formal training centrally; but, generally speaking, less than 1 out of 100 supermarket meat department employees is trained centrally.

An advantage of on-the-job in-store training is that it avoids the artificial classroom atmosphere of central training, thereby eliminating the need for the trainee to adjust from the controlled situation of the classroom to the reality of the store meat department. The most serious disadvantage to typical on-the-job training is that the new employee is usually trained by someone who is not a qualified teacher and who is more than likely a poor teacher. In addition to the disadvantages outlined previously for the so-called osmosis or emulation type of training which is so common in the industry today, another disadvantage to on-the-job training is that the trainee is too often pulled off the training program and used to close the gap when emergencies arise.

One of the major advantages of central training is that learning is not affected by the inevitable interruptions and distractions that occur in the store. Moreover, standardized instruction can be given by trainers who are carefully selected and qualified to teach. This more tightly controlled training situation assures that the employee will receive more thorough instruction as well as a better induction.

Centralized training, however, usually costs more than other forms of training and may be impractical when stores are spread over a wide geographical area. Perhaps a more important disadvantage is that when training is conducted centrally, there is a tendency for store and department managers to feel relieved of all training responsibilities. The most serious disadvantage to central training is that it tends to encourage a pass-the-buck attitude among meat department managers who, rather than assuming any responsibility for the employee, very often tend to blame the central training program for problems caused by other factors—problems such as low productivity, poor planning and scheduling, and low employee morale.

Training in model departments, which is probably the fastest growing training innovation in the supermarket industry, is designed to combine the virtues of on-the-job and central training. In this type of training, a meat department in one store serves as the company training base for all the apprentice meat cutters in all the stores in one geographical area, usually a district or zone containing anywhere from 5 to 20 supermarkets.

The model meat department is carefully selected and is made to serve as a model in every respect. All company policies and standard operating practices are installed and followed to the letter. And, equally important, the department manager has had the opportunity to become thoroughly familiar with modern training principles and techniques.

As in the central training program approach, standardized instruction can be provided in the model department by trainers who are well prepared and qualified to train. On the other hand, model department training resembles on-the-job training in that instruction is conducted under actual operating conditions. Thus, trainees contribute to production and line employees gain training experience.

Considering the pros and cons of the three methods of training, the model department appears to offer the optimum solution. Those few supermarket chains that have made the greatest progress in the direction of professional training have adopted the model department training concept.

However, no matter which method is used, the eventual responsibility for training will rest on the shoulders of line personnel. Every meat manager must understand that whether meat employees are trained centrally or in a model department, such training is not completed when the employee leaves the training program. Therefore, every meat manager should learn and practice sound principles and techniques of training so that he not only can follow through on the initial training that has taken place, but can also be qualified to train employees in any future changes in standard operating procedures.

Selecting the Meat Trainer

When a company decides to move in the direction of a structured training program for the first time, one of the questions that invariably arises is, "Should we go outside the company to find a qualified trainer and teach him the meat business, or should we look for someone inside the company who has meat knowledge and skills and teach him to train people?" There is only one good answer to this question and that is expressed in the second alternative. It is far easier to make a meat man into a trainer than vice-versa.

Still, contrary to popular belief, training is not a simple task which can be performed equally well by all managers. There is also a general misconception in the supermarket industry that every manager has certain innate qualities which make him an expert trainer when, in fact, there are very few trainers in the managerial ranks, even up to and including those holding senior positions. The reasons for this are simply that most managers have not been exposed to modern training principles and techniques, and competent trainers are made, not born.

Selecting a company meat trainer is a critically important decision. Just because a person knows the company's meat operation, or runs a profitable department, or is highly productive, or has seniority does not necessarily mean he will become a good meat trainer. Choosing the best person for this task, if it is done right, often means that rules of succession are broken. The man with the most seniority or the man who is next in line for promotion frequently must be bypassed, which often leads to resentment among some of the older employees. Still, if the right man is chosen and does a professional job in developing and implementing the meat training department, this resentment usually can be overcome.

The person selected to become the company meat trainer should have certain qualifications and qualities. First, he must know the meat business, although he need not be the most skilled meat cutter in the company. He must want the job. Also, he must like the idea of teaching and have the ability and desire to communicate with others. Moreover, he should be patient, articulate, and capable of acquiring a sound knowledge of training principles and techniques.

Qualifying the Company Meat Trainer

Acquiring the knowledge and skills of a good trainer does not occur by chance. When one company appointed a new meat trainer, he was somewhat astonished to learn that he had to spend many weeks of concentrated study and effort to prepare himself for the job. The new trainer said, "After all, I have been training people in my meat departments in different stores for several years. I know as much about training as any meat man in this company." He was right, but what he failed to understand was that his knowledge of training was limited to training by osmosis and that he was not a professional trainer. Just as it takes many months for a person to learn the necessary skills of a top-notch meat department manager, it is equally true that similar study and learning efforts are required if he is to acquire the knowledge and skills of a good trainer.

Several options are available to teach the man the skills he will need to qualify as a company meat trainer. One approach used by several chains is to have the newly-selected trainer visit and learn from another company that has developed and is using an effective, well organized, well planned meat training program. Many supermarket companies willingly cooperate in this manner. Another approach is to have the new trainer attend one of the supermarket industry meetings on training that are held several times each year. The American Management Association conducts similar training seminars each year and also has a programmed instruction course called "Train the Trainer" that can be taken by the new trainer either at the company's offices or at home. Also, Proctor & Gamble has developed a short "How to Train Others" programmed instruction booklet which it offers free to the supermarket industry. The AMA programmed instruction course and the P & G instruction booklet should be made available to the company meat trainer and to each of the model department trainers. Additionally, the P & G booklet should be made available to every meat department manager in the company.

A note of caution is in order. Attending seminars or meetings or taking programmed instruction courses does not guarantee that the individual will apply effectively what he has learned. All too often, newly trained meat trainers revert to their own improvised methods and techniques if they are not properly supervised, and the training program falls apart. There is no substitute for capable guidance and direction to guarantee that the principles learned are properly applied.

Developing a Standard Practices Manual

The standard practices manual is the heart of any meat training program. It contains all departmental policies and practices that have been adopted as standard operating procedures by the company. The manual is the guideline for what is to be taught, and extreme care must be exercised in the way it is developed.

One well intentioned supermarket company learned the importance of this fact from a very costly experience. The personnel and training directors had convinced top management that a professionally developed training program was the best answer to their turnover problem in the meat department.

They understood the importance of a standard practices manual as the foundation of the training program and started developing one by having the vice-president of meat operations identify each of the standard practices for the various manual operations in the meat department. Based on the information supplied by the vice-president, a standard practices manual was developed and distributed to each meat specialist in the company for review. A meeting was then held with the vice-president and the meat specialists and, after considerable discussion, agreement was reached on the standard practices.

The training department, assuming that this agreement finalized the adoption of the standard practices, printed the manual, assured of the specialists' commitment to follow through on its implementation. A copy of the printed manual was sent to each meat department manager in the company, with a covering note from the training department, asking that each of the standard practices identified be implemented.

The results were disastrous. Since the company had never before identified or specified standard practices, the methods used in different operations varied substantially among the stores. The new standard practices were rejected almost universally for the simple reason that none of the meat department managers had a voice in determining what they should be.

Some years after this early failure, another attempt was made by the same company to develop a professional training program, this time using the model department training concept. The personnel and training directors had learned from their first experience that without the commitment of the people who would be responsible for implementing the standard practices, the program was doomed to failure.

The two men prepared a detailed outline of the topics to be covered in the new standard practices manual. They discussed the outline with the vice-president of meat operations and made changes and additions, based on his input.

At weekly meetings, which were attended by the meat vice-president, the training director assigned one major topic in the outline to each meat specialist. The meat specialist was instructed to discuss the topic with the department managers under his supervision and, based on their consensus, to submit the recommended standard practices at the next weekly meeting.

At the same time, the department managers who had been selected to be the future model department meat trainers were also assigned topics and asked to submit their proposals for standard practices. The recommendations submitted by the specialists and model department trainers were discussed at each meeting. Twelve weekly meetings were required to cover all the topics. No meeting was concluded until the meat vice-president, the specialists, and the model department trainers reached agreement on the identification of each of the standard practices under consideration.

Involving the meat department managers, the meat specialists, and the vice-president of meat operations in developing and identifying standard practices resulted in their total commitment once the practices had been agreed to. After each weekly meeting, the future model department trainers returned to their respective stores and implemented each of the standard practices that had been accepted. The identification, acceptance, and implementation of the standard practices in meat departments throughout the company had been accomplished.

Many good supermarket training programs have been short-circuited by failing to involve those who will be responsible for implementing the program in identifying the standard practices that they will teach to their trainees. Literally dozens of standard practices manuals have been prepared by various companies, but because of lack of involvement and commitment, they exist only on paper.

It is not uncommon to find that most supermarket companies embarking on their first effort at a professionally designed meat training program have no standard practices. As a result, the methods and procedures used in one store may vary considerably from those used in another. For any meat training program to be successful, it is necessary to have standardized methods and practices used in all stores in the company. Otherwise, the trainee who is taught a particular method for an activity in the model training department faces the very real likelihood that that particular method will not be used in the store to which he is permanently assigned after his training. This creates confusion and conflict within the company. His meat department manager is more than likely to say, "That may be the way you were taught to perform this activity in the training store, but we don't do it that way here."

If a company does not have an up-to-date standard practices manual, one of the first tasks of the company meat trainer is to prepare such a manual. Unfortunately, as indicated earlier, this is not as simple as it sounds. The company meat trainer cannot simply put down on paper the standard practices which he believes are best for the company. After all, for any standard practices manual to be adopted company-wide, it must have the support and commitment of top management, field supervisors, and store and meat managers. In order to attain this commitment, it is necessary for the company meat trainer to involve people from various positions within the company in the development and implementation of the various standard practices that are eventually adopted. This involvement should include at the very minimum the top meat officials in the company, a representative sample of meat specialists, and a representative sample of meat department managers within the company. Without such involvement, there is likely to be little commitment to the standard practices identified by the company meat trainer; and without such commitment, the whole training program is likely to fail.

Another difficulty in the preparation of the standard practices manual is to identify the best of the methods or procedures that exist in the various meat department operations in the company. For this reason, the meat trainer should have some knowledge of industrial engineering or methods analysis principles; or he should have assistance from skilled technicians in that area so that the one best way to perform each task can be identified.

One by-product of developing a standard practices manual is that the practices eventually adopted for the whole company are superior to those previously used in any one store. In addition, it often happens that simply through the re-examination of methods in current use, a new and improved method or procedure is developed. Thus, part of the productivity improvement that invariably results from the implementation of a well planned, structured meat department training program can be traced to standardizing the best methods and procedures in use, as well as developing improvements.

Training Meat Department Employees

Following is a list of subjects included in the standard practices manual for the meat department of one company:

1. Packaging
    A. Tray sizes for various items
    B. Film sizes for various items
    C. Wrapping methods
2. Pricing and labeling
    A. Code-dating fresh meats
    B. Case (display) life
    C. Tare weights
    D. Prepackaged merchandise
        1. Code-dating
        2. Returning out-of-code merchandise
3. Handling price changes
4. Displaying
    A. Rotation
    B. Advertised items
    C. Case line-up
    D. Required items
    E. Seasonal items
    F. Optional items
5. Customer relations and customer complaints
6. Special orders
    A. Keeping variety of servings and item thickness on display
    B. Use of conventional packaging materials
7. Sanitation
    A. Effect on product life
    B. Cleaning schedule and methods
8. Temperature and humidity control
    A. Effect on product life
    B. Cooler, cutting, packaging, and display areas
9. Ordering
    A. Principles and guidelines
    B. Inventory control
    C. Weekend carry-over
    D. Primal cuts
    E. Advertised items
10. Receiving
    A. Back door security
    B. Product inspection

  C. Weighing
  D. Handling invoices
  E. Storage of product
11. Breaking
  A. Beef forequarters
  B. Beef hindquarters
  C. Veal
  D. Lamb
12. Retail cutting—boning and trimming
  A. Beef
  B. Veal
  C. Lamb
  D. Pork
  E. Poultry
13. Ground Meats
  A. Importance
  B. Fat-lean ratio
    1. Ground beef or hamburger
    2. Ground chuck
    3. Ground round
  C. Handling discolored product
14. Merchandising profitable items
15. Rehandling (rewraps)
  A. Rates and losses
  B. Discolored product
  C. Torn and leaky packages
  D. Policy on markdowns
  E. Conversion to profitable cuts
16. Cutting tests
  A. Method
  B. Frequency
17. Meat Inventory
  A. Frequency
  B. Procedure
  C. Computation of department gross profit

  The reader may wonder about the sequence of the various topics listed in this company's standard practices manual, which is not accidental. An important principle of teaching is that simple tasks must be taught first. The outline of this standard practices manual is designed with this principle in mind, with subjects becoming more and more complex as the trainee is exposed to various activities within the department.

It cannot be overemphasized that no meat department training program will be successful—in fact is doomed to failure—unless standard practices have been identified, recorded, and implemented in all existing meat departments of the company.

Installing Standard Practices in All Meat Departments

After the standard practices have been agreed upon by the various meat personnel who serve as the consulting group to the company meat trainer, it is necessary that they become part of the normal operating procedure in each meat department of the company. The best way to accomplish this is through a series of classroom meetings and on-the-job demonstrations.

The first classroom meeting and demonstration, which will require only a few hours, should be attended by the director of store operations, all district managers, all meat specialists, and the director of meat operations. They should be asked to examine the standard practices manual in complete detail prior to the meeting. The objective of this first meeting should be to obtain the agreement and commitment of each of these individuals to implementing the standard practices throughout the company.

Next, the company meat trainer should plan a series of meetings for store managers and meat department managers, following a somewhat different format. The basic objective of this series of meetings is the retraining of meat department managers, as well as the implementation of the standard practices included in the manual. These retraining classes are normally scheduled for two to three hours on one afternoon or evening each week for five or six weeks, depending on the content of the program. The maximum number of people attending any one class meeting should be limited to 20 individuals. The value in having the store manager attend each session with his meat department manager is that both are exposed to exactly the same information at the same time. Moreover, these classroom and demonstration sessions, so organized, help to involve the store manager in the meat department and to further his knowledge of meat operations, thereby reducing his inclination to avoid the meat department because he considers it a mystery. The value of spacing these retraining meetings a week apart is to provide each manager with the time and opportunity to implement the standard practices learned at each meeting and to allow the store manager and his meat manager to report back at each succeeding meeting on the success (or problems) they have had with implementing the standard practices.

Normally the retraining program consists of both classroom and on-the-job training. Each attendee is given a copy of the standard practices manual to study so that he can review the material to be covered in advance of the forthcoming meeting. The on-the-job part of this series of retraining meetings normally consists of demonstrations of methods or procedures that previously have not been adopted uniformly in all stores in the company. Since some of these demonstrations will require the actual handling of meat products, it is desirable, wherever possible, for the classroom setting in each zone or district to be in one of the stores within that district. This will allow the class to move to the meat department of that store for on-the-job demonstration and training.

Several companies have found that it is highly desirable to give written tests to each person attending the retraining sessions at the beginning of each session, covering those subjects discussed at the previous meeting, and to request a written report from each store indicating those standard practices that have been implemented since the previous week's session.

It is also desirable that the district manager and meat specialist attend all meetings of their store and meat managers. It should be made clear to each of these supervisors that one of their major responsibilities is to follow through to ensure that the standard practices taught at each meeting are implemented by their store and meat managers during the week that follows. Moreover, the company meat trainer should visit a representative number of stores in each district as they are being retrained to guarantee that questions regarding the standard practices are answered and misunderstandings are corrected.

Developing the Instructor's Manual

There is no professional meat trainer who can recall from memory every point that should be covered in the discussion of a given subject. For this reason, it is mandatory that an instructor's manual be prepared for any training course. The meat instructor's manual, like the standard practices manual, should cover in proper sequence every point to be discussed in each of the training sessions.

In preparing the instructor's manual, the company meat trainer should keep in mind that trainees will learn best when they understand why a given practice has been adopted. Therefore, any well planned instructor's manual will be divided into three major segments for each item covered: (1) what is to be done, (2) how it is to be done, and (3) why it is to be done in a particular way.

In several companies the instructor's manual is designed with each page containing three vertical columns. The first column identifies what is to be done or the steps to be taken. The second column identifies how that step is to be performed and is often called "key points." The third column identifies why the step is required and/or why it is to be done in the way specified.

Following is an illustration of the three-column breakdown for a small segment of one operation.

Hand Wrapping Boneless Roasts

Steps	Key Points	Reasons Why
1. Select proper roll width	1. Guidelines (a) 11" for small roasts (under 2 lbs.) (b) 14" for medium roasts (2-5 lbs.) (c) 17" for large roasts (over 5 lbs.)	1. Costs (a) improved productivity (b) fewer rewraps (c) lower film costs (d) better package appearance
2. Obtain unwrapped roast and place on wrapping pedestal with the long axis of the product parallel to the long axis of the pedestal	2. With right hand (a) align length and width of roast with pedestal	2. Eliminates rehandling (a) wrapping is easier (b) film size is more accurately estimated
3. Grasp film and pull from roll	3. With both hands (a) cut off for 1½" overlap	3. Improves accuracy in cutting off optimum film size; reduces film cost
4. Fold film over narrow roast width	4. With both hands (a) overwrap from near side to far side of roast	4. Improves wrapping speed
5. Overwrap both ends of roast	5. Grasp loose film at each end of roast (a) with both hands simultaneously	5. Improves productivity
6. Complete overwrap	6. Raise roast from pedestal (a) fold ends of film under roast (b) should be snug wrap	6. Easiest method (a) better productivity (b) improved package appearance
7. Dispose wrapped roast to sealing belt and grasp next unwrapped roast	7. Dispose wrapped roast with left hand & simultaneously grasp next unwrapped roast with right hand (a) press wrapped package lightly against sealing plate as disposed	7. Eliminates rehandling (a) saves time (b) improves seal

In many instances, the key points and the reasons why contain memory joggers or words designed to remind the trainer of various points or reasons to be covered in the on-the-job training. Because every manual task in the meat department must be broken down into the same degree of detail as in the above illustration, the preparation of the instructor's manual becomes a sizeable task. Yet, this is absolutely necessary if training is to be done in a thorough and expert fashion. Moreover, the manual must be kept up to date as changes are made in standard practices. Once it is developed, the manual greatly simplifies the task of training; and as meat managers become qualified in training principles and techniques, it assures standardization of training procedures and operating techniques in all meat departments of the company.

TRAINING MEAT DEPARTMENT MANAGERS TO TRAIN

Whereas the standard practices should be developed by line personnel, the preparation of such training material as the standard practices manual and the instructor's manual is usually a staff function, often handled by the training department. On the other hand, the training of meat department apprentices, wrappers, and other clerks is a line responsibility—that is, the training should be conducted by managers on the firing line. This is true whether a company follows the model department concept or whether new employees are trained by the department manager in the store in which they will work.

The ideal solution to on-the-job training would be for every meat department manager to become a highly skilled and qualified trainer. However, since that is not a realistic goal, many supermarket companies solve this problem by training in model departments. Nevertheless, even in those companies following the model department training concept, every meat department manager should be given instructions in how to train new employees. This is necessary so that he can follow up on employees who have been trained in the model department and, also, because he must know how to retrain experienced employees when changes in standard operating procedures are adopted by the company.

Any meat manager who is provided with the company's standard operating practices manual and with an instructor's manual and who is properly taught and religiously applies the principles of learning and the principles of teaching, can do a satisfactory job of training employees on the job.

TRAINING PRINCIPLES

Whatever the approach used to qualify the new trainer, he must become thoroughly familiar with training principles and techniques.

Training principles are usually divided into two groups: principles of learning and principles of teaching. It is impossible for any training program to succeed if either the learning or teaching principles are misunderstood or improperly applied.

The principles of learning specify that the trainee's ability to learn is affected by five major factors:

1. The trainee's capability and attitude
2. The trainee's background, previous training, and experience
3. The nature of the task being taught
4. The instruction method and techniques that are employed
5. The capabilities and attitude of the trainer

Sound knowledge of the principles of teaching are as important to the trainer as his knowledge of the principles of learning. Teaching principles, for the most part, relate to the thorough, advance planning of the training program and take into account the following six basic factors:

1. The simple tasks must be taught first
2. Each task must be broken down into its basic component parts
3. Only the correct methods should be taught
4. Teaching cycles should be short and should be reinforced immediately by practice
5. Skills should be developed through repetition
6. The trainee must be motivated [1]

The new trainer becomes skilled through practice, just as the trainee does. Moreover, he must learn when, where, and how to use training aids as well as the types of teaching aids that will be most

---
[1] For a detailed discussion on training, see Edward M. Harwell, *Personnel Management and Training* (New York: Chain Store Publishing Corp., 1969), pp. 87-160.

effective. He must learn how to test the trainee during the training period to ensure that the trainee has acquired the desired knowledge or knows the correct method. He must know how to measure the trainee's productivity on various tasks taught at various times during the training period so that he and the trainee are kept informed as to the trainee's learning progress to ensure that the trainee is neither overtrained nor undertrained on any particular activity. Finally, the trainer must learn how to follow-up to be certain that the methods and techniques he has taught are used by the trainee. After all, the use of the methods and techniques, when combined with the speed, accuracy, and attitude of the trained employee, are the true measures of a professional training program.

The Trainee's Capability and Attitude

Any training effort will fail unless the trainee has the ability and the desire to learn. In fact, the success of any learning experience is the sum of ability multiplied by desire. If either factor is zero, the result will be zero. If both are near 100 percent, success in learning will be guaranteed.

A person who is physically handicapped—for example, someone with only one arm—could have all the desire in the world to become a cutter or a meat wrapper, but no matter how much effort he expends, he could never be successful. He has the desire but not the ability. On the other hand, a new employee who has all the mental and physical qualifications to become a skilled cutter will not really be successful unless he has an interest in retail meat operations and a desire to learn.

There is not much that can be done to influence the ability of the individual to learn. However, the skilled trainer who understands the principles of learning knows that it is possible to influence the attitude of an employee in an on-the-job training situation by properly motivating him.

To encourage the trainee, the trainer must capture the trainee's undivided attention and gain his confidence and cooperation. Because almost everyone is apprehensive and nervous when confronted with a new task, the trainer must first put the employee at ease. When the trainee first arrives on the job he should be greeted in a friendly manner. Next, the trainee's previous experience should be explored. In this way the trainer can discover precisely what the trainee already knows about the tasks to be learned and can estimate the amount of time needed for training. Encouraging the trainee to talk about himself also helps him to relax.

During this first meeting, before formal training actually begins, the trainee should be told what he will learn and, without extensive detail, be given an overall preview of the entire job. Since learning is improved by the promise of rewards, the trainer should explain how the trainee will benefit from the learning experience. The trainee should also understand that no one expects perfect performance on the first day and that speed in performing manual tasks will come through practice.

The trainer must recognize that because different people have different capabilities and attitudes, their progress and learning speeds will vary. Unfortunately, in most supermarket companies training periods for meat apprentices, for example, are fixed. In fact, some union contracts require that a man spend "x" number of months in his apprenticeship before he can be considered a journeyman meat cutter, which is often unfair to both the employee and the company. It is also one of the major causes of the difficulties in attracting bright young people to the retail meat business and the primary cause of turnover among employees during their meat apprenticeship period.

Some new meat wrapper trainees will become proficient within a week, whereas others will take two or even three weeks to reach their eventual level of performance. This means that there should be no fixed or inflexible training periods that apply across the board to all new employees. Trainees must be allowed to progress as their ability and desire dictate, and every training program should be flexible to allow for these variations in learning speed from one person to another.

The Trainee's Background and Experience

One of the trainer's initial responsibilities is to learn something about the new employee's background and experience. Obviously, if a man has worked in a packing plant handling fresh meat, he will have a considerable advantage over another new employee who has not had such experience. He is likely to learn the retail meat business rapidly, and the trainer must take this into consideration in planning his on-the-job training program. However, such previous experience does not guarantee success. The capability and attitude of the employee are far more important to his learning ability than his previous experience.

The Nature of the Job

Naturally, learning is influenced by the simplicity or complexity of the task that is being taught. More time is required for a trainee to become a skilled meat cutter than for him to become a skilled wrapper. And, contrary to popular belief, it requires more time to become a skilled meat manager than it does to become a skilled meat cutter. So, the difficulty of the task to be learned, coupled with the ability, the attitude, and the background and experience of the trainee, have a major influence on the length of the learning period and the amount of practice required to become skilled at any given task.

Instruction Methods

The training method used by the instructor will also have a great influence on the trainee's rate of learning. The trainee must be made to understand everything about the task he is learning. The trainer must make certain that the trainee understands the answers to such questions as: Why is the task necessary? Why must it be performed using the methods being taught? Why is it performed at a certain point in a sequence of operations? How does the task fit into the overall picture of the department operation? Once the trainee understands the purpose and objective of the task, the learning process is reinforced and he is likely to make fewer mistakes.

The importance of understanding the reasons why a task is performed in a certain way can be illustrated by the experience of Kay Adams, who had been working in the meat department of a Midwestern supermarket for one week. On Monday of the second week, the meat manager decided to train Kay in the weighing, pricing, and labeling operation. He taught her how to set the price per pound, insert the commodity slugs into the label printer, and set the tare on the scale. He also told Kay that in addition to the tare for the weight of the packaging material, she should also follow a chart that indicated how much additional tare should be added for different specified fresh and smoked meat items. He neglected to tell Kay that the added tare weight was to compensate for loss of weight while the wrapped product was in the display case. When the manager left the store to attend a meeting that Monday afternoon, Kay decided it did not make sense to charge the customer less than the actual weight of the meat item, so she began setting the tare for various commodities based on the actual weight of the packaging materials alone, making no allowance for product shrinkage.

On Wednesday afternoon of that same week, a weights and measures inspector came into the store and began removing selected packages of different commodities from the display cases. He took the packages into the backroom, removed the packaging material, weighed each item on the scale, and found all those packaged on previous days to weigh slightly less than the weight indicated. As a result, the store was charged with deceptive pricing practices and the company was fined $1,000. If the manager had told Kay during her training period that the added tare was required by law to compensate for possible loss in weight during the two or three-day period the package might be in the display case, it is unlikely that she would have made this serious mistake which not only cost the company money, but also led to adverse publicity in local papers.

Every trainee should be given specific information on how he is progressing with regard to his learning speed. This requires that the trainee's performance be measured at various points during the learning period. There is no way for the trainee to know how he is progressing unless his performance is measured against the average performance of typical trainees. Without some guidance he cannot set his own performance goals. Furthermore, without such standards, the effectiveness of the trainer and the training program cannot be fully evaluated.

Capability and Attitude of the Trainer

One can talk forever about enlightened training principles; but if the trainer himself is not a suitable teacher, or if the methods he uses are slipshod or do not follow sound principles, the entire program will be a waste of time and money. Moreover, if the trainer himself is not well motivated, if he is impatient or unconcerned, the meat department will continue to lose one of its most valuable potential assets—the trainee with promise.

As is true in the case of the trainee, if the trainer has the right attitude and the ability and desire to learn, the chances of his developing into an excellent, skilled trainer are good. But even with these qualifications, it takes many months of diligent practice to become skilled, as any professional trainer will readily admit.

A qualified trainer needs a familiarity with modern training methods, as well as a thorough knowledge of the subject he is teaching. He must possess the capacity to express himself coherently, to communicate with others, to recognize employees' needs, and to plan and organize efficiently. In addition, he requires an understanding of what motivates learning and a constructive attitude toward trainees and training.

PRINCIPLES OF TEACHING

Training success depends in large measure on whether the program is thoroughly planned. The workplace and training area must be properly arranged in advance of the training session. Good lighting and ventilation are important. Moreover, the workplace should be organized exactly as the trainee would be expected to maintain it, with tools, materials, supplies, and training aids in place and ready for use. Obviously, interruptions and distractions should be kept to a minimum.

Simple Tasks Must Be Taught First

Regardless of the job to be learned, the trainee must first be well grounded in the fundamental simple tasks. The sequence in which jobs are performed in a department is seldom the best sequence to follow in training. A meat apprentice trainee, for example, should not start to learn the meat business by first writing a meat order, then by receiving, breaking into primal cuts, retail cutting, traying, wrapping, and displaying. Although this procedure may represent the actual sequence of tasks he will eventually perform on the job, it is not the best sequence for effective learning. The introduction of complex tasks at the beginning of a training program will confuse the trainee, and his self-confidence can be destroyed if he is unable to succeed with these more complex tasks.

In most well planned meat apprentice training programs, the trainee begins his training on the wrapping operation. At this stage, he not only learns proper wrapping methods, but he is also given the opportunity to become familiar with different types of retail cuts. He then usually moves to the pricing operation where he learns the mechanics of the scale and label printer and something about the pricing policies in the company. Only after he has mastered these two basic operations is he exposed to some of the more complex tasks in the department.

Breaking the Task Down into Basic Components

As discussed previously, each task must be broken down into its detailed, component parts by listing the successive steps to be performed, the key points for each step, and the reason the task is done in the method outlined. By following such an instructor's manual, the trainer ensures thorough coverage of the job; equally important, he provides the trainee with an understanding of all activities in the department.

Only the Correct Method Should Be Taught

The trainer who explains or demonstrates the wrong way to perform a task runs the risk of being misunderstood by the trainee. Recently, a trainer was instructing an apprentice in retail cutting methods. He first demonstrated the correct method of trimming fat and removing excess tail from T-bone steaks; however, he did not point out the key points in each step or the reasons why he used certain methods in performing this operation. Then, in rapid succession, he demonstrated three incorrect methods that should be avoided in trimming fat and removing excess tail from the T-bone.

At that point the trainer was called to the telephone. "Practice the correct method I showed you first," he said, "I'll be right back." When he returned 15 minutes later, 30 T-bones had been trimmed incorrectly and the trainee had cut his left thumb to the bone.

As is so often the case with inept trainers, this one blamed the accident on the trainee. When he returned and saw the mess, his comment was, "This would not have happened had you paid attention. I told you to do it the way I showed you the first time."

But if the trainee has not learned, it can be assumed that the trainer has not properly taught. The trainer's demonstration of one correct and three incorrect methods had thoroughly confused the trainee. The trainer must realize that he cannot describe a procedure in one fashion and perform it in another. To the trainee, the demonstrated way is the right way regardless of what is said. If the trainer demonstrates the task in a sloppy way to show how it should not be done, the trainee is likely to learn the sloppy method of performing the task.

Errors committed during practice must be corrected immediately before they solidify as bad habits. A bad habit is developed through repetition and the longer it is practiced, the more natural it becomes and the more difficult it is to root out. Errors that occur during the performance of a task are often due to the trainee's desire to work too rapidly in order to make a good impression. The trainer must emphasize that speed is a product of practice, and the trainee's initial goal should be accuracy rather than speed.

Teaching Cycles Should Be Short and Immediately Reinforced by Practice

A meat trainer in one company, following an excellent instructor's manual, showed a trainee how to break a beef forequarter into primal cuts. He demonstrated each successive step of the task, stated its key points and reasons why each was necessary, and why it was done in a given manner. He began his demonstration by conditioning the neck (removing discolored parts) and ended 35 minutes and 73 steps later by working up all the trimmings. When he finished, he handed the trainee a knife and told him to go to work on a fresh forequarter. It is not difficult to imagine the predicament of the trainee.

Although the trainer had followed an excellent manual and had provided the proper explanation, he made the mistake of giving the trainee too much to digest at one time without the opportunity to practice each step in succession. Such an approach never succeeds because a trainee requires time to assimilate what he has been told and shown. He can retain the information only if it is presented to him in small units and if he is allowed to practice each short cycle immediately after it is demonstrated. Each cycle should contain three to six steps, depending on the complexity of the steps. For example, the meat trainer first should have explained and demonstrated the conditioning of the neck; then he should have asked the trainee to practice this cycle on several forequarters before proceeding to the next cycle. Likewise, the balance of the breaking operation should have been presented, demonstrated, and practiced in short segments.

However, the trainer should also take time out to describe the total job. For example, before beginning instruction on the breakdown of a forequarter, he should briefly discuss the total forequarter breakdown, identifying the various primals on the carcass that will eventually become the products of the breaking job. Such a summary enables the trainee to visualize and understand the end result and to relate each successive step to the final goal.

Skills Should Be Developed Through Repetition

Repetition builds skill. The retention of information and the development of skills are directly related to the amount of practice the trainee is allowed. In the early stages of learning, the apprentice usually retains three to four times the knowledge, and retains it longer, if he is allowed to practice the task two times instead of once, or four cycles instead of two.

Immediately after the initial demonstration, the trainee should repeat the cycle until he performs it correctly without hesitation or false movement. When he performs a segment of an operation for the first time, he should be permitted to continue working undisturbed at his own rate of speed as long as he is performing the task correctly. If he recognizes a mistake himself he should be allowed to correct it without interference. On the other hand, if the trainee fails to recognize a mistake, he must be interrupted and corrected in a friendly manner, preferably in private, because no one likes to be corrected in the presence of others. To make certain the trainee understands the correct methods, the trainer should question him about the key points of the steps performed. Moreover, the trainee should be praised whenever he performs the job properly.

The amount of repetition required will vary from trainee to trainee and from job to job. However, at the time of initial instruction, each cycle should be performed by the trainee a minimum of three times before proceeding to the next cycle in the task. But even a procedure such as this does not guarantee that the trainee will master every step, and further practice is often necessary. In any case, the training program must provide sufficient time for practice. The amount of time that is allotted depends on the number of steps to be learned, the complexity or difficulty of the task, and the ability of the trainee as well as the trainer. After each of the cycles in an operation has been individually mastered, the trainee should be guided through the complete operation and permitted to practice until he can perform it accurately and completely.

The Trainee Must Be Motivated

The degree to which the trainee is motivated often determines whether he will put his whole heart into learning or whether he will perform half-heartedly. Thus, a trainer who knows how to motivate people has a great advantage over one who does not. There are three fundamental ways to motivate an employee during the training period: (1) by emphasizing the importance of each task being taught; (2) by encouraging the trainee through analyzing his attitudes and needs; and (3) by informing him of his progress and having him set his own learning goals.

Even though the required skill, dexterity, and leadership capability vary significantly from one job to another, there is no such thing as an unimportant job in the meat department. Every job is important. Just as a supermarket cannot stay in business without a meat cutter or a meat department manager, so it cannot function without a wrapper or a clean-up man. Therefore, no matter what job is being taught, the trainee should be aware of its importance to the overall success of the department and the store so that he will be proud and want to perform well.

The trainer must watch closely for clues which will identify and, perhaps, explain the trainee's needs and attitudes. One trainee may require more recognition for a job well done than another. A second trainee may lack self-confidence and need more reassurance than another. A third may require closer supervision. A fourth trainee may be frustrated and concerned over how well he is doing, and his learning ability may consequently be impaired. Such anxiety may be avoided if the trainee is kept informed of the nature of the job he is learning and of his progress. When he finds the motivating key, the trainer should use it to unlock the trainee's talents. A well motivated trainee will learn faster and better than one who is not properly motivated.

When a trainee learns slowly, some trainers tend to become impatient. Although the job now seems simple to them, such trainers tend to forget that it was not so simple when they first learned it themselves. A trainer should avoid showing impatience either in word, deed, or facial expression. Any expression of impatience makes the trainee apprehensive and nervous and further retards his learning ability.

The trainer who is satisfied that his trainee knows how to perform an operation should gradually allow him to work on his own.

Over-supervision or "snoopervision" tends to kill initiative. Nevertheless, the trainee should occasionally be checked and watched, particularly for the repetition of mistakes he might have made earlier in training.

Perhaps the most critical factor in motivating an employee is keeping him informed of his performance or learning progress. For example, how many forequarters is a trainee expected to break into primals per hour, after 10 hours of training and practice? After 20 hours? How many one-pound packages of ground beef should the trainee wrap per hour at the end of her first day? At the end of her first week? Without such standards against which to measure performance, everyone, the trainer and the trainee included, is working in the dark.

Measuring employee performance during training allows the trainee to compete not only against the standard, but also against other trainees. The development of a friendly, competitive atmosphere can do much to instill enthusiasm, to motivate the trainee, and thus to stimulate learning. Moreover, measured performance provides the opportunity for deserved recognition of achievement which is also a strong motivating force.

Keeping the trainee informed is not nearly as difficult as it might seem. One meat trainer, for example, keeps a record of the time required by each new trainee to cut loins into T-bone, porterhouse, and strip steaks. For each trainee who goes through the training program, the trainer records the average time required to process the 3rd, 5th, 10th, 15th, 20th, and 25th loins. On the basis of these averages, he has established learning standards for processing short loins up to 25 cycles. He has recorded and drawn charts showing the same information for every major activity in the training program. The figures are posted in the cutting room of the model meat department, and each trainee is encouraged to compare his performance with the average for 3rd, 5th, 10th, 15th, 20th, and 25th cycles. As additional trainees are trained, the trainer revises his average performance figures.

This is an excellent way to keep the trainee informed of his progress since it eliminates guesswork and opinion from performance evaluation. The establishment of standards for various stages in the learning process also permits the trainee to establish his own learning goals on the basis of the progress he is making. Self-imposed learning goals are particularly effective in motivating the average trainee.

WHAT DOES TRAINING REALLY COST?

Studies conducted by a number of supermarket companies have indicated that there is a 30 percent loss in productivity during the training period required to learn a manual task. Thus, if it takes 20 months to train an apprentice meat cutter to perform all manual operations correctly and repeatedly using osmosis training, the cost of that training is 30 percent of the employee's salary for the 20-month period. If the new employee, for example, earns $5 an hour, including benefits, or about $866 per month, he will gross $17,320 during the 20-month period, but will be unproductive for 30 percent of that time. Translated into dollars, his training by osmosis will cost the company $5,196.

If the training period for that same employee can be reduced to three or four months through a structured training program (and it can), the cost to the company will be between $779 and $1,039 or a minimum saving of $4,000 per trainee.

Every company that employs new people has a training cost, but most underestimate the cost of osmosis training because the costs are hidden in loss of productivity. On the other hand, when a professional training program is developed and implemented, the costs surface and are more readily observable.

The major costs involved in developing an effective training program are: (1) the cost of the training department personnel, or the meat trainer who is taken out of a store or district to head up the development of the training program; (2) the cost of the time of the people involved in developing standard practices and implementing them in existing stores; and (3) the cost of teaching the meat trainer and the model department training managers to know and to apply the principles of teaching and the principles of learning.

To learn the principles of teaching and the principles of learning, it is recommended that only the new meat trainer be sent to visit other companies and that he, in turn, train the model department training managers. He should probably spend two or three days at two companies, reviewing the materials they have available and observing the actual training in progress. Such visits will expose him to the techniques, methods, and training aids that are used in more progressive companies, which he can adapt to his own needs.

Who Pays the Cost of the Trainee?

The area that creates the greatest problem with regard to the cost of training is that of reimbursing the trainee during the training period. Many excellent training programs have fallen apart because this problem has not been resolved satisfactorily.

More often than not, top management recommends that the trainee's salary be absorbed by the store in which he is being trained. However, the meat manager responsible for training the new employee is also responsible and accountable for controlling wage expenses. Therefore, rather than absorb the cost of the trainee's lost productivity during his training period, the meat manager has a natural tendency to remove the trainee from the training program and to assign him to the least skilled jobs in the department where he can be more productive. As a result, the training program as developed and planned often is never implemented. Unless a company solves this dilemma in advance, the trainer will not be motivated to teach the trainee anything complicated; and the training program will continue for many months beyond what is actually required.

In the model department concept, because one store is training employees who will be placed in other stores at the end of the training program, it makes sense that the training costs be spread out over the stores in the district. In other words, the cost of the employee during his training period should be distributed among the stores that will benefit from the training program.

There are several alternative solutions to this program. One is to charge a portion (perhaps 50 percent) of the trainee's salary to the training store, based on the theory that even though the trainee is not skilled, he is still making some contribution to the department's production. The balance of his salary would be charged to a general training budget set up for the entire company.

Another alternative is not to charge any costs to the training store, but to set up a training budget for the district based on the anticipated number of meat department employees who must be trained in a given quarter, six months, or annual period. At the end of the fiscal quarter (or other period), the costs are allocated to all the stores in the district on an equal basis or they are distributed only among those stores that will receive the new employees after training is completed.

Normally, no more than two people are trained in a model department at one time. This is a reasonable number for a district of from 5 to 12 stores when an expertly developed 13-week meat apprentice program is used. If turnover within the district is not excessive, two trainees during each quarter should adequately fill the district's replacement needs.

It is recommended that model department training be used for such skilled jobs as apprentice meat cutter but not for the less skilled jobs such as wrappers or pricers. These less skilled tasks should be taught by the meat manager in each individual store, which again emphasizes the need to qualify each meat department manager in knowing not only how to follow through on training but also in knowing the principles of learning and teaching. When the department manager is capable of using effective training techniques, rather than osmosis training, the trainee will learn more quickly, he will learn the correct methods to use, he will be motivated, and, most important from a cost point of view, he will be more productive.

SUMMARY

In comparison with the cost of a conventional osmosis-type training program, the application of sound training principles in a structured training program can, according to several highly successful supermarket chains, reduce training time and costs by from 50 to 75 percent. The other obvious advantages that accrue from professional training are reduced employee turnover, higher productivity, and improved accuracy. Companies using such training programs have found that the return on their investment can be realized solely from the 50 to 75 percent reduction in training time and costs.

13

The Role of the Meat Department Manager

It is traditional in the supermarket industry to evaluate meat department managers on the basis of their performance in five major areas of measurable results: (1) total meat sales, (2) meat sales as a percent of total store sales (i.e., distribution percent), (3) gross profit percent, (4) wage expense, and (5) supply and linen costs. The manager who attains the best record in each of these five areas is usually considered the best performer in the company. The fallacy in this type of evaluation, which is probably used in 9 out of 10 companies, is that the customer has as much, if not more, influence over three of these factors as does the department manager.

Distribution, gross profit, and wage expense are directly affected by the department's product mix, which in turn is affected and largely determined by customer shopping preferences. This is not to suggest that the manager is impotent in merchandising the department to influence the product mix. On the contrary, his merchandising skills are usually the determining factor in the profitability of the department. But what must be kept in mind when evaluating managerial performance is that a manager with a 22-percent gross profit percentage may be doing an equal or superior job to a manager with a 23-percent gross profit percentage.

Two meat departments in the same company located only one mile apart with the same pricing structure and supervised by managers of equal ability could vary in gross profit by 2 percentage points. The reason is that the customers in each of the stores buy in such a manner that the resulting product mix has a significant effect on the gross profit percentage that is realistically attainable in either store. Pork is normally a higher profit item than beef. Therefore, a store located in an area where customer demand for pork is high should have a higher gross profit percentage than a store located in an area where beef demand is high. The same is true for distribution, which can vary by as much as 10 percentage points or more from one store to another because of the product mix, which is affected by the location of the store and the demands of the customers it serves. Such differences could also be influenced by one store having extensive non-foods, service delicatessen, and bakery departments, while the other did not. Wage expense will also vary from one store to another depending on the customers' demand for service and the amount of processing that is required at store level because of the product mix required to meet customer demand, as well as variations in average wage rates.

Nevertheless, most companies continue to use a constant standard to evaluate meat managers on factors over which the customer exerts significant influence. Literally thousands of meat managers have been unfairly demoted, discharged, or promoted because the company has failed to take into consideration the variations that exist from store to store when customer demand determines, to a large extent, the product mix, and therefore the department's performance. Yet, if the department manager's performance is to be evaluated fairly, consideration must be given to the variations created by the customer. The company should establish standards, for example, for man-hour requirements and for gross profit percentage for the major commodity groups, and determine over an historical period the normal demands for each commodity group on a store-by-store basis. In other words, the customer (i.e., the product mix) must be evaluated before the manager can be. Then, by translating variations in product mix into standards of performance, a company will know that Store

A, for example, with the same degree of managerial skills as Store B, should be attaining a 1½-percent higher gross profit because the product mix of Store A makes that level of performance realistic.

Once such standards are established for each store in the company, the performance of each department manager can be measured, and it can be determined whether his performance is above, below, or at the average standard established for his store. He can be evaluated on his ability to order properly so that there is adequate product on display, minimal shrinkage, and few out-of-stocks; to schedule people so that labor costs are minimized; to train people so that they are promotable; to motivate people so that turnover is kept to a minimum; to ensure that his people use the proper size film and trays so that supply costs are not excessive; to enforce processing and wrapping procedures that will minimize linen costs consistent with proper sanitation; and to be an innovative merchandiser so that he influences, to the greatest extent possible, what the customer buys, which in turn is reflected in higher gross profit dollars, higher sales and distribution, and lower labor and material costs.

IDENTIFYING CANDIDATES FOR PROMOTION

Just as stores have different characteristics which affect performance, so do employees. Therefore, each company must select from its available manpower pool those employees who, by virtue of their past performance, have demonstrated the greatest potential for success as department managers. Obviously, the most likely candidates will be among those who have had successful track records as assistant meat managers or assistant head meat cutters. But within that group, despite equal success at their current jobs, there will be both good and poor prospects for promotion. The best candidates will be among those employees who, first and foremost, *want* to be department managers. This point cannot be overemphasized. It is sometimes difficult for management to accept the fact that some employees do not want to be promoted to positions requiring supervisory skills, and many a satisfied "working employee" has had a successful employment record shattered by being placed in an unwanted position of leadership.

Therefore, the candidate must want to be a manager and should show evidence of that desire by his aggressiveness, his willingness to learn and to assume responsibility, his open-mindedness to new ideas, and his creative ability, particularly with regard to innovative merchandising ideas. Moreover, he should have earned the respect of his superiors, his peers, and his subordinates in his present position. And, he obviously must have the technical skills required to operate a meat department. While his physical capabilities are also important, it can be assumed that he has shown evidence, in his present position, of physical coordination and strength and that he is willing to work in below-normal temperatures. Individuals with serious hernia or back troubles should not work in supermarkets; moreover, people with chest or kidney difficulties will be adversely affected by the cold.

One way to evaluate the assistant's managerial potential is to monitor his performance while he assumes the responsibility for the department during the manager's vacation period, day off, or other absence. He can also be appraised for his leadership skills through tests such as the Leadership Appraisal which might help to identify promotable employees.[1]

WHAT IS A MANAGER?

The two basic components of managing are (1) knowing the department's operation, and (2) applying to the operation the four vital managerial skills of planning, organizing, supervising, and controlling.

Details of the Operation

Because the department manager of a $15,000 to $25,000 weekly volume meat department will spend much of his day supervising, training, and developing his employees as well as performing the physical operations in the department, it is essential that he have expert knowledge of the department's operation, especially in areas such as product knowledge, standard practices, and merchandising.

Product knowledge is extremely important to the department manager who is held accountable for customer relations and merchandising practices, which affect gross profits. A manager must know his products, including seasonality, quality, perishability, cooking methods, and ethnic preferences if he is to offer suggestions and advice to his customers. Product knowledge is also important from a merchandising point of view if the manager is to develop and capitalize on tie-in displays, seasonal promotions, and other special

---

[1] Glenn Mitchell and Edward M. Harwell, *Leadership Appraisal* (New York: Chain Store Publishing Corp., 1971).

display opportunities. In addition, if a manager is to be held responsible for the gross profits of his department, he must know gross profit percentages and be taught the basics of costs and markups.

While no company would want to withhold from its department managers knowledge that relates to the physical characteristics of the product, there is a wide difference of opinion regarding disseminating pricing and markup information. In some companies, the meat department manager is given the actual gross profit percentage on each item. Other companies assign codes to indicate a gross profit range; for example, Code A might indicate an item with a gross profit of less than 10 percent, whereas Code E would refer to items grossing more than 40 percent. In still other companies, gross profit information is limited to a few highly profitable items on which weekly merchandising bulletins are issued. And, there are those companies that give their meat department managers no information whatsoever on the profitability of the various items in the department. Yet, it should be obvious that there is no way that a manager can be held accountable for the performance of his department, in terms of gross profit, without having such knowledge on various items.

Companies that withhold individual item gross profit information from their meat department managers explain their actions on the following basis: The company spends large sums of money on advertising to bring customers into the store, and meat items are often used as the drawing card. The meat manager sees only his operation, rather than the total merchandising picture. If he knows that certain items bring a lower profit than others, he might be tempted not to display those lower profit items, which would defeat the company's total store merchandising campaign.

In such companies, costs, retails, and gross profit percentages are made available to the meat supervisors on all items; the department manager is merely told, on a week-to-week basis, which items will generate the most profit, but he is not given specific figures, and especially not on low-profit items. However, no department manager can be held accountable for the performance of his department without such information, and a company that does otherwise is really admitting that it is incapable of exerting the kind of discipline required at store level to ensure that product is on display in accordance with the standards that the company has established.

In addition to product knowledge, a manager must know the company's standard practices for the equipment, tools, and supplies that are being used in the department; the approved methods of ordering, receiving, processing, packaging, product rotation, and price changing; and the requirements for maintaining proper levels of sanitation, temperature, safety, maintenance, and security. To be a successful merchandiser, the department manager must understand how performance is affected by impulse buying, customer traffic patterns, item profitability, product grouping, product presentation, space allocation, in-store merchandising, tie-in merchandising, interdepartment merchandising, merchandising private or controlled label items, ethnic items, and advertised, promotional, new, and seasonal items, as well as how to dispose of discontinued or distress items.

Some companies feel that to round out his role as an expert in department operations, the department manager should also have an understanding of the company's service operations and how buying, warehousing, transportation, advertising, accounting, and personnel are related to the department's operation.

While it is assumed that candidates for the department manager position will have acquired, as assistants in the department, varying degrees of knowledge in department operations (i.e., product knowledge, standard practices, and merchandising techniques), in most cases they will have had little opportunity to develop their managerial skills in planning, organizing, supervising, and controlling. And, more often than not, employees who are discharged from management positions are those who have not been properly trained in these four vital managerial skills.

Managerial Skills

To be an effective planner, a meat department manager should know how to forecast weekly sales volume and tonnage by commodity group and the labor required to fill those needs adequately. He should also be capable of developing courses of action to improve his department's performance and to establish realistic goals and target dates for their completion. In some companies, he is responsible for projecting the percent of department sales to total store sales, tonnage, gross profit, and wage, supply, and linen expenses.

As an organizer, he will be responsible for scheduling employees to match production requirements, for assigning primary and secondary responsibilities to employees to make the best possible use of the available man-hours, and for delegating authority, not only so that more of his own time may be spent in managing the department, but also so that his employees are given the opportunity to gain the experience required for their own career advancement.

Under supervisory skills, the meat department manager must be capable of inducting, motivating, training, and developing employees. He also will be expected to handle employee grievances in a manner that will improve morale, and he must be a good listener and counselor to his employees. Moreover, as the department's link to management, he must be capable of communicating effectively within the organizational structure. In addition, he will be expected to supervise the department's operation so that plans are successfully executed and so that customer relations are handled in a manner that will benefit the department and the entire store.

A manager who is properly controlling his department will be skillful in evaluating performance, measuring results at preplanned intervals, and analyzing problems and making decisions. Additionally, he will know how to evaluate the results of any actions, how to discipline and commend employees, and how to follow through on any aspect of the department's operation.

Manual skills alone no longer suffice; the manager's ability to plan, organize, supervise, and control will be critical to his success.[2]

TRAINING FOR MANAGERIAL RESPONSIBILITIES

Invariably, the new department manager will have been trained in technical skills by his own department manager. In fact, if he has not been, it is an indication of the department manager's inability to delegate responsibility and to train his staff. Day-to-day pressures are often cited as the reason for not having trained subordinates, but often this is an excuse used by an insecure manager who fears losing his own job. Because many meat department managers do not want to transfer to other store departments or even to store management positions because of the inequities that exist in wage rates and hours, the mobility of a meat department manager within a company is very much limited.

Thus, many meat managers are covetous of their present positions and shy away from developing subordinates who might become competitive. However, one of the primary responsibilities of any

---

[2] For a detailed discussion of these subjects, see Edward M. Harwell, *Personnel Management and Training* (New York: Chain Store Publishing Corp., 1969).

department manager is to train and develop subordinates, and a company that allows a department manager to shirk that responsibility will not have available the pool of promotable people it needs for normal turnover and growth. For this reason, it is unwise for a company to use relief managers to fill in on a roving basis as needed because this practice relieves the department manager of the responsibility to train the second man in his department and eliminates the opportunity for management to observe the assistant's performance and evaluate his potential as a future department manager.

Each company should develop a program to train those meat cutters and assistant department managers who have been identified as promotable. Without a well planned training program, training will be done by osmosis in the department, if at all. For example, the manager-trainee will probably have no experience in writing an order unless it is part of a planned training program. Yet, such experience is necessary in the development of any future manager. It is only with a carefully planned training program that the trainee will learn to exercise judgment and to evaluate factors such as paydays, holidays, advertised items, sales for the corresponding week the previous year, sales for the previous week, and other factors such as the inventory on hand, competitive situations, merchandising opportunities, etc., all of which enter into writing an intelligent order.

Moreover, companies without some type of formal training program are often forced to raid their competition to fill vacancies. This is an unwise practice not only because it is discouraging to and destroys the confidence and loyalty of meat department employees who seek advancement, but also because employees from other companies will not have the required technical skills and knowledge with regard to standards for cutting, trimming, and processing product as well as other important details of the operation.

In-store Training

Training in meat department operations is usually done at store level or in a model department, whereas training in managerial skills is most often handled centrally. Some companies develop their store level training programs around the major areas of the department manager's responsibilities. Such a program might take the following form:

A. Display case:
   1. Developing effective customer relations
   2. Knowing cooking methods for all items
   3. Making sure that required items are on display
   4. Maintaining proper load levels
   5. Supervising cleanliness of cases and floor in sales area
   6. Maintaining proper case temperatures
   7. Supervising shelf life, code-dating, and product rotation
   8. Removing discolored items, torn or leaky packages
   9. Preventing freezer burn on frozen items
   10. Maintaining correct prices on all items
   11. Checking to ensure that signs are on advertised items and that all advertised items are on display at all times
   12. Merchandising effectively
B. Receiving and processing:
   1. Enforcing receiving procedures and standards
   2. Maintaining sanitation and temperature control
   3. Making sure that merchandise is refrigerated unless it is being processed
   4. Knowing trimming policies on all items
   5. Scheduling production, workloads, and people so that proper quantities are processed in the proper order each day
   6. Controlling wage expense, gross profit, and supply costs
   7. Knowing shrinkage and tare allowances
   8. Performing cutting tests
   9. Enforcing safety standards
C. Cooler management:
   1. Knowing ordering procedures
   2. Conditioning rail stock properly
   3. Maintaining sanitation and temperature control
   4. Maintaining proper inventory control
   5. Enforcing ground beef quality control
   6. Checking that no odds and ends are in cooler except returns of guaranteed sale merchandise

These general headings indicate the breadth and scope of the department manager's major responsibilities. They also indicate the need for a planned training program that will equip him to perform effectively. The simple fact that the man has been loyal and dedicated and has performed well as a meat cutter will be of little help to him in getting work done through others, planning the workload, scheduling people, controlling shrinkage, generating sales, achieving a satisfactory distribution percentage, developing subordinates, handling special orders and customer complaints, taking an accurate inventory, dealing with government inspectors or union representatives, and the myriad of other activities that enter into running a successful department. It is only through a planned training program that he will have the arsenal of skills required for successful performance.

Only with a background of training and experience can an individual be expected to evaluate his operation and to make the types of decisions that will spell the difference between operating at a level above or below the standard set for his department. For example, on the surface, at least, it would appear that any company should be able to establish guidelines for scheduling people, but the fact is that there is no one best schedule to recommend. Yet, there are scheduling principles which should be followed, and every company has the obligation of training managers in these principles. Application of these principles requires judgment, of course, and whether a particular meat department is using the best schedule for its operation will depend on the manager's ability to exercise good judgment.

Because the scheduling of hours in a meat department is one of the most important components in a successful operation, this function provides a good example of the value of the combination of good training and good judgment.

Assuming that meat cutters should be assigned the earliest lunch hours, while the wrappers and pricers remain behind to package product left out of refrigeration on the production line, it would seem logical also to assume that meat cutters should be scheduled to begin their working day earlier than other department employees. However, whether or not this is the best solution will depend on the various jobs assigned to the department employees. If the wrappers are responsible for checking or cleaning the display cases or setting up the luncheon meat displays, they should probably start work at the same time as the meat cutters; otherwise they will fall far behind the cutters in wrapping product that has been processed. On the other hand, if the wrappers have no other specific assignments to perform when the store opens, they should be scheduled to start and end their working day perhaps one-half hour after the cutters. This, too, however, will depend on how much flexibility the department has. While it is preferable to set up the luncheon meat case in the evening, if the store closes at 9 P.M. and the last employee in the department leaves at 7 or 8 P.M., the department manager will have no option but to schedule the wrappers to spend some time (which will vary depending on the day of the week) setting up the luncheon meats, bacon, turkeys, and so on before they can perform any wrapping duties in the morning.

If a store opens for business at 9 A.M., the meat cutters should be scheduled to start work at 8 A.M., except on Monday (if the store is closed on Sunday) when they would start working at 5 or 6 A.M., to allow them the hours they will need to process product after a Sunday closing. Moreover, time must be allowed to wash and clean the display cases, which is done each Monday morning in some companies. However, whether all the meat cutters will be brought in at the same time or on a staggered schedule will depend on several factors, including the department's volume, the hours the store is open, and the expected workload for each day of the week. For example, if the department consists of two cutters and a manager, and the store opens at 9 A.M., it might be advisable to start one cutter at 8 A.M. and the second cutter at 8:30 because, while it takes only one man to mix the trimmings for ground beef (the first item processed in the morning), it might take two men to grind the meat—one to feed the trimmings into the grinder and another to catch the ground meat as it is extruded. This, too, will depend on the equipment that the store has available. On the other hand, if there are four cutters in the department, it might be advisable for one to begin work at 8, two to start at 8:30, and the fourth to begin his day at 12:30, working until the 9 P.M. store closing.

The number of cutters and wrappers scheduled to work in the department will depend to some extent on how the manager decides to spend his own time. Some managers prefer to work in the backroom and delegate the display counters to a clerk. In such cases, it would be possible to have one less cutter but an additional clerk might be required to handle the display cases. While most managers are working managers and have the option of where and how they prefer to spend their time, it is not advisable to allow a manager to spend too much of his working day in retail cutting, boning, and trimming; if he concentrates his time and energies there, he will spend little time supervising and otherwise managing the department. Therefore, while it is reasonable for a manager to seek some variety in his work and to want to spend some time in the backroom, he should be expected to move about the entire department and to fill in wherever necessary. He should be discouraged from working on the saw or becoming involved in any backroom activity which he cannot easily leave when he is needed elsewhere. While this is the ideal arrangement, it obviously cannot and will not work in a small department where there is only one cutter and a manager. In such a situation, the manager will have to schedule himself to perform some of the cutting in addition to working the display area.

Scheduling days off is also subject to variation. Most companies agree that the department manager should never take Monday off if the store is closed on Sunday. Because of the heavy Monday workload and the decisions that may have to be made on a Monday morning, such as what to do with product that has been left over from Saturday, he must be available the first day of the week. However, there are differences of opinion with regard to a manager not working on Saturday. Some companies prohibit this practice, while others feel that the manager should be allowed to be off at least part of the day. The rationale behind the second opinion is that if the manager has not properly prepared the department by Saturday morning, he will be incapable of doing so during the rest of the day and that it is far more important that he be on the job on Thursday and Friday, which are very heavy processing days. However, this too depends on whether the store is closed on Sunday, the capabilities of the assistant in the department, and the reliability of the entire staff.

Moreover, unless the meat manager has a reliable and experienced assistant to whom the job can be delegated, he should schedule himself to work late on the Saturdays when period-ending inventories are taken. In some companies, an inventory is taken weekly; in others, bi-weekly or monthly. Often the cooler and display case are piece counted. The meat manager is asked to send headquarters the number of pieces on hand, by type of cut; using average weights headquarters extends these figures to establish the closing inventory at cost. In other companies, the cooler and display case are inventoried by primal, by weight. For example, the manager sends headquarters the actual weight of all product in the cooler by commodity and the total weight of each item in the display case, grouped according to the primal from which the cuts were made. Headquarters then translates the weights to retail value and cost. Other companies only take a cooler inventory and assume a constant display case inventory at closing time on Saturday night. Stores that take monthly inventories will usually take weekly inventories in problem stores and a weekly inventory in one store in each district on a rotating basis. In many companies the meat manager must be available when such inventories are taken to guarantee that they are taken accurately.

The meat manager should also schedule himself to work on the busiest night of the week. If that night is Friday, and the store closes at 9 P.M., the meat department manager should schedule himself to begin work at noon, if he works an eight-hour day. However, meat department managers typically work a 42 to 45-hour week, including planned overtime. In some companies, overtime is given to top-performing meat managers as a means of rewarding them for their performance.

Thus, while the variations in the meat department manager's own schedule are somewhat limited, the possible combinations in scheduling lunch hours, breaks, and days-off for full-time wrappers and cutters, plus working part-timers into the schedule to maintain flexibility are many. The meat manager must exercise his judgment to maximize his available labor hours so that product is available in the proper quantities at the proper time and at the lowest possible labor cost.

While he will usually plan his schedule with his store manager, it is the meat manager's intimate knowledge of the department's activities and requirements that will result in the optimum work schedule being executed.

Central Training

Qualifying a man to become a manager, in the true sense of the word, is no simple task because training in managerial skills requires a classroom setting which can be costly. While a number of training programs are available through industry and management groups, few companies can afford to enroll their department managers in those programs which require him to be off the job for one or two weeks or more. Moreover, many of these programs are not supermarket-oriented, as they should be if the training in planning, supervising, organizing, and controlling is to be meaningful to the meat department manager.

Therefore, the best approach is for a company to develop its own training program, using training aids and materials that are available from outside sources, but customizing them to its own operation. For example, the American Management Association has two programs—"The Basic Skills of Supervisory Management" and

"Developing Supervisory Leadership Skills." Each of these courses is divided into eight units. For each unit the AMA supplies general films, as well as short filmed case studies dramatizing actual problems, role-playing scripts, programmed instruction texts, and other materials for in-company classroom or home study. Each course unit contains sufficient instructional materials for a two or three-hour training session.

The strength of the AMA programs is their complete coverage of the subject and the technical competence of those who have developed the training materials. Their weakness is that they are not oriented to the supermarket industry. However, many companies have made effective use of these materials to teach basic principles, while developing their own systems and techniques, case studies, and role playing situations tailored to everyday supermarket problems, to illustrate the principles.

The Xerox Corporation has also developed some outstanding training materials, including tapes, films, and programmed instruction courses on specific managerial skills. However, these, too, are most effective when adapted to supermarket situations and problems.

Any company that sincerely wants a management skills training program can locate or develop the necessary materials. The basic problem is not in developing the program, but rather in allowing a trainee the opportunity to develop his managerial skills by applying on the job what he has learned in the classroom. The difficulty is not to acquire knowledge of good managerial techniques, but to develop skills through experience in using them.

Thus, the trainee must be given the opportunity to practice these skills. Moreover, without proper follow-through, any manager training program is doomed to failure; this is the point where manager training programs often fall apart. Therefore, the final vital ingredient is to set up feedback mechanisms that will provide accurate reports regarding on-the-job application of managerial techniques to ensure that they are successfully and repeatedly performed to a point where skills are acquired in their use.

THE MANAGER'S INFLUENCE ON DEPARTMENT PERFORMANCE

While a managerial skills training program is costly to develop, not doing so can be even more costly, considering that the department manager will be responsible for sales, gross profits, wage and supply expense, and other factors that will affect the profits not only of the meat department but also of the entire store. As discussed earlier, customer preferences will affect the product mix which in turn affects the department's performance level. In the area of sales, for example, there are many influencing factors, not all of which are under the department manager's control. He has little control over setting prices, establishing policies on trimming product, deciding what items are to be advertised, what and how much equipment is to be used, the number of display cases, the location or layout of the department, the accuracy of the checkers in ringing up items, and other factors which affect sales.

However, despite the external influences on product mix and the limitations described above, the manager does control such highly important factors as ordering the proper amount of product for various days of delivery. Moreover, it is his responsibility to enforce company standards on packaging and to see that packages are priced correctly.

Sales are also influenced by the quality of the product—that is, the condition in which it is received, the amount of fat and bone left on each retail cut, the freshness of all product (especially the trimmings), the cleanliness of the department which affects product shelf life, as well as the temperature at which product is stored, processed, and displayed. Department managers are also responsible for customer service, which involves filling special orders, offering advice to customers, and talking with customers to learn the cause of any unhappy experience with meat items bought in the store, all of which affect sales.

With regard to gross profit, again, the department manager exerts considerable influence. He has the responsibility to ensure that product is of proper quality when received; he influences the product mix by the variety of product he has on display and the space allocated to each item; and he enforces standards with regard to properly boning and trimming product.

Just as the merchandiser uses cutting tests to establish prices for the retail cuts on a company-wide basis (see Chapter 9), so every good manager will periodically perform cutting tests to be certain that he is attaining the proper cutability and gross profit percentage from each type of meat sold in his store. Either he or his meat cutters will weigh a beef forequarter, for example, and break it down into retail cuts. All of the product that comes out of the forequarter is segregated, including all of the trimmings that go into stew meats, cubed steaks, and ground meats, all of the fat and bone, and all of the retail cuts. The weight for each type of product taken from the forequarter is indicated on the cutting test form. Either the manager or headquarters will then translate the cost per pound of the forequarter into the retail value of the items actually put into the case. The current price of all of the retail cuts taken from the forequarter will be related to the cost per pound of the forequarter and in this manner the gross profit of the retail cuts will be determined. A theoretical gross profit figure is arrived at by dividing the retail value of the trimmings, retail cuts, bones, and fat into the difference between the cost of the product and the retail value.

The gross profit percentage is considered theoretical for two reasons: (1) it assumes a proper fat-lean mixture of trimmings (a maximum of 30 percent fat), and (2) it assumes no loss due to rewraps or errors at the checkout. However, if the department manager performs his cutting test accurately with respect to how much of the fat content of the animal will actually be saleable, and makes an allowance for product shrinkage while it is in the display case, based on the company's standards, and also has a factor to apply for checker errors, he will be able to determine exactly whether his meat cutters are processing product correctly and whether he is achieving a gross profit percentage that falls within the acceptable range that the company has specified for the product mix in his store.

By analyzing the cutting test, the meat manager can determine whether his meat cutters are cutting according to company standards. For example, he can tell whether all of the beef stew is being taken from the quarter, rather than being put into trimmings for ground meat, whether the cuts are being overtrimmed or undertrimmed, and so on. Some companies require that a piece count be indicated on the cutting form, in addition to the number of pounds of retail cuts. With this information, the manager and/or headquarters can determine whether company standards are being followed with regard to the thickness and the weight of the retail cuts.

Figure 45 shows the results of a cutting test made on two boxes of pork loins. The loins were weighed and the total entered. Then the retail cuts were made and the weights of all the retail cuts and

The Role of the Meat Department Manager   331

the trimmings, fat, and bone were recorded. Next, the selling price was entered and multiplied by the weight of each type of retail cut to get the sales value. In this particular store, the fat and bones had no resale value. Adding the totals shows that the 123.26 pounds of product have a retail value of $147.75. However, from past experience, the company knows that losses due to rewraps and other factors will amount to 4 percent, which is deducted from the sales value. Dividing the total sales value ($141.84) by the weight (123.26) shows that the price per pound return is $1.15. If the two boxes of pork loins were purchased at 80 cents per pound, or a total of $98.61, the profit is $43.23, or a 30.5 percent gross margin ($141.84—98.61÷141.84×100=30.5).

FIGURE 45
Cutting Test on Pork Loin

Taken by: **Date**

Piece count: 2 boxes
Weight: 123.26 LBS.
Cost: $.80 per LB.
Total Cost: 98.61

	Weight	Selling Price	Sales Value
Rib End Roast	17.00	.88	14.96
Loin End Roast	28.30	1.08	30.56
Center Cut Loin Chops	21.08	1.68	35.41
Center Cut Rib Chops	29.25	1.58	46.22
Country Style Ribs	17.01	1.08	18.37
Trimmings	2.50	.89	2.23
Fat	4.40		
Bones	3.19		
Cutting Loss	.53		
Sales Value			$147.75
Shrinkage @ 4%			5.91
Total			$141.84
Price per Pound Return			$1.15
Gross Profit %			30.5%

By making cutting tests, the cutability and profitability of product that comes out of the forequarter or hindquarter of beef, veal, lamb, pork primals and poultry can be determined.

A department manager can have tremendous influence on the profitability of his department, and the difference between a good and poor manager can often be reflected in significant percentage point differences in gross profit and distribution. A typical experience occurred in one Western chain where the meat distribution in one store, over a two-year period, was between $1\frac{3}{4}$ to 2 percent above the company average. The department also ran first or second in gross profit percentage in this 40-store chain. When the company opened a new and larger store, the meat manager in this store was transferred and a new manager was placed into the older, smaller store. Under the new manager, within 60 days both distribution and gross profit percentages began to slip. It wasn't too long before this pace-setting meat department was running below company average in distribution, showing a decrease of about 3 percent. And while the department's gross profit percent was not affected as drastically, it was still off about 1 percent, but running at company average.

While this poor showing could have been caused by poor display techniques, overtrimming, leaving discolored meat in the case, or a combination of these and other factors, it was finally determined that the major source of the problem was frequent out-of-stocks on important items. The effect on distribution was even more serious than the effect on gross profit because when a meat department is out of stock, it is a safe assumption that the store will lose customers in other departments as well. Moreover, the benefits of improving distribution even though the profit percent remains the same are fairly obvious. A higher distribution percentage means increased sales in the department and increased sales mean increased gross profit dollars. If the meat department has a 25 percent distribution, (i.e., it accounts for 25 percent of the total store sales) in a $100,000 weekly volume store it will generate $25,000 in sales. If, however, the distribution percentage is increased to 27 percent, that translates into an additional $2,000 in sales, at, say, 20 percent gross profit, or an additional $400 in profit; and the gross profit in the meat department is generally higher than in most other departments. But what is even more important, and what is so difficult to measure, is what effect lost sales in the meat department have on the total store—how many customers are lost as a result of poor product presentation or frequent out-of-stocks.

Within one week after this manager was replaced, there was an immediate improvement in distribution. During the first week, the department ran 1 percent above company average and ¾ of 1 percent above during the second week. Eventually this store's meat department regained its leadership role in both distribution and gross profit. Primarily through eliminating out-of-stocks, the department manager influenced the product mix which, in turn, influenced sales and gross profit.

An economy-minded department manager also can bring more profits to the company through controlling his supply and labor costs. In a company that establishes labor standards on the basis of dollar sales per man-hour, each meat department manager has the opportunity to schedule labor hours up to the maximum allowed. But not every store requires the same amount of labor, and this figure will vary according to the store's product mix. For example, in a store where customer demand makes possible sales of a high percentage of prepackaged product, labor and supply costs will be lower than in a store where customers demand a higher than average percentage of product that must be processed, packaged, and labeled at the store. Moreover, the volume generated in each product category will affect the amount of labor and supplies required. Processing baby beef, for example, requires more labor and more supplies per 100 pounds of product than processing heavier beef. Therefore, a department manager has an obligation to his company to limit his expenditures to the needs of his particular department's product mix and not to spend any more dollars than are required to run his operation, even though that money might be readily available to him because of the company's standard allowance for labor and materials.

A department manager who really knows the details of the operation, and has the ability to get work done through people by mastering the four vital managerial skills, can be a tremendous asset to any meat department, as well as to the store and the company.

He will be a leader and a trainer. He will know how to delegate responsibility and authority to develop his people, how to motivate people, how to communicate with people, how to discipline, how to handle conflicts within his department, how to plan, organize, supervise, and control—the four basics of managerial skills training. In fact, the basic leadership qualities for a meat department manager are exactly the same as for a store manager or any executive, including the president of the company.

CAPITALIZING THE MEAT MANAGER'S TALENTS

One of the major reasons why few meat department managers move to store management positions is that there is little financial incentive for them to do so. But another reason is that they are not encouraged by their supervisors who are often reluctant to promote the more talented meat managers and thus discourage them from making such moves. However, from the total company point of view, this is shortsighted because a store manager knowledgeable in meat department operations is a tremendous asset.

In those companies bound by tradition, the meat department manager normally has only one opportunity for advancement and that is to the position of meat specialist. However, in more progressive companies, the talented meat manager is perhaps the one most sought after for development into a store manager because in most companies the typical store manager's greatest weakness is in meat department operations; therefore, a store manager with knowledge of meat operations is more likely to solve the day-to-day problems that arise in the meat department. Not only should talented meat department managers be considered for store manager positions, but those who have exhibited the ability to manage, to handle people, and to get work done through people can easily be qualified for district manager and higher supervisory positions because the management skills required in the meat department are transferable to any other operation.

When supervisors tend not to promote meat managers into other positions because of the vacuum that will be created in the meat department, it is an indication that the company lacks an effective training program. It is also equally true that a successful meat department manager is one who has trained a subordinate to take his place by teaching his assistant the standard practices; by delegating to his subordinates responsibilities for such areas as receiving and checking in product, matching product against company standards, and writing orders; and by training his subordinates to schedule people and product, and other such details of the operation. In this respect, it is a truism in management that no manager is really promotable unless he has developed a subordinate who is qualified to take his place.

The benefits that can accrue to any company willing to make the investment in training department managers are many. There is the obvious advantage of being able to promote from within, which builds loyalty and morale and provides the pool of talent needed for turnover and expansion purposes. There are the financial rewards that come from a department that is run on a profitable basis. Increased productivity comes from a satisfied staff that is being properly supervised and disciplined. In addition, there are the savings in supervisory costs when a manager can really manage and run his department. Moreover, there is the reduction in turnover, either voluntary or involuntary, that goes hand-in-hand with a man knowing and being able to perform his job. And in those companies not burdened by tradition, there are opportunities in other departments in the company for the meat department manager that will discourage him from seeking his future elsewhere. All in all, an effective training program for meat department managers is the starting point and the bedrock on which not only a viable meat department but also a successful company can be built.

Appendix

The following master list of recommended names for retail cuts of beef, veal, pork, and lamb was developed by the Industrywide Cooperative Meat Identification Standards Committee and is reprinted with permission from the National Live Stock and Meat Board. For more information, including illustrations of each retail cut, the primal cuts from which they originate, and the commonly used names, the reader should contact the National Live Stock and Meat Board (36 South Wabash Avenue, Chicago, Ill. 60603) to obtain a copy of the *Uniform Retail Meat Identity Standards* manual.

Abbreviations Used*

BAR B Q	Barbecue	POT-RST	Pot-Roast
BI	Bone In	RND	Round
BLD	Blade	RST	Roast
BNLS	Boneless	SHLDR	Shoulder
DBLE	Double	SQ	Square
LGE	Large	STK	Steak
PK	Pork	TRMD	Trimmed

BEEF CHUCK (Arm Half)
   ARM POT-ROAST
   ARM POT-RST BNLS
   CROSS RIB POT-ROAST
   CROSS RIB POT-RST BNLS
   SHOULDER POT-RST BNLS
   BEEF SOUP BONE
   ARM STEAK
   ARM STEAK BNLS
   SHORT RIBS

* Abbreviations are used because no line may contain more than 22 characters and spaces. Generally a label should contain no more than two lines of type.

Appendix

SHOULDER STEAK BNLS
SHOULDER POT-RST BNLS
SHOULDER STEAK BNLS
BEEF FOR STEW
FLAT RIBS
SHORT RIBS
FLANKEN STYLE RIB
BEEF MARROW BONES

BEEF CHUCK (Blade Half)
  NECK POT-ROAST
  NECK POT-ROAST BNLS
  NECK BONES
  BEEF FOR STEW
  POT-ROAST BNLS
  7-BONE POT-ROAST
  7-BONE STEAK
  BLADE ROAST
  BLADE STEAK
  BLADE STEAK CAP OFF
  TOP BLADE POT-ROAST
  TOP BLADE STEAK
  UNDER BLADE POT-ROAST
  UNDER BLADE STEAK
  UNDER BLD POT-RST BNLS
  UNDER BLADE STEAK BNLS
  MOCK TENDER
  TOP BLADE ROAST BNLS
  TOP BLADE STEAK BNLS
  EYE ROAST BNLS
  EYE STEAK BNLS
  EYE EDGE POT-ROAST

BEEF SHANK
  CROSS CUTS
  CROSS CUTS BNLS
  CENTER CUT
  SOUP BONES

BEEF BRISKET
  WHOLE BNLS
  POINT HLF BNLS
  FLAT HALF BNLS
  POINT CUT BNLS
  MIDDLE CUT BNLS
  FLAT CUT BNLS
  EDGE CUT BNLS
  HALF POINT BNLS
  CORNED BNLS

BEEF PLATE
  SHORT RIBS
  SPARERIBS
  RIBS
  SKIRT STEAK BNLS
  SKIRT STK CUBED BNLS
  SKIRT STEAK ROLLS BNLS
  ROLLED BNLS

BEEF FLANK
  STEAK
  STEAK CUBED
  STEAK CUBED ROLLED
  STEAK ROLLS

BEEF RIB
  ROAST LARGE END
  EXTRA TRIM RST LGE END
  STEAK LARGE END
  ROAST SMALL END
  STEAK SMALL END
  STEAK SMALL END BNLS
  EYE STEAK
  RIB EYE ROAST
  SHORT RIBS
  BACK RIBS
  ROLLED CAP POT-RST

BEEF LOIN
  TOP LOIN STEAK
  (or Strip Steak)
  TOP LOIN STEAK BNLS
  (or Strip Steak)
  T-BONE STEAK
  PORTERHOUSE STEAK
  SIRLOIN STEAK
    WEDGE BONE
    ROUND BONE
    FLAT BONE
    PIN BONE
  SHELL SIRLOIN STEAK
  SIRLOIN STEAK BNLS
  TOP SIRLOIN STEAK BNLS
  TENDERLOIN ROAST
  TENDERLOIN STEAK
  (or Filet Mignon)
  TENDERLOIN TIPS

BEEF ROUND
  STEAK
  STEAK BNLS

RUMP ROAST
RUMP RST BNLS
HEEL OF ROUND
BEEF FOR STEW
TOP ROUND STK 1st CUT
TOP ROUND STEAK
TOP RND STK BUTTERFLY
TOP ROUND ROAST
BEEF CUBED STEAK
BOTTOM ROUND RUMP RST
BOTTOM ROUND ROAST
BOTTOM ROUND STEAK
EYE ROUND ROAST
EYE ROUND STEAK
TIP ROAST
TIP STEAK
TIP STEAK CAP OFF
TIP ROAST CAP OFF
CUBES FOR KABOBS

FRESH PORK SHOULDER
PORK SHOULDER WHOLE
PORK SHOULDER RST BNLS
ARM PICNIC
ARM PICNIC BNLS
ARM ROAST
ARM STEAK
BLADE BOSTON ROAST
BLADE BOSTON RST BNLS
BLADE STEAK
PORK CUBED STEAK
CUBES FOR KABOBS
PORK HOCK

FRESH PORK LOIN
BLADE ROAST
BLADE CHOPS
COUNTRY STYLE RIBS
BACK RIBS
CENTER RIB ROAST
RIB CHOPS
(or Center Cut Chops)
RIB CHOPS FOR STUFFING
CENTER LOIN ROAST
TOP LOIN CHOPS
BUTTERFLY CHOPS
TOP LOIN ROAST BNLS

TOP LOIN CHOPS BNLS
(or Center Cut Chops Bnls)
LOIN CHOPS
SIRLOIN ROAST
SIRLOIN CHOPS
SIRLOIN CUTLETS
RIB HALF
SIRLOIN HALF
TENDERLOIN WHOLE
TIPLESS TENDERLOIN
ASSORTED CHOPS

FRESH PORK SIDE
FRESH SIDE PORK
FRESH SIDE PORK SLICED
SPARERIBS

PORK LEG (FRESH HAM)
WHOLE
ROAST BNLS
RUMP PORTION
CENTER ROAST
CENTER SLICE
SHANK PORTION
RUMP HALF
SHANK HALF
PORK CUBED STEAK

SMOKED PORK SHOULDER
SHOULDER ROLL
PICNIC WHOLE
SMOKED PORK HOCK

MISC. SMOKED PORK
JOWL
JOWL SLICES
NECKBONES
PIGS FEET

SMOKED PORK LOIN
CANADIAN STYLE BACON
ROAST
CHOPS
RIB CHOPS
BACK RIBS

SMOKED PORK BELLY
SLAB BACON
SLICED BACON
SPARERIBS

SMOKED HAM
  WHOLE
  SHANK PORTION
  SHANK HALF
  CUBES FOR KABOBS
  RUMP HALF
  RUMP PORTION
  CENTER ROAST
  CENTER SLICES
  CENTER SLICES BNLS
LAMB SHOULDER
  SQUARE CUT WHOLE
  ROAST BNLS
  CUSHION ROAST BNLS
  BLADE ROAST
  BLADE CHOPS
  ARM ROAST
  ARM CHOPS
  NECK SLICES
  CUBES FOR KABOBS
  LAMB FOR STEW
  COMBINATION
LAMB FORESHANK AND BREAST
  LAMB BREAST
  BREAST FOR STUFFING
  BREAST ROLLED
  RIBLETS
  SPARERIBS
  SHANK
LAMB RIB
  ROAST
  ROAST BNLS
  RIB CHOPS
  CROWN ROAST
  FRENCHED CHOPS
LAMB LOIN
  ROAST
  CHOPS
  DOUBLE CHOPS
  DOUBLE CHOPS BNLS
  DOUBLE ROAST BNLS
LAMB LEG
  WHOLE
  ROAST BONELESS
  SHORT CUT SIRLOIN OFF
  COMBINATION
  SIRLOIN CHOPS
  SIRLOIN HALF
  SHANK HALF
  CENTER ROAST
  CENTER SLICE
  FRENCHED STYLE ROAST
  AMERICAN STYLE ROAST
  CUBES FOR KABOBS
  LAMB FOR STEW
  LAMB CUBED STEAK
VEAL SHOULDER
  ARM ROAST
  ARM STEAK
  BLADE ROAST
  BLADE STEAK
  ROAST BONELESS
  VEAL FOR STEW
VEAL FORESHANK AND BREAST
  VEAL BREAST
  RIBLETS
  SHANK CROSS CUTS
VEAL RIB
  ROAST
  CHOPS
  CHOPS BNLS
  CROWN ROAST
VEAL LOIN
  ROAST
  ROAST BONELESS
  KIDNEY CHOPS
  LOIN CHOPS
  TOP LOIN CHOPS
VEAL LEG
  SIRLOIN ROAST
  SIRLOIN STEAK
  SIRLOIN ROAST BNLS
  ROUND ROAST
  ROUND STEAK
  RUMP ROAST
  RUMP ROAST BNLS
  HEEL ROAST
  VEAL CUBED STEAK
  CUBES FOR KABOBS
  CUTLETS

SUPPLEMENTARY MATERIAL FOR CHAPTER 4

Comparison of Yields of Retail Cuts and Retail Sales Values for Choice Beef Carcasses, by Yield Grade *
May 1974

Retail Cut	Price per Pound	Yield Grade 1 % of Carcass	Yield Grade 1 Value/cwt.	Yield Grade 2 % of Carcass	Yield Grade 2 Value/cwt.	Yield Grade 3 % of Carcass	Yield Grade 3 Value/cwt.	Yield Grade 4 % of Carcass	Yield Grade 4 Value/cwt.	Yield Grade 5 % of Carcass	Yield Grade 5 Value/cwt.
Rump, boneless	$1.70	3.7%	$ 6.29	3.5%	$ 5.95	3.3%	$ 5.61	3.1%	$ 5.27	2.9%	$ 4.93
Inside round, boneless	1.82	4.9	8.92	4.5	8.19	4.1	7.46	3.7	6.73	3.3	6.01
Outside round, boneless	1.74	4.8	8.36	4.6	8.00	4.4	7.67	4.2	7.31	4.0	6.96
Round tip, boneless	1.80	2.7	4.86	2.6	4.68	2.5	4.50	2.4	4.32	2.3	4.14
Sirloin, bone-in	1.71	9.1	15.56	8.7	14.88	8.3	14.19	7.9	13.51	7.5	12.82
Short loin, bone-in	1.97	5.3	10.44	5.2	10.24	5.1	10.05	5.0	9.85	4.9	9.65
Blade chuck, bone-in	.87	9.9	8.61	9.4	8.18	8.9	7.74	8.4	7.31	7.9	6.87
Rib, short cut (7"), bone-in	1.60	6.3	10.08	6.2	9.92	6.1	9.76	6.0	9.60	5.9	9.44
Chuck, arm boneless	1.29	6.4	8.26	6.1	7.87	5.8	7.48	5.5	7.10	5.2	6.71
Brisket, boneless	1.54	2.5	3.85	2.3	3.54	2.1	3.23	1.9	2.90	1.7	2.62
Flank steak	2.06	.5	1.03	.5	1.03	.5	1.03	.5	1.03	.5	1.03
Lean trim	1.21	12.3	14.88	11.3	13.67	10.3	12.46	9.3	11.25	8.3	10.04
Ground beef	.93	13.3	12.37	12.2	11.35	11.1	10.32	10.0	9.30	8.9	8.28
Kidney	.66	.3	.20	.3	.20	.3	.20	.3	.20	.3	.20
Fat	.02	7.6	.15	12.7	.25	17.8	.36	22.9	.46	28.0	.56
Bone	.01	10.4	.10	9.9	.10	9.4	.09	8.9	.09	8.4	.08
Total		100.0	$113.96	100.0	$108.05	100.0	$102.15	100.0	$96.25	100.0	$90.34

Difference in retail value between yield grades—$5.90 per cwt. of carcass.

* These comparisons reflect average yields of retail cuts from beef carcasses typical of the midpoint of each of the USDA yield grades and average prices (including salepriced items) for USDA Choice beef during May, 1974 as furnished to the Economic Research Service, U.S. Department of Agriculture by a large number of selected retailers throughout the country. For further information about yield grades for beef contact Livestock Division, AMS, USDA, Washington, D. C. 20250.

Appendix 341

Comparison of Yields of Retail Cuts and Retail Sales Values for Choice Lamb Carcasses, by Yield Grade *
May 1974

Retail Cut (Bone-in)	Price per Pound	Yield Grade 1 % of Carcass	Yield Grade 1 Value/cwt.	Yield Grade 2 % of Carcass	Yield Grade 2 Value/cwt.	Yield Grade 3 % of Carcass	Yield Grade 3 Value/cwt.	Yield Grade 4 % of Carcass	Yield Grade 4 Value/cwt.	Yield Grade 5 % of Carcass	Yield Grade 5 Value/cwt.
Leg, short cut	$1.43	23.6%	$33.75	22.2%	$31.75	20.8%	$29.74	19.4%	$27.74	18.0%	$25.74
Sirloin	1.94	6.7	13.00	6.4	12.42	6.1	11.83	5.8	11.25	5.5	10.67
Short loin	2.34	10.4	24.34	10.1	23.63	9.8	22.93	9.5	22.23	9.2	21.53
Rack	2.14	8.1	17.33	7.9	16.91	7.7	16.48	7.5	16.05	7.3	15.62
Shoulder	1.36	24.9	33.87	23.8	32.37	22.7	30.87	21.6	29.38	20.5	27.87
Neck	.82	2.2	1.80	2.1	1.72	2.0	1.64	1.9	1.56	1.8	1.48
Breast	.67	9.8	6.57	9.8	6.57	9.8	6.57	9.8	6.57	9.8	6.57
Foreshank	1.06	3.5	3.71	3.4	3.60	3.3	3.50	3.2	3.39	3.1	3.29
Flank	1.17	2.3	2.69	2.3	2.69	2.3	2.69	2.3	2.69	2.3	2.69
Kidney	.94	0.5	.47	0.5	.47	0.5	.47	0.5	.47	0.5	.47
Fat	.02	4.6	.09	8.2	.16	11.8	.24	15.4	.31	19.0	.38
Bone	.01	3.4	.03	3.3	.03	3.2	.03	3.1	.03	3.0	.03
Total		100.0	$137.65	100.0	$132.32	100.0	$126.99	100.0	$121.67	100.0	$116.34

Difference in retail value between yield grades—$5.33 per cwt. of carcass.
* These comparisons reflect average yields of retail cuts from lamb carcasses typical of the midpoint of each of the USDA yield grades and average prices (including salepriced items) for USDA Choice lamb during May, 1974 as furnished to the Economic Research Service, U.S. Department of Agriculture by a large number of selected retailers throughout the country. For further information about yield grades for lamb, contact Livestock Division, AMS, USDA, Washington, D. C. 20250.

Glossary of Common Meat Industry Terms

Aging: Holding beef at 34° to 38°F., usually for two to four weeks, which allows enzymatic activity to break down complex proteins, improving flavor and tenderness. Quick aging is accomplished in two to three days by holding beef at about 65°F. A relatively high humidity is maintained to prevent dehydration of carcasses, and ultraviolet lamps help prevent microbial growth.

Baby Beef: Meat from cattle between four and eight months of age at the time of slaughter.

Bake: To cook by dry heat. Now usually done in an oven, but may be in ashes, under coals, or on heated metals or stones. When applied to meat, it is called roasting.

Barbecue: To roast meat slowly on a grill, spit, or over coals in a specially-prepared trench. The carcass may be left whole or cut in pieces. While cooking, it usually is basted with a highly seasoned sauce.

Baste: To moisten meat while cooking to add flavor and to prevent drying of the surface.

Bloom: The color of meat that is associated with freshness. The color of each species of animal varies, depending on how much myoglobin pigment is present in the tissues and muscles. Beef, for example, contains more than pork. When a cut surface of beef is exposed to oxygen, the original purplish-red pigment changes to a bright red color. The better the sanitation and temperature controls, the longer the meat will retain its bloom.

Boil: To cook in water or a liquid, mostly water, in which bubbles rise continually and break on the surface. (See Simmer.)

Boxed Beef: Trimmed primals or subprimals shipped in boxes.

Glossary of Common Meat Industry Terms

Braise: To brown meat in a small amount of fat, then cook slowly in a covered utensil in a small amount of liquid.

Bread: To coat meat with bread crumbs.

Broil: To cook by direct heat; to grill.

Butterfly: To cut double slices of desired thickness from a boneless piece of meat, leaving slices hinged on one side.

Calf: The offspring of a cow. (See Veal.)

Carcass: The dressed, slaughtered animal.

Cartage Company: A receiver and shipper of goods; often referred to as a distributor.

Cattle Grower: One who raises meat animals; also called a producer.

Chill-Packed Poultry: A form in which poultry is distributed. The poultry is processed into retail cuts, packaged, and usually price-marked at the source. After packaging, the poultry is stored, shipped, and delivered at 26° to 28°F., which forms a crust of ice on the surface of the product.

Clod (Shoulder): The large outside muscle of the chuck. It extends from the elbow of the shank to the ridge of the blade bone.

Club Steak: A name commonly used for a top loin steak; also called a strip steak.

Consumer Price Index: A measure of the changes in prices for goods and services, published monthly by the Bureau of Labor Statistics, and based upon a sample of 400 commodities and services. The Index includes changes in food retail prices for about 100 items, based on prices in retail stores in 56 cities or metropolitan areas.

CO_2-Packed Poultry: A form in which poultry is distributed. After some processing at the source, the poultry is shipped to the stores for retail processing, packaging, and pricing. The whole poultry is shipped and delivered in boxes to which dry ice snow or pellets have been added.

Cottage Butt (Roll): A selected portion of a boneless pork shoulder Blade Boston Roast which has been cured and smoked. It is also called smoked pork shoulder roll.

Cubed Steak: A boneless piece of meat which has been put through a mechanical tenderizer, forming a steak.

Cutability: The proportion of lean to fat of the carcass that is saleable as trimmed (boned or partially boned) retail cuts.

Cutlet: A thin, boneless piece of lean meat, usually from veal leg or pork loin.

Deckle: The layer of connective tissue, lean meat, and fat lying between rib bones and the primary brisket muscle.

Disposable Personal Income: The amount left from income after the payment of federal, state, and local taxes.

Department Distribution: The dollar sales in any one department, expressed as a percentage of total store sales.

Distributor: A middleman who sells and delivers product that he has purchased from a processor, or trans-ships product that the retailer has purchased from the processor.

Dredge: To sprinkle or coat meat with a fine substance, such as flour.

Enzyme: A complex protein compound produced by animals and plants which has the ability to accelerate organic reactions.

Establishment Number: The number granted an establishment or plant when it complies with all requirements for government inspection. The number appears on the inspection stamp and identifies the processing plant.

Feeders: Calves that are held back from market for fattening. They graze and are formula-fed until they are full-grown cattle, weighing about 1,100 pounds at 15 months of age.

Filet Mignon: A beef tenderloin steak.

Filet (Fillet): A boneless strip of meat or fish.

Fixed Functions: Those activities which are relatively unaffected by variations in volume—for example, sanitation, ordering, etc.

Forequarter: The anterior portion of a side that has been cut from top to bottom.

Foresaddle: The anterior portion of a veal or lamb carcass that has not been split from front to back into sides; instead the carcass is split from top to bottom to yield a foresaddle and a hindsaddle.

Freezer Burn: Discoloration due to loss of moisture and to oxidation in freezer-stored meats caused by improper packaging.

Fresh Meat: Meat that has not been salted, cured, or cured and smoked.

Fricasee: Meat cut into pieces and then braised.

Frozen Meat: Fresh meat that has been frozen.

Fry: To cook in fat; applied especially (1) to cooking in a small amount of fat—also called pan frying and (2) to cooking in a deep layer of fat—also called deep-fat frying.

Grades: (See Quality Grades and Yield Grades.)

Grill: (See Broil.)

Gross Margin or Gross Profit: That part of the selling price that remains after the cost of the goods sold has been deducted; expressed either in dollars or as a percentage.

Ground Beef Patties: Shaped patties made of ground fresh or frozen beef. (See Meat Patties.)

Ham: Meat from the hind leg of pork which has been cured and smoked.

Ham, Cooked: A term usually seen on packages of thinly-sliced boneless, fully-cooked ham that has been cured but not smoked.

Ham, Country or Country-Style: A dry-cured, smoked ham. Called country ham if produced in a rural area, country-style if produced elsewhere.

Ham, Fresh: Meat from the hind leg of pork which has not been cured or cured and smoked. Often called pork leg or leg of pork.

Glossary of Common Meat Industry Terms 345

Ham, Fully-Cooked: Ham cooked to an internal temperature of at least 150°F. Does not require further heating. To serve hot, should be heated to 140°F. before serving.

Ham, Nonperishable: Term applied to a canned ham which has been cooked to an internal temperature of at least 250°F. during processing. It can be stored without refrigeration.

Ham, Perishable: Term applied to canned hams which have been cooked to at least 150°F. during processing. To serve hot, should be heated to 140°F.

Ham, Smithfield: A ham made in Smithfield, Va. It is hand-rubbed with salt, dry-cured in the salt and then smoked and dried. Hams cured elsewhere by this process must be labeled Smithfield Style Ham and indicate place of processing.

Ham, Water Added: Ham with up to 10 percent added weight due to retention of the curing solution.

Hamburger: Ground or chopped fresh or frozen beef. Must not contain more than 30 percent fat. (See Meat Patties and Patties with Meat.)

Hindquarter: The posterior portion of a side that has been cut from top to bottom.

Hindsaddle: The posterior portion of a veal or lamb carcass that has not been split from front to back into sides; instead the carcass is split from top to bottom to yield a foresaddle and a hindsaddle.

Hotel Rack: An unsplit rib portion from the foresaddle of a lamb or veal carcass.

Inspection Mark: A round stamp placed on meat products to ensure inspection for wholesomeness. Each inspected product bears the mark of inspection and the number of the establishment where it was last processed. (See Establishment Number.)

Ice-Packed Poultry: A form in which poultry is distributed. After a limited amount of processing at the source, the poultry is shipped to the stores for retail processing, packaging, and pricing. The poultry is shipped and delivered in boxes to which ice has been added.

Jowl Bacon (Bacon Square): Cured and smoked pork jowl.

Loin Eye: One of three muscles in the loin. It is a part of the tender longissimus dorsi muscle that lies along the backbone in the rib and loin.

Marbling: Intramuscular flecks or streaks of fat within the lean. Marbling is an important factor affecting quality in meat. It enhances palatability by increasing juiciness and flavor.

Marinade: An acid (vinegar, lemon juice, lime juice) liquid, usually with seasoning and with or without oil, in which meat is allowed to stand before cooking to enrich flavor. Can also have a tenderizing effect.

Marinate: To treat with a marinade.

Meat Patties: Patties prepared from fresh or frozen chopped and/or ground meat with or without seasonings, and containing no more than 30 percent fat. If labeled with species names, must contain only meat of the named species. (See Patties with Meat.)

Miscut: A retail cut that has not been processed according to company standards with regard to thickness, fat trim, etc.

Neck Bones: Usually refers to the cervical vertebrae. Pork neck bones have two thoracic vertebrae with ribs and sternum attached.

Nitrates, Nitrites: Used in curing and preserving meats. Sodium nitrite protects meat from growth of *Clostridium botulinum* spores (cause of botulism); it gives flavor and color to processed meat. Nitrates (sodium and potassium) convert into nitrites.

Nonfat Dry Milk: Milk residue after removal of fat and moisture. Used as extender in some meat products such as sausage and meat loaves. Must be listed under "ingredients" on label.

Offal: (See Variety Meats.)

Osmosis Training: An unstructured training environment which relies upon the trainee absorbing what he observes.

Overtrimming: Removing more fat and/or bone from the retail cut than is specified in the company's standards.

Packer: A plant that processes carcasses for sale to a distributor or retailer; for example, breaking beef into quarters, manufacturing sausages, etc. In some cases the packer is also a slaughterer.

Pan Broil: To cook uncovered on a hot surface, usually in a frying pan. The fat is poured off as it accumulates.

Pan Fry: Cooking meat in a small amount of fat.

Papain: An enzyme obtained from the juice of the papaya. The enzyme action breaks down the protein in the meat and creates a tenderizing effect like aging.

Parboil: To boil for a short time preliminary to cooking by another method. Meat is precooked rather than parboiled. (See Precook.)

Patties with Meat: Patties prepared from at least 60 percent chopped and/or ground fresh or frozen meat (with a maximum of 30 percent fat); may contain water, binder and/or extender materials, poultry products, and meat by-products. Must contain not less than 13.5 percent protein with a minimum protein efficiency ration (PER) that is not less than 90 percent of PER of "Meat Patties."

Patty, Patties: Ground or chopped meat mechanically formed into a round, oval, or square patty. May be with or without other ingredients.

Per Capita Consumption: The average number of pounds consumed annually by each individual in the population.

Picnic: A front shoulder cut of pork, usually cured or smoked, and often canned.

Pigs Feet: Feet of pigs removed from the shoulder slightly above the knee joints. They may be fresh, cured, cooked, or pickled.

Portion Control Cuts: Steaks and chops which have been cut to specified weights and/or thicknesses.

Pot-Roast: A chunky piece of meat cooked by braising.

Precook: To simmer for a short time preliminary to cooking by another method. (See Simmer.) Meat is precooked rather than parboiled.

Glossary of Common Meat Industry Terms

Primal: A major section cut from a beef, lamb, or veal quarter or saddle (chuck, shoulder, rib, round, etc.) or a major section cut from a pork carcass (ham, loin, spareribs, shoulder, etc.); sometimes referred to as a wholesale cut.

Processor: (See Packer.)

Quality Grades: Official standards established by the USDA Agricultural Marketing Service for grading meat. Each grade name (for example, Prime, Choice, etc.) is associated with a specific degree of quality.

Rail Stock: Major sections of a carcass hung on overhead rails with hooks (sides, quarters) or trees (primals).

Red Meat: Beef, veal, lamb, and pork.

Retail Cuts: Meat cut into retail portions for the consumer—for example, steaks, roasts, etc.

Rewrap: A retail cut that is pulled from the display case, and in some cases reprocessed, rewrapped, reweighed, and repriced. The cause may be an expired code date, a torn package, a miscut, discoloration, etc.

Rib Eye: The major muscle in the rib primal. It is a part of the tender longissimus dorsi muscle that lies along the back bone in the rib and loin.

Roast: To cook meat, uncovered, by dry heat in an oven. (See Bake.)

Rough Cut: Cuts that result from the primal breaking operation, such as short ribs, which are removed before the major retail cuts are made.

Saddle: (See Foresaddle and Hindsaddle.)

Sear: To brown the surface of meat by a short application of intense heat.

Shelf Life: The time period during which a retail package can be left on display.

Shell Loin: A beef short loin from which the tenderloin has been removed.

Short Plate: The portion of the forequarter immediately below the primal rib.

Shrinkage: An erosion of profits, caused by weight loss, spoilage, markdowns, or pilferage.

Side: One-half of a carcass that has been split from front to back without quartering, or one matched forequarter and hindquarter.

Side Pork Belly: That portion of the pork side middle after removal of the loin, fat back, and spareribs. Must be boneless and contain no major cartilages of sternum and ribs. Sold fresh or as slab or sliced bacon.

Simmer: To cook in a liquid at a temperature of approximately 185°F., causing bubbles to form slowly and break below the surface.

Skeletal Muscle: Muscle which is connected to the skeleton.

Skirt: The diaphragm muscle which separates the thoracic cavity from the abdominal cavity.

Slab Bacon: Bacon made from Side Pork Belly. (See Side Pork Belly.)

Slaughterer: One who kills live animals. In some cases, the slaughterer is also the cattle grower. Most slaughterers also process carcasses.

Smoking: A method of processing meat by hanging over burning hardwood chips in a smokehouse.

Sodium Nitrate: A curing agent that converts into sodium nitrite. (See Nitrates, Nitrites.)

Spring Lamb: New-crop lambs slaughtered between March 1 and the end of the week that contains the first Monday in October.

Steam: To cook in steam with or without pressure.

Stew: Small pieces of meat simmered in water or other liquid barely to cover. May be with or without vegetables. The meat is usually browned before adding liquid.

Subprimal: A major section cut from a primal, from which the retail cuts are made. The top round, bottom round, eye round, and sirloin tip, for example, are subprimals of the primal beef round.

Tare Weight: The weight of the packaging film and tray, which is deducted before the retail cut is priced. In some states, anticipated shrinkage from weight loss while the product is in the display case must also be included in the tare weight.

Tenderize: To break down the muscle tissues either mechanically or chemically, so that the meat is more palatable.

Tonnage: A quantity of product, expressed in pounds.

Undertrimming: Leaving more fat and/or bone on the retail cut than is specified in the company's standards.

Vacuum Packaging: Sealing product in an air-tight, moisture-proof film, which reduces weight loss and surface spoilage and allows product to be safely held for at least two weeks, when maintained at proper temperatures.

Variable Functions: Those activities which are directly or significantly affected by variations in volume—for example, processing, wrapping, etc.

Variety Meats: The edible organs and glands of a meat animal. Included are heart, tongue, liver, thymus (sweetbreads), kidney, spleen (melt), brain, stomach walls (tripe), hog intestines (chitterlings) and testicles (fries). Also commonly referred to as meat by-products and offals.

Veal: Meat from very young milk-fed calves usually not over 12 to 14 weeks of age at the time of slaughter.

Wholesale Cut: (See Primal.)

Wholesomeness: Refers to freedom from pathogenic microorganisms or other harmful bacteria. This is influenced by the health of the animal and by proper sanitation, handling, and storage temperature.

Yearling: An animal between one and two years of age.

Yield Grade: Official standards established by the USDA Agricultural Marketing Service for grading carcasses. The grades (for example, Yield Grade 1, Yield Grade 2, etc.) are designed to identify carcasses for differences in cutability or yield of boneless, closely-trimmed retail cuts from the round, loin, rib, and chuck.

Index

A–B

Adjustments in grading, 86
Advertising, 190-92
Advertising directors, 31
Age in grading standards, 82, 84
Aging of meats, 117-18
Agriculture, Department of, *see*
    Product—inspecting and grading
Area of rib eye in grading beef, 88
Baby beef, 21
Bacteria
  sanitation and, 220-21; *see also*
    Sanitation
  temperature and, 249
Beef
  braising, 103
  breaking, 47-48
  broiling, 95
    timetable for, 96
  buying, 131-33; *see also* Procurement
  canned, 70
  cooking guide for, 93
  cooking in liquid, 102, 104, 105
  cured or smoked, 67-68
  in forecasting and scheduling system, 279
  frozen, 25
  grades of, 80, 82-84
  inspecting and grading, *see*
    Product—inspecting and grading

  inspecting processed, 77
  order breakdown chart for, 168-69
  per capita consumption of, 18-19
  primal cuts and bone structure of, 49
  processing trimmings of, 156-58
  in production run, 253
  retail cuts of
    basic cuts, 55-56
    bones identifying seven groups of, 56-57
    defined, 48
    muscles identifying, 57-65
    nomenclature for, 52-55
    retail operations principles and, 254-57
  roasting, 99, 100
  sales of, by yield grades, 90
  sausages and luncheon meats from, 68-70
  secret to success of operation, 250
  source of, 46-47
  storage of, 119-22
    of cooked foods in home, 120
    time charts for, 121, 122
  tonnage and man-hour forecast for, 276
  variety meats of, 65-66
  yield grade standards for, 88
  yield and value of cuts of, 87
  See also Veal
Beef chart, 60
Bloom, 219-21
  bacteria and, 220-21
  bacteria, temperature and, 220

349

Brains, 65
Braising, 102
  beef, 103
  poultry, 111-13
    timetable for, 103
Breaking
  of beef, 47-48
  of pork, 48-49
  in standard practices manual, 296
Breasts of veal and lamb, 48
Brisket, defined, 48
Broiling
  of beef, 95
    timetable for, 96
  described, 94-98
  griddle, of sausage, 117
  oven, of sausage, 117
  pan, 98
  of poultry, 113-14
  timetable for, 96-97
Buyer-supplier relationship, 123-26
  deciding on the supplier, 124-26
Buying function, 126-31
  buying alternatives in, 129-31
  establishing prices in, 126-29

C-D

Canned meats, 43, 70-71
  minimum requirements in grading, 78
Carcass
  defined, 47
  straight, defined, 48
Carcass weight in grading beef, 88
Cattle, 46-47; *see also* Beef
Chickens, 66
  cooking, *see* Cooking methods
  frozen, 71
  grading, 84-85
  ideal temperature for, 250
Chitterlings, 65, 66
Choice (beef grade)
  cooking guide for, 93
  defined, 82
  roasting, 99
Choice (lamb grade), 84
Chuck, defined, 48
Cleaning schedule, 226
Color in grading standards, 82, 84

Commercial (beef grade)
  braising, 102
  defined, 83
Company specifications for receiving, 174-75
Conformation
  in grading standards, 82, 84
  of the legs, in lamb grading, 89
Contests, as merchandising supports, 211-13
Cooking aids, as merchandising supports, 210-11
Cooking methods, 92-122
  with dry heat, 94-100
    broiling, 94-97; *see also* Broiling
    pan broiling, 98
    pan frying, 98; *see also* Frying
    roasting, 99; *see also* Roasting
  for fresh red meats, 94
  with moist heat, 100-4
    braising, 102; *see also* Braising
    cooking in liquid, 102, 104, 105
    timetable for braising, 103
    timetable for roasting, 100-1
  for poultry, 108-16
    braising, 111-13
    broiling, 113-14
    cooking giblets and neck, 115-16
    frying, 114-15
    roasting, 110-11
    roasting guide, 112
    simmering or stewing, 115
  sausage, 116-17
  for variety meats, 104-9
    heart, 106
    kidney, 106-7
    liver, 105-6
    sweetbreads, 106
    timetable for cooking, 109
    tongue, 107-8
    tripe, 107
Coolers, sanitation in, 229-30
Cull (lamb grade), 84
Cured and smoked meats, 43
Customer preferences, 195-97
Customer relations
  merchandising and, 197-98, 213-15
  in standard practices manual, 295
Customer service, retail operations principles for, 270-72
Cutter and canner (beef grade), 83
Cutter techniques and merchandising, 203-6

Index 351

Cutting test, 187, 329-32
Demonstrators, as merchandising supports, 209-10
Directors
 advertising and operations, 31
 of sales and merchandising, 30-31
Discoloration, 219-21
 bacteria and, 220-21
 bacteria, temperature and, 220
 "first loss is best loss" and, 255-56
 of ground meat, 259-60
 merchandising product suffering from, 206-8
Display areas
 height and width of, 269-70
 sanitation in, 230
 in standard practices manual, 295
Disposable income, percent of, spent on food, 18
Distribution and processing, central, 145-64
 CO_2, 161
 determining need for, 146-52
 operating a central packaging plant, 162-64
 packaging primal cuts, 158-61
 processing, 155-56
 processing beef trimmings, 156-58
 pros and cons of operating a distribution center, 152-53
 soft-film overwrap, 160-61
 vacuum pack, 159-60
Dry heat cooking, *see* Cooking methods
Ducks, 66, 67; *see also* Cooking methods

E–F

Education, labor shortage and rise in level of, 283
Employees, 281-314
 developing a training program for, 287-301
 determining the method of training, 288-89
 developing instructor's manual, 298-300
 developing a standard practices manual, 291-97
 installing standard in all meat departments, 297-98
 qualifying the company meat trainer, 290-91
 selecting the meat trainer, 289-90
 training managers to train, 300-1
 injuries to, 242
 managers, *see* Managers
 manpower shortage, 283-87
 female trainee, 285-86
 problems in holding new recruits, 286-87
 sources of new employees, 284-85
 principles of teaching, 306-11
 breaking the task down into basic components, 307
 only the correct method should be taught, 307-8
 simple tasks must be taught first, 306-7
 skills should be developed through repetition, 309
 teaching cycles should be short and reinforced by practice, 308-9
 trainee must be motivated, 310-11
 real cost of training, 312-14
 who pays, 313-14
 safety for, 233-45
 checklist, 243-45
 sanitation facilities for, 229, 231-33
 training principles, 301-6
 capability and attitude of the trainer, 305-6
 instruction methods, 304-5
 nature of the job, 304
 trainee's background and experience, 303-4
 trainee's capability and attitude, 302-3
 unique qualities of, 26-27
Equipment, 27
 sanitation and, 225-30
 cleaning schedule, 226
 cooler, 229-30
 display area, 230
 processing area, 228-29
 processing room floor, 226-28
 in processing and packaging, 221-24
 retail operations principles and, 251
 in standard practices manual, 295
External fat
 in grading beef, 88
 in grading lamb, 89
Fat
 external
  in grading beef, 88
  in grading lamb, 89
 See also Trimmings

Federal Meat Inspection Act (1906), 73-74
Federal Wholesale Meat Act (1967), 74
Firmness in grading standards, 82, 84
Flank, defined, 48
Food and Drug Administration,
    nutrition labeling under, 79
Forequarters
  of beef, defined, 47
  of veal and lamb, defined, 48
Foresaddles, defined, 48
Freezing of fresh product at home, 120-21
Fresh meats
  grading, 79-81
  present practices in retailing, 16-18
  as product type, 43; *see also* Product
Frozen meats
  inspecting processing of, 78
  as product type, 43
  types of, 24-26, 71-72
Frying
  pan, 98
  of poultry, 114-15
  of sausage, 116

G–I

Geese, 66, 67; *see also* Cooking methods
Giblets, cooking poultry, 115-16
Good (beef grade)
  cooking guide for, 93
  defined, 82-83
  roasting, 99
Good (lamb grade), 84
Grade A (poultry grade), 84-85
Grade B (poultry grade), 84-85
Grade C (poultry grade), 84-85
Grading, 73-91
  adjustments in, 86
  beef grades, 80, 82-84
  beef and lamb sales by yield grades, 90
  of fresh product, 79-81
  lamb, 80, 84
  pork, 80, 90-91
  poultry, 84-86
  USDA standards for, 82
  yield grade standards for lamb, 89
  yield grades, 86-87
  yield grades for beef, 88
Griddle broiling of sausage, 117

Ground meat, 75-76
  as first item in production run, 252
  retail operations principles and, 259-62
  trimmings for, 257-59
  in standard practices manual, 296
Guinea hens, 66, 67; *see also* Cooking
    methods
Hard-to-sell items, merchandising, 203-8
  cutting techniques in, 203-6
  discolored product and, 206-8
  new items as, 208
Hearts
  cooking, 106
  in variety meats, 65
Hindquarters
  of beef, defined, 47
  of veal and lamb, defined, 48
Hindsaddles, defined, 48
Hogs, 47; *see also* Pork
Impulse sales, 198-203
  interdepartment merchandising and,
      200-1
  store-wide promotions and, 202-3
  sub-departments and, 201-2
Industrywide Cooperative Meat
    Identification Standards Committee
    (ICMISC), 54
Inspection, 73-91
  of fresh product, 73-77
  of processed product, 77-79
Inspectors
  safety, 233-34, 235
  and weighing and pricing, 264
Instructor's manual, developing an, 298-300
Inventory control, 272-73
Invoice, approving, in receiving, 177-80

K–L

Kidney, pelvic, and heart fat in grading
    beef, 88
Kidney and pelvic fat in lamb grading, 89
Kidneys, 65
  cooking, 106-7
Labeling in standard practices manual, 295
Labor
  as controllable expense, 273-79
  time involved to buy one steak, 18
  See also Employees

Index

Lamb
  braising, 103
  breaking, 48
  broiling, 95-97
    timetable for, 97
  buying, 133-34
  cooking in liquid, 102, 104, 105
  forecasting and scheduling system for, 279
  frozen, 25
  grades of, 80, 84; *see also*
    Product—inspecting and grading
  per capita consumption of, 21
  primal cuts and bone structure of, 51
  in production run, 253
  retail cuts of
    basic cuts, 55-56
    bones identifying seven groups of, 56-57
    defined, 48
    muscles identifying, 57-65
    nomenclature for, 52-55
    retail operations principles and, 254-57
  roasting, 99-101
  sales of, by yield grade, 90
  storage of, 119-22
    of cooked foods in home, 120
    time charts for, 121, 122
  sausages and luncheon meats from, 68-70
  tonnage and man-hour forecast for, 276
  variety meats of, 65-66
  yield grade standards for, 89
  yield and value of cuts of, 87
Lamb chart, 62
Laws regulating nomenclature for retail cuts, 52-53
Legs of veal and lamb, 48
Linens, as controllable expense, 273, 278-79
Liquid, cooking in, 102, 104
  timetable for, 105
Livers, 65
  cooking, 105-6
  frozen, 71
Loins
  of beef, 48
  of pork, 51-52
  of veal and lamb, 48
Luncheon meats
  shelf life of, 16
  sources for, 68-70
  storing temperatures for, 250-51

M

Man-hour requirements for fixed functions, 275
Managers, 315-35
  capitalizing talents of, 334-35
  department performance influenced by, 328-33
  functions of, 318-21
    details of the operation, 318-20
    managerial skills, 320-21
  identifying candidates for promotion to, 317-18
  traditional evaluation of, 315
  training, 321-28
    central training, 327-28
    in-store training, 322-27
    training to train, 300-1
Manpower forecast, tonnage and, 276
Manpower shortage, 283-87
  female trainees and, 285-86
  problems in holding new recruits, 286-87
  sources of new employees and, 284-85
Marbling in grading standards, 82, 84
Marinating meats, 119
Meat department, 13-42
  contribution to sales and gross profits from, 14-16
  cooked and frozen items in, 24-26
  current practices of, 16-18
  history of, 14-16
  installing standards in, 297-98
  organizational structure of, 29-42
    choosing the optimum, 42
    director of advertising, 31
    director of operations, 31
    director of sales and merchandising, 30-31
    responsibility for performance, 32
    upper echelon organization, 30
    variations in organizational structure (charts), 32-41
  per capita consumption and, 18-23
    future trends, 23-26
  share of total store sales from, 23-24
  unique qualities of, 26-27
Meat grade stamps, USDA, 81
Meat inspection stamps, 74
Merchandising
  advertising and, 190-92
  and customer relations, 197-98, 213-15

Merchandising (cont'd)
    getting customer reaction and, 197-98
    of hard-to-sell items, 203-8
        cutting techniques and, 203-6
        discolored product and, 206-8
        new items and, 208
    by impulse sales, *see* Impulse sales
    in product placement, 192-95
    responding to customer preference in, 195-97
    in standard practices manual, 296
    supports for, 208-13
        contests, 211-13
        cooking aids, 210-11
        demonstrators, 209-10
Merchandising directors, 30-31
Miscuts, 254-55
Moist heat cooking, *see* Cooking methods

N–O

National Institute for Occupational Safety and Health (NIOSH), 233, 242
National Live Stock and Meat Board, 54
Necks, cooking poultry, 115-16
Occupational Safety and Health Act (1970), 233
Occupational Safety and Health Administration (OSHA), 216, 233-42
    requirements of, 234-42
Operations directors, 31
Operations principles, *see* Retail operations principles
Order breakdown chart, 168-69
Ordering, 165-73
    procedures for, 171-73
        adjustments and transfers, 172-73
    retail operations principles and special, 270
    in standard practices manual, 295
    telephone, 271-72
    transmitting, 170-71
    writing the order, 165-70
        order breakdown chart, 168-69
Organization, store level, 41-42
Organizational structure, 29-42
    choosing the optimum, 42
    director of advertising in, 31
    director of operations in, 31
    director of sales and merchandising in, 30-31
    responsibility for performance in, 32
    upper echelon organization in, 30
    variations in (charts), 32-41
Oven broiling of sausage, 117
Oven cooking of sausage, 116-17

P

Packaging
    prepackaged products, 137-38
    of primal cuts, 158-61
    in retail operations principles, 263-64
    rewraps, 252
        profits and, 262-63
    and sanitation, 221-24
    soft-film overwrap, 160-61
    in standard practices manual, 295
    vacuum pack, 159-60
Packaging plant, operating a central, 162-64
Pan broiling, 98, 117
Pan frying, 98, 116
Per capita consumption, 18-23
    future trends in, 23-26
Personnel, *see* Employees
Plate, defined, 48
Pork
    braising, 102, 103
    breaking, 48-49
    broiling, 95, 96
        timetable for, 97
    buying, 134-37; *see also* Procurement
    canned, 70-71
    cooking in liquid, 102, 104, 105
    cured or smoked, 68
    cutting test on, 331
    expected yield on, 91
    in forecasting and scheduling system, 279
    frozen sausages of, 71
    grades of, 80, 90-91
        grade standards, 90-91
    inspecting and grading, *see* Product—inspecting and grading
    inspecting processed, 77
    order breakdown chart for, 168-69
    per capita consumption of, 22
    primal cuts and bone structure of, 53

Index

Pork (cont'd)
  retail cuts of
    basic cuts, 55-56
    bones identifying seven groups of, 56-57
    defined, 48
    muscles identifying, 57-65
    nomenclature for, 52-55
    retail operations principles and, 254-57
  roasting, 99-101
  sanitization and smoked, 228
  sausages and luncheon meats from, 68-70
  storage of, 119-22
    of cooked foods in home, 120
    time charts for, 121, 122
  tonnage and man-hour forecast for, 276
  variety meats of, 65-66
Pork chart, 63
Poultry, 66-67
  buying, 138-42; see also Procurement
  cooking, 108-16
    braising, 111-13
    broiling, 113-14
    cooking giblets and necks, 115-16
    frying, 114-15
    roasting, 110-11
    roasting guide, 112
    simmering or stewing, 115
  in forecasting and scheduling system, 279
  grades of, 84-86
  inspection of, 75; see also
    Product—inspecting and grading
  per capita consumption of, 18, 22-23
  storage of, 119-22
    of cooked foods in the home, 120
    time charts for, 121, 122
  tonnage and man-hour forecast for, 276
  See also Chickens; Turkeys
Poultry class name, 85
Poultry grade shield, 85
Poultry inspection mark, 76, 85
Poultry Products Inspection Act (1957), 75
Power tools
  safety of, 242-44
  sanitizing, 228-29
Prepackaged products, buying, 137-38
Prices
  establishing, in buying function, 126-29
  establishing, and setting goals for profits, 184-85
  inspectors and, 264
  to meet profit goals, 185-89

  retail operations principles for weights and, 264-66
  in standard practices manual, 295
Primal cuts
  defined, 47
  packaging of, 158-61
Prime (beef grade)
  cooking guide for, 93
  defined, 82
  roasting, 99-100
Prime (lamb grade), 84
Processing
  central, see Distribution and processing
  inspecting sausage, 77-78
  sanitation and, 221-24
    sanitation in area of, 228-29
    room floor, 226-28
Processing plant, operating a central, 153-55, 161-62
Procurement, 123-44
  of beef, 131-33
  buyer-supplier relationship in, 123-26
    deciding on the supplier, 124-26
  buying function in, 126-31
    buying alternatives, 129-31
    establishing prices, 126-29
  of lamb, 133-34
  of pork, 134-37
  of poultry, 138-42
    chill packing, 139-41
    dry-ice packing, 141
    ice packing, 139
    turkeys, 141-42
  of prepackaged products, 137-38
  rail vs. truck deliveries of, 142-43
  store-door deliveries of, 143-44
Product
  inspecting and grading, 73-91
    adjustments in grades, 86
    beef grades, 80, 82-84
    beef and lamb sales by yield grades, 90
    grade standards for pork, 90-91
    grading fresh product, 79-81
    inspecting fresh product, 73-77
    inspecting processed product, 77-79
    lamb grades, 84
    poultry grades, 84-86
    USDA grading standards, 82
    yield grade standards for lamb, 89
    yield grades, 86-87
    yield grades for beef, 88
  merchandising and placement of, 192-95

Product (cont'd)
   procurement of, *see* Procurement
   retail operations principles and
      availability of, 267-69
   retail operations principles and
      rehandling of, 262-63
   See also Beef; Lamb; Pork; Poultry;
      Variety meats; Veal
Profits
   contribution of meat department to
      sales and gross, 14-16
   managers and, 329-33
   merchandising and, *see* Merchandising
   product availability and gross, 267-68
   and rehandling products, 262-63
   setting goals for, 182-90
      contribution to total sales and gross
         margin dollars, 183
      establishing prices and, 184-85
      evaluating performance, 189-90
      pricing to meet goals, 185-89
      saw-ready round cutting test, 187

R

Rail, truck deliveries vs. deliveries by,
   142-43
Receiving, 174-81
   approving the invoice in, 177-80
   backroom security and, 180-81
   company specifications for, 174-75
   retail operations principles for, 247-48
   sanitation and, 221-24
   in standard practices manual, 295-96
   at the store, 175-77
Record keeping, safety, 235-40
Red meat, wholesale cuts of, 47-52
Red meat animals (cattle; hogs; sheep),
   46-47; *see also* Beef; Lamb; Pork
Retail cuts
   basic, 55-56
   bones identifying seven groups of, 56-57
   defined, 48
   muscles identifying, 57-65
   nomenclature for, 52-55
   retail operations principles and, 254-57
   in student practices manual, 296
Retail operations principles, 246-80
   for code-dating and shelf life, 266-67
   for controllable expenses, 273-79

   for customer service, 270-72
   for display height and width, 269-70
   for forecasting and scheduling system,
      279
   for ground meat, 259-62
   for inventory control, 272-73
   for legal compliance, 276-80
   for man-hour requirements for fixed
      functions, 275
   for meat department tonnage and
      man-hour forecast, 276
   for packaging materials, 263-64
   for product availability, 267-69
   for production scheduling, 251-53
   for receiving, 247-48
   for rehandling product, 262-63
   for retail cutting and trimming, 254-57
   for sanitation and safety, 251
   for special orders, 270
   for temperature, 248-51
   for trimmings for ground meat, 257-59
   for weighing and pricing, 264-66
Rib
   defined, 48
   of veal and lamb, 48
Rib eye, area of, in grading beef, 88
Roasting, 99-101
   of poultry, 110-11
      roasting guide, 112
Roasts, hand wrapping boneless, 299
Round, defined, 48

S

Saddles, defined, 48
Safety, 233-45
   checklist, 243-45
   retail operations principles and, 251
Sales
   of beef by yield grade, 90
   contribution of meat department to
      gross profits and, 14-16
   impulse, 198-203
      interdepartment merchandising and,
         200-1
      store-wide promotions and, 202-3
      sub-departments and, 201-2
   meat department share of total store,
      23-24

Sales (cont'd)
   merchandising hard-to-sell items, 203-8
      cutting techniques and, 203-6
      discolored product and, 206-8
      new items and, 208
Sales directors, 30-31
Sales ranges by product, typical, 45
Sanitation, 216-33
   bloom, discoloration and, 219-21
      bacteria and, 220-21
      bacteria and temperature, 220
   economics of, 217-19
   employees and, 231-33
   equipment and, 225-30
      cleaning schedule, 226
      cooler, 229-30
      display area, 230
      processing area, 228-29
      processing room floor, 226-28
   in processing and packaging, 221-24
   retail operations principles and, 251
   in standard practices manual, 295
Sanitizers, 225
Sausages
   cooking, 116-17
   inspecting processing of, 77-78
   meat for, 68-70, 74-75
Sawdust, 226-27
Saw-ready primals, defined, 48
Security, receiving and backroom, 180-81
Sheep, 47
Shelf life
   code-dating and, 266-67
   influences of, *see* Discoloration;
      Packaging; Processing
Shoulders of veal and lamb, 48
Simmering
   of poultry, 115
   of sausage, 117
Special orders, 270
Specifications for receiving, 174-75
Standard (beef grade)
   braising, 102
   cooking guide for, 93
   defined, 83
Standard practices, developing, 291-97
Standard practices manual, 295-96
Standards
   grading, 82, 84; *see also* Grading
   installing, in meat departments, 297-98
   safety, 234-42
   See also Retail operations principles

Stewing of poultry, 115
Storage, 119-22
   of cooked foods in home, 120
   time charts for, 121, 122
Store-door deliveries, 143-44
Store equipment, *see* Equipment
Store-wide promotions, 202-3
Subprimals, defined, 48
Supplies, as controllable expense, 273
Sweetbreads, 65, 106

T

Teaching principles
   principles of teaching, 306-11
      breaking the task down into basic
         components, 307
      only the correct method should be
         taught, 307-8
      simple tasks must be taught first, 306-7
      skills should be developed through
         repetition, 309
      teaching cycles should be short and
         reinforced by practice, 308-9
      trainee must be motivated, 310-11
   See also Training
Telephone orders, 271-72
Temperature
   cleaning schedule and, 226
   of coolers, 248, 250
   in processing area, 248-51
   receiving and, 247
   retail operations principles for, 248-51
   of water, for cleaning, 227
Tenderizing of meats, 118-19
Texture in grading standards, 82, 84
Tongue, 65
   cooking, 107-8
Training
   of managers, 321-28
      central training, 327-28
      in-store training, 322-27
      training to train, 300-1
   real cost of, 312-14
      who pays, 313-14
   See also Teaching principles
Training principles, 301-6
   capability and attitude of the trainer,
      305-6

Training principles (cont'd)
  instruction methods, 304-5
  nature of the job, 304
  trainee's background and experience, 303-4
  trainee's capability and attitude, 302-3
Training program, 287-301
  determining the method of training, 288-89
  developing instructors manual, 298-300
  developing a standard practices manual, 291-97
  installing standard in all meat departments, 297-98
  qualifying the company meat trainer, 290-91
  selecting the meat trainer, 289-90
  training managers to train, 300-1
Trimmings
  processing beef, 156-58
  retail operations principles and, 254-57
  ground meat and, 257-59
Tripe, 65, 107
Truck deliveries, rail deliveries vs., 142-43
Turkeys, 16-17, 66-67
  cooking, *see* Cooking methods
  frozen, 25-26, 71

U–Y

Uniform Retail Meat Identity Standards (manual), 54
USDA (U.S. Department of Agriculture), *see* Product—inspecting and grading
Utility (beef grade), 83
Utility (lamb grade), 84
Variety meats
  cooking methods for, 104-8
    heart, 106
    kidney, 106-7
    liver, 105-6
    sweetbreads, 106
    timetable for cooking, 109
    tongue, 107-8
    tripe, 107
  sources of, 65-66
Veal
  braising, 102, 103
  breaking, 48
  buying, *see* Procurement
  cooking in liquid, 102, 104, 105
  forecasting and scheduling system, 279
  frozen, 25
  grades of, 80
  inspecting and grading, *see* Product—inspecting and grading
  per capita consumption of, 20-21
  primal cuts and bone structure of, 50
  in production run, 253
  retail cuts of
    basic, 55-56
    bones identifying seven groups of, 56-57
    defined, 48
    muscles identifying, 57-65
    nomenclature for, 52-55
    retail operations principles and, 254-57
  roasting, 100, 101
  sausages and luncheon meats from, 68-70
  source of, 46-47
  storage of, 119-22
    cooked foods in home, 120
    time charts for, 121, 122
  tonnage and man-hour forecast for, 276
  variety meats of, 65-66
Veal chart, 61
Wholesome Poultry Products Act (1968), 75
Williams-Steiger Occupational Safety and Health Act (1970), 233
Wrapping, *see* Packaging
Yield grade stamps, 87
Yield grades, 86-91
  for beef, 88
  beef and lamb sales by, 90
  for lamb, 89